GED® TEST
MATHEMATICAL
REASONING
REVIEW

Related Titles

GED® Test Preparation
GED® Test Power Practice
GED® Test Mathematical Reasoning Flash Review
GED® Test RLA Flash Review
GED® Test Science Flash Review
GED® Test Social Studies Flash Review

GED® TEST MATHEMATICAL REASONING REVIEW

LEARNING EXPRESS®

NEW YORK

Cataloging-in-Publication Data is on file with the Library of Congress.

ISBN 978-1-61103-059-4

Printed in the United States of America

9 8 7 6 5 4 3 2 1

For more information on LearningExpress, other LearningExpress products, or bulk sales,
please write to us at:
    224 W. 29th Street
    3rd Floor
    New York, NY 10001

CONTRIBUTOR ▶

Kimberly Stafford majored in mathematics and education at Colgate University in upstate New York. She taught math, science, and English in Japan, Virginia, and Oregon before settling in Los Angeles. Kimberly began her work in Southern California as an educator in the classroom but soon decided to launch her own private tutoring business so she could individualize her math instruction. She believes that a solid foundation in math empowers people by enabling them to make the best work, consumer, and personal decisions. Kimberly is unfazed by the ubiquitous student gripe, "When am I going to use this in real life?" She stresses that the mastery of math concepts that are less applicable to everyday life helps teach a critical skill—problem solving. The very ability to apply a set of tools to solve new and complex problems is an invaluable skill in both the workforce and personal life. Kimberly believes that mathematics is a beautiful arena for developing organized systems of thinking, clear and supported rationale, and effective problem solving.

CONTENTS ▶

1 ▶ ABOUT THE GED® MATHEMATICAL REASONING TEST

The test of General Education Development, or GED® test, measures how well you understand high-school-level math, reading, writing, science, and social studies. Passing a GED® test in a specific area proves you have a high-school-level education in that subject. If you pass all four of the GED® tests, you will be awarded with a GED® diploma, the equivalent of a high school diploma.

The four separate modules of the GED® test include:

1. Reasoning through Language Arts
2. Social Studies
3. Science
4. Mathematical Reasoning

To pass each test, not only will you need to know the basics of each subject, but you'll also need to use critical thinking, writing, and problem solving skills.

If you would like to receive a high school diploma, but you are unable or do not wish to graduate via the traditional path of attending high school, the GED® test might be a great fit for you.

The GED® Mathematical Reasoning Test

The purpose of the Mathematical Reasoning test is to assess your *depth* of math knowledge. In addition to performing computations correctly, you will need to demonstrate your ability to reason mathematically: to build solution pathways and to evaluate the lines of reasoning as you solve problems. In other words, are you able to identify how to start a problem? Can you change your course of action when your original solution pathway is not working? Can you recognize flaws in your reasoning or in that of others? Do you understand *why* you are doing what you are doing, or are you simply following a memorized procedure?

Improving your conceptual understanding of math will not only help you pass the GED® Mathematical Reasoning Test, but will also aid you in furthering your education and in securing and maintaining future jobs.

How Is the Test Delivered?

You will take your GED® test on a computer at an official testing center. Although you do not need to be a computer expert to pass the GED® test, you should be comfortable using a mouse and typing on a keyboard.

The GED® Testing Service has put together a useful GED® Test Tutorial to familiarize GED® candidates with important aspects of the exam. It's important to watch this tutorial in order to:

- learn how to use the computer to navigate the questions on the test,
- learn how to operate the online calculator that will be provided during the GED® test,
- become familiar with the five different styles of questions that will be on the exam, and
- understand how to access and use several different math reference tools that will be available during your GED® Mathematical Reasoning Test.

You can find this useful tutorial here: http://www.gedtestingservice.com/2014cbttutorialview/

When and Where Can I Take the Test?

Now that the GED® tests are given online, the testing dates are no longer restricted to just three times a year. The first step is to create an account at www.GED.com. Use this account to select an official Testing Center, a date, and the time that you would like to take any of the four different tests. If you do not pass a particular module on your first attempt, you may take that test up to two more times with no waiting period between test dates. If you still do not pass on your third attempt, you will need to wait 60 days before you can retake that particular test.

How Much Do the GED® Tests Cost?

The exact price of the GED® tests varies from state to state. On average, each of the four GED® Tests costs around $30, for an average total of $120 for all four tests. You can pay for any or all parts of the test you are ready to take. If you don't pass a module on your first attempt, you will have the opportunity to take two reduced fee retakes for each module purchased. (You will receive at least $20 off of two retake tests and certain states may waive additional fees as well.)

How Are the Tests Scored?

The GED® tests are all scored on a scale of 100 to 200 points. A minimum score of 145 is required for passing each test. Each question on the GED® test is assigned a different point value depending on its difficulty. Students who score 170 points or more will receive an Honors Passing Score. You will find out your score (or scores) on the same day you take the test. After you take any of the GED® tests, you will receive an Enhanced Score Report from the GED® Testing Service. This personalized report will help you learn more about your score. In the event that you do not pass on your first attempt, it will help you identify what skills need more attention. Here are the breakdowns of scores:

- Below Passing: 100–144
- Passing Score: 145–169
- Honors Passing Score: 170–200

How Long Is the Test?

You can choose to take all four GED® tests at once, or you can take each test separately. In total, the four different subject tests take about seven hours to complete. The Mathematical Reasoning Test is composed of two separate parts that are timed together as a single test. You will have 115 minutes (just under 2 hours) to answer 46 questions.

What Topics Are Covered on the GED® Mathematical Reasoning Test?

More than half of the math portion of the GED® test contains problems that require algebraic thinking. Don't let this scare you! Algebra is a way to demonstrate mathematical reasoning skills in a sometimes abstract, yet logical, way. Algebraic thinking is ingrained in everyday life; it's likely that you are already using this way of thinking without even realizing it to solve problems in your daily routine. The questions on the Mathematical Reasoning Test will fall under two areas: Quantitative Problem Solving and Algebraic Problem Solving.

- **Quantitative Problem Solving** math questions cover basic math concepts like multiples, factors, exponents, absolute value, ratios, percentages, averages, geometry, probability, and more. Approximately 45% of the questions will fall into this category.
- **Algebraic Problem Solving** math questions ask you to use your knowledge of the basic building blocks of math to solve problems using algebra, including linear equations, quadratic equations, functions, linear inequalities, and more. Approximately 55% of the questions will fall into this category.

What Types of Questions Are on the Mathematical Reasoning Test?

Since the GED® Mathematical Reasoning Test is given on a computer, you will see several different types of questions. The questions may ask you to use the mouse to move images around or use the keyboard to type in your answer. It is important to preview the GED® Test Tutorial mentioned above so that you are familiar with the different formats of questions you will be asked to answer. Here are different formats of questions you will encounter on the actual test:

1. Multiple Choice

More than 50% of the questions on the GED® test will be multiple-choice. You will have to pick the best answer out of four given choices: A, B, C, and D. To select an answer, you will click your mouse in the circle next to that answer choice. To change your answer, click the circle of another answer choice. In this book, you will simply circle the correct response to a multiple-choice question.

2. Fill-in-the-Blank

For fill-in-the-blank questions, rather than being presented with a selection of possible answers from which to choose, you will need to type in an answer or answers. In this book, you can practice by writing in the correct answer on the given line or lines.

> Henry has $5 more than Oliver, and the same amount of money as Murray. Together, they have $85. How much money does Oliver have?
>
> _____ dollars.

3. Drop-Down

For drop-down questions, you will need to select the correct numerical answer or phrase to complete a sentence or problem. You will click your mouse on the arrow to show all of the answer choices. Then, you will click on your chosen answer to complete the sentence, paragraph, or equation. This type of question is similar to a multiple-choice item.

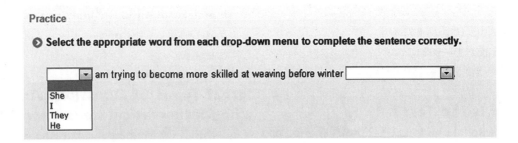

Practice

> Select the appropriate word from each drop-down menu to complete the sentence correctly.

[____ ▾] am trying to become more skilled at weaving before winter [_____ ▾]

She
I
They
He

4. Drag-and-Drop

To answer drag-and-drop questions, you will need to click on the correct object, hold down the mouse, and drag the object to the appropriate place in the problem, diagram, chart, or graph. In this book, you can practice this type of question by identifying which object will complete the problem, diagram, chart, or graph. Instead of dragging it, you will need to write your answer in.

Practice

❯ Drag and drop the seasons in the order in which they occur from December to November.

5. Hot Spot

For hot-spot questions, you will need to click on an area of the screen to indicate where the correct answer is located. For instance, you may be asked to plot a point by clicking on an empty graph. In this book, you can practice by identifying where the correct answer is located and marking the location on paper in the appropriate spot.

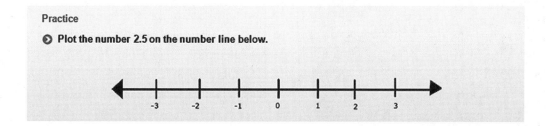

Practice

❯ Plot the number 2.5 on the number line below.

Can I Use a Calculator?

An online calculator, called the *TI-30XS MultiView* (pictured below), will be available to you for most of the questions within the Mathematical Reasoning Test.

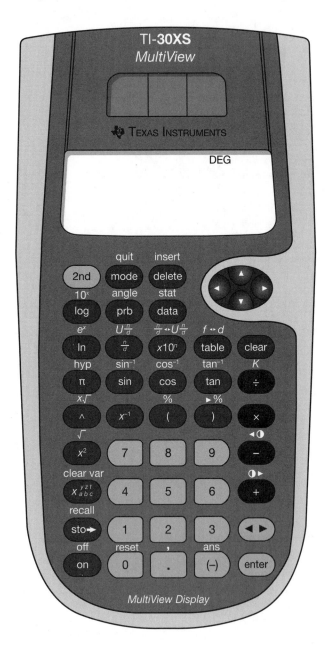

MultiView Display

The first five math questions on the test will be non-calculator questions and they will comprise Part 1. These questions may deal with ordering fractions and decimals, using the least common multiple (LCM) and the greatest common factor (GCF), using the distributive property, simplifying or solving problems using the rules of exponents, or identifying absolute value, among other computational skills and concepts. Part 2 of the test will have the on-screen calculator available for you to use. Most states will permit you to bring in a *TI-30XS MultiView* calculator, but you should check with your individual testing center regarding this. No other calculators will be permitted.

Carefully going through Chapter 12 in this book, Calculator Skills on the TI-30XS, is a great way to help build your calculator skills. It is also a good idea to carefully study the tutorials and reference sheets on the official GED® Testing Service website before you take the actual test.

CALCULATOR RESOURCES

The GED® Testing Service has created a calculator reference sheet and tutorial videos on its website to help you get the most out of the *TI-30XS MultiView* calculator. Although the reference sheet will be available for you to use during the test, you should be comfortable with the functions of the calculator *before* taking the test. You will not want to take extra time to read through the reference sheet's illustrated steps while trying to complete the problems in limited time.

Visit www.gedtestingservice.com/testers/calculator to learn all about the *TI-30XS MultiView*.

Formula Reference Sheet

A list of formulas will be available for you to use during the test. Although it will include basic formulas such as the area of a rectangle or triangle, circumference of a circle, and perimeter of geometric figures, it will benefit you greatly to be able to recall these formulas from memory and work with them comfortably without having to rely on the Formula Reference Sheet. These formulas will be covered in Chapter 10 of this book. Visit the Appendix on page

277 to see the list of formulas you will be given on test day.

How to Use This Book

Now that you are familiar with the structure and guidelines of the GED® test, you can begin focusing on mastering the math content. The next chapter is a Diagnostic GED® Mathematical Reasoning test. This exam is designed to model as closely as possible the actual GED® test. Each question is accompanied by a detailed answer explanation—not only will you be able to see why the correct answer is right, but you will also be able to see why some of the other choices are incorrect.

After completing this diagnostic test, the following review chapters will help you brush up on concepts and skills:

Chapter 3: Fractions and Decimals
Chapter 4: Negatives, Exponents, and PEMDAS
Chapter 5: Rates, Proportions, and Percents
Chapter 6: Variables and Linear Equations
Chapter 7: Graphs of Linear Equations and Inequalities
Chapter 8: Quadratics and Functions
Chapter 9: Interpreting Data in Graphs and Tables
Chapter 10: Geometry Basics
Chapter 11: Statistics and Probability
Chapter 12: Calculator Skills on the TI-30XS

As you work through the skills and content in Chapters 3 through 11, pay close attention to the detailed explanations for any of the questions you have gotten wrong. It is important that you learn from your mistakes and understand the correct way to tackle each problem.

It will also benefit you to spend extra time studying the shaded boxes in each chapter. These boxes highlight important concepts, pitfalls, vocabulary, and techniques. There are several types of shaded boxes that you will encounter:

Sneak Preview Question

These boxes give you an idea of what types of questions you are going to be able to answer after completing a particular section. Don't panic if initially you cannot understand or answer the question!

Don't Do This!

These boxes help you stay out of trouble by showing you mistakes that students commonly make. Study these boxes carefully so you know what errors to steer clear of!

Rule

We will put some of the important rules that you need for the GED® test in shaded boxes.

Vocabulary Alert!

If certain terms are critical to your understanding of the content being presented, or to your ability to interpret questions on the GED® test, we'll highlight these terms in a shaded box.

Calculator Tip!

We'll let you know if the concept being presented is something that you can also learn how to do on your TI-30XS in Chapter 12.

Chapter 12 gives you the opportunity to learn some very beneficial calculator skills. Before moving on to the second full-length GED® Mathematical Reasoning Practice Test in Chapter 13, make sure you are comfortable using all the formulas on the reference sheet provided in the Appendix. These will be provided when you take the actual test, but having these formulas committed to memory will be very beneficial to you.

If you practice a little bit of math every day, not only will you see an improvement in your test scores, but you will also notice that you are retaining your math skills better and longer. Best of luck on your GED® test study journey and with your test-taking experience!

For additional information on the GED®, visit www.gedtestingservice.com/testers/mygedfaqs.

2 ▶ GED® MATHEMATICAL REASONING DIAGNOSTIC TEST

This practice test is modeled on the format, content, and timing of the official GED® Mathematical Reasoning test. Like the official exam, the questions focus on your quantitative and algebraic problem-solving skills.

You may refer to the formula sheet in the Appendix on page 277 as you take this exam. Answer questions 1–5 *without* using a calculator. You may use a scientific calculator (or a calculator of any kind) for the remaining exam questions.

Work carefully, but do not spend too much time on any one question. Be sure you answer every question.

Set a timer for 115 minutes (1 hour and 55 minutes), and try to take this test uninterrupted, under quiet conditions.

Complete answer explanations for every test question follow the exam. Good luck!

45 questions

115 minutes

1. The product of two consecutive integers is 42. If the smaller integer is x, which of the following equations must be true?

    a. $x + 1 = 42$

    b. $x^2 + x = 42$

    c. $2x + 1 = 42$

    d. $2x^2 + x = 42$

2.

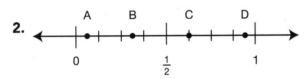

If x is a rational number such that $\frac{1}{2} < x < \frac{3}{4}$, then which of the points on the number line above may represent x?

    a. Point A

    b. Point B

    c. Point C

    d. Point D

3. A real-estate agent has found that the asking price of a home in his area can be estimated by taking the square footage, multiplying by 84, and adding 1,065. If the square footage is represented by S and the asking price by P, then which of the following formulas represents this estimation?

    a. $P = 1,149S$

    b. $P = 84(S + 1,065)$

    c. $P = 84S + 1,065$

    d. $P = S + 1,149$

4. In the x-y coordinate plane below, draw a dot on the point that is represented by the ordered pair (4,–2).

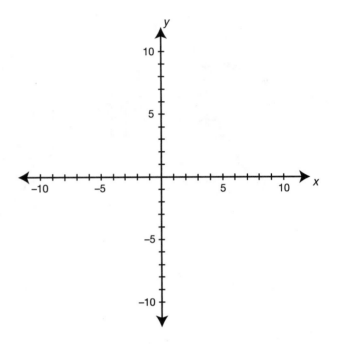

5. Which of the following is equivalent to $\frac{2^5}{2^2}$?

    a. 2

    b. 2^3

    c. 2^7

    d. 2^{10}

6. Which of the following graphs shows n as a function of m?

a.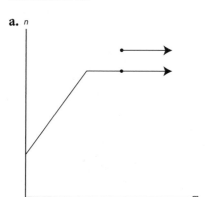

b.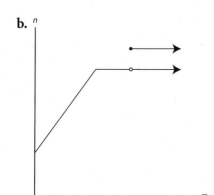

c.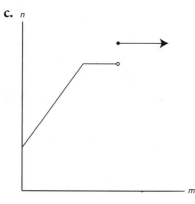

d.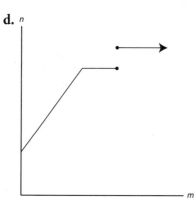

7. As a simplified fraction, $\frac{1}{4}\left(\frac{5}{2} - \frac{1}{6}\right) =$

   a. $-\frac{1}{4}$

   b. $\frac{1}{6}$

   c. $\frac{7}{12}$

   d. $\frac{3}{2}$

8. Suppose that for a rational number x, $3(x - 5) = 3$. Select which of the following must be true.

   a. $x - 5 = 1$

   b. $3x - 15 = 9$

   c. $x = 5$

   d. $3x = 8$

9. For input a, the function f is defined as $f(a) = -2a^2 + 1$. What is the value of $f(-8)$?

   a. -127

   b. -34

   c. 33

   d. 129

10. Which of the following represents the solution set of the inequality $4x - 9 < 3x + 1$?

   a. $x < -\frac{8}{7}$

   b. $x < -8$

   c. $x < 10$

   d. $x < \frac{10}{7}$

11. $(x - 5)(2x + 1) =$

   a. $2x^2 - 3x + 1$

   b. $2x^2 - 9x - 5$

   c. $2x^2 - 5$

   d. $2x^2 - 10$

12. What is the largest possible value of x if $x^2 - 14x + 35 = -10$? Write your answer in the box below.

13. The figure below shows the graph of a function and all of its turning points.

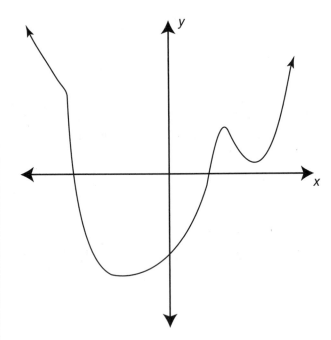

How many *x*-intercepts does the function have?

a. None

b. 1

c. 2

d. infinitely many

14. A website is selling a laptop computer for $375.00 plus 6.5% state sales tax. A student wishes to purchase two of these computers: one for his brother and one for himself. Including tax, what will be the total cost of his order? Write your answer in the box below.

$ _____

15. A small town has a population of 20,510 and an area of 86.8 square miles. To the nearest tenth, what is the population density as measured by the value "people per square mile"?

a. 2.72

b. 236.3

c. 2,201.4

d. 55,833.1

16. $\dfrac{2}{x(x-1)} + \dfrac{1}{x-1} =$

a. $\dfrac{3}{2x(x-1)}$

b. $\dfrac{2+x}{x(x-1)}$

c. $\dfrac{3}{x(x-1)}$

d. $\dfrac{2}{x-1}$

17.

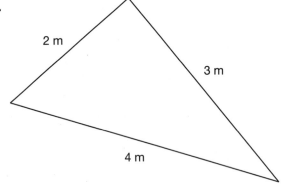

In meters, what is the perimeter of the given triangle?

a. 3 m

b. 6 m

c. 7 m

d. 9 m

18. Two friends go to a restaurant for lunch and receive a final bill of $24.36. One friend believes they should tip 15%, while the other believes they should tip 20%. To the nearest cent, what is the difference between the two possible tips?

a. $1.22

b. $3.65

c. $4.87

d. $8.52

19. Two high-school biology classes hosted a bird watching day where students kept track of how many different species of birds they observed in a nearby park. The dot plot represents the number of species observed by many of the students.

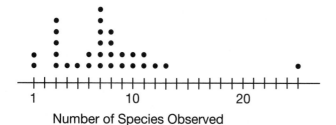

Number of Species Observed

Four of the students have not been included on the plot. The number of species these students observed was:

STUDENT	NUMBER OF SPECIES OBSERVED
Amy	14
Scott	14
Crystal	21
Gilbert	9

Draw as many dots on the graph above as is necessary to add these students' observations to the plot.

20. Which of the following is equivalent to the expression $2x + 3(x-2)^2$?
a. $3x^2 - 10x + 12$
b. $3x^2 + 3x - 4$
c. $3x^2 - 2x + 4$
d. $3x^2 - 10x + 4$

21. The histogram below represents the data collected through a survey of students at a large commuter college. Each student surveyed provided the one-way distance he or she travels to campus.

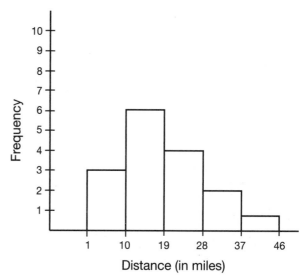

Distance (in miles)

Based on the data, which of the following statements must be true?
a. A total of 46 students were surveyed.
b. There is one student who travels exactly 46 miles to campus, one way.
c. Between 10 and 19 students travel exactly 6 miles to campus, one way.
d. Fewer than 5 students travel less than 10 miles to campus, one way.

22. The figure below represents the cumulative number of packages loaded onto trucks in one day at a small warehouse. When the day began, there were already 50 packages loaded.

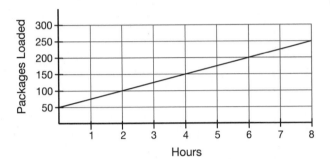

Based on this graph, how many packages were loaded each hour?

a. 25

b. 50

c. 125

d. 250

23. A right triangle has legs of length 7 and 4. To the nearest tenth, what is the length of its hypotenuse?

a. 3.3

b. 5.7

c. 8.1

d. 11.0

24.

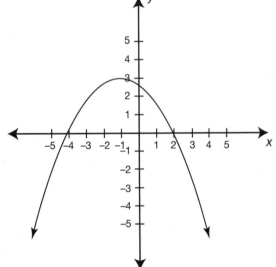

The graph shown here represents a function $y = g(x)$. Select the correct description of the function from the options that follow.

a. The function has a maximum value of -1 when $x = 3$.

b. The function has a maximum value of 3 when $x = -1$.

c. The function has a minimum value of 3 when $x = -1$.

d. The function has a minimum value of -1 when $x = 3$.

25. A map is drawn such that 2.5 inches on the map represents a true distance of 10 miles. If two cities are 7.1 inches apart on the map, then to the nearest tenth of a mile, what is the true distance between the two cities?

a. 14.6

b. 17.8

c. 28.4

d. 71.0

26. Over the last six months, a company's monthly revenue has increased by 28%. If the revenue this month is $246,990, then what was the revenue six months ago? Round your answer to the nearest cent. Write your answer in the box below.

$ ☐

27. The chart below represents the enrollment in an annual professional training program for several nonconsecutive years. Circle the year for which there was the largest difference between the number of men enrolled and the number of women enrolled in the program.

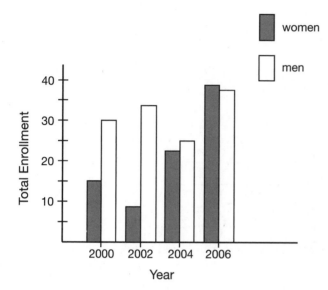

28. A line p passes through the point $(-8,4)$ and has a slope of $\frac{4}{5}$. Which of the following represents the equation for the line p?
  a. $4x - y = -52$
  b. $4x - y = -60$
  c. $4x - 5y = -60$
  d. $4x - 5y = -52$

29.

x	0	2	4	6
y	1	4	7	10

The table above shows some points in the x-y coordinate plane that the graph of a line $y = mx + b$ passes through. Based on this information, what is the value of the slope m?
  a. $\frac{1}{2}$
  b. $\frac{2}{3}$
  c. $\frac{3}{2}$
  d. 2

30. What are the two linear factors of the polynomial $2x^2 - x$?
  a. x and $2x - 1$
  b. $2x$ and $x - 1$
  c. $2x$ and x
  d. $2x$ and $x - 2$

31. A line P graphed in the x-y coordinate plane crosses the x-axis at a point $(-5,0)$. If another line Q has an equation of $y = 3x - 2$, then which of the following statements is true?
  a. The x-intercept of line P is closer to the origin than the x-intercept of line Q.
  b. The x-coordinate of the x-intercept of line P is smaller than the x-coordinate of the x-intercept of line Q.
  c. The x-intercepts of both lines lie to the right of the y-axis.
  d. The x-intercept of line Q cannot be determined from the given information.

32. A remote-controlled vehicle travels at a constant speed around a testing track for a period of 12 hours. In those 12 hours, the vehicle covers 156 kilometers. In terms of kilometers per hour, at what rate was the vehicle traveling? Write your answer in the box below.

$\boxed{}$ km/hr

33. The chart represents the number of households in selected cities that have subscribed to a new company's Internet service.

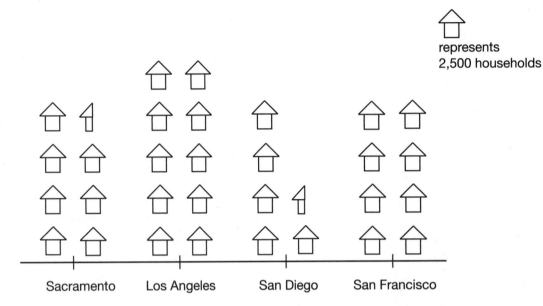

represents
2,500 households

Based on this data, how many households have subscribed to the service in San Diego?

a. 13,750

b. 15,000

c. 18,750

d. 20,000

34. A teacher would like to pick 2 students from her class of 30 (16 girls and 14 boys) to be class leaders. If she picks these students one at a time, without replacement, what is the probability that both class leaders are boys? Round your answer to the nearest whole percent.

a. 14%

b. 21%

c. 47%

d. 91%

35. If $\frac{3}{4}x = 12$, then $x =$

a. 9

b. $11\frac{1}{4}$

c. $12\frac{3}{4}$

d. 16

36. Which of the following lines is parallel to the line $y = \frac{2}{9}x - \frac{1}{5}$?

a. $y = -\frac{9}{2}x + 1$

b. $y = \frac{3}{4}x + 5$

c. $y = \frac{2}{9}x - 8$

d. $y = \frac{3}{4}x - \frac{1}{5}$

37. The figure below is a rectangle with a half-circle attached.

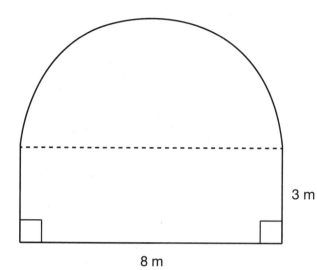

3 m

8 m

Given the indicated dimensions, what is the area of the region in terms of π?

a. $14 + 4\pi$ meters

b. $14 + 16\pi$ meters

c. $24 + 8\pi$ meters

d. $24 + 16\pi$ meters

38. What is the value of the expression $-3x + 10y$ when $x = -4$ and $y = -2$?

a. -34

b. 32

c. -8

d. 1

39. $-x^2(x + 1) - (x^3 + 4x^2) =$

a. $-6x^3 - x^2$

b. $-2x^3 - 5x^2$

c. $-2x^3 + 3x^2$

d. $-2x^3 + 4x^2 + 1$

40. Which of the following is the equation of the line that passes through the points $(-8,1)$ and $(4,9)$ in the x-y coordinate plane?

a. $y = \frac{2}{3}x + \frac{19}{3}$

b. $y = \frac{2}{3}x + 9$

c. $y = \frac{3}{2}x + \frac{21}{2}$

d. $y = \frac{3}{2}x + 13$

41. The figure below represents a composite part to be manufactured by fusing together two solid cubes.

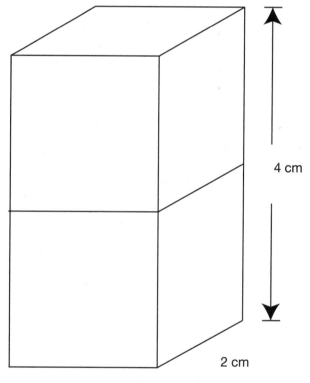

4 cm

2 cm

2 cm

If the cubes used are identical, what is the volume of the resulting part?

a. 4 cm^3

b. 8 cm^3

c. 16 cm^3

d. 40 cm^3

42. An IT consultant charges a company $75 an hour to analyze its current systems. Additionally, he charges a 3% project fee and a 1% telecommunications fee on the cost of the billed hours. If a project requires 20 hours for the consultant to complete, what will be the final amount charged to the company?

  a. $1,515
  b. $1,545
  c. $1,560
  d. $2,100

43. What expression is equivalent to the sum of $\frac{1}{2}x$ and $\frac{3}{4}x - 5$?

Select from the numbers and expressions listed below, and write the correct values into the boxes to find an equivalent expression.

$\frac{5}{4}x$

$\frac{2}{3}x$

$\frac{3}{4}$

$\frac{5}{2}$

$\frac{1}{2}x$

$\boxed{} - \boxed{}$

44. The ratio of full-time employees to part-time employees in a midsize law firm is 4:3. If there is a total of 20 full-time employees, how many part-time employees work at the firm?

  a. 15
  b. 19
  c. 23
  d. 27

45. What is the value of $\frac{x-5}{x^2+1}$ when $x = -3$?

  a. $-\frac{3}{2}$
  b. $-\frac{4}{5}$
  c. $\frac{8}{5}$
  d. 1

Answers and Explanations

1. **Choice b is correct.** If the first integer is x, then the second integer is $x + 1$ and their product is $x(x + 1) = x^2 + x = 42$.
   Choice **a** is incorrect. The second integer would be $x + 1$, but the product of both integers should be included in the equation.
   Choice **c** is incorrect. The question asks for the *product*, not the *sum*.
   Choice **d** is incorrect. While there are two integers, neither integer will be represented by $2x$.

2. **Choice c is correct.** The middle hash mark between one-half and one represents three-fourths. Point C is between this mark and the one-half mark, indicating it satisfies the given inequality.
   Choice **a** is incorrect. This point is much smaller than one-half. In fact, it is smaller than one-fourth.
   Choice **b** is incorrect. This point is between one-fourth and one-half.
   Choice **d** is incorrect. This point is larger than three-fourths.

3. **Choice c is correct.** Multiplying by 84 is the first step, and this is represented by $84S$. The 1,065 is added to this term, leading to the model $P = 84S + 1,065$.
   Choice **a** is incorrect. This model represents multiplying the square footage by 1,149.
   Choice **b** is incorrect. This model represents multiplying by 84 as the last step and would produce different results.
   Choice **d** is incorrect. This model represents just adding 84 and then 1,065 to the square footage.

4.

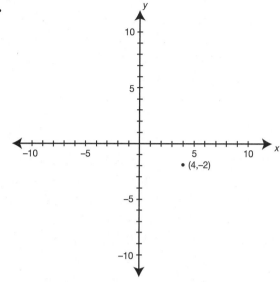

5. Choice b is correct. By the laws of exponents, $\frac{2^5}{2^2} = 2^{5-2} = 2^3$.

Choice **a** is incorrect. When subtracted according to the laws of exponents, there will be a final exponent larger than 1.

Choice **c** is incorrect. The laws of exponents require subtraction here instead of addition.

Choice **d** is incorrect. The laws of exponents require subtraction here instead of multiplication.

6. Choice c is correct. For each possible value of m, there is only one possible value of n.

Choice **a** is incorrect. After and including the indicated point, there are two possible values of n for each value of m.

Choice **b** is incorrect. After the indicated point, there are two possible values of n for each value of m.

Choice **d** is incorrect. At the indicated point, there are two possible values of n for that value of m.

7. Choice c is correct. $\frac{1}{4}\left(\frac{5}{2} - \frac{1}{6}\right) = \frac{1}{4}\left(\frac{15}{6} - \frac{1}{6}\right) = \frac{1}{4}\left(\frac{14}{6}\right) = \frac{7}{12}$.

Choice **a** is incorrect. Denominators are never subtracted when subtracting two fractions.

Choice **b** is incorrect. When rewriting the first fraction with the common denominator of 6, the numerator must also be multiplied by 2.

Choice **d** is incorrect. Parentheses indicate multiplication, not addition. Further, addition of fractions doesn't involve adding the denominators.

8. Choice a is correct. Dividing both sides by three shows that $x - 5 = 1$.

Choice **b** is incorrect. Multiplying the expressions on the left side yields $3x - 15 = 3$, **not** $3x - 15 = 9$.

Choice **c** is incorrect. Dividing both sides by three shows that $x - 5 = 1$. This can be further reduced to $x = 6$, **not** $x = 5$.

Choice **d** is incorrect. Multiplying the expressions on the left side yields $3x - 15 = 3$. This can be further reduced to $3x = 18$, **not** $3x = 8$.

9. Choice a is correct. $f(-8) = -2(-8)^2 + 1 = -2(64) + 1 = -128 + 1 = -127$.

Choice **b** is incorrect. The exponent on the a indicates a should be squared, not multiplied by 2. Further, the result of this will be positive instead of negative.

Choice **c** is incorrect. The exponent on the a indicates a should be squared, not multiplied by 2.

Choice **d** is incorrect. The value of $(-8)^2$ is positive, not negative.

10. Choice c is correct. After subtracting $3x$ from both sides, the resulting inequality is $x - 9 < 1$. Adding 9 to both sides results in the final solution of $x < 10$.

Choice **a** is incorrect. Since the sign of $3x$ is positive, it should be subtracted from both sides. Similarly, in the next step, the 9 should be added to both sides since it is subtracted from $4x$.

Choice **b** is incorrect. After subtracting the $3x$ from both sides, the 9 should be added to both sides since it is subtracted from $4x$.

Choice **d** is incorrect. Since the sign of $3x$ is positive, it should be subtracted from both sides.

11. Choice b is correct. Using FOIL, $(x - 5)(2x + 1) = 2x^2 + x - 10x - 5 = 2x^2 - 9x - 5$.

Choice **a** is incorrect. Using FOIL involves the multiplication of the inner terms instead of the addition of them.

Choice **c** is incorrect. This is the product of only the first two and the last two terms, but FOIL requires the product of the inner and outer terms be included.

Choice **d** is incorrect. While the first term is $2x^2$, the FOIL technique will add many more terms to the final product.

12. The correct answer is 9. Adding 10 to both sides yields the equation $x^2 - 14x + 45 = 0$. The left-hand side of the equation factors into $(x - 5)(x - 9)$, resulting in solutions of 5 and 9. Nine is, of course, the larger of the two solutions to the equation.

13. Choice c is correct. The graph crosses the x-axis at exactly two points, and the fact that all of the turning points are shown indicates it will not cross it again.

Choice **a** is incorrect. A graph with no x-intercepts does not cross the x-axis at any point.

Choice **b** is incorrect. A graph with only one x-intercept would cross the x-axis exactly once. This graph crosses the x-axis more than that.

Choice **d** is incorrect. A graph with infinitely many x-intercepts would have to curve back toward the x-axis and cross it in a regular pattern. That behavior is not indicated by this graph since all the turning points are shown.

14. The correct answer is $798.75. The student will spend $375 \times 2 = \$750$ on the two computers and $\$750 \times 0.065 = \$48.75$ on the tax: $\$750 + \$48.75 = \$798.75$.

15. Choice b is correct. Dividing the number of people by the area yields $236.29 \approx 236.3$.

Choice **a** is incorrect. The term *square miles* does not imply that the 86.8 must be squared. It is instead a unit of measure for area.

Choice **c** is incorrect. Since the final result will be people per square miles, taking the square root before dividing is not a needed step.

Choice **d** is incorrect. Although the area is measured in square miles, the values of the population and the area do not need to be squared.

16. Choice b is correct. $\frac{2}{x(x-1)} + \frac{1}{x-1} = \frac{2}{x(x-1)} + \frac{x}{x(x-1)} = \frac{2+x}{x(x-1)}$.

Choice **a** is incorrect. The fractions must have a common denominator before they can be added and once they do, only the numerators are combined.

Choice **c** is incorrect. While the common denominator is $x(x-1)$, $\frac{1}{x-1} \neq \frac{x}{x(x-1)}$.

Choice **d** is incorrect. The x terms in the numerator and denominator are not factors and therefore cannot be canceled.

17. Choice d is correct. The perimeter is the sum of all side lengths: $2 + 4 + 3 = 9$.

Choice **a** is incorrect. The area of the triangle is 3 square meters, not the perimeter.

Choices **b** and **c** are incorrect. The lengths of all sides must be added to find the perimeter, not just two of them.

18. **Choice a is correct.** $0.2 \times 24.36 - 0.15 \times 24.36$
= 1.22.
Choice **b** is incorrect. This represents a tip of
15%, not the difference between the two tips.
Choice **c** is incorrect. This represents a tip of
20%, not the difference between the two tips.
Choice **d** is incorrect. The *difference* refers to
subtraction, not addition.

19. The scores are added to the dot plot by placing
repeated dots over the value on the scale. The
circled dots represent the four added students.

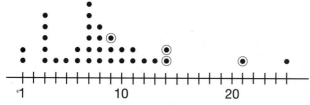

Number of Species Observed

20. **Choice a is correct.** Following the order of
operations, the binomial must first be squared,
the 3 distributed, and then like terms combined:
$2x + 3(x - 2)^2 = 2x + 3(x^2 - 4x + 4) = 2x + 3x^2$
$- 12x + 12 = 3x^2 - 10x + 12$.
Choice **b** is incorrect. FOIL must be used to
expand the squared term: $(x - 2)^2 \neq x^2 + 4$.
Choice **c** is incorrect. When simplifying, the 3
must multiply each term within the
parentheses.
Choice **d** is incorrect. When simplifying, the 3
must multiply the constant term 4.

21. **Choice d is correct.** The bar representing
distances from 1 up to 10 miles has a height of
3, meaning 3 students reported traveling less
than 10 miles to campus.
Choice **a** is incorrect. The total number of
students surveyed can be found by adding the
frequencies. There were $3 + 6 + 4 + 2 + 1 = 16$
students surveyed.
Choice **b** is incorrect. While there was only one
student who travels between 37 and 46 miles to
campus, there is no way to tell the exact number
of miles he travels using this graph.

Choice **c** is incorrect. The 10 and 19 on the
horizontal axis represent distance, not
frequency.

22. **Choice a is correct.** The slope of the line
represents the unit rate. Using the start point
(0,50) and the end point (8, 250), the slope is
$\frac{250 - 50}{8 - 0} = \frac{200}{8} = 25$.
Choice **b** is incorrect. The point 50 on the
vertical axis represents the number of packages
loaded at the beginning of the day.
Choice **c** is incorrect. There were 125 packages
loaded a little after 3 hours, so it cannot be the
hourly rate.
Choice **d** is incorrect. This cannot represent the
hourly rate because there were 250 packages
loaded after 8 hours.

23. **Choice c is correct.** Using the Pythagorean
theorem, $7^2 + 4^2 = c^2$ where c is the length of the
hypotenuse. Solving for c, $c^2 = 65$ and $c = \sqrt{65}$
≈ 8.1.
Choice **a** is incorrect. The Pythagorean theorem
requires that all of the terms be squared, not
just the length of the hypotenuse.
Choice **b** is incorrect. When using the
Pythagorean theorem $a^2 + b^2 = c^2$, a and b
represent the lengths of the legs.
Choice **d** is incorrect. While the Pythagorean
theorem does contain a sum, the terms are also
squared.

24. **Choice b is correct.** The highest point in the
graph is the maximum, which is 3. This occurs
at $x = -1$. This is the vertex of the parabola.
Choice **a** is incorrect. The highest point in the
graph is the maximum, which is 3. This occurs
at $x = -1$. This is the vertex of the parabola.
Choice **c** is incorrect. The highest point in the
graph is the maximum, not the minimum.
Choice **d** is incorrect. The highest point in the
graph is the maximum, which is 3. This occurs
at $x = -1$. This is the vertex of the parabola.

25. Choice c is correct. If x is the number of miles between the two cities, then $\frac{2.5 \text{ in.}}{10 \text{ mi}} = \frac{7.1 \text{ in.}}{x \text{ mi}}$. Cross multiply and solve the resulting equation:

$$2.5x = 71$$
$$x = \frac{71}{2.5} = 28.4$$

Choice **a** is incorrect. This is a proportional relationship, so subtraction does not apply in general.

Choice **b** is incorrect. The final result must be in miles, but multiplying two values that are measured in inches will yield a result in square inches.

Choice **d** is incorrect. This would be the number of miles if each inch represented 10 miles.

26. The correct answer is $192,960.94. If x represents the revenue six months ago, then the equation $1.28x = 246,990$ must be true. Dividing both sides by 1.28 yields $x = 192,960.94$.

27. The correct answer is 2002. The largest difference is indicated by the bars representing the enrollment in one year having the largest discrepancy in height. In 2002, the program had an enrollment of approximately 34 male students and 8 female students. This is the largest height discrepancy shown on the graph.

28. Choice d is correct. Using the point-slope formula, the equation of the line must be

$$y - 4 = \frac{4}{5}(x - (-8))$$
$$y - 4 = \frac{4}{5}(x + 8)$$
$$y - 4 = \frac{4}{5}x + \frac{32}{5}$$
$$y = \frac{4}{5}x + \frac{52}{5}$$

To rewrite this in $Ax + By = C$ form, bring the x term to the left-hand side and multiply both sides of the equation by -5.

Choice **a** is incorrect. When rewriting the equation in $Ax + By = C$ form, the -5 must be distributed to all of the terms.

Choice **b** is incorrect. In the point-slope formula, the slope must be distributed to both the x term and the constant term. Further, when rewriting the equation in $Ax + By = C$ form, the -5 must be distributed to all of the terms.

Choice **c** is incorrect. In the point-slope formula, the slope must be distributed to both the x term and the constant term.

29. Choice c is correct. Using the first two points, $m = \frac{4 - 1}{2 - 0} = \frac{3}{2}$.

Choice **a** is incorrect. The slope formula is not $\frac{x_1 - y_1}{x_2 - y_2}$. In other words, the formula involves subtracting values from different points.

Choice **b** is incorrect. The change in y is represented in the numerator of the slope formula, not the denominator.

Choice **d** is incorrect. The slope formula is not $\frac{x_2 - y_2}{x_1 - y_1}$. In other words, the formula involves subtracting values from different points.

30. Choice a is correct. Both terms only share x as a factor. When this term is factored out, the resulting expression is $x(2x - 1)$.

Choice **b** is incorrect. The second term does not have a factor of 2, so $2x$ cannot be factored out of the polynomial.

Choice **c** is incorrect. These two expressions are the factors of the first term. Both are not factors of the second term.

Choice **d** is incorrect. The second term does not have a factor of 2, so $2x$ cannot be factored out of the polynomial. Further, $x - 2$ is not a factor of the polynomial.

31. Choice b is correct. The x-coordinate of the x-intercept of line P is -5, while the x-coordinate of the x-intercept of line Q is $\frac{2}{3}$.

Choice **a** is incorrect. The x-intercept of line P is 5 units away from the origin, while the x-intercept of line Q is less than 1 unit away.

Choice **c** is incorrect. The x-coordinate of the x-intercept of line P is negative.

Choice **d** is incorrect. The x-intercept of line Q can be found by letting $y = 0$ and solving for x.

32. The correct answer is 13.

$$\frac{156 \text{ km}}{12 \text{ hr}} = \frac{\frac{156}{12} \text{ km}}{\frac{12}{12} \text{ hr}} = \frac{13 \text{ km}}{1 \text{ hr}}$$

33. **Choice a is correct.** There are 5.5 house symbols used in the chart for San Diego, indicating $5.5 \times 2,500 = 13,750$ subscribing households in that city.

Choice **b** is incorrect. There are 5.5 house symbols, not 6 (which would result in 15,000 subscribing households).

Choice **c** is incorrect. This is the number of subscribing households in Sacramento.

Choice **d** is incorrect. This is the number of subscribing households in San Francisco.

34. **Choice b is correct.** Using the multiplication rule for probability, the probability is $\frac{14}{30} \times \frac{13}{29} \approx 0.21$ or 21%.

Choice **a** is incorrect. Since the students are being selected from the entire class, the denominator should be 30 and not 14.

Choice **c** is incorrect. This represents the probability that one girl is randomly selected. The question is asking for a compound probability of both selected leaders being boys.

Choice **d** is incorrect. The probability of an "and" event should use the multiplication rule, not the addition rule.

35. **Choice d is correct.** To isolate the x, multiply both sides of the equation by the reciprocal of $\frac{3}{4}$. Thus $x = \frac{4}{3}(12) = 16$.

Choice **a** is incorrect. To cancel out the $\frac{3}{4}$, both sides should be multiplied by the reciprocal instead of the original fraction.

Choice **b** is incorrect. Subtracting the fraction from both sides will not isolate the x since the x is multiplied by the fraction.

Choice **c** is incorrect. Adding the fraction to both sides will not isolate the x since the x is multiplied by the fraction.

36. **Choice c is correct.** This line has the same slope and therefore, by definition, is a line that is parallel to the original.

Choice **a** is incorrect. This line is perpendicular to the given line.

Choice **b** is incorrect. Although the y-intercept is the negative reciprocal of the y-intercept of the original line, this has no effect on whether the line is parallel.

Choice **d** is incorrect. Although the y-intercept is the same as the y-intercept of the original line, this has no effect on whether the line is parallel.

37. **Choice c is correct.** The area of the rectangular region is $8 \times 3 = 24$ square meters, while the area of the half circle is $\frac{1}{2}\pi r^2 = \frac{1}{2}\pi(\frac{8}{2})^2 = \frac{1}{2}\pi(16) = 8\pi$.

Choice **a** is incorrect. This is the perimeter of the region.

Choice **b** is incorrect. This would be the perimeter of the region if the radius was 8 meters (this is the diameter) and if it was a full circle instead of a half circle.

Choice **d** is incorrect. The area of the half circle is half of the usual area formula πr^2. This is the area if the full circle was used.

38. **Choice c is correct.** $-3(-4) + 10(-2) = 12 - 20 = -8$.

Choice **a** is incorrect. This results from mixing up the substitution of x and y. The term multiplied by -3 should be -4.

Choice **b** is incorrect. The product of -3 and -4 is positive since both signs are negative.

Choice **d** is incorrect. When substituting values into the expression, the notation $-3x$ and $10y$ indicates multiplication and not addition.

39. Choice b is correct. $-x^2(x + 1) - (x^3 + 4x^2) =$
$-x^3 - x^2 - x^3 - 4x^2 = -2x^3 - 5x^2$.
Choice **a** is incorrect. The terms within the second set of parentheses are not like terms and therefore cannot be combined.
Choice **c** is incorrect. The negative must be distributed to every term in the second set of parentheses.
Choice **d** is incorrect. The terms in front of both sets of parentheses must be distributed to every term within the parentheses.

40. Choice a is correct. The slope of the line is $m = \frac{9 - 1}{4 - (-8)} = \frac{8}{12} = \frac{2}{3}$. Using this in the point-slope formula along with the first point, the equation can be found with the following steps.

$$y - 1 = \tfrac{2}{3}(x - (-8))$$
$$y - 1 = \tfrac{2}{3}(x + 8)$$
$$y - 1 = \tfrac{2}{3}x + \tfrac{16}{3}$$
$$y = \tfrac{2}{3}x + \tfrac{19}{3}$$

Choice **b** is incorrect. In the point-slope formula, the slope should multiply the entire term $(x - x_1)$.
Choice **c** is incorrect. The slope of the line should be the change in y divided by the change in x. Additionally, only one point should be used in the formula instead of an x value from one point and a y value from another.
Choice **d** is incorrect. The slope of the line should be $\frac{2}{3}$, the change in y divided by the change in x.

41. Choice c is correct. The volume of one of the cubes is $2 \times 2 \times 2 = 8$ cm^3. Since the part consists of two cubes, the final volume is double this, or 16 cm^3.
Choice **a** is incorrect. This is the area of one face of one of the cubes.
Choice **b** is incorrect. This is the volume of only one of the cubes used to make the part.
Choice **d** is incorrect. This is the surface area of the final part.

42. Choice c is correct. $75 \times 20 = 1,500$, $0.01 \times 1,500 = 15$, and $0.03 \times 1,500 = 45$ for a total of $1,500 + 15 + 45 = 1,560$.
Choice **a** is incorrect. This includes only the telecommunications fee, but there is also a 3% project fee.
Choice **b** is incorrect. This includes only the project fee, but there is also a 1% telecommunications fee.
Choice **d** is incorrect. Three percent of a total is found by multiplying by 0.03, not 0.3. Similarly, one percent is found by multiplying by 0.01 instead of 0.1.

43. The correct answer is $\frac{5}{4}x - 5$.
$\frac{1}{2}x + \frac{3}{4}x - 5 = \frac{2}{4}x + \frac{3}{4}x - 5 = \frac{5}{4}x - 5$.

44. Choice a is correct. To maintain the ratio, the fraction of full-time employees to part-time employees must be equivalent to $\frac{4}{3}$. The number of full-time employees can be found by multiplying 4 by 5; therefore, the number of part-time employees can be found by multiplying 3 by 5 to get 15.
Choice **b** is incorrect. Although the difference between 20 and 4 is 16, it can't be used to find the final answer. Ratios work with a common multiplier, not a common sum.
Choice **c** is incorrect. This will not maintain the ratio, since it did not use a common multiplier.
Choice **d** is incorrect. This is approximately correct if the number of part-time employees was 20 instead of full-time employees.

45. Choice b is correct. $\frac{(-3) - 5}{(-3)^2 + 1} = \frac{-8}{10} = -\frac{4}{5}$.
Choice **a** is incorrect. The numerator of the fraction shows subtraction of 5 from x, not multiplication.
Choice **c** is incorrect. The value of $(-3)^2$ is 9, not 6.
Choice **d** is incorrect. The value of $(-3)^2$ is 9, not -9.

3 ▶ NUMBER FOUNDATIONS PART I: FRACTIONS AND DECIMALS

In this chapter you will begin to learn the arithmetic concepts that are the foundations of algebra. Since algebra is used to model and solve complex problems, algebra is an important skill to have in your personal life as well as in the work force. Solving problems accurately with careful math will help you make good consumer decisions and avoid expensive mistakes on the job or at home—as well as do well on the GED® test!

This chapter covers:

- Vocabulary used to define arithmetic operations
- Least common multiples (LCMs) and greatest common factors (GCFs)
- Simplifying and creating equivalent fractions
- Operations with fractions
- Comparing and ordering decimals, fractions, and negative numbers in lists as well as on number lines

Throughout this chapter there are practice exercises that will help reinforce the concepts in each section. At the end of the chapter you will find a comprehensive set of questions that model the types of questions you will find on the GED® test. The answers and explanations for all the practice questions and review questions can be found at the end of the chapter.

The Language of Math

In order to be ready to learn the arithmetic foundations of algebra, you must become completely comfortable with the language used to represent the four basic math operations: addition, subtraction, division, and multiplication. Let's begin our exploration by investigating which mathematical operations are represented by various everyday words.

GED® QUESTION SNEAK PREVIEW!

These *Sneak Preview* boxes will give you an idea of what you may see on your GED® Mathematical Reasoning Test. Read the following section to learn how to answer these types of questions:

- *What is triple the difference of 65 and 50?*
- Use numbers and variables to represent the following: *What is 7 less than the product of 10 and a number x?*

English-to-Math Translations

Algebra is used to model real world situations, but first you must get comfortable with translating words into math. Let's begin with the four key words that represent addition, subtraction, division, and multiplication. In this chapter we'll use these words with numbers, and we will review these terms in a later chapter once we begin applying them with variables.

Sum: A *sum* of two or more numbers is the answer to an *addition* problem.
- *The sum of 3 and 5 is 8 (i.e., 3 + 5 = 8).*
- *If Jane has 4 guitars and James has 5 guitars, the sum of their guitars is 9.*

Difference: A *difference* between two numbers is the answer to a *subtraction* problem.
- *The difference of 5 and 4 is 1 (i.e., 5 − 4 = 1).*
- *If Jane is 60 inches tall and James is 52 inches tall, the difference in their heights is 8 inches.*

Quotient: A *quotient* is the answer to a *division* problem.
- *The quotient of 18 and 6 is 3 (i.e., 18 ÷ 6 = 3).*
- *If Jane is 30 and James is 15, the quotient of their ages is 2.*

Product: A *product* is the answer to a *multiplication* problem.
- *The product of 8 and 9 is 72 (i.e., 8 × 9 = 72).*
- *If Jane's lucky number is 8 and James's lucky number is 11, the product of their lucky numbers is 88.*

Don't expect to see the words above all the time—just like there are many ways to say "hello," there are lots of other ways to indicate the four operations. Let's consider 6 + 7, which could be described the following ways:

- *the sum of six and seven*
- *six plus seven*
- *six more than seven*
- *six increased by seven*
- *the total of six and seven*

Each of these phrases contains a different keyword that signals addition: *plus*, *more than*, *increased*, and *total*. The four basic operations have a handful of keywords that act as a clue to which operation will be used.

The following chart lists several of the most common keywords for each operation:

ADDITION	SUBTRACTION	MULTIPLICATION	DIVISION
sum	difference	product	quotient
combine	take away	times	percent
total	less than	of	out of
plus	minus	every	share
and	decrease	each	split
altogether	left	factors	average
increase	fewer	double (× 2)	each
more than	remove	triple (× 3)	per

Words That Symbolize Grouping in Parentheses

In addition to words that indicate the four basic arithmetic operations, keep your eyes out for special words and phrases that combine more than one operation and sometimes require parentheses:

The quantity of: *The quantity of* indicates that there are two or more terms combined to make one term. This combination of multiple terms into a single term requires *parentheses*.

- *6 times the quantity of 5 plus 10 is written* 6(5 + 10)

The sum of and **the difference of:** These two terms are like *the quantity of* in that they are used to symbolize that parentheses must be used.

- *5 times the difference of 8 and 3 is written* 5(8 − 3)
- *The sum of 20 and 19 divided by 3 is written* (20 + 19) ÷ 3

DON'T DO THIS!

Many students forget to use parentheses when they are presented with the terms *the quantity of*, *the sum of*, and *the difference of*. Remember that these special phrases require grouping. Don't fall for this common mistake! (Note: The symbol ≠ is read "does not equal" and you will see it in lots of these *Don't Do This!* boxes.)

NO! *2 times the sum of 12 and 10* ≠ 2 × 12 + 10

YES . . . Instead, *2 times the sum of 12 and 10* = 2(12 + 10)

Tricky Subtraction Clues

Sometimes words for subtraction can be tricky. For example, *from* and *less than* indicate subtraction, but the order of the terms must be reversed:

- **From:** *Subtract 8 from 10 is written as* 10 − 8 and **not** *8 − 10*. This is because the phrase indicates that 8 is the number being subtracted, not 10.

■ **Less than:** *2 less than 20* is written *20 – 2* and **not** *2 – 20*. The phrasing indicates that 20 is the starting number, which is being reduced by 2.

DON'T DO THIS!

Many students forget that when translating *from* and *less than* into mathematical equations it is necessary to flip the order that the numbers or terms are presented in.)

NO! *10 less than 5 ≠ 10 – 5*

YES . . . Instead, *10 less than 5 = 5 – 10*

Special Multiplication Words

The word *twice* represents multiplication by 2 and *triple* signifies multiplication by 3:

Twice: *Twice as much as the original $50 price* is written as *2 × $50*

Triple: *Triple the number of last year's 4,000 attendees* is written as *3 × 4,000*

Practice

Represent each phrase as a numerical expression. Do not combine the numbers to evaluate them for a final answer.

1. 10 passengers increased by 20 and then decreased by 7

2. $85 is shared by three siblings

3. Four less than the product of six and twelve

4. Triple the sum of their $500 October sales and their $700 November sales

5. They split the difference of her expenses of $3,200 and his expenses of $2,800

6. $40 less than $100 is increased by $80 and then doubled

Multiples, Factors, and Simplifying Fractions

Multiples and *factors* are important vocabulary words that are commonly used when explaining how to perform important operations on numbers. Multiples and factors are especially useful when working with fractions and later, in algebraic equations.

GED® QUESTION SNEAK PREVIEW!

You may be asked a question like this on your GED® Mathematical Reasoning test! We haven't introduced variables yet, so you might not know how to answer this, but this also requires a solid understanding of factors.

■ *What is the greatest common factor of $14x^4yz^2$ and $35xy^3$?*

Multiples

Multiples are numbers that result when multiplying one number by whole numbers such as 1, 2, 3, 4, 5, and so forth. For example, if we wanted to find the multiples of 6, we would start out with:

- $6 \times 1 = \underline{6}$
- $6 \times 2 = \underline{12}$
- $6 \times 3 = \underline{18}$
- $6 \times 4 = \underline{24}$

Every number has an infinite number of multiples. However, here, we will just list the first several multiples of 6:

Multiples of 6: 6, 12, 18, 24, 30, 36, 42, 48, 54 . . .

The Least Common Multiple

The **LCM** or **least common multiple** is the smallest multiple that two different numbers or terms have in common. For example, in order to find the LCM of 8 and 12, write out the beginning of the multiple lists for 8 and 12.

First create multiple lists for 8 and 12:

Multiples of 8: 8, 16, **24**, 32, 40, **48**, 56
Multiples of 12: 12, **24**, 36, **48**, 60

Looking at these lists, you can see 24 and 48 are *both* multiples of 8 and 12. Since 24 is the smallest multiple 8 and 12 have in *common, 24 is the least common multiple of 8 and 12.*

Knowing how to find least common multiples is critical for adding, subtracting, and comparing fractions, which we will learn about later in this chapter.

The Greatest Common Factor

A number that divides evenly into another number is a **factor** of the second number. For instance, the factors of 12 are 1, 2, 3, 4, 6, and 12 since all these numbers evenly divide into 12. It is also true that 7 is a factor of 7, 14, 21, and 28. (Can you see the relationship between *factors* and *multiples*?)

The **greatest common factor**, commonly referred to as the **GCF**, is a special factor that is shared by two or more numbers. The GCF is the *largest factor* that the numbers being considered have in common. In order to find the GFC of two numbers, write out the factor lists for both numbers and select the greatest factor they have in common. For example, let's find the greatest common factor of 32 and 40.

Make factor lists for 32 and 40:

Factors of 32: 1, <u>2</u>, <u>4</u>, **8**, 16, 32
Factors of 40: 1, <u>2</u>, <u>4</u>, 5, **8**, 10, 20, 40

Although 2, 4, and 8 are all factors of both 32 and 40, 8 is the GCF.

Finding the GCF between two or more numbers is necessary when reducing fractions, which we will discuss next. Being able to identify the greatest common factor is also helpful when simplifying complex algebraic expressions, which will be covered in later chapters.

VOCABULARY ALERT!

The **least common multiple** is the smallest multiple that two or more numbers have in common. *36 is the least common multiple of 9 and 12.*

The **greatest common factor** is the largest factor that two or more numbers have in common. *10 is the greatest common factor of 10 and 20.*

Simplifying Fractions

Before we jump into fractions, let's review some important vocabulary: the number on the *top* of a fraction is called the **numerator** and the number on the bottom of a fraction is called the **denominator**. Commit these terms to memory so that you can understand explanations and instructions in your future math studies.

VOCABULARY ALERT!

The number located on the top of a fraction is called the **numerator** and the number located on the bottom is called the **denominator**:

$$\frac{\text{numerator}}{\text{denominator}}$$

Simplest Form

A fraction is in **simplest form**, or **lowest terms**, when its numerator and denominator cannot be divided by any like factor. In order to reduce a fraction into simplest form, divide the numerator and denominator by the greatest common factor. This is a critical skill required for the GED® test since all answer choices will be presented in lowest terms. Therefore, in order to identify the correct answer choice from a multiple choice list, you'll need to reduce fractional answers to simplest form.

Example

What is $\frac{24}{42}$ in simplest form?

First identify that the GCF of 24 and 42 is 6. Then divide both the numerator and denominator by the GCF:

$$\frac{24}{42} = \frac{24 \div 6}{42 \div 6} = \frac{4}{7}$$

Therefore, $\frac{24}{42}$ reduced to lowest terms is equivalent to $\frac{4}{7}$.

Even though $\frac{24}{42}$ and $\frac{4}{7}$ are equivalent, the fraction $\frac{4}{7}$ is in *simplest form* because it cannot be reduced any further. All multiple-choice answers will be presented in simplest form.

Practice

7. What is the least common multiple of 6 and 20?

8. What is the least common multiple of 12, 18, and 6?

9. What is the greatest common factor of 15 and 60?

10. Is there ever a time when the greatest common factor of two numbers will be 1?

11. Reduce the fraction $\frac{48}{72}$ to lowest terms.

Working with Fractions

Fractions are one of the most important building blocks of mathematics since we encounter fractions every day: in recipes ($\frac{1}{3}$ cup of milk), driving ($\frac{3}{4}$ of a mile), land measurements ($5\frac{1}{2}$ acres), money (half a dollar), and so forth. Many arithmetic problems involve fractions in one way or another. Decimals, percents, ratios, and proportions, which are covered in later chapters, require proficiency with fractions.

GED® QUESTION SNEAK PREVIEW!

The GED® Mathematical Reasoning Test may ask you to represent the fractional total that certain quantities represent. Read the following section to learn how to answer questions like this:

- *If Emma uses 8 inches of a yard of fabric and Jackson uses 14 inches from that same yard, what fraction of the yard of fabric did they use together?*

Representing Measurements with Fractions

A fraction is a representation of a *part to a whole*. The denominator represents the total number of units that make up one whole, while the numerator represents the number of units that are being considered.

Example

What fraction of an hour does 15 minutes represent?

Start with the part to whole relationship and fill in the given and known information:

$$\frac{\text{part}}{\text{whole}} = \frac{\text{\# of minutes being considered}}{\text{\# of minutes in one whole hour}} = \frac{15}{60}$$

So, 15 minutes is $\frac{15}{60}$ of an hour. Now reduce that to simplest terms:

$$\frac{15}{60} = \frac{15 \div 15}{60 \div 15} = \frac{1}{4}$$

Therefore, 15 minutes is equivalent to $\frac{1}{4}$ of an hour.

DON'T DO THIS!

When writing fractions, the numerator and denominator must be in the same units. For example, consider a situation where Sophia has 3 feet of ribbon and she uses 7 inches of it to make a bow. It would be incorrect to say that she used $\frac{7}{3}$ of her ribbon since the 7 would be in inches and the 3 would be in feet. Instead, both the numerator and the denominator must be in the same units. Therefore, turn the 3 feet into inches by multiplying it by the 12 inches that are in each foot: 3 ft. × 12 in. = 36 inches. Now we can say that Sophia used $\frac{7}{36}$ of her ribbon since both the numerator and denominator are in inches.

Proper Fractions, Improper Fractions, and Mixed Numbers

You need to know some important terms used to describe fractions so that you can understand the instructions for adding, subtracting, multiplying, and dividing fractions that will follow. Fractions are broken down into three types:

- **Proper fractions** have a numerator that is less than the denominator: $\frac{1}{3}$, $\frac{2}{5}$, and $\frac{4}{7}$.
- **Improper fractions** have a numerator that is greater than the denominator: $\frac{3}{2}$, $\frac{5}{3}$, and $\frac{7}{5}$. All improper fractions have a value greater than one.

- **Mixed numbers** contain a whole number along with a proper fraction written to the right of it: $4\frac{1}{2}$, $7\frac{2}{3}$, and $10\frac{1}{3}$.

Similarly to how fractions are always reduced to simplest terms before giving the final answer to a question, improper fractions are typically converted to mixed numbers when answering questions. A mixed number is easier to understand in context than an improper fraction.

Think about this: If Jimbo tells his employer he has $\frac{7}{3}$ bags of cement left to build a retaining wall, this information is not entirely easy for his boss to picture. However, if Jimbo tells her that he has $2\frac{1}{3}$ bags of cement remaining, that gives his employer a much clearer picture of his remaining supplies. Read on to learn how to convert a mixed number into an improper fraction.

Changing Improper Fractions into Mixed Numbers

In order to change improper fractions into mixed numbers, use the following steps:

1. Divide the denominator into the numerator.
2. If there is a remainder, change it into a fraction by writing the remainder over the original denominator of the improper fraction. Write it next to the whole number.

Example

Change $\frac{13}{2}$ into a mixed number.

1. Divide the denominator (2) into the numerator (13) to get the whole number portion (6) of the mixed number:

$$\begin{array}{r} 6 \\ 2\overline{)13} \\ \underline{12} \end{array}$$

2. Write the remainder of the division (1) over the original denominator (2):

$$\begin{array}{r} 1 \\ \frac{1}{2} \end{array}$$

3. Write the two numbers together: $6\frac{1}{2}$

4. Check: Change the mixed number back into an improper fraction (see below). If you get the original improper fraction, your answer is correct.

Changing Mixed Numbers into Improper Fractions

Mixed numbers must be turned into improper fractions before you can multiply and divide them. Convert mixed numbers into improper fractions using the following steps:

1. Multiply the whole number by the denominator.
2. Add the product from step 1 to the numerator.
3. Write that sum as the numerator of a fraction over the original denominator.

Example

Change $\frac{12}{4}$ into a mixed number.

1. Divide the denominator (4) into the numerator (12) to get the whole number portion (3) of the mixed number:

$$\begin{array}{r} 3 \\ 4\overline{)12} \\ \underline{12} \\ 0 \end{array}$$

2. Since the remainder of the division is zero, you're done. The improper fraction $\frac{12}{4}$ is actually a whole number: 3

3. Check: Multiply 3 by the original bottom number (4) to make sure you get the original top number (12) as the answer.

Raising Fractions to Higher Terms

We have already discussed simplifying fractions by dividing the numerator and denominator by their GCF. The opposite of reducing a fraction is raising it to higher terms. It is often necessary to raise a fraction to higher terms in order to create common denominators, which are needed to add and subtract fractions. To create an equivalent fraction that is in higher terms, multiply the numerator and denominator by the same number and rewrite the products as a new fraction.

Example

Rewrite $\frac{2}{3}$ as an equivalent fraction with a denominator of 27:

Starting with $\frac{2}{3}$, determine that both the numerator and denominator must be multiplied by 9 in order to create a denominator of 27:

$$\frac{2}{3} = \frac{2 \times 9}{3 \times 9} = \frac{18}{27}$$

In this manner, $\frac{2}{3}$ can be rewritten as $\frac{18}{27}$, and they are equivalent fractions:

Practice

12. 25¢ is what fraction of 75¢?

13. $20.00 is what fraction of $200.00?

14. 8 inches is what fraction of a foot?

15. 8 inches is what fraction of a yard? (Hint: 1 yard = 36 inches)

16. 1,320 feet is what fraction of a mile? (Hint: 1 mile = 5,280 feet)

17. 3 minutes is what fraction of an hour?

18. 30 seconds is what fraction of an hour? (Hint: How many seconds are in an hour?)

19. 80 minutes is what fraction of a day? (Hint: How many minutes are in a day?)

20. Convert $4\frac{3}{5}$ into an improper fraction.

21. Convert $\frac{20}{3}$ into a mixed number.

Operations on Fractions

Now that you understand fractions as *part to whole* relationships and how to manipulate them into equivalent fractions, let's review how to add, subtract, multiply, and divide fractions.

Adding and Subtracting Fractions

Fractions must have **common denominators** before adding or subtracting them. When two fractions have the same denominator, it means that all the pieces are the same size, and therefore you can just combine the numerators. When adding or subtracting two fractions that have common denominators, *add or subtract the numerators together and keep the denominator the same*. For example, $\frac{1}{2} + \frac{1}{2}$ would be done as such:

$$\frac{1}{2} + \frac{1}{2} = \frac{1+1}{2} = \frac{2}{2}$$

DON'T DO THIS!

Remember, do NOT add the denominators! Keep the denominator the same!

NO! $\frac{1}{2} + \frac{1}{2} \neq \frac{1+1}{2+2} = \frac{2}{4} = \frac{1}{2}$

Since $\frac{2}{4}$ reduces to $\frac{1}{2}$, it wouldn't make any sense for $\frac{1}{2} + \frac{1}{2} = \frac{2}{4}$.

YES . . . $\frac{1}{2} + \frac{1}{2} = \frac{1+1}{2} = \frac{2}{2} = 1$

If you get confused about this rule, you can always comes back to this example that $\frac{1}{2} + \frac{1}{2}$ should equal 1, and not $\frac{1}{2}$!

Making Common Denominators

Oftentimes, two or more fractions will not have common denominators and you will need to create common denominators by raising fractions to higher terms. It is always a good idea to use the **least common multiple** as the common denominator because there will be less reducing required at the end. In this example, one of the denominators was a factor of the other denominator, so only one fraction needed to be changed:

Example
$\frac{1}{6} + \frac{7}{12}$

1. Notice that the smaller denominator (6) evenly divides into the larger denominator (12), so find the LCD by raising $\frac{1}{6}$ to 12ths:
$$\frac{1}{6} = \frac{1 \times 2}{6 \times 2} = \frac{2}{12}$$

2. Add the numerators and keep the denominator the same:
$$\frac{2}{12} + \frac{7}{12} = \frac{9}{12}$$

3. Reduce to lowest terms or write as a mixed number, if applicable:
$$\frac{9}{12} = \frac{3}{4}$$

In this next example, neither of the denominators were factors of each other, so both fractions get manipulated:

Example

$\frac{2}{3} + \frac{4}{5}$

1. Here, 3 does not divide evenly into 5, so find a common denominator by multiplying the denominators by each other:

$3 \times 5 = 15$

2. Raise each fraction to 15ths, the LCD:

$\frac{2}{3} = \frac{10}{15}$

$\frac{4}{5} = \frac{12}{15}$

3. Add numerators and keep the denominator the same:

$\frac{22}{15}$

4. Reduce to lowest terms or write as an equivalent mixed number, if applicable:

$\frac{22}{15} = 1\frac{7}{15}$

Multiplying Fractions

The good news is that multiplication and division with fractions is actually much easier than addition and subtraction. Multiplication and division do NOT require common denominators. When you multiply fractions, you can simply multiply both the numerators and the denominators straight across:

$$\frac{1}{2} \times \frac{2}{3} = \frac{1 \times 2}{2 \times 3} = \frac{2}{6} = \frac{1}{3}$$

After you multiply or divide fractions, always reduce your answer to lowest terms.

Dividing Fractions

Dividing fractions is almost just as easy as multiplying fractions! To divide fractions, multiply the first fraction by the reciprocal of the second fraction. The **reciprocal** is the flipped version of that fraction, where the numerator and denominator have switched places. Notice in the following example that the reciprocal of $\frac{2}{3}$ is $\frac{3}{2}$ once the problem has been changed from division to multiplication:

$$\frac{1}{2} \div \frac{2}{3} = \frac{1}{2} \times \frac{3}{2} = \frac{1 \times 3}{2 \times 2} = \frac{3}{4}$$

DON'T DO THIS!

When dividing fractions, do NOT use the reciprocal of the first fraction. You must keep the first fraction the same and use the reciprocal of the second fraction:

NO! $\frac{5}{7} \div \frac{1}{10} \neq \frac{7}{5} \times \frac{1}{10}$

YES . . . $\frac{5}{7} \div \frac{1}{10} = \frac{5}{7} \times \frac{10}{1}$

Adding Mixed Numbers

Mixed numbers, you remember, consist of a whole number and a proper fraction. To add mixed numbers:

1. Add the fractional parts of the mixed numbers. If the sum is an improper fraction, change it to a mixed number.
2. Add the whole number parts of the original mixed numbers.
3. Add the results of steps 1 and 2.

Example

$2\frac{3}{5} + 1\frac{4}{5}$

1. Add the fractional parts of the mixed numbers and change the improper fraction into a mixed number:

$$\frac{3}{5} + \frac{4}{5} = \frac{7}{5} = 1\frac{2}{5}$$

2. Add the whole number parts of the original mixed numbers:

$$2 + 1 = 3$$

3. Add the results of steps 1 and 2:

$$1\frac{2}{5} + 3 = 4\frac{2}{5}$$

Watch Out! Subtracting Mixed Numbers

Consider the problem $5\frac{1}{2} - 2\frac{7}{8}$. Notice that the fractional portion of $2\frac{7}{8}$ is larger than the fractional portion of $5\frac{1}{2}$. There are a few different ways to handle this type of situation, but the easiest and most reliable method is to turn both mixed numbers into improper fractions and then proceed with the subtraction:

Example

Calculate: $5\frac{1}{2} - 2\frac{7}{8}$

1. Make common denominators to subtract the fractions: $5\frac{1}{2} = 5\frac{1 \times 4}{2 \times 4} = 5\frac{4}{8}$

2. After noticing that the second fractional part is larger than the first fractional part, rewrite mixed numbers as improper fractions:

$$5\frac{4}{8} - 2\frac{7}{8} \Rightarrow \frac{44}{8} - \frac{23}{8}$$

3. Subtract the numerators and keep the denominator the same, then rewrite the answer as a mixed number:

$$\frac{44 - 23}{8} = \frac{21}{8} = 2\frac{5}{8}$$

Multiplying and Dividing Mixed Numbers

It is necessary to change mixed numbers into improper fractions before they can be multiplied or divided.

Example

$4\frac{2}{3} \times 5\frac{1}{2}$

1. Change $4\frac{2}{3}$ to an improper fraction:

$$4\frac{2}{3} = \frac{4 \times 3 + 2}{3} = \frac{14}{3}$$

2. Change $5\frac{1}{2}$ to an improper fraction:

$$5\frac{1}{2} = \frac{5 \times 2 + 1}{2} = \frac{11}{2}$$

3. Multiply the fractions:
   Notice that you can cancel a 2 from both the 14 and the 2.

$$\frac{\overset{7}{\cancel{14}}}{3} \times \frac{11}{\underset{1}{\cancel{2}}}$$

4. Change the improper fraction to a mixed number.

$$\frac{77}{3} = 25\frac{2}{3}$$

DON'T DO THIS!

When multiplying mixed numbers, it is tempting but incorrect to multiply the whole numbers by each other and then multiply the fractions by each other. Do not fall for this common mistake! Instead, convert mixed numbers to improper fractions before performing multiplication or division!

NO! $2\frac{1}{3} \times 5\frac{1}{2} \neq (2 \times 5) + (\frac{1}{3} \times \frac{1}{2})$

YES . . . $2\frac{1}{3} \times 5\frac{1}{2} = \frac{7}{3} \times \frac{11}{2}$

When dividing mixed numbers, it is still necessary to take the reciprocal of the second improper fraction:

Example

$2\frac{3}{4} \div \frac{1}{6}$

1. Change $2\frac{3}{4}$ to an improper fraction:

$$2\frac{3}{4} = \frac{2 \times 4 + 3}{4} = \frac{11}{4}$$

2. Rewrite the division problem:

$$\frac{11}{4} \div \frac{1}{6}$$

3. Find the reciprocal of the $\frac{1}{6}$ and multiply:

$$\frac{11}{\underset{2}{\cancel{4}}} \times \frac{\overset{3}{\cancel{6}}}{1} = \frac{11 \times 3}{2 \times 1} = \frac{33}{2}$$

4. Change the improper fraction to a mixed number.

$$\frac{33}{2} = 16\frac{1}{2}$$

Practice

22. $\frac{1}{6} + \frac{7}{12}$

23. $\frac{1}{4} - \frac{1}{6}$

24. $\frac{3}{4} \times \frac{5}{6}$

25. $\frac{3}{4} \div \frac{5}{6}$

26. $2\frac{1}{3} \times 4\frac{2}{5}$

Ordering Fractions and Decimals

On the GED® test it is likely that you will be asked to put fractions, decimals, and rational numbers in order, either presented as a list or on a number line. In this section you will learn how to how to read and order decimals, how to compare fractions, and how to order negative numbers.

GED® QUESTION SNEAK PREVIEW!

On the GED test you need to be ready for ordering questions such as this:

- Click and drag these numbers so they are ordered from least to greatest: 0.2, –0.045, 0.06, 0.053, –0.44

Understanding and Ordering Decimals

Place values to the right of the decimal point represent parts of a whole. The names of the place values look similar to those of numbers to the left of the decimal point. However, note the *-ths* at the end of each name in the chart.

ONES	.	TENTHS	HUNDREDTHS	THOUSANDTHS	TEN THOUSANDTHS	. . .
4	.	3				
3	.	4	5			
5	.	2	3	5		

The first number listed in the table, 4.3, is read, "Four and three tenths." To illustrate this as a mixed number

(a whole number and a fraction), it is written like it sounds: $4\frac{3}{10}$.

The second number listed, 3.45, is read as "three and forty-five hundredths." As a mixed number, it is written $3\frac{45}{100}$.

The third number listed in the chart, 523.5, is read as "five and two hundred thirty-five thousandths." It is written $5\frac{235}{1,000}$.

To order decimals on the number line, you can use the previous strategy of writing decimals as fractions with a power of 10 (10, 100, 1,000, 10,000, and so forth).

For example, let's order the following decimals from least to greatest:

1.2, 1.40, 1.15, 1.67, and 1.53.

Each of these decimals has two digits to the right of the decimal point except the number 1.2. However, adding zeros at the end of a decimal number does not change the value: 1.2 is equivalent to 1.20, which is also equivalent to 1.200. The pattern continues.

To make the comparison easier, simply add a zero to 1.2 so that each number has the same number of digits to the right of the decimal point. Then, note that each denominator will be 100 since there are two digits to the right of each decimal point (the hundredths place).

$$1.20 = 1\frac{20}{100}$$
$$1.40 = 1\frac{40}{100}$$
$$1.15 = 1\frac{15}{100}$$
$$1.67 = 1\frac{67}{100}$$
$$1.53 = 1\frac{53}{100}$$

Since each fraction has the same denominator, it is easy to determine the order of the numbers: 1.15, 1.2, 1.4, 1.53, and 1.67.

It is also helpful to think about decimals in terms of money. For instance, 1.2 is like $1.20. We all know that this amount is a little more than $1. Another example: 3.76 is like $3.76—it is about $\frac{3}{4}$ of the way between $3 and $4. The following number line illustrates this concept.

Comparing Fractions

Which fraction is larger, $\frac{3}{8}$ or $\frac{3}{5}$? Don't be fooled into thinking that $\frac{3}{8}$ is larger just because it has the larger denominator. Use any of these three reliable ways to compare fractions:

- **Compare the fractions to $\frac{1}{2}$.** Both $\frac{3}{8}$ and $\frac{3}{5}$ are close to $\frac{1}{2}$. However, $\frac{3}{5}$ is more than $\frac{1}{2}$, while $\frac{3}{8}$ is less than $\frac{1}{2}$. Therefore, $\frac{3}{5}$ is larger than $\frac{3}{8}$. Comparing fractions to $\frac{1}{2}$ is actually quite simple. The fraction $\frac{3}{8}$ is less than $\frac{4}{8}$, which is the same as $\frac{1}{2}$; in a similar fashion, $\frac{3}{5}$ is more than $\frac{2.5}{5}$, which is the same as $\frac{1}{2}$. ($\frac{2.5}{5}$ may sound like a strange fraction, but you can easily see that it's the same as $\frac{1}{2}$ by considering a pizza cut into 5 slices. If you were to eat half the pizza, you'd eat 2.5 slices.)

- **Raise both fractions to higher terms with the same denominator.** When both fractions have the same denominator, then all you need to do is compare their numerators.

$$\frac{3}{5} = \frac{3 \times 8}{5 \times 8} = \frac{24}{40} \quad \text{and} \quad \frac{3}{8} = \frac{3 \times 5}{8 \times 5} = \frac{15}{40}$$

Since 24 is greater than 15, $\frac{24}{40}$ is greater than $\frac{15}{40}$.

This shows that $\frac{3}{5}$ is greater than $\frac{3}{8}$.

- **Shortcut: cross multiply.** "Cross multiply" means to perform diagonal multiplication between the denominators of each fraction with the numerators of the other fraction. To compare fractions through cross multiplication, write the cross multiplication results above the fractions and compare them. The cross product that was larger will be sitting above the larger fraction.

$$\overset{\textcircled{24}}{\tfrac{3}{5}} \underset{\text{vs}}{\times} \overset{\textcircled{15}}{\tfrac{3}{8}}$$

Since 24 is greater than 15, this indicates that $\frac{3}{5}$ is larger than $\frac{3}{8}$.

Comparing Fractions and Decimals Together

Sometimes the GED® test will ask you to order a list of numbers that contains both decimals and fractions. There are two different ways you can approach this:

1. Turn the fractions into decimals, so the list contains only decimals.
2. Turn the decimals into fractions, so the list contains only fractions.

These are both valuable skills to have for other mathematical tasks other than ordering lists of numbers, so make sure you are comfortable with both of the following conversion techniques.

Converting Fractions into Decimals

Convert fractions into decimals to make them easier to work with or to compare to other decimals. This is not a difficult task since **a fraction simply means "divide."** The numerator of the fraction is divided by the denominator. Thus, $\frac{3}{4}$ means "3 divided by 4," which may also be written as $3 \div 4$ or $4\overline{)3}$. The value of $\frac{3}{4}$ is the same as the *quotient* (result) you get when

you perform the division. $3 \div 4 = 0.75$, which is the **decimal value** of the fraction.

Converting Decimals into Fractions

Converting a decimal into a fraction can make it easier to compare to other fractions. Earlier you reviewed the names of different decimal places: tenths, hundredths, thousandths, and so on. To change a decimal to a fraction:

1. Write the digits of the decimal as the top number of a fraction.
2. Write the decimal's name as the bottom number of the fraction.

Example

Change 0.018 to a fraction.

1. Write 18 as the top of the fraction: $\qquad$ $\frac{18}{}$
2. Since there are three places to the right of the decimal, it's thousandths.
3. Write 1,000 as the bottom number: $\qquad$ $\frac{18}{1,000}$
4. Reduce by dividing 2 into the top and bottom numbers: $\qquad$ $\frac{18 \div 2}{1,000 \div 2} = \frac{9}{500}$

Ordering with Negative Numbers

When ordering values that include negative numbers, it is critical to remember that the larger a negative number is, the smaller its value is.

If negative numbers scare you, just think about them in terms of money. If you keep spending more money than you have in your bank account, you go deeper and deeper into debt. If you have only $3 in your bank account and you buy a sandwich for $5, you will be $2 in the hole. That number is located two spaces to the left of 0 on this number line:

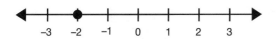

This is true for bigger numbers as well. If you have $100 in your checking account and you spend $150, you owe $50. So your bank account—before overdraft fees, of course—is negative $50. On a number line like the next one, −50 would be 50 spaces to the left of 0.

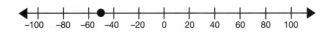

Ordering with Absolute Value

We will go more into absolute value in the next chapter, but a basic way to think about the absolute value of a number is the number without its sign. So the absolute value of −8 is 8. Think about a negative temperature on a freezing cold night. You can probably imagine that it would be much colder on a −20 degree night than on a −3 degree night. This is because −20 is a *smaller number* than −3. However, the absolute value of −20, written |−20|, is actually a bigger number than the absolute value of −3, |−3|. This is because |−20| is farther from 0 on a number line than |−3|.

Ordering on Number Lines

Sometimes you'll be given a question that requires you to place numbers on a number line or use a number line to estimate a value. This still tests your understanding of fractions and decimals. A good tool to keep in mind for this is the "comparing fractions to $\frac{1}{2}$" tip given previously. For example, if asked to plot $\frac{2}{3}$, $-1\frac{1}{4}$, $1\frac{2}{5}$, and $-\frac{7}{8}$ on a number line, we would start by considering each number and how it compares to increments of $\frac{1}{2}$:

- $\frac{2}{3}$ is between 0 and 1, and is bigger than $\frac{1}{2}$, so it will be closer to 1 than it is to 0:

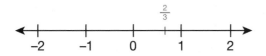

- $-1\frac{1}{4}$. Be careful with negative numbers. Think about spending money. If you spent a dollar and change you have spent more than a dollar, but you didn't spend two dollars, so this number will need to go between −1 and −2. Since the fractional part of $-1\frac{1}{4}$ is less than $\frac{1}{2}$, that means the number will sit closer to the −1 on the number line:

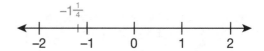

- $1\frac{2}{5}$ is between 1 and 2. The fraction part of this mixed number is smaller than $\frac{1}{2}$, so it will be closer to 1 than it is to 2:

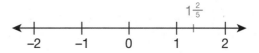

- $-\frac{7}{8}$. Be careful with negative numbers. Think again about spending money. If you spend a fractional part of a dollar, but you didn't spend a whole dollar, that means you spent between 0 and $1. Since $\frac{7}{8}$ is larger than $\frac{1}{2}$, you need to plot $-\frac{7}{8}$ closer to −1 than to 0:

Now when you put all of these numbers together on the number line you can see how they relate to one another:

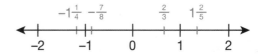

Practice

Write the following lists in order of least to greatest.

27. $\frac{2}{3}, \frac{5}{2}, \frac{3}{4}, \frac{4}{9}$

28. $-0.3, 3.29, 3.031, -0.03, 3.3$

29. $0.34, \frac{1}{5}, -0.4, -\frac{3}{2}, \frac{1}{3}$

CALCULATOR TIPS!

Although it is important to be able to perform all of the fraction and decimal skills presented here by hand, many of these tasks can also be done on the TI-30XS calculator. This calculator will be a great help when working with fractions and decimals, but it will take some time to learn how to use all of its features correctly. Do the following Chapter Review questions without using any of the special calculator functions. After you have read through *Chapter 12: Calculator Skills on the TI-30XS*, you can complete them again with the aid of your calculator.

Summary

After completing this chapter you'll have a thorough understanding of the vocabulary used to describe mathematical operations; how to break numbers down in their factors and multiples; how to work with fractions in several different capacities; and how to order decimals, fractions, and negative numbers. Practice the following questions, which are similar to what you will see on your GED® test day. Good luck!

Number Foundations Part I Review

1. What is the sum of 12.03 and 4.5?
   a. 7.53
   b. 12.48
   c. 16.53
   d. 57.03

2. The table shows Ms. Kayla's GED® students' results from a keyboarding quiz. What is the difference in words per minute (wpm) between the fastest- and the slowest-typing student?

_____

NAME	WORDS TYPED	MINUTES
Percy	90	2
Derrick	67	2
Toneshia	84	2
Connie	70	2
Frank	59	2

3. Using the table from the previous question, how many words would Percy type in 5 minutes?
   a. 450
   b. 180
   c. 350
   d. 225

4. What expression represents *7 less than the product of 10 and a number h.*
   a. $7 - (10 \times h)$
   b. $7 - (10 \div h)$
   c. $(10 \times h) - 7$
   d. $(10 \div h) - 7$

5. What is the greatest common factor of 12, 24, and 48?
   a. 6
   b. 8
   c. 12
   d. 48

6. Gina sells $\frac{5}{8}$ of a mushroom pizza and $\frac{3}{4}$ of an onion pizza to the same family. How much pizza in all did the family buy?

   a. $1\frac{3}{8}$

   b. $1\frac{1}{2}$

   c. $\frac{8}{12}$

   d. $\frac{15}{32}$

7. Katherine has $5\frac{4}{5}$ yards of red silk fabric. Steve uses $1\frac{1}{3}$ yards of it. How many yards of red silk fabric are remaining?

   a. $6\frac{5}{8}$

   b. $4\frac{3}{2}$

   c. $4\frac{7}{15}$

   d. $4\frac{2}{5}$

8. Ryan has 30 pounds of cactus sand and is making tiny pots of various succulents to sell at the Mississippi Avenue Weekend Fair. If each tiny pot requires $\frac{1}{4}$ pound of sand, how many tiny succulent pots can he prepare for the fair?

   _____

9. Put the following numbers in order from least to greatest:
15, 1.0005, $\frac{3}{2}$, 1.005. _____

10. Put the following list of fractions and decimals in order of least to greatest:

0.068, $\frac{2}{3}$, -1.7, $\frac{8}{5}$, 0.61, $-1\frac{2}{3}$

(Note: This would be a drag and drop question on your GED® test, but instead, just list them in order.)

Answers and Explanations

Chapter Practice

1. **10 + 20 − 7.** Start with 10 passengers. Then remember that "increased" means addition and "decreased" means subtraction.

2. **$85 ÷ 3.** When something is "shared" it means it is divided. Since the 3 siblings were sharing $85, divide $85 by 3.

3. **(6 × 12) − 4.** The term "less than" means subtraction. "Less than" requires you to switch the order that the items are presented in, so the 4 comes last. The word "product" lets you know that you have to multiply the two numbers in a set of parentheses.

4. **3($500 + $700).** The word "sum" symbolizes two numbers being added in a set of parentheses, so the "sum of their $500 October sales and $700 November sales" is ($500 + $700). Then, "triple that" means to multiply this expression by three.

5. $\frac{1}{2}$**($3,200 − $2,800) or ($3,200 − $2,800) ÷ 2.** The word "difference" symbolizes two numbers being subtracted in a set of parentheses. The "difference of her expenses of $3,200 and his expenses of $2,800" is ($3,200 − $2,800). Then, to "split" it means dividing that expression by two. Dividing by two can also be expressed as multiplying by $\frac{1}{2}$, so there are two possible answers provided.

6. **($100 − $40 + $80)2; or 2($100 − $40 + $80).** First, interpret "$40 less than $100" to mean $100 − $40, since "less than" means subtraction in the opposite order. Increasing that by $80 means adding $80 to $100 − $40. Finally, "and then doubled" is asking the $100 − $40 + $80 to be put in parentheses before multiplying it by two, so that everything is doubled, and not just the first or last term.

7. **60.** Make two lists of the multiples for both 6 and 20:

6: 6, 12, 18, 24, 30, 36, 42, 48, 54, <u>60</u>, 66

20: 20, 40, <u>60</u>

60 is the least common multiple on these lists.

8. **36.** Make lists of the multiples for 12, 18, and 6:

12: 12, 24, <u>36</u>

18: 18, <u>36</u>

6: 6, 12, 18, 24, 30, <u>36</u>

36 is the least common multiple on these lists.

9. **15.** Make lists of the factors for 15 and 60:

15: 1, 3, 5, <u>15</u>

60: 1, 2, 3, 4, 5, 12, <u>15</u>, 20, 30, 60

15 is the greatest factor on both of these lists.

10. **Yes.** When working with two or more prime numbers, the greatest common factor will be 1.

11. $\frac{2}{3}$. Divide the numerator and denominator by 8 to start: $\frac{48 \div 8}{72 \div 8} = \frac{6}{9}$. Then reduce again by a factor of 3: $\frac{6 \div 3}{9 \div 3} = \frac{2}{3}$

12. $\frac{1}{3}$. Since 25¢ is the part and 75¢ is the whole, write these numbers in $\frac{part}{whole}$ format and reduce: $\frac{part}{whole} = \frac{25}{75} = \frac{1}{3}$

13. $\frac{1}{10}$. Since \$20 is the part and \$200 is the whole, write these numbers in $\frac{part}{whole}$ format and reduce: $\frac{part}{whole} = \frac{20}{200} = \frac{1}{10}$

14. $\frac{2}{3}$. It is important here to convert both measurements to the same unit: inches. Since there are 12 inches in 1 foot, write the *part*, 8 inches, over the *whole*, 12 inches: $\frac{part}{whole} = \frac{8}{12} = \frac{2}{3}$

15. $\frac{2}{9}$. It is important here to convert both measurements to the same unit: inches. Now we are comparing 8 inches to 36 inches, since it takes 36 inches to make 1 yard. $\frac{part}{whole} = \frac{8}{36} = \frac{2}{9}$

16. $\frac{1}{4}$. It is important here to convert both measurements to the same unit: feet. 1,320 feet is the part and since 1 mile = 5,280 feet, 5,280 is the *whole*: $\frac{part}{whole} = \frac{1,320}{5,280} = \frac{1}{4}$

17. $\frac{1}{20}$. It is important here to convert both measurements to the same unit: minutes. Since 1 hour = 60 minutes, use 60 as the *whole* and 3 as the *part*: $\frac{part}{whole} = \frac{3}{60} = \frac{1}{20}$

18. $\frac{1}{120}$. It is important here to convert both measurements to the same unit: seconds. Since there are 60 minutes in an hour, and 60 seconds in each minute, multiply 60 by 60 to determine how many seconds are in an hour: $60 \times 60 = 3,600$. Now 30 seconds will be the *part* and 3,600 seconds will be the *whole*: $\frac{part}{whole} = \frac{30}{3,600} = \frac{1}{120}$

19. $\frac{1}{18}$. It is important here to convert both measurements to the same unit: minutes. Since there are 24 hours in a day and 60 minutes in each hour, perform $24 \times 60 = 1,440$ to get the number of minutes in a day. $\frac{part}{whole} = \frac{80}{1,440} = \frac{1}{18}$

20. $\frac{23}{5}$. To convert $4\frac{3}{5}$ into an improper fraction, multiply 4 by 5 , add that product to 3, and put that sum over the original denominator, 5: $\frac{4 \times 5 + 3}{5} = \frac{23}{5}$

21. $6\frac{2}{3}$. To convert $\frac{20}{3}$ into a mixed number, divide 20 by 3 to get 6 with a remainder of 2. Put that remainder over 3: $20 \div 3 = 6$ Remainder 2; $\frac{20}{3} = 6\frac{2}{3}$

22. $\frac{3}{4}$. Notice that the smaller denominator (6) evenly divides into the larger denominator (12), so find the LCD by raising $\frac{1}{6}$ to 12ths: $\frac{1}{6} = \frac{1 \times 2}{6 \times 2} = \frac{2}{12}$. Add the numerators and keep the denominator the same and then reduce your answer: $\frac{2}{12} + \frac{7}{12} = \frac{9}{12} = \frac{9 \div 3}{12 \div 3} = \frac{3}{4}$

23. $\frac{1}{12}$. The least common denominator for 4 and 6 is 12, so raise both of these fractions to 12ths:

$\frac{1}{4} = \frac{1 \times 3}{4 \times 3} = \frac{3}{12}$

$\frac{1}{6} = \frac{1 \times 2}{6 \times 2} = \frac{2}{12}$

So $\frac{3}{12} - \frac{2}{12} = \frac{1}{12}$.

24. $\frac{5}{8}$. When multiplying fractions, multiply straight across the numerators and straight across the denominators: $\frac{3 \times 5}{4 \times 6} = \frac{15}{24} = \frac{5}{8}$

25. $\frac{9}{10}$. When dividing fractions, multiply the first fraction by the reciprocal of the second fraction:

$\frac{3}{4} \div \frac{5}{6} = \frac{3}{4} \times \frac{6}{5} = \frac{18}{20}$

Then reduce this by 2 to get $\frac{9}{10}$.

26. $\frac{48}{5}$ **or** $9\frac{3}{5}$**.** When multiplying mixed numbers, turn them both into improper fractions and then multiply straight across the numerators and the denominators: $2\frac{1}{3} = \frac{7}{3}$ and $4\frac{2}{5} = \frac{22}{5}$ and $\frac{7}{3} \times \frac{22}{5} = \frac{144}{15} = \frac{48}{5}$ or $9\frac{3}{5}$.

27. $\frac{4}{9}, \frac{2}{3}, \frac{3}{4}, \frac{5}{2}$**.** To compare all of the given fractions, turn them all into decimals: $\frac{2}{3} = 0.\overline{66}$, $\frac{5}{2} = 2.5$, $\frac{3}{4} = 0.75$, $\frac{4}{9} = 0.\overline{44}$.

Now you can see that they should be arranged in the following order: $\frac{4}{9}, \frac{2}{3}, \frac{3}{4}, \frac{5}{2}$.

28. **−0.3, −0.03, 3.031, 3.29, 3.3.** To compare all of the given fractions, add zeros to the right of all of the decimals so that they are all out of thousandths. The two negatives will come first with −0.030 being closer to 0 on the number line than -0.300, so the −0.300 is the smallest number. $3\frac{31}{1,000}$ is the smallest of the remaining three numbers and $3\frac{300}{1,000}$ is larger than $3\frac{290}{1,000}$, so the final order is −0.3, −0.03, 3.031, 3.29, 3.3.

29. $-\frac{3}{2}, -0.4, \frac{1}{5}, 0.34, \frac{1}{3}$**.** To compare these terms, turn all of them into decimals with the same number of digits to the right of the decimal sign:

0.34

$\frac{1}{5} = 0.20$

$-0.4 = -0.40$

$-\frac{3}{2} = -1.50$

$\frac{1}{3} = 0.\overline{66}$

The farthest number to the left of 0 on a number line would be −1.5, followed by −0.40. Then for the positive numbers, the correct ordering is 0.20, 0.34, 0.$\overline{66}$.

Number Foundations Part I Review

1. c. *Sum* is a key word that means add. You need to add the numbers 12.03 and 4.5. Place the numbers one over the other and line up the decimal points.

12.03

+4.5

Because 4.5 does not show as many decimal places as 12.03, add a zero on the end of 4.5 to make 4.50. Then each number will show the same number of places to the right of the decimal. These will be easier to add.

12.03

+4.50

Now add each column one at a time starting on the right.

12.03

+4.50

16.53

2. 15.5 wpm. To answer this question, it is helpful to recall that words per minute is a rate. First, notice that the quiz results were for 2 minutes, not 1 minute. We need to find words per minute. To do this, simply divide each number of words typed by 2 to find the words per minute for each person. Since each number is being divided by the same number, we only need to do this for the greatest and the smallest number of words typed. $\frac{90 \text{ words}}{2 \text{ minutes}} = 45$ wpm. $\frac{59 \text{ words}}{2 \text{ minutes}} = 29.5$ wpm. To find the difference, simply subtract 29.5 from 45 to get 15.5 wpm. Alternatively, subtract the smallest number of words typed from the largest number and divide the difference by 2.

3. d. Since Percy typed 90 words in 2 minutes, divide 90 by 2 to see how many words Percy typed per minute: 90 ÷ 2 = 45 words per minute. To see how many words Percy would type in 5 minutes, multiply 45 words by 5: 225

4. c. The phrase *product of 10 and a number h* implied that 10 and *h* should be multiplied in a set of parentheses. The phrase *less than* means subtraction, but you have to switch the order of the terms, so the 7 will come last: $(10 \times h) - 7$.

5. c. To find the greatest common factor of 12, 24, and 48, write out the factor lists for each of these numbers:

12: 1, 2, 3, 4, 6, <u>12</u>
24: 1, 2, 3, 4, 6, 8, <u>12</u>, 24
48: 1, 2, 3, 4, 6, 8, <u>12</u>, 16, 24, 48

12 is the greatest factor in all of these lists.

6. a. We need to add $\frac{5}{8}$ and $\frac{3}{4}$ in order to see how much pizza that single family bought. To find the LCD, check to see whether the smaller denominator (4) evenly divides into the larger denominator (8). Since it does, we only need to raise the smaller fraction ($\frac{3}{4}$) to higher terms to have common denominators. Multiply the numerator and denominator by 2 to raise $\frac{3}{4}$ to $\frac{6}{8}$. Then add the numerators and keep the denominator the same: $\frac{5}{8} + \frac{6}{8} = \frac{11}{8}$. This simplifies to $1\frac{3}{8}$.

7. c. For this question, we need to subtract the $1\frac{1}{3}$ yards of silk that Steve used from the $5\frac{4}{5}$ yards of red silk fabric that Katherine has. Use a common denominator of 15:

$$5\frac{4}{5} = 5\frac{12}{15}$$
$$1\frac{1}{3} = 1\frac{5}{15}$$

Since the second fraction has a smaller value than the first fraction, we can perform the subtraction by subtracting the whole number and the fractions separately:

$$5\frac{12}{15} - 1\frac{5}{15} = 4\frac{7}{15}$$

8. 120. Our task is to take 30 pounds of soil and divide it into equal portions of $\frac{1}{4}$ pound each. To do this, we need to perform $30 \div \frac{1}{4}$. When dividing with fractions, multiply the first number by the reciprocal of the second fraction: $30 \div \frac{1}{4} = 30 \times \frac{4}{1} = 120$. Ryan will be able to make 120 tiny succulent pots for the fair.

9. 1.0005, 1.005, $\frac{3}{2}$, 15. All of these numbers, when rewritten, contain the digits 1 and 5. The number $1.005 = 1\frac{5}{1,000}$, the number $1.0005 = 1\frac{5}{10,000}$, and $\frac{3}{2} = 1\frac{1}{2} = 1.5$. Therefore, 1.0005 is less than 1.005, which, in turn, is less than 1.5. The greatest number is 15.

10. $-1.7, -1\frac{2}{3}, 0.068, 0.61, \frac{2}{3}, \frac{8}{5}$. Convert the fractions into decimals and add zeros so that they all have three places to the right of the decimal. Written in this fashion, they are all in *thousandths* and can be compared:

$$0.068 = \frac{68}{1,000}$$
$$\frac{2}{3} = 0.667 = \frac{667}{1,000}$$
$$-1.7 = -1.700 = \frac{-1,700}{1,000}$$
$$\frac{8}{5} = 1.600 = \frac{1,600}{1,000}$$
$$0.61 = 0.610 = \frac{610}{1,000}$$
$$-1\frac{2}{3} = -1.667 = \frac{-1,667}{1,000}$$

Since all the fractions above are now out of 1,000, we can ignore the denominators and just focus on the numerators: $-1,700, -1,667, 68, 610, 667, 1,600$.

NUMBER FOUNDATIONS PART II: NEGATIVES, EXPONENTS, AND PEMDAS

This chapter expands upon the arithmetic concepts that were introduced in the previous chapter. Here you will learn how to incorporate and work with negative numbers, which is a highly valuable skill. Why? Because negative numbers come up in life just as much as positive numbers. Stock prices fall, money gets spent, and temperatures drop—all of these are illustrations of negative numbers in action. Additionally, mastering the skills in this chapter is critical to your ability to perform the algebra skills in subsequent chapters. The answers and explanations for all practice questions are at the end of the chapter.

This chapter covers:

- Rules for working with signed numbers
- Order of operations (PEMDAS)
- Laws of exponents
- Square roots and cube roots
- Absolute value
- Scientific notation
- Recognizing rational, irrational, and undefined numbers

Signed Numbers

Signed numbers include all real numbers that are positive or negative. It's very important that you feel totally comfortable adding, subtracting, multiplying, and dividing positive and negative numbers. Aside from helping you reach your goal of passing the GED® Mathematical Reasoning test, being able to work with negative numbers will help you make well-informed career and financial decisions in your personal life!

GED® QUESTION SNEAK PREVIEW!

You may have to evaluate expressions with signed numbers on your GED® Mathematical Reasoning test. Read the following section to learn how to get this type of question correct:

- *Evaluate $-3 + -10(-5 - 14)$*

Adding Like Signs

The term *like signs* refers to operations on either all positive numbers or all negative numbers. It's helpful to think of positive numbers as money you've earned and negative numbers as money you've spent. It shouldn't be a surprise that if you earn $20 and then you earn $10, you have earned $30. A positive plus a positive always equals a bigger positive.

Conversely, you can probably understand that if you spend $10 on a movie ticket and then you spend $5 on popcorn, you just spent $15. This scenario is modeled as such:

$$(-\$10) + (-\$5) = -\$15$$

The parentheses in this equation do not have any mathematical significance—they simply compartmentalize each negative number. The previous equation can also be written like this:

$$-10 + -5 = -15$$

The scenario of spending money twice can be generalized as the rule that *a negative plus a negative equals a bigger negative.*

RULE: ADDING LIKE SIGNS

Adding like signs always results in the *same sign* of the numbers being added. A positive plus a positive will always be a positive. A negative plus a negative will always be a negative.

- **Positive + Positive = Positive:**
  $20 + 10 = 30$
- **Negative + Negative = Negative:**
  $-10 + -5 = -15$

Adding Opposite Signs

The term *opposite signs* refers to operations on both positive and negative integers. In the following examples, earned money is a positive number, spent money is a negative number, and *debt* is money you owe to someone, so debt is a negative number too.

Case 1: If you earn $25 and spend $20, you will have $5 left over. This is modeled as:

$$25 + (-20) = 5$$

In this case, a positive plus a negative equals a positive.

Case 2: If you earn $20 and spend $25, you are in debt by $5. You owe someone $5 so you have –$5. This is modeled as:

$$20 + (-25) = -5$$

In this case, a positive plus a negative equals a negative.

Looking at both cases, notice that each time the answer had the same sign as the larger number. When adding numbers with opposite signs, *ignore the signs of the numbers, subtract the numbers, and give the answer the sign of the larger number.*

RULE: ADDING OPPOSITE SIGNS

When adding numbers with opposite signs, sometimes the answer will be negative and sometimes it will be positive. Follow these steps to add opposite signed numbers:

- *Ignore the signs.*
- *Subtract the two numbers.*
- *Give the answer the sign of the larger number.*

So, to perform $20 + (-25)$, we subtracted 20 from 25 and gave the difference of 5 the negative sign from the larger number. This equation has the same answer if the order of the numbers is switched around: $-25 + 20 = -5$. In addition problems, it is not significant if the negative number is on the left or right.

Subtracting Signed Numbers

What do you do when asked to subtract signed numbers? *Don't do it!* It is way too easy to make careless errors when subtracting mixed numbers. Life is tough enough, and there are many things out there that will try to ruin your day, so don't allow subtracting signed integers be one of them! Look at how confusing the expressions $5 - (-3)$ and $-26 - (-8)$ are. Luckily, there is an easy way to turn subtraction problems into addition problems:

> *Turn subtraction problems into addition by adding the opposite value of the number being subtracted.*

For example, $10 - 9$ is the same thing as $10 + (-9)$. We will refer to this technique as *keep-switch-switch* and it can always be used to turn subtraction into addition:

> *keep* the sign of the first number,
> *switch* the subtraction to addition, and
> *switch* the sign of the second number.

If you use *keep-switch-switch* to turn subtraction into addition, you just need to remember your rules for *adding* signed numbers and you don't have to worry about another set of rules for subtracting signed numbers.

Of course you shouldn't turn easy problems like $10 - 2$ into $10 + -2$, but *keep-switch-switch* will help turn odd-looking problems into problems that are much more clear:

> $5 - (-3)$ will become $5 + (3)$.
> $-26 - (-8)$ will become $-26 + 8$

Notice in the first example of $5 - (-3)$, *subtracting a negative is the same as adding a positive.* That is a really good fact to be comfortable with since it comes up a lot. Once you have rewritten your subtraction problem as addition, follow the rules for addition.

RULE: TURN SUBTRACTION INTO ADDITION

Turn odd-looking subtraction problems into addition by using keep-switch-switch:

- *Keep* the sign of the first number.
- *Switch* the subtraction to addition.
- *Switch* the sign of the second number.

Example:

−30 − (−10) will become *−30 + 10*
Then follow the rules for addition.

Multiplying and Dividing Signed Numbers

Multiplication and division follow the same rules for signed numbers.

Multiplying and Dividing Opposite Signs

When you multiply or divide opposite signs, the answer will always be negative. Think of −$5 × 4 as a model of spending $5 on 4 separate occasions. In total, you would have spent $20, which is expressed as −20. Therefore, −5 × 4 = −20.

Multiplying and Dividing Like Signs

When you multiply or divide numbers with the same signs, the answer will always be positive. Think of −$5 × −4 as representing someone canceling out a $5 debt you owe them 4 times in a row. (Having that debt canceled would be like you earning $20.) Therefore, −5 × −4 = 20 and the same relationship holds true for division: −8 ÷ −4 = 2.

RULE: MULTIPLYING AND DIVIDING WITH NEGATIVES

Multiplying and dividing signed numbers follow the same rules:

Opposite signs:

(−) × / ÷ (+) = (−)
(+) × / ÷ (−) = (−)

Same signs:

(−) × / ÷ (−) = (+)
(+) × / ÷ (+) = (+)

Now read the information in the following box carefully, because it illustrates one of the most common mistakes made with signed numbers.

DON'T DO THIS!

The most common mistake students make when working with signed numbers is to apply the "two negatives yield a positive" to *addition*, instead of limiting that rule to multiplication and division. It is a very easy mistake to make. Remember that adding two negatives is like spending money twice, so adding two negatives is always a bigger negative!

NO! −8 + −2 ≠ 10
YES . . . −8 + −2 = −10

Practice

1. $-4.5 \times 6 =$ _____

2. $-\$6.60 - \$18.50 =$ _____

3. $-18 + -10 - 12 =$ _____

4. Olivia bought 20 T-shirts for her soccer team. If the T-shirts cost $18 each, write an expression to represent Olivia's purchase and show how much money she spent in total.

5. A group of five people split a dinner bill of $110. Write an expression to represent how they shared the bill and then show how much money each person spent.

Exponents

You will be able to easily recognize when an exponent is being used. An **exponent** is written as a small number above the upper right-hand corner of a regular sized number. The number being raised to an exponent is called the **base**. In the expression 3^4, 4 is the exponent and 3 is the base.

GED® QUESTION SNEAK PREVIEW!

On the GED® test you will need to be able to evaluate expressions with exponents:

- *Find the value of the following expression:* $(-5)^2 - (-4)^3$.

How to Use Exponents

Exponents are a mathematical shorthand notation for representing repeated multiplication. Instead of writing $3 \times 3 \times 3 \times 3$, an exponent of 4 can be used as an instruction that the number 3 be multiplied by itself 4 times:

$$3 \times 3 \times 3 \times 3 = 3^4$$

The exponent always gives instructions for how many times the base will be multiplied by itself. Therefore, 10^6 means 10 multiplied by itself 6 times:

$$10^6 = 10 \times 10 \times 10 \times 10 \times 10 \times 10 = 1,000,000$$

DON'T DO THIS!

Although students know that exponents are shorthand for repeated multiplication, it is all too easy to make careless errors. 2^4 does not equal 8! Do not multiply the base by the exponent!

NO! $2^4 \neq 2 \times 4$

YES . . . $2^4 = 2 \times 2 \times 2 \times 2 = 16$

Powers, Squares, and Cubes

Exponents are normally referred to as **powers**. The expression 3^4 is said as *three to the fourth power* or *three raised to the power of 4*. The exponents two and three have their own special names:

Squared: When a base is raised to a power of two, the base is being squared. 5^2 is said as *five squared*. Since $5^2 = 5 \times 5$, $5^2 = 25$.

Cubed: When a base is raised to a power of three, the base is being cubed. 5^3 is said as *five cubed*. Since $5^3 = 5 \times 5 \times 5$, $5^3 = 125$.

Example

Write $4 \times 4 \times 4$ in exponential form and evaluate it.

Since 4 is being multiplied by itself 3 times, the exponential notation for this is 4^3. We can then write that $4^3 = 64$.

Example

Write 2 to the power of five in exponential form and evaluate it.

2 to the power of five is 2^5: $2 \times 2 \times 2 \times 2 \times 2 = 32$

Square Roots and Cube Roots

Roots undo exponents. Square rooting and cube rooting involve backwards thinking. For instance, if a problem states, "What is the square root of 16?" it is asking you for the number that equals 16 when multiplied by itself. Mathematically, it is written

$$\sqrt{16} = ?$$

So, what number, when multiplied by itself (i.e., when squared), yields 16? Four!

$$4 \times 4 = 16$$
$$4^2 = 16$$

So, $\sqrt{16} = 4$.

Cube roots function in the same way. To find a cube root of a number, ask yourself, "What number used three times in multiplication gives me this number?" Mathematically, cube roots are written like the following: $\sqrt[3]{27}$.

So, what is the $\sqrt[3]{27}$? What number multiplied by itself three times yields 27? Three!

$$3 \times 3 \times 3 = 27$$
$$3^3 = 27$$

So, $\sqrt[3]{27} = 3$

It is also important to understand how to simplify expressions that contain roots. We will review this process with two forms—whole numbers and fractions.

Whole Numbers
$$\sqrt{a \cdot b} = \sqrt{a} \cdot \sqrt{b}$$

Example: Simplify $\sqrt{27}$.
$$\sqrt{27} = \sqrt{3 \cdot 9} = \sqrt{3} \cdot \sqrt{9} = 3\sqrt{3}$$

Fractions
$$\sqrt{\frac{a}{b}} = \frac{\sqrt{a}}{\sqrt{b}}$$

Example: Simplify $\sqrt{\frac{4}{9}}$.
$$\sqrt{\frac{4}{9}} = \frac{\sqrt{4}}{\sqrt{9}} = \frac{2}{3}$$

Laws of Exponents

There are six laws of exponents that are used when working with exponents. For each law we'll give a general rule using variables and we'll give an example using numbers. These laws work the same regardless of whether the bases and exponents are numbers or variables. Notice that the first two rules *only* apply to situations where the bases are the same.

1. Multiplying Like Bases: *When multiplying like bases, simply add the exponents and keep the base the same to create a simplified term:*
General Rule: $x^a \cdot x^b = x^{(a+b)}$
Example: $2^3 \times 2^4 = 2^{(3+4)} = 2^7$

2. Dividing Like Bases: *When dividing like bases, subtract the exponents and keep the base the same to create a simplified term.*

General Rule: $\frac{x^a}{x^b} = x^{(a-b)}$

Example: $\frac{2^6}{2^2} = 2^{(6-2)} = 2^4$

3. Raising a Power to a Power: *When a base with a power is raised to another power, multiply the exponents and keep the base the same to create a simplified term.*

General Rule: $(x^a)^b = x^{a \cdot b}$

Example: $(5^2)^3 = 5^{2 \cdot 3} = 5^6$

4. Raising a Product to a Power: *When a product is raised to a power, raise each factor inside the parentheses to the power outside the parentheses. (This rule may often be combined with the previous rule. Don't forget to raise the coefficient to the power as well.)*

General Rule: $(xy)^a = x^a y^a$

Example: $(2x^4 y)^3 = 2^3 x^{4 \cdot 3} y^3 = 8x^{12} y^3$

5. Raising to a Power of Zero: *Any base raised to a power of zero equals 1.*

General Rule: $x^0 = 1$

Example: $78^0 = 1$

6. Negative Exponents: *A base raised to a negative power is equivalent to the reciprocal of that base with the positive value of the power.*

General Rule: $x^{-a} = \frac{1}{x^a}$

Example: $3^{-2} = \frac{1}{3^2}$

Practice

6. What is the value of *5 squared*?

7. What is the value of *negative 5 squared*?

8. What is the value of *negative 5 cubed*?

9. Compare and contrast your answers to questions 6, 7, and 8.

10. What is the value of k if $5^4 \times 5^2 = 5^k$?

11. What is the value of k if $5^8 \div 5^k = 5^2$?

12. What is the value of $\sqrt[3]{-8}$?

13. Simplify $\sqrt{40} \times \sqrt{5}$.

Order of Operations

In order to correctly solve problems that include more than one operation, there is a specific order of operations that must be followed.

GED® QUESTION SNEAK PREVIEW!

You will need to demonstrate a knowledge of correct order in which to do operations on the GED® Mathematical Reasoning test. Read the following section to learn how to answer a question like this:

- *Simplify:* $\frac{4 + 3 \times 2}{7 - 14 \div 7}$

PEMDAS

PEMDAS is an acronym used to remember the correct order to perform operations. You can remember *PEMDAS* by reciting *Please Excuse My Dear Aunt Sally*. The Order of Operations to follow when evaluating numerical or variable expressions is:

1. **P**arentheses
2. **E**xponents and Roots*
3. **M**ultiplication and **D**ivision*
4. **A**ddition and **S**ubtraction*

*These operations are performed as they arise from left to right in a problem.

PEMDAS will help you correctly evaluate mathematical expressions, but only if you pay attention to the small, but *very* important asterisk at the end of the list above! It is critical that you treat the operations that are on the same line together as equal partners that are evaluated from left to right. Doing multiplication before division can get you in some hot water—read on!

DON'T DO THIS!

The most common mistake with PEMDAS is doing multiplication before division instead of going left to right. Notice that in solving $24 \div 6 \times 2$, you will get two different answers depending on whether you prioritize multiplication or move from left to right:

NO! Don't think that you must always do multiplication *before* division:

$24 \div 6 \times 2 \neq 24 \div 12 = 2$ (Incorrect!)

YES . . . Instead, perform multiplication and division from *left to right*:

$24 \div 6 \times 2 = 4 \times 2 = 8$ (Correct!)

Notice that each method gives a different answer. Therefore, only one method can be correct: Move from left to right when performing multiplication and division.

Distributive Property

A distribution center is the place from which something is distributed, or sent, to many other locations. In math, the **distributive property** distributes a number or term to other numbers or terms through *multiplication*. Whenever you see a set of parentheses containing a sum or difference, and there is a number or variable directly before or after the parentheses, you can use the distributive property. In order to perform the distributive property, multiply the term outside the parentheses by each of the terms separated by + or – inside the parentheses.

Example

Expand the expression $3(4 + 1)$ and then solve.

First we notice that there is a sum contained inside a set of parentheses and there's another number directly outside the parentheses. We would distribute the factor of 3 to the 4 and the 1 by multiplying 3 to each of those numbers. After doing this we will add the products:

$$3 \cdot (4 + 1) = 3 \cdot 4 + 3 \cdot 1$$
$$12 + 3$$
$$\boxed{15}$$

Of course, in the previous case, it is not *necessary* that you use the distributive property to simplify the expression. However, the distributive property will be required when dealing with expressions that have variables.

Example

Expand the problem $5(x + 6)$ into an equivalent expression.

In this case, it is impossible to add the x and 6 first since variables and constants cannot be combined. Here, the only way to proceed is to multiply the 5 by each of the terms inside the parentheses and keep your answer as two separate terms:

$$5(x + 6)$$
$$5x + 30$$

DON'T DO THIS!

The distributive property is only used when the numbers or variables inside the parentheses are being *added* or *subtracted*. Do not make the common error of using the distributive property when the parentheses contain numbers that are being multiplied:

NO! $7(4 \times 8) \neq 7 \cdot 4 \times 7 \cdot 8$

YES . . . Instead, $7(4 \times 8) = 7 \times 4 \times 8$

Negative Bases with Exponents

Negative bases with exponents cause problems for many students because a small change in notation results in a completely different answer. Look at how the two following examples produce opposite answers depending on the presence or absence of parentheses:

Negative *Within* Parentheses

$(-5)^2 =$

$-5 \times -5 =$

$\underline{25}$

When the negative is within a set of parentheses, it gets canceled out when squared.

Negative *Without* Parentheses

$-5^2 =$

$-1 \times 5 \times 5 =$

$\underline{-25}$

When the negative is *not* within a set of parentheses, it acts as a -1 being multiplied by the square of 5. In this case, the negative does *not* cancel out.

When a negative value is subbed in for a variable, the problem is treated as if there are parentheses around the negative number: if $x = -6$, then x^2 will equal $(-6)^2 = 36$.

Notice that a negative base raised to an *odd* power will *not* cancel out since there will be one negative sign remaining, after all the pairs have canceled out:

$$(-2)^5 = (-2) \times (-2) \times (-2) \times (-2) \times (-2)$$
$$= 4 \times 4 \times -2 = -32$$

RAISING A NEGATIVE BASE TO A POWER

When a set of parentheses is around a negative number that has an exponent:

- *Even* exponents will cancel out the sign of a negative base: $(-3)^2 = (-3)(-3) = 9$
- *Odd* exponents will preserve the sign of a negative base: $(-2)^3 = (-2)(-2)(-2) = -8$

Now let's tackle a problem that combines what you've learn about signed numbers, exponents, PEMDAS, and the distributive property:

Example

Solve $4x^2 + 3(1 - x)$, when $x = -2$.

    a. 21

    b. 25

    c. 73

    d. 77

First, let's substitute –2 for every x and rewrite the expression:

$$4(-2)^2 + 3(1 - -2)$$

While it may be tempting to go from left to right, we need to be careful. We cannot multiply -2×4 and then square the answer because **E**xponents come before **M**ultiplication in the order of operations. Plus, we also have **P**arentheses in the second half of the problem, and the order of operations indicates we do them *first*. Always.

So let's go through the steps one by one:

1. We have **P**arentheses: $(1 - -2)$. When subtracting a negative number, the negatives turn into addition. Thus, $(1 - -2)$ really is $(1 + 2)$, which equals 3. Our problem now reads:
   $$4(-2)^2 + 3(3)$$
2. We have **E**xponents: $(-2)^2$. This is 4. Our problem now reads:
   $$4(4) + 3(3)$$
3. We have **M**ultiplication: $4(4)$ and $3(3)$. $4(4) = 16$ and $3(3) = 9$. Our problem now reads:
   $$16 + 9$$
4. We have **A**ddition: $16 + 9$, which equals 25.

Therefore, the answer is choice **b**, 25!

You get choice **a**, 21, if you don't do the parentheses first and just multiply 3×1 and then subtract –2. You get choice **c**, 73, if you multiply 4×-2 and then square it, along with not computing the parentheses first. You get choice **d**, 78, if you multiply 4×-2 and then square it but still compute the second half correctly.

Practice

14. Solve $(52 + \sqrt{64}) \div 10$. _____

15. Evaluate $-3 + -10(-5 - 14)$

16. Simplify $\frac{4 + 3 \times 2}{7 - 14 \div 7}$

17. Evaluate $4(2)^2 + (1 - (-2))^3$

Absolute Value

The absolute value of a number has a special notation of straight-lined brackets. Do not confuse $|-5|$ with (-5) since they have very different meanings.

Distance from Zero

The absolute value of a number tells us how far away it is from zero. For instance, the number 8 is a distance of 8 from zero. The number 400 is a distance of 400 from zero. What about the number –10? Think about it. Even though it is a negative number, it is still a distance of 10 from zero—just to the left of zero instead of to the right.

The absolute value is written mathematically like the following examples:

- $|8| = 8$ (Read: the absolute value of 8 is 8)
- $|-10| = 10$ (Read: the absolute value of –10 is 10)

You may be asked to find the absolute value of the distance between two numbers. What does that mean? It means to find the difference between the numbers (subtract) and then record the absolute value of the answer.

DON'T DO THIS!

With parentheses, a negative on the outside will cancel out a negative on the inside: –(–4) = +4. However, with the absolute value bracket, you must take the absolute value of the inside number *first*, and *then* apply the negative symbol on the outside. Therefore, absolute values with a negative on the outside always return a negative answer. Don't make the mistake of canceling out the two negatives with absolute values:

NO! –|–8| ≠ +8

YES . . . –|–8| = –8

Practice

18. Find $|x - y|$ when $x = 3$ and $y = 8$. _____

19. Find the absolute value of the difference between 5 and 3. _____

20. Simplify: $|-20 + 5| - |-40|$

Scientific Notation

Scientific notation is a special format used to write extremely big or small numbers in shorthand. Science, finance, and population research are just some areas that involve very large or small numbers. Scientists writing papers about outer space don't want to have to keep writing huge numbers like 93,000,000 miles (the distance from the sun to the Earth) and 300,000,000 (the speed of light in meters per second) so scientific notation gives us a universally accepted way to discuss and compare very large and small numbers.

GED® QUESTION SNEAK PREVIEW!

Be ready to express extremely large or small numbers in scientific notation on the GED® test:

■ *The sun is 93,000,000 miles from earth. Which of the following expressions represents this distance in scientific notation?*

 a. 93×10^6

 b. 93×10^5

 c. 9.3×10^7

 d. 0.93×10^8

Scientific Notation Format

The general format for a number written in scientific notation is $a \times 10^b$, with specific requirements for the types of numbers a and b can be:

1. a must always be a number greater than or equal to 1 and less than 10.
2. b is a positive or negative integer. It determines the number of spaces the decimal point moves to the left or to the right. (b can also be 0)

When $b \geq 0$, the value of the scientifically notated number is greater than 1. When $b < 0$, the value of the scientifically notated number is a decimal between 0 and 1.

VOCABULARY ALERT!

Scientific notation represents numbers in the format: $a \times 10^b$, where $1 \leq a < 10$ and b is an integer. When $b \geq 0$ the number will be greater than or equal to 1. Conversely, when $b < 0$ the number will be less than 1.

Converting from Scientific Notation to Standard Notation

To convert a number from scientific notation to standard notation, look at b to get the instructions on how many times to move the decimal right or left:

Example

What is 5.9×10^4 in standard notation?

Since 10^4 has four zeros (10,000), the decimal in 5.9 will move to the right four times. 5.9×10^4 translates to 59,000.

Negative exponents will move the decimal the other direction.

Example

Write the following number in standard notation: 8.5×10^{-3}

The 10^{-3} is giving instructions to move the decimal point three places to the left. The expression 8.5×10^{-3} represents the decimal 0.0085 after moving the decimal point three times to the left.

Converting from Standard Notation to Scientific Notation

Converting a number from standard notation to scientific notation can be a little trickier for students. Let's convert 9,800,000 in scientific notation. Since 9,800,000 must be written in the format $a \times 10^b$, where a is between 1 and 10, our decimal must go between the 9 and the 8, make $a = 9.8$. Since this placement moved the *original* decimal 6 places six to the left, our scientific notation instructions must move the decimal 6 places to the right. Write 9,800,000 as 9.8×10^6. Check the answer by sliding the decimal point in 9.8 six times to the *right*. This gives 9,800,000, indicating that we have the correct scientific notation.

Suppose we have a really small number that needs to be written in scientific notation, like 0.000047. We are going to approach this task the same way. First, select an a that is between 1 and 10: put the decimal between the 4 and 7 to get 4.7. Next, we need to multiply by a power of 10 to make the scientific notation represent the original number. To get to 4.7, we moved the decimal point five spaces to the *right*. To express a small number, use a negative exponent: 4.7×10^{-5}. We can verify that this answer is correct by sliding the decimal point in 4.7 five times to the *left*; since this gives us our original value 0.000047, 4.7×10^{-5} must be the correct scientific notation.

Practice

21. Translate 316.72 into scientific notation.

22. Express 0.00205 in scientific notation.

23. Pluto is 5,914,000,000 km from the sun. Represent this distance in scientific notation.

24. The width of a specialized medical probe is 0.0008 centimeters. Represent this width in scientific notation.

Rational, Irrational, and Undefined Numbers

Before moving on to our next chapter, let's cover three important types of numbers that you should be familiar with.

Rational Versus Irrational Numbers

A **rational number** is any number that can be represented in the form $\frac{p}{q}$, where p and q are both integers and q does not equal 0. In decimal form, rational numbers will either end or have a repeating decimal (example, $\frac{1}{3} = 0.\overline{33}$).

Irrational numbers have non-repeating decimals that never end and they cannot be written as fractions. A common irrational number is π, which has a value of 3.141592 . . . Square roots often produce irrational numbers. The first irrational square roots are $\sqrt{2}$, $\sqrt{3}$, and $\sqrt{5}$, but there are infinite irrational numbers.

Undefined Numbers

Undefined numbers are very important in math—these are numbers that cannot exist. An **undefined number** occurs when any number is divided by 0. That quotient is undefined since it is impossible to split a quantity into 0 parts. Therefore, any fraction with a denominator of 0 is undefined. Fractions are the most common place where you will encounter undefined numbers. Pay close attention to the two important types of fractions in the following box:

DON'T DO THIS!

It is important to understand what "0" represents in a fraction. Is $\frac{0}{8}$ the same as $\frac{8}{0}$? Definitely not! $\frac{0}{8} = 0$, because there are 0 out of 8 parts. But $\frac{8}{0}$ is undefined, because it is impossible to have 8 parts of 0. (The symbol for undefined is "∅"). Zero is never allowed to be the denominator of a fraction, so don't make the mistake of interpreting fractions with 0 in the bottom as having a value of 0!

$$\text{NO! } \frac{8}{0} \neq 0$$
$$\text{YES} \ldots \frac{0}{8} = 0$$
$$\text{YES} \ldots \frac{8}{0} = \varnothing \text{ or undefined}$$

CALCULATOR TIPS!

Although it is important to be able to perform all of the fraction and decimal skills presented here by hand, many of these tasks can also be done on the TI-30XS calculator. This calculator will be a great help when working with negatives and scientific notation, but it will take some time to learn how to use all of its features correctly. It is very easy to make mistakes with order of operations when using calculators, so these types of questions are best done by hand. Do the following Chapter Review questions without the special calculator functions. After you have read through *Chapter 12: Calculator Skills on the TI-30XS*, you can complete them again with the aid of your calculator.

Summary

You have now completed the Number Foundations Review and have some new skills under your belt: working with signed numbers and exponents; using PEMDAS to correctly navigate the order of operations; understanding absolute value; and converting between scientific notation and standard notation. Practice these questions to get a feel for what you may see on your GED® test day!

Number Foundations Part II Review

1. Evaluate the following expression:
   $$(5 - 3) \times (4 + 4 \div 2)$$
   a. 6
   b. 8
   c. 10
   d. 12

2. Simplify the following problem: $\sqrt{\frac{75}{72}}$.
   a. $\frac{5\sqrt{3}}{3\sqrt{8}}$
   b. $\frac{3\sqrt{5}}{8\sqrt{3}}$
   c. $\frac{25 \cdot 3}{8 \cdot 9}$
   d. $\sqrt{\frac{75}{72}}$

3. Simplify. $\sqrt[3]{-1,000} - 3^2$ _____

4. Which absolute value expression illustrates the distance between point A and point B on the following number line?

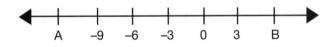

   a. $|12 - 6|$
   b. $|-12 + 6|$
   c. $|-12 - 6|$
   d. $|6 - 12|$

5. How many units is h from 0 on the number line below?

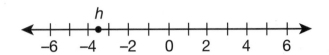

   a. $-4\frac{1}{2}$
   b. $-3\frac{1}{2}$
   c. $4\frac{1}{2}$
   d. $3\frac{1}{2}$

6. Which of the following is the number 316.72 written in scientific notation?
   a. 3.1672×10^{-2}
   b. 3.1672×10^2
   c. 3.1672×10^3
   d. 3.1672×10^1

7. Pluto is 5,914,000,000 km from the sun. This distance can be written in scientific notation as:
   a. 59.14×10^8
   b. 5.914×10^9
   c. 0.5914×10^{10}
   d. 5.914×10^6

8. Which of the following is an irrational number?
   a. $\sqrt{12}$
   b. $\sqrt{9}$
   c. $\frac{7}{3}$
   d. $\frac{0}{11}$

9. For what two values of x is the following numerical expression undefined? $\frac{12x}{x^2 - 25}$.

   _____

Answers and Explanations

Chapter Practice

1. **−27.** Multiplying opposite signs always results in a negative answer, so $-4.5 \times 6 = -27$.

2. **−$25.10.** Adding two negatives always gives a bigger negative answer, so $-\$6.60 - \$18.50 = -\$25.10$.

3. **−40.** To solve this problem, first add the −18 to the −10 to get −28. Then the problem reads $-28 - 12$. Use *keep-switch-switch* to turn this into addition: $-28 + (-12)$. Now we again are adding two negatives, which will give us a bigger negative: $-28 + (-12) = -40$.

4. **$20 \times -18 = -360$.** Spending money should be represented as a negative value. Since Olivia bought 20 T-shirts at $18 each, express this as $20 \times -18 = -360$.

5. **$-110 \div 5 = -\$22$.** Paying a bill of $110 can be written as −110. Splitting it 5 ways means dividing it by 5: $-110 \div 5 = -\$22$. Each person spent $22.

6. **25.** Write *five squared* as $(5)^2$. This is equivalent to $(5)(5) = 25$.

7. **25.** Write *negative five squared* as $(-5)^2$. This is equivalent to $(-5)(-5) = 25$.

8. **−125.** Write *negative five cubed* as $(-5)^3$. This is equivalent to $(-5)(-5)(-5) = -125$.

9. When (−5) was squared, the negative sign canceled out and gave the same answer as 5^2. However, when (−5) was cubed, the final answer remained negative.

10. **$k = 6$.** Use the law $x^a \cdot x^b = x^{(a+b)}$ to rewrite $5^4 \times 5^2$ as $5^{4+2} = 5^6$. Therefore $k = 6$.

11. **$k = 6$.** First use the law $\frac{x^a}{x^b} = x^{(a-b)}$ to rewrite $5^8 \div 5^k = 5^2$ as $5^{(8-k)} = 5^2$. Now, since both the left and right side of the equation are 5 to a power, we can see that both of the powers must be equal. Therefore, $8 - k = 2$, which leads to $k = 6$.

12. **−2.** The cube root (−8) means the number that will yield 8 when it is multiplied by itself 3 times. Since $(-2) \times (-2) \times (-2) = -8$, the cube root of −8 must be −2.

13. **$10\sqrt{2}$.** To simplify radicals, multiply the two terms under a single radical: $\sqrt{40} \times \sqrt{5} = \sqrt{200}$. Then, simplify this radical by rewriting it as a product with a perfect square: $\sqrt{200} = \sqrt{100} \times \sqrt{2} = 10\sqrt{2}$.

14. **6.** Taking the steps one by one:
We have parentheses, $(52 + \sqrt{64})$. In the parentheses we have a square root, so we need to solve that in order to add it to 52. The $\sqrt{64} = 8$. $52 + 8 = 60$.
We have division: $60 \div 10$, which equals 6, so $(52 + \sqrt{64}) \div 10 = 6$.
It is important that the order of operations is followed to find the right answer.

15. **187.** Use PEMDAS to help you perform the correct order of operations.
First do Parentheses: $-3 + -10(-5 - 14)$
$= -3 + -10(-19)$
Then do Multiplication: $-3 + -10(-19)$
$= -3 + 190$
Lastly, do Addition: $-3 + 190 = 187$.

16. **2.** Use PEMDAS to help you perform the correct order of operations. With complex fractions, the numerator and denominator must each be done before the final addition. This is because the equation $\frac{4+3\times 2}{7-14\div 7}$ is really equivalent to $\frac{(4+3\times 2)}{(7-14\div 7)}$.
Do multiplication and division first:
$\frac{(4+3\times 2)}{(7-14\div 7)} = \frac{4+6}{7-2}$.
Then do the addition and substraction in both parts of the fraction: $\frac{4+6}{7-2} = \frac{10}{5}$.
Lastly, perform the final division: $\frac{10}{5} = 2$.

17. **43.** While it may be tempting to go from left to right, we cannot multiply 2 by 4 and then square it because <u>E</u>xponents come before <u>M</u>ultiplication. Plus, we also have <u>P</u>arentheses in the second half of the problem, and the order of operations indicates we do that FIRST. <u>P</u>arentheses: $(1 - -2)$. Subtracting a negative number is like adding a positive, so turn the subtraction into addition by using *keep-switch-switch*: $(1 - (-2))$ becomes $(1 + 2)$ which equals 3. The problem now reads: $4(2)^2 + 3^3$. <u>E</u>xponents: $(2)^2$. This is 4. The problem now reads: $4(4) + 3^3$. <u>M</u>ultiplication: $4(4) = 16$ and $3^3 = 27$. The problem now reads: $16 + 27$ so the answer is 43.

18. $|3 - 8| = |-5| = 5$

19. **2.** $|5 - 3| = |2| = 2$. If the numbers were reversed, the absolute value of the difference would be $|3 - 5| = |-2| = 2$. Either way you write the numbers, as long as you are taking the absolute value of the difference between the two numbers, you will always get the same answer.

20. **–25.** Begin by taking care of the first absolute value bracket: $|-20 + 5| - |-40| = |-15| - |-40|$. Then take the absolute value of both numbers and subtract them to find the final answer: $15 - 40 = -25$.

21. $\mathbf{3.1672 \times 10^2}$. Scientific notation requires the number to be written in the form $a \times 10^b$ where a must be between 1 and 10. Move the decimal twice to the left to write a as 3.1672. Now b must dictate that the decimal place be moved twice to the right, so $b = 2$: 3.1672×10^2.

22. $\mathbf{2.05 \times 10^{-3}}$. Scientific notation requires the number to be written in the form $a \times 10^b$ where a must be between 1 and 10. Move the decimal three times to the right to write a as 2.05. Now b must dictate that the decimal place be moved three times to the left, so b must be –3: 2.05×10^{-3}.

23. $\mathbf{5{,}914{,}000{,}000 = 5.914 \times 10^9}$. Scientific notation requires the number to be written in the form $a \times 10^b$ where a must be between 1 and 10. Move the decimal nine times to the left to write a as 5.914. Now b must dictate that the decimal place be moved nine times to the right, so b must be 9: $5{,}914{,}000{,}000 = 5.914 \times 10^9$.

24. $\mathbf{0.0008 = 8 \times 10^{-4}}$. Scientific notation requires the number to be written in the form $a \times 10^b$ where a must be between 1 and 10. Move the decimal four times to the right to write a as 8. Now b must dictate that the decimal place be moved four times to the left, so b must be –4: $0.0008 = 8 \times 10^{-4}$.

Number Foundations Part II Review

1. d. Order of operations says that you should first perform any operations in parentheses, and then perform all multiplication and division, moving from left to right; then perform all addition and subtraction, again moving from left to right.
Start by simplifying the expressions inside both sets of parentheses, and in the second expression, be sure to divide 4 by 2 before adding 4:
$(5 - 3) \times (4 + 4 \div 2)$
$= 2 \times (4 + 2)$
$= 2 \times 6$
$= 12$

2. a. To simplify this expression, knowledge of the laws of roots is needed. The square root of a fraction is equivalent to the square root of the numerator and the square root of the denominator: $\dfrac{\sqrt{75}}{\sqrt{72}}$. It is also important to recognize that if we rewrite each term as a product of two factors, we may be able to further simplify. $\dfrac{\sqrt{75}}{\sqrt{72}}$ can be written as $\dfrac{\sqrt{25}\cdot\sqrt{3}}{\sqrt{9}\cdot\sqrt{8}}$. This can be further simplified because 25 and 9 are both perfect squares. $\dfrac{\sqrt{25}\cdot\sqrt{3}}{\sqrt{9}\cdot\sqrt{8}} = \dfrac{5\sqrt{3}}{3\sqrt{8}}$. Choice **b** has the square root signs assigned to the wrong numbers. Option **c** reflects a factorization of 75 and 72 but lost the square root. Choice **d** suggests that this problem cannot be simplified, when in fact it can.

3. −19. The cubed root of −1,000 is −10, since $-10 \times -10 \times -10 = -1{,}000$. 3^2 is equal to 9, so rewrite $\sqrt[3]{-1{,}000} - 3^2$ as $-10 - 9$. −19 is the final answer.

4. c. To answer this question, it is helpful to remember that the absolute value of the number is the distance between that number and 0. The scale of the number line is 3-unit increments. Thus, point A is −12 and point B is 6. To find the difference between these two numbers, simply make a subtraction problem and take the absolute value. Choice **a** includes +12, not −12. Choice **b** reflects the sum, not the difference. For choice **d** to be correct, it should read $|6 - (-12)|$.

5. b. Even though only even numbers are drawn into this number line, we can see that each tick mark represents 1. h is halfway between the tick marks for −3 and −4, so the value for h must be $-3\frac{1}{2}$. Answer choices **c** and **d** are incorrect since these positive numbers sit on the right side of the 0 on the number line. Answer choice **a** is not correct because if h had a value of $-4\frac{1}{2}$, it would have to be sitting on the left side of 4 on the number line.

6. b. Scientific notation expresses a number as the product of a number between 1 and 10, including 1 but excluding 10, and a power of 10. If the number is greater than 1, then the exponent of 10 is non-negative. So, to write 316.72 in scientific notation, move the decimal point two places to the left to get a number between 1 and 10, and write the power of 10 as 2 because you moved the decimal point two places to the left.

7. b. A number in scientific notation is written as a number that is at least 1 but less than 10, multiplied by a power of 10. The power of 10 is the number of places that the decimal is moved to transform the number into decimal notation (regular numbers). If the decimal point in the number 5.914 is moved nine places to the right, the number becomes 5,914,000,000.

8. a. Irrational numbers cannot be written as a fraction, so we know that answer choices **c** and **d** are incorrect. (Remember that $\frac{0}{11}$ has a value of 0.) Irrational numbers have a decimal value that does not terminate or repeat. Since the value of $\sqrt{9}$ is 3, this means that choice **b** can also not represent an irrational number. Therefore, $\sqrt{12}$ is the only possible choice for an irrational number.

9. **–5 and 5.** We are only concerned with the denominator when talking about undefined expressions. We need to find the two values of x that make the denominator equal to zero. Let's set up an equation and solve for x:

$x^2 - 25 = 0$

$x^2 = 25$

$\sqrt{x^2} = \sqrt{25}$

$x = 5$ and -5

Remember, a square root is the number that, when multiplied by itself, gives you the number you start with. In this problem, we are looking for the number that when multiplied by itself yields 25, which is 5. Also, when you square a negative number, you get a positive answer. So, -5×-5 *also* equals 25. Therefore, the two values of x that make the equation undefined are 5 and –5.

5 ▶ RATES, PROPORTIONS, AND PERCENTS

In this chapter, you'll learn some extremely useful skills that can be applied to your personal and work life. Rates, proportions, and percents are concepts that we encounter all around us: miles per hour, price per pound, percentage discounts, and commissions. In addition to being useful in your everyday life, mastery of the skills in this chapter will be critical to your success on the GED® test. The answers and explanations for all practice questions are at the end of the chapter.

This chapter covers:

- Rates and unit rate
- Setting up and solving proportions
- Working with percentages
- Solving word problems with percentages

Rates and Unit Rate

Before diving into rates and unit rate, we need to become familiar with ratios. A ratio is a fraction that compares two numbers. We use ratios every day. A city map might have a scale where 2 cm represents 500 meters. This information could be recorded as 2:500 or $\frac{2}{500}$. If a class has 12 girls and 14 boys, the ratio of $\frac{12}{14}$ demonstrates that relationship. Since $\frac{12}{14}$ reduces to $\frac{6}{7}$, it can also be said that the ratio of girls to boys in the class is $\frac{6}{7}$.

This ratio of $\frac{6}{7}$ means that for every 6 girls in the class, there are 7 boys.

GED® QUESTION SNEAK PREVIEW!

You will be using ratios and proportions to solve questions like this on the GED® test:

- *Ava bought 2.5 pounds of organic grapes at the farmer's market for $9. Liam bought 3.2 pounds of organic grapes at the store for $12. How much more per pound were the grapes that Liam bought at the store?*

Rate and Unit Rate Defined

A **rate** is a special type of ratio that compares two measurements that have different units. Consider this example of comparing lawns to days: *Polina mowed 12 lawns in 3 days*. The rate is 12 to 3.

A **unit rate** is a rate that compares the first type of measurement to just 1 unit of the second type of measurement. The rate of *12 lawns in 3 days* can be expressed as a unit rate by reducing both numbers to simplest terms, by diving by 3: *Polina mowed 4 lawns per day*. Rates are often presented in fractional form and a *unit rate* is a fraction with a denominator of 1.

VOCABULARY ALERT!

Unit rates are presented most commonly as a phrase in the *per unit* language. Questions that contain the word *per* often require the unit rate to be found through division. Unit rate shows how many units of one type of quantity correspond to *one unit* of a second type of quantity. Some examples are words per minute, price per pound, and persons per square mile. In each of these, the second word is on the bottom of a ratio and has been reduced to 1.

Although unit rate is used in many different contexts, we are going to focus here on examples of unit rate in speed, price, and population density.

Speed

It took Denise 1 hour and 45 minutes to walk a four-mile trail. How many miles per hour did she walk, rounded to the nearest tenth of a mile?

To find how many miles per hour, we write our fraction with the number of miles as the numerator and the number of hours as the denominator: $\frac{4 \text{ miles}}{1.75 \text{ hours}}$. This is now a simple division problem: $4 \div 1.75 = 2.28$. Rounded to the nearest tenth, Denise walked 2.3 miles per hour.

Price

Rick's Market is selling 12-pound turkeys for $19.50 each, and Mike's Meats is selling 15-pound turkeys for $23.85. Which store offers the better price per pound of turkey?

To find the better price per pound of turkey, we need to calculate the rate for each turkey. The price per pound at Rick's Market is $\frac{\$19.50}{12 \text{ lbs}}$, or $1.63/lb. The price per pound at Mike's Meats is $\frac{\$23.85}{15 \text{ lbs}}$, or $1.59/lb. Even though a turkey costs more at Mike's Meats, it offers a better price per pound of turkey.

Density

An estimated 392,880 people live within 58 square miles in Minneapolis, MN. Approximately 3.82 million people live within 503 square miles in Los Angeles, CA. What is the difference of people per square mile between these two cities?

To find the persons per square mile in Minneapolis, we need to first write our fraction: $\frac{392,880 \text{ people}}{58 \text{ square miles}}$. There are 6,774 people per square mile in Minneapolis (rounded from 6,773.79).

To find the people per square mile in Los Angeles, we write another fraction: $\frac{3,820,000 \text{ people}}{503 \text{ square miles}}$. There are 7,594 people per square mile in Los Angeles (rounded from 7,594.43).

To find the difference of people per square mile between Minneapolis and Los Angeles, we subtract 6,774 from 7,594.

$7,594 - 6,774 = 820$ people per square mile

Practice

1. Anita made 28 necklaces in 8 hours. How many necklaces does Anita make in an hour?

2. Use the information from question 1 to determine how many necklaces Anita can make in a 40-hour workweek.

3. Pete, Celia, and Lauren are planning a road trip to Zion National Park. Pete's car has a 12-gallon tank that gets 540 miles per tank of gas. Celia's car has a 15-gallon tank that gets 585 miles on one tank. Lauren's car has a 21-gallon tank that gets 798 miles. Help them determine who should drive by calculating who gets the most miles per gallon with their cars.

4. A space shuttle orbits at a distance of 2,430 miles in $4\frac{1}{2}$ hours. Find the shuttle's average speed in miles per hour.

5. Eliseo made $90.00 babysitting for 12 hours for the Goonan family. At that same rate, how much will he earn if he works Monday through Friday, 6 hours a day for the Goonan family?

Proportions

A **proportion** is an equation where two ratios are set equal to each other. Proportions are commonly used to solve real world problems. If a recipe makes 12 cupcakes, but you want to make 36 cupcakes, knowing that you need to multiply all the ingredients by 3 is actually utilizing proportions! Take a look at the following sample GED® question and then read on to see how to work with and solve proportions.

A proportion question on your GED® test might look like this:

■ *Nine out of ten professional athletes suffer at least one injury each season. If there are 120 players in a professional league, estimate how many of them experienced at least one injury last season.*

Solving Proportions with Equivalent Fractions

Let's consider this *Sneak Preview* problem. The phrase *nine out of ten* is the ratio $\frac{9}{10}$, representing that 9 out of 10 professional athletes suffer at least one injury each season. Since we are considering a league of 120 players, we need to set an equivalent ratio that is equal to $\frac{9}{10}$, but representative of 120 players. A proportion can be set up that puts the number of *injured* athletes in the numerator and the *total* number of athletes in the denominator:

$$\frac{9 \text{ injured}}{10 \text{ total}} = \frac{? \text{ injured}}{120 \text{ total}}$$

Now use equivalent fractions to determine what the new numerator would be. In this case, multiply the numerator and denominator by 12 to create an equivalent fraction:

$$\frac{9 \text{ injured}}{10 \text{ total}} \times \frac{12}{12} = \frac{108 \text{ injured}}{120 \text{ total}}$$

Therefore, in a league of 120 professional athletes, it is likely that 108 of them suffered an injury last season.

Understanding Cross Products

In the previous example, it was easy to see that a factor of 12 would help us arrive at the equivalent ratio we needed to obtain. When it's not so easy to recognize how to create the required equivalent fraction, cross products are used to solve proportional equations. The **cross products** of a proportion are the products when multiplying diagonally across the two ratios. *The cross products in a proportional equation*

are always equal. In the following illustration, you can see that the equivalent fractions $\frac{3}{5}$ and $\frac{6}{10}$ have identical cross products:

$$5 \times 6 = 3 \times 10$$

RULE: CROSS PRODUCTS

For all proportional relationships in the form $\frac{a}{b} = \frac{c}{d}$, the cross products ad and bc will be equal in value.

If $\frac{a}{b} = \frac{c}{d}$, then $ad = bc$

Solving Proportions with Cross Products

Let's use cross products to consider a lemonade recipe that calls for a sugar to lemon juice ratio of 3 to 4. If you have 50 tablespoons of lemon juice and want to use it all to make as much lemonade as possible, you could use cross products to solve for how many tablespoons of sugar you would use.

1. First, write the given ratio information in words and numbers: $\frac{sugar}{lemon} = \frac{3}{4}$
2. Then, use the additional information to create a proportion that will allow you to solve for the missing information. Make sure to fill in the

given information into the correct part of the second ratio: $\frac{3}{4} = \frac{sugar}{50}$

3. Next, use the cross products to write an equation: $3(50) = 4(sugar)$

4. Solve the equation by dividing both sides by 4 to get sugar alone: $\frac{150}{4} = sugar$, so 37.5 tablespoons of sugar will be needed.

DON'T DO THIS!

When setting up a proportion, it is very important that both ratios are written with like items in the same respective place. An easy mistake to make when working quickly through a proportion problem is to input your given information incorrectly. Consider this problem:

There are 3 red marbles for every 4 blue marbles in a drawer. If there are 24 blue marbles in total, how many red marbles are there?

NO! $\frac{3}{4} = \frac{24}{red}$

YES . . . $\frac{red}{blue} = \frac{3}{4} = \frac{24}{red}$

Notice that in the mistaken proportion above, the *24 blue marbles* were put in the numerator of the second fraction, but that the *4 blue marbles* had been represented in the denominator of the first fraction. It's a good habit to write your ratio out in words first, as $\frac{red}{blue}$, so that you are sure to input your information correctly!

Practice

6. If K.P. can read 1,000 words in 5 minutes, how many words could he read in 12 minutes?

7. The ratio of men to women at a certain meeting is 3 to 5. If there are 18 men at the meeting, how many people are at the meeting?

8. A certain model of calculator is known to have approximately 8 malfunctioning calculators out of every 2,000. If an office supply store in Los Angeles is going to order 750 of these calculators to stock their stores for back to school shopping in August, approximately how many returns due to defect should they anticipate having later in the fall?

9. The Robb family wants to have the carpet in their vacation home steam cleaned. They received a special offer in the mail advertising $3 for every 10 square feet of carpeting cleaned. If they don't want to spend more than $250, how many square feet of carpeting can they have cleaned with this offer?

10. Sandy's Treasures sells used books in bundles at a great discount. According to the table, how much would it cost to buy nine used books?

BUNDLES OF BOOKS	PRICE
3	$15
6	$30
9	x
12	$60
15	$75

Understanding Percents

What, exactly, is a percent? Let's break down the word to see. The prefix, *per*, means *for every*, and the root, *cent*, means *100*. Put these two parts together and you should see that the word *percent* means *for every 100*. A **percent** is a special kind of ratio that is *out of 100*. Let's see what kind of percent question you might see on test day.

GED® QUESTION SNEAK PREVIEW!

Most of the percent questions on the GED® test will be word problems, but it's possible you'll encounter a question like this:

- *320 is 40% of what number?*

Percentages as Fractions and Decimals

Since a percentage conveys a number that is a fraction out of 100, all percentages can be written as fractions or decimals. For instance, 5% means *5 for every 100* or *5 out of 100*. This is $\frac{5}{100}$ as a fraction, which is equivalent to 0.05 as a decimal:

$$5\% = \frac{5}{100} = 0.05$$

Since percentage is really just a shorthand notation for a fractional relationship out of 100, you must always change a percentage to its fractional or decimal equivalent whenever performing mathematical operations with percentages. *To change a percentage to a decimal, simply move the decimal point two spaces to the left.*

DON'T DO THIS!

Percentages are only used in writing and are never used in calculations. They must be converted into their decimal or fraction equivalent before being used in calculations. Notice that the percent symbol (%) looks like a jumbled up "100." Let that remind you to change a percentage into a fraction (by putting it over 100), or into its decimal equivalent (by moving the decimal 2 spaces to the left), before doing any calculations. For example, when needing to take 40% of a number, you will not use "40" in your calculations, but you will instead use $\frac{40}{100}$ or 0.40:

NO! 40% of 50 ≠ 40 × 50 = 2,000
YES . . . 40% of 50 = 0.40 × 50 = <u>20</u>

Three Different Types of Percentage Skills

There are three different percentage skills that you will most commonly face. Each type is listed below with an example and the method to solve it.

1. Finding a percentage of a whole number
Example

You want to buy a suitcase that normally costs $70 and is currently 20% off. How much will the discount be?

Finding the percentage of a whole number is one of the most useful skills to have with percentages. You will use this skill to calculate tax, sale prices, markups, and many other things. **To find the percent of a whole number, simply turn the percentage into a decimal and multiply it by the number you're finding the percentage of:**

20% of $70 = 0.20 × $70 = <u>$14</u>

2. Finding what percentage one number is of another number
Example
Customers in a supermarket are polled regarding their preference between nonfat milk and low-fat milk. If 18 out of 60 people surveyed prefer nonfat milk, what percentage of customers prefer nonfat milk?

If you've ever received a percentage grade on a test in school, then you are already familiar with this type of percentage application, since percentage grades are normally found by dividing the points you got correct by the total points. **To find what percentage one number is of another number, divide the "part" by the "whole." Then multiply the quotient by 100 and add the % symbol:**

18 out of 60 = $\frac{18}{60}$ = 0.3; and 0.3 × 100 = <u>30%</u>

3. Finding the whole when the percentage and part are given
Example
If 15% of a shipment of eggs arrived broken, and 30 eggs arrived broken, how many eggs were in the total shipment?

Although this particular type of problem is the least common, at times it is necessary to work backward by using the percentage and the part to figure out the whole. **To find the *whole* when the % and *part* are given, set up and solve a proportion in the form** $\frac{part}{whole} = \frac{\%}{100}$.

If 30 is 15% of the whole, fill in 15% for the % and 30 for the part:

so $\frac{30}{whole} = \frac{15}{100}$

Now set the cross products equal to each other:

$30(100)$ = whole(15)
$\frac{3,000}{15}$ = whole
<u>200</u> = whole

The entire order must have consisted of 200 eggs.

DON'T DO THIS!

A common error is for students to always use division instead of multiplication when working with percents. One way to avoid this mistake is to remember that the word *of* means *multiplication* in math. Be careful when you are working with percentage problems like *what is 20% of 60?*

NO! *20% of 60 ≠ 60 ÷ 20*
YES . . . *20% of 60 = 60 × 0.20 = <u>12</u>*

Practice
11. What is 25% of 600 students?

12. What is $\frac{1}{2}$% of 400,000 deer?

13. 14 out of 80 customers got sick after eating undercooked meat at a new restaurant. What percentage got ill?

14. 560 people were in the test audience for a film. If 70 of them thought it was too violent for viewers under 18, what percentage thought the movie was *not* too violent for viewers under 18?

15. 15 red pens is 12% of how many pens?

Problem Solving with Percentages

Now that you are familiar with how to work with percentages in several different contexts, in this section we will look at how to handle some common applications of percentages.

GED® QUESTION SNEAK PREVIEW!

Not only do you need percentages for the GED® test, but they are also helpful to understand in your everyday life.

- *Lucas is buying a drill that costs $120 but on July 4 it is on a one-day sale for 30% off. If sales tax is 7.5%, what will the total price be after calculating the 30% discount and tax?*

Simple Interest

It costs money to borrow money. *Interest* is the money a bank or lending institution charges someone for borrowing money. Lenders usually charge a percentage of the loan for every year it is borrowed. **Principal** is the initial amount of the money borrowed and **interest** is the charge the borrower pays for his or her loan. **Simple interest** is a type of interest that is calculated by multiplying the following three components:

Simple Interest = (Principal) × (Interest Rate) × (# of Years Borrowed)

Suppose you took out a five-year car loan for $12,000, with an interest rate of 6.5% per year. You might want to figure out how much money you will be paying in interest.

To solve this problem, we need to use the simple interest formula: $I = prt$, where p = the principal balance, r = the interest rate, and t = the duration or time.

Before we start substituting numbers to solve this problem, we need to convert the percentage to a decimal. Remember, we just move the decimal point two spaces to the left. So 6.5% becomes 0.065.

When we substitute values into the formula, we get the following equation:

$$I = (12,000)(0.065)(5)$$
$$I = 3,900$$

Therefore, you will be paying a total amount of $3,900 in interest over the course of the five-year loan.

Remember that $3,900 is just the fee you have to pay to borrow that money. You'll need to pay back the $12,000 *plus* the $3,900 for your 5-year car loan.

Tax

If you buy something that costs $100 in a city that has an 8% sales tax, you will have to pay an additional fee of 8% of $100 for your purchase. That would be an extra $8! Tax is always presented as a percentage. The dollar amount of tax is calculated by multiplying the cost of an item by the percentage expressed as a decimal.

Example

Elie buys a bike helmet for $38.50 and the tax is 7%. Calculate the total cost.

First, we can calculate the cost of the tax by multiplying $38.50 by 0.07:

$$\$38.50 \times 0.07 = \$2.695$$
$$\$2.695 \text{ rounds to } \$2.70$$

Then, find the total cost of Elie's bike helmet by adding the original price of $38.50 to the tax of $2.70:

$$\$38.50 + \$2.70 = \$41.20, \text{ so Elie's total purchase}$$
will be $41.20.

DON'T DO THIS!

Be careful to read the entire question carefully when doing questions involving tax. Sometimes you might be asked to find *just the tax* but it is more likely that you will be asked to find *the total cost*. A common mistake that students make is to forget to add the tax to the original price—so pay special attention to answering the question carefully!

Markups and Sale Prices

Two common types of questions involve determining discounted sale prices or marked-up retail prices. To find a sale price, calculate a percentage of an item and *subtract* it from the original cost. Markups require you to find the percentage of an item and *add* that answer to the original cost. Follow along in the following example to get the hang of it:

Every month you budget for fun money. You are able to put aside $30 each month. You see a pair of shoes that you really want for $90, but you have only

$65 saved. The next week the shoes go on sale for 25% off. Do you have enough money to buy them?

To solve this problem, we need to figure out the sale price of the shoes. The first step is to convert the percentage to a decimal. So 25% becomes 0.25 when we move the decimal point two spaces to the left. Multiply 0.25 by 90, the price of the shoes, to figure out how much they are marked down to:

$$90 \times 0.25 = 22.5$$

Remember, $22.50 is not the sale price of the shoes, but the amount taken off the original $90. So, you need to subtract $22.50 from $90, which results in $67.50. If you have only $65, unfortunately you do not have enough money.

DON'T DO THIS!

A very typical mistake that students make is to find the actual dollar amount for the *markup* or *discount* and to mistake that for the final price. Use common sense to help you recognize when you are making a mistake. If a $70 desk is 20% off, that is not a huge discount, so it wouldn't make sense for the sale price to be $14!

Example: Find the final price of a $70 desk that is 20% off:

  NO! $70 × 0.20 = $14 (this is the *discount*, not the final price)
  YES . . . $70 × 0.20 = $14, so $70 − $14 = $56 is the final price

---

Commissions

Commission is a form of job payment that is often found in sales-oriented fields. Real estate agents, art dealers, and certain retail sales associates all earn commissions either as their entire paycheck or as a bonus payment. Commission is generally paid as a percentage of the service rendered or a percentage of the product sold. Follow along in the next example to understand how to answer commission questions:

Example

Terri is a real estate agent for a family looking for a new home. She finds them a home they love for $380,000 and will earn a 2.5% commission from the seller of the home. How much money will Terri earn for helping to negotiate this property sale?

Since Terri earns 2.5% of the $380,000, we need to find 2.5% of $380,000. To do this, change 2.5% to a decimal and multiply that by $380,000:

$$0.025 \times \$380,000 = \$9,500$$

Terri will earn $9,500 on the sale of that house.

Percentage Increase and Decrease

If I tell you that something is $10 off, can you say for certain if this is a worthwhile discount? Since you don't know if I'm offering you $10 off a $12 meal or $10 off a $3,200 bike, your answer should be "no." Without knowing what the *original* cost was, it's not possible to judge if a $10 discount is a good deal.

The concept we will now investigate is **percent of change**. Percent of change is a measure that compares the *amount of change* to the *original amount*. Whether you are finding the **percentage increase** or **percentage decrease**, the percent of change is easiest to find by using the formula:

$$\text{Percent of change} = \frac{amount\ of\ change}{original\ amount} \times 100$$

In this formula, the *amount of change* is the exact amount of decrease or increase, which is calculated by *subtracting* the original and new amounts. The following problem illustrates how to calculate the percentage increase:

Example

Your rent went from $800 a month to $875 per month. Determine whether this rent hike is within the 6% maximum increase allowed by city law by calculating the percentage of increase.

Start with the *Percent of Change* formula:

$$\text{Percent of change} = \frac{amount\ of\ increase}{original\ amount} \times 100$$

Calculate the *amount of change* in the numerator by subtracting the original rent from the new rent:

$$\text{Percent of change} = \frac{875 - 800}{800} \times 100$$
$$\text{Percent of change} = \frac{75}{800} \times 100$$

Being able to calculate your rent increase as 9.375% allows you to tell your landlord that his rent hike is illegal and that he needs to lower the increase. It literally *pays* to know your math!

Practice

16. What will the total payback be if Stan borrows $68,000 at 4.5% simple interest for a period of 8 years?

17. What is the total price for a paper order if the tax is 8.5% and the paper costs $90?

18. Wilderness Sports gives their employees 60% off gear for one weekend of the year. Sierra selects a collection of gear that totals $1,450. What will her discounted price be?

19. Eleanor sold a full-page advertisement in *The New York Times* for $12,000. If she gets a commission of 7.25%, how much money did she earn for that sale?

20. Last year, A Stone's Throw sales were $56,000, but this year the business's sales were $60,000. What was the percentage increase rounded to the nearest tenth?

CALCULATOR TIPS!

Although it is beneficial to have a fundamental understanding of what percentages represent, you are able to perform percentage calculations on the TI-30XS calculator. You will still need to know *how* to set up the problems, but the calculator can turn the percentages into decimals for you, and vice versa. Do the following Chapter Review questions without the special calculator functions, and after you have read through *Chapter 12: Calculator Skills on the TI-30XS*, you can complete them again with the aid of your calculator.

Summary

You now have a gamut of important and practical new skills under your belt: understanding and working with rates; problem-solving with proportions; and powerful calculating with percentages. Your GED® test will most certainly have questions like these on test day, so take your time and review any sections that you need a little more focus on!

Rates, Proportions, and Percents Review

1. Suppose a jet can fly a distance of 5,100 miles in three hours. If the jet travels at the same average speed throughout its flight, how many hours will it take the jet to travel 22,950 miles?
 a. 4.5 hours
 b. 13.5 hours
 c. 15.3 hours
 d. 18 hours

2. Joe made $90 babysitting for 12 hours. At this rate, how long will it take him to make an additional $300?
 a. 25 hours
 b. 7.5 hours
 c. 40 hours
 d. 28 hours

3. Jeremy purchased six cans of tomatoes for $5.34. At this rate, how much would he pay for 11 cans of tomatoes?
 a. $10.68
 b. $9.79
 c. $9.90
 d. $11.00

4. Solve for x: $\frac{8}{10} = \frac{x}{100}$. _____

5. The scale on a state map is 1 inch:24 miles. How many miles apart are two cities if they are 3 inches apart on the map?
 a. 32 miles
 b. 72 miles
 c. 80 miles
 d. 96 miles

6. A survey of 1,000 registered voters shows that 650 people would choose Candidate A in an upcoming election. If 240,000 people vote in the upcoming election, according to the survey, how many votes will Candidate A receive?

7. Samantha went to a local restaurant to celebrate her birthday with a friend. The charge for the meal was $15. Samantha paid with a $20 bill and tipped the waiter 15% of the cost of the meal. How much change did she have left?

a. $2.25
b. $2.75
c. $3.50
d. $3.75

8. If Veronica deposits $5,000 in her savings account with a yearly interest rate of 9% and leaves the money in the account for eight years, how much interest will her money earn?

a. $360,000
b. $45,000
c. $3,600
d. $450

9. Mr. Jordan is planning to buy a treadmill. The treadmill he wants is on sale at 10% off the retail price of $700. Mr. Jordan has an additional coupon for 5% off after the discount has been applied. What is the final cost of the treadmill, not including any taxes or assembly fees?

a. $587.50
b. $598.50
c. $630.00
d. $668.50

10. Alexis bought a gardening shed for $339. She loved it so much that the next summer she went to buy another one but the price had gone up to $419. What was the percentage increase in price of her beloved garden shed, rounded to the nearest whole number?

a. 24%
b. 36%
c. 19%
d. 80%

Answers and Explanations

Chapter Practice

1. **3.5.** This question is asking us to find Anita's unit rate since it's wanting to know how many necklaces she made in one hour. Divide the necklaces made by the time she worked: $\frac{28 \text{ necklaces} \div 8}{8 \text{ hours} \div 8} = \frac{3.5 \text{ necklaces}}{1 \text{ hour}}$. Anita made 3.5 necklaces per hour.

2. **140.** Since Anita makes 3.5 necklaces per hour, multiply 3.5 by 40 to see how many necklaces she can make in a 40-hour work week: $3.5 \times 40 = 140$.

3. **Pete has the best mileage at 45 miles per gallon.** To find the miles per gallon for each car, divide the number of miles traveled by the number of gallons:

Pete: $\frac{540 \text{ miles} \div 12}{12 \text{ gallons} \div 12} = \frac{45 \text{ miles}}{1 \text{ gallon}} = 45$ miles per gallon.

Celia's: $\frac{585 \text{ miles} \div 15}{15 \text{ gallons} \div 15} = \frac{39 \text{ miles}}{1 \text{ gallon}} = 39$ miles per gallon.

Lauren's: $\frac{798 \text{ miles} \div 21}{21 \text{ gallons} \div 21} = \frac{38 \text{ miles}}{1 \text{ gallon}} = 38$ miles per gallon.

Pete gets the most miles per gallon in his car so he should drive.

4. **540 miles per hour.** To find the miles per hour, divide the miles traveled by the space shuttle by the hours: $\frac{2{,}430 \text{ miles} \div 4.5}{4.5 \text{ hours} \div 4.5} = \frac{540 \text{ miles}}{1 \text{ hour}} = 540$ miles per hour.

5. **$225.** First find Eliseo's hourly rate: $90 ÷ 12 hours = $7.50 per hour. A Monday – Friday workweek of 6 hours per day contains 5 days at 6 hours per day, so that is a total of 30 hours. Therefore, multiplying 30 hours by Eliseo's $7.50 hourly rate will show how much money he will make in that one week: 30 hours × $7.50/hour = $225.

6. 2,400 words. Let's set up a proportional relationship by writing two fractions. Let's use x to represent the number of words per 12 minutes:

$$\frac{1,000}{5} = \frac{x}{12}$$

Cross multiply to solve for x:

$$1,000 \times 12 = 5x$$
$$12,000 = 5x$$
$$\frac{12,000}{5} = 2,400$$

7. 48. The first step of the solution is to use the ratio $\frac{men}{women}$ to record the given information of there being 3 men and 5 women: $\frac{men}{women} = \frac{3}{5}$. Next, we want to turn this relationship into a proportion where the second ratio shows 18 men. Since we don't know the number of women at the meeting, we used w to represent them: $\frac{men}{women} = \frac{3}{5} = \frac{18}{w}$. Solve this proportion using equivalent cross products: $3w = 5(18)$. Divide both side by 3 to get $w = 30$. This is not our answer to the question though, which asked for the *total* number of men and women. Since there are 30 men and 18 women, there are 48 people in total at the meeting.

8. 3. Since 8 out of every 2,000 calculators are malfunctioning, and we are looking to see how many calculators out of 750 will be likely to have a malfunctioning problem, set up the following proportion:

$$\frac{malfunctioning}{total} = \frac{8}{2,000} = \frac{m}{750}$$

Begin to solve this proportion using cross products:

$$8(750) = 2,000m$$
$$6,000 = 2,000m$$

$m = 3$, so the store should expect to have approximately 3 returns if they sell all 750 calculators.

9. 833 square feet. Since every 10 square feet cost $3, and the Robb family wants their maximum cost to be $250, set up the following proportion, where f represents the number of square feet that would correspond to a cost of $250:

$$\frac{cost}{sq.\ ft.} = \frac{\$3}{10} = \frac{\$250}{f}$$

Begin to solve this proportion using cross products:

$$10(250) = 3f$$
$$2,500 = 3f$$
$$\frac{2,500}{3} = 833.\overline{3} = f$$

So the Robb family can clean up to 833 square feet of carpet without spending more than $250.

10. $45. One way to find the cost of nine used books is to figure out the relationship between the number of books and the price of the other bundles. Do you notice a pattern? Do you see that each time the number of books is multiplied by 5 to get the price of each bundle? If we multiply 9 by 5, the answer is $45.

Another way to find the cost of the bundle of 9 books is to set up two equivalent fractions and solve for x:

$$\frac{6}{30} = \frac{9}{x}$$
$$6x = 30 \times 9$$
$$6x = 270$$
$$x = \frac{270}{6}$$
$$x = 45$$

11. 150. First, recall that the word *of* requires multiplication: 25% of 600 students will be solved by doing 25% $\times$ 600. Next, remember that percentages must be changed to their decimal equivalent before they can be used in calculations. Do this by moving the decimal point twice to the left and then perform the multiplication: $0.25 \times 600 = 150$.

12. 2,000. First let's rewrite $\frac{1}{2}\%$ as 0.5%. Next, let's remember that the word *of* means we need to multiply 0.5% by 400,000 deer. Since we need to change percents to their decimal equivalents before using them in calculations, move the decimal twice to the left and set up the problem as $0.005 \times 400,000 = 2,000$.

13. 17.5%. To find what percent one number is of another number, divide the part by the whole. Then multiply the quotient by 100 and add the % symbol:

$$\frac{14}{80} \times 100 = 17.5\%$$

14. 87.5%. Watch out for the questions that give you the number of people who satisfy a specific criterion, but then ask you to find the percentage of the opposite criterion! We are asked to find the percentage of the test audience that thought the movie was not too violent for viewers under 18. 70 out of 560 thought it was too violent, so subtract 70 from 560 to see how many thought it *was not* too violent. $560 - 70 = 490$. To find what percent 490 is out of 560, divide the part by the whole. Then multiply the quotient by 100 and add the % symbol:

$$\frac{490}{560} \times 100 = 87.5\%$$

15. 125. To find the *whole* when the % and *part* are given, set up and solve a proportion in the form $\frac{part}{whole} = \frac{\%}{100}$. Fill in 15 as the *part*, 12 as the percent, and let w represent the *whole* you are solving for: $\frac{15}{w} = \frac{12}{100}$. Now use cross multiplication to simplify this to $15(100) = 12w$. Dividing both sides by 12 gives $w = 125$.

16. $92,480. First, calculate the simple interest using the simple interest formula:

Simple Interest = (Principal) × (Interest Rate) × (# of Years Borrowed)

Plug in $68,000 as the principal, 8 as the years borrowed, and 0.045 as the interest rate (change 4.5% to its decimal equivalent):

Simple Interest = (68,000) × (0.045) × (8)
Simple Interest = $24,480.

Since we must find the *total payback*, add the simple interest to the $68,000 borrowed to calculate the total payback as $92,480.

17. $97.65. To find the cost of 8.5% tax on a $90 purchase, multiply 0.085 by 90: $0.085 \times 90 =$ $7.65. Now add the tax to the original price of $90: $90 + $7.65 = $97.65.

18. $580. Since Wilderness Sports gives their employees a 60% discount, that means that Sierra will pay 40% of the $1,450 of gear she's selected. (Since 100% − 60% = 40%.) Therefore, Sierra's discounted price be will be $1,450 × 0.40 = $580. Sierra will pay $580 for her gear on the discount weekend. Alternatively, you could find 60% of the original $1,450, and then subtract that from $1,450. This will give you the same answer, but it takes two separate calculations instead of just one!

19. $870. $7.25\% = \frac{7.25}{100} = 0.0725$. Find the 7.25% commission Eleanor made on $12,000 by multiplying 0.0725 by $12,000: $0.0725 \times $12,000 =$ $870.

20. 7.1%. Since A Stone's Throw sales went from $56,000 up to $60,000, we know that the *amount of increase* is $4,000. (We got this by subtracting the previous sales numbers.) We also know that the original sales were $56,000. Find the percentage increase by putting these figures into the *Percent of Change* formula:

$$\text{Percent of change} = \frac{amount\ of\ increase}{original\ amount} \times 100$$

$$\text{Percent of change} = \frac{4,000}{56,000} \times 100 \approx 7.1\%$$

Rates, Proportions, and Percents Review

1. b. Dividing 5,100 miles by three hours gives you the speed of the jet in miles per hour:
$$\frac{5,100}{3} = 1,700 \text{ miles per hour}$$
Therefore, to fly a distance of 22,950 miles, divide the distance 22,950 miles by 1,700 miles per hour, which equals $\frac{22,950}{1,700} = 13.5$ hours.

2. c. Find how much Joe makes per hour:
$$\$90 \div 12 = \$7.50$$
Joe makes $7.50 per hour.
To find how many hours he will need to babysit to earn $300, divide $300 by $7.50:
$$\$300 \div 7.50 = 40$$
It will take Joe 40 hours to earn an additional $300.

3. b. To find the cost of one can of tomatoes, divide the cost of six cans ($5.34) by 6:
$$\$5.34 \div 6 = \$0.89$$
Each can of tomatoes costs $0.89.
Next, to find the cost of 11 cans, multiply $0.89 by 11:
$$\$0.89 \times 11 = \$9.79$$
The cost of 11 cans of tomatoes is $9.79.

4. $x = 80.$ Solve the proportion $\frac{8}{10} = \frac{x}{100}$ by setting the cross products equal to one another:
$$8(100)=10(x)$$
$$800 = 10x$$
$$\frac{800}{10} = x$$
$$x = 80.$$

5. b. Because 1 inch on the map represents 24 miles, 3 inches on the map represent 3×24, or 72 miles.

6. 156,000. Solve this word problem by setting a proportion that compares Candidate A Voters to Total Voters. The given information tells us that the first ratio will be 650 Candidate A Voters to 1,000 Total Voters:
$$\frac{\text{Candidate A Voters}}{\text{Total Voters}} = \frac{650}{1,000}$$
Set this ratio equal to a ratio with 240,000 as the Total Voters and A as the Candidate A Voters:
$$\frac{\text{Candidate A Voters}}{\text{Total Voters}} = \frac{650}{1,000} = \frac{A}{240,000}$$
Now solve this using cross products:
$$650(240,000)=1,000A$$
$$156,000,000 = 1,000A$$
$$A = 156,000.$$
Therefore, it can be anticipated that Candidate A will receive 156,000 out of the 240,000 votes.

7. b. A 15% tip on a charge of $15 equals $2.25. Therefore, the total amount that Samantha paid was $15.00 + $2.25 = $17.25. The difference equals $20.00 − $17.25 = $2.75.

8. c. In the formula $I = prt$, the amount of money deposited is called the principal, p. The interest rate per year is represented by r, and t represents the number of years. The interest rate must be written as a decimal. Here, $p = 5,000$, $r = 9\% = 0.09$, and $t = 8$. Substitute these numbers for the respective variables and multiply: $I = 5,000 \times 0.09 \times 8 = \$3,600$.

9. b. This question requires taking your time and making sure you do all the required steps. Do one step at a time to arrive at the correct answer.

First, find the sale price after the 10% has been deducted (remember, 10% is the same as 0.10):

$$\$700 - 0.10(\$700) = \$700 - \$70$$
$$= \$630$$

Now, apply the 5% coupon to the discounted price of $630. Remember, 5% is the same as 0.05. Be sure to subtract from $630, not from the original price of $700.

$$\$630 - 0.05(\$630) = \$630 - \$31.50$$
$$= \$598.50$$

10. a. Use the formula for % of increase by subtracting the original price from the new price:

$$\% \text{ of increase: } = \frac{amount\ of\ increase}{original\ amount} \times 100$$

$$\% \text{ of increase} = \frac{419 - 339}{339} \times 100 = 23.59\%$$

So the percentage increase rounded to 24%. Answer choice **c**, 19%, is what you get if you divided the amount of increase by the new price of $419, but instead you have to divide it by the original price. Answer choice **d**, 80%, is just the difference in price from last year to this year, without it being divided by the original price.

CHAPTER

6 ▶

ALGEBRA PART I: VARIABLES AND LINEAR EQUATIONS

N ow that you've completed the important foundational work in the past few chapters, you are ready to move on to algebra. Algebra is an organized system of rules that is used to help solve problems for **unknowns**. It is because of algebra that engineers can build bridges, cell phones, and engines. In all of these cases, equations are written to determine the values of unknowns. As you work through this material, be sure to pay special attention to any new words you may encounter. It is important that you build a strong foundation for the more advanced algebraic concepts presented in the following chapters. Answers and explanations for all practice questions are at the end of the chapter.

This chapter covers:

- $+, -, \times,$ and $\div$ algebraic expressions
- The distributive property on linear expressions
- Evaluating algebraic expressions through substitution
- Solving linear equations
- Modeling word problems with algebra

The Language of Algebra

In Chapter 3, you practiced translating words into numerical expressions. Here you'll learn how to translate words into algebraic expressions. What is the difference between numerical phrases and algebraic expressions? Numerical phrases contain only numbers while **algebraic expressions** contain at least one unknown value. That unknown may often be referred to as *a number*, such as in *5 times a number*. If there is a second unknown, it may be referred to as *another number* or *a second number*.

GED® QUESTION SNEAK PREVIEW!

It is important to be able to model real-world situations with algebraic equations on your GED® Mathematical Reasoning test. The following section will teach you how to answer this type of question:

- *Which expression models 4 times the quantity of 5 less than a number?*

Using Variables in Algebraic Expressions

A **variable** is a letter or symbol used to represent an unknown number. Although the variable x is most commonly used to represent an unknown quantity in algebraic expressions, any letter or symbol can be used. The phrase *5 more than 10* is translated as $5 + 10$, and the phrase *5 more than a number* can be written as $5 + x$, $5 + m$, or even $5 + K$. When a phrase refers to two unknown values, it is common to represent the first unknown number with x and the second unknown number as y. Using this convention, the phrase *twice a number plus four times another number* would be written $2x + 4y$, but it would also be correct to choose any two different variables and represent the phrase as $2g + 4h$.

Recognizing Key Words

Remember to look for key words that represent addition, subtraction, multiplication, and division. We discussed these words and gave examples in Chapter 3, so you may want to review this before moving on. Here is a reminder of words to keep your eye out for:

ADDITION	SUBTRACTION	MULTIPLICATION	DIVISION
sum	difference	product	quotient
combine	take away	times	percent
total	less than	of	out of
plus	minus	every	share
and	decrease	each	split
all together	left	factors	average
increase	fewer	double (× 2)	each
more than	remove	triple (× 3)	per

Tricky Phrases

As discussed in Chapter 3, these phrases indicate that two items must be grouped together in parentheses: *quantity*, *sum of*, and *difference of*.

Example: *10 times the sum of five and a number*

The sum of indicates that $5 + x$ must be grouped together as a single term in parentheses: $10(5 + x)$

Also recall that some phrases for subtraction can be misleading. For example, *from* and *less than* indicate subtraction, but the order of the terms must be reversed:

Example: *What is 8 less than twice y?*

Less than indicates subtracting in the reverse order that the expressions are presented. Since *twice y* means $2y$, represent *8 less than twice y* as $2y - 8$.

Defining the Parts of Algebraic Expressions

If I tell you how to do something in Latin, but you only speak English, then you will not know how to follow my instructions. Learning the correct math language is necessary in order to be able to follow mathematical instructions. Become familiar with the following vocabulary since these terms will be used to explain more involved procedures with algebraic equations:

Constant: An independent fixed number that remains the same and does not change.
    Example: $y = 3x + 7$; 7 is the *constant*

Variable: A letter or symbol that represents a number in an algebraic expression.
    Example: $-2x + 8y$; x and y are *variables*

Coefficient: The number or symbol multiplied by a variable in an algebraic expression. It is very important to remember that when a variable is on its own, its coefficient is 1:
    Example: $4x^2 + 3x + y + 2$; 4, 3, and 1 are *coefficients*, but 2 is a constant

Term: A number, a variable, or a coefficient multiplied by one or more variables. *Terms* in algebraic expressions are separated by addition or subtraction.
    Example: $5t$; there is one term: $5t$
    Example: $-12x + 3y - 10$; there are 3 terms: $-12x$, $3y$, and 10

Factor: Numbers that are multiplied together in an algebraic expression—because of PEMDAS, terms that are added or subtracted within a set of parentheses are treated as a single factor.
    Example: $9xy$; there is one term with three *factors*: 9, x, y
    Example: $9(x + y)$; there are two *factors*: 9 and $(x + y)$

Algebraic Expression: A mathematical sequence containing one or more variables or numbers connected by addition or subtraction.
    Example: $-12x + 3y - 10$ is an *algebraic expression* with three terms

Practice

Represent each phrase as an algebraic expression.

1. The sum of 5 and twice a number w

2. One-third of the difference of 6 and a number

3. 30 more than a number squared

4. The quantity 13 less than a number is tripled and then added to another number

5. Combine $48.90, $20.20, and a number; then cut it in half

6. A dozen fewer than a cubed number

Evaluating Expressions

Evaluating algebraic expressions means replacing the variables in an expression with given numbers and performing the arithmetic operations in the expression. Although this sounds easy enough, it is critical to carefully follow the correct order of operations dictated by PEMDAS, since it is easy to mix this up and get an incorrect answer.

GED® QUESTION SNEAK PREVIEW!

The GED® Mathematical Reasoning test wants you to demonstrate the ability to use real-life formulas to make accurate calculations. You may get a question like this:

- *A jewelry design firm uses the formula $r = \frac{80 + 35n}{n}$ to determine the price per ring, r, when n rings are made. If the firm chooses to make 20 rings in August, determine the cost per ring.*

Evaluating Single Variable Expressions

The most basic algebraic expressions contain only one variable and are called *single-variable expressions*. You may already have experience evaluating single-variable expressions since the *perimeter* of a square is a single-variable expression. (Remember that the perimeter of a shape is the distance around it.)

Perimeter of square = 4*s*, where *s* represents the side length.

If we want to find the perimeter of a square piece of property that has a side length of 62 feet, we replace the *s* in the formula with the value of 62:

Perimeter = 4*s*, evaluate for *s* = 62 feet
Perimeter = 4(62)
Perimeter = 248 feet

Sometimes there will be a single variable, but it will appear more than once. In this case, replace the variable with its numerical equivalent each time the variable appears. Then use PEMDAS:

Example
Evaluate the expression $-3x^2 + 10x$ for $x = -5$.

Replace both x variables with -5 and follow the appropriate order of operations as dictated by PEMDAS:

$-3(-5)^2 + 10(-5)$

Take care of the exponent first: $(-5)^2 = -5 \times -5 = 25$

$-3(25) + 10(-5)$

Next do the multiplication:

$-75 + -50$

The last step is to add:

-125 is your final answer

Subbing Negative Values in for Variables

Notice that when –5 was substituted in for x^2, the negative sign canceled out when $(-5)^2$ was performed. It's critical to understand that when substituting a negative value in for a variable, use parentheses and include the negative sign in the operation instructed by the exponent. Therefore, *even exponents* cancel out the negative sign of a negative base since the product of two negative factors is positive. Conversely, all odd exponents will preserve the negative sign of a negative base.

RULE: SUBBING NEGATIVE VALUES INTO EXPONENTIAL EXPRESSIONS

When substituting a negative number in for a variable that has an exponent:

- **Even exponents** will cancel out the sign of a negative base: $(-3)^2 = (-3)(-3) = 9$
- **Odd exponents** will preserve the sign of a negative base: $(-2)^3 = (-2)(-2)(-2) = -8$

The information in the previous box sometimes misleads students to think that an even exponent will *always* result in a positive answer. The information in the following box is one of the most difficult exponent nuances for students to master.

DON'T DO THIS!

A common mistake students make is using a negative coefficient to cancel out a negative base *before* acting upon the exponent. This is an especially easy mistake to make when the coefficient is –1! For example, when evaluating $-x^2$ for $x = -4$, be aware that the coefficient of x^2 is –1. PEMDAS requires that *negative four squared* is done first, before multiplying it by the –1 coefficient:

Example

Evaluate $-y^2$ for $y = -4$

$-y^2 = -1 \times y^2$

$-y^2 = -1 \times (-4)^2$

$-y^2 = -1 \times (-4)(-4)$

$-y^2 = -1 \times 16$

$-y^2 = \underline{-16}$

Notice that even though the exponent is even, the answer is negative since the coefficient is negative. Test writers love to trick students with this concept, so make sure you understand how to avoid making this error!

Evaluating Multivariable Expressions

Algebraic expressions that contain more than one variable are called **multivariable expressions**. If you've ever calculated the *perimeter* of a rectangle using the formula *perimeter = 2l + 2w*, then you already have some experience with multivariable expressions. To evaluate a multivariable expression, replace each variable in the expression with the given value for that variable, then work through the correct order of operations.

Example

Evaluate the expression $-3m - 10n$ for $m = -5$ and $n = -2$

Replace *m* with –5 and *n* with –2:

$$-3m - 10n$$
$$-3(-5) - 10(-2)$$

Now let PEMDAS guide you through the correct order of operations. Do the multiplication first:

$$15 - (-20)$$

Now use *keep-switch-switch* to rewrite subtraction as addition:

$$15 + 20$$

Add to get 35 as the final answer.

Practice

7. Evaluate $\frac{-10 + 3c}{4c}$ for $c = -2$

8. What is the value of the expression $3.14r^2h$ at $r = 10$ and $h = 2$?

9. Evaluate the expression $2(lw + wh + hl)$ for $l = 6, w = 4, h = 2$.

10. Let *w* represent any real number other than 0. Will the value of the expression $-w^2$ sometimes, always, or never be negative? Explain your reasoning.

11. Let *v* represent any real number other than 0. Will the value of the expression $-v^3$ sometimes, always, or never be negative? Explain your reasoning.

12. Evaluate the expression $-v^2 + v^3$ for $v = -3$.

13. Marco and Polo are making props for the school play. The prop is a cube that will be used as a pulpit. Marco wants to make a cube that has a side length of 2 feet and Polo thinks it would be better to make a cube with a side length of 3 feet. How much bigger is the surface area of Polo's cube than Marco's cube? (Use the formula for the surface area of a cube, *Surface Area* = $6s^2$, where *s* is the side length of the cube.)

14. Interest is the money an investment pays you. One formula used to calculate the new amount of your money including interest is $C(1 + r)^t$ where C stands for your beginning investment, *r* is the interest rate as a decimal, and *t* is the time in years. If Paula invests \$10,000 at an interest rate of 5%, what will the value of her investment be after 4 years? Round your answer to the nearest dollar.

Performing Operations on Expressions

In this section you will learn how to add, subtract, multiply, and divide algebraic expressions.

GED® QUESTION SNEAK PREVIEW!

You may be asked to multiply binomials on your GED® Mathematical Reasoning test.

- *Multiply* $(2x - 5)(x + 8)$

Although this question seems like it might be simple, it actually requires a lot of knowledge and practice to be solved correctly. We will cover these skills in this section.

Keeping in the theme of operations, let's look at the rules and methods used to perform operations on algebraic expressions.

Distributive Property with Linear Expressions

We looked at the distributive property in a previous chapter. Remember, it does exactly what it sounds like it does—distributes a number or term to other numbers or terms. Parentheses and multiplication are always involved.

For instance, if we needed to expand the problem $5(3 + y)$, we would distribute the 5 to the 3 by multiplying 5×3, and then distribute the 5 to the y by multiplying $5 \times y$. The result would be $15 + 5y$.

Sometimes the factor may be on the right side of a set of parentheses, but that doesn't change how the distributive property will function. For instance, if we needed to expand the problem $(9 - h)4$, we would distribute the 4 to the 9 and the h using multiplication:

$$(9 - h)4 =$$
$$(4)(9) - (4)(h) =$$
$$36 - 4h$$

DON'T DO THIS!

A difficult application of the distributive property is when a constant is being added to an expression that requires the distributive property. One example of this is $2 + 7(3 - y)$. In this case, it is always tempting for students to add $2 + 7$ before distributing the 7 to $(3 - y)$. However, since PEMDAS dictates that multiplication must come before addition, adding $2 + 7$ is incorrect. Instead, refrain from doing the addition until the 7 has been distributed:

NO! $2 + 7(3 - y) \neq 9(3 - y)$

YES . . . $2 + 7(3 - y) = 2 + 7(3 - y)$

$$2 + 7(3) - 7(y)$$
$$2 + 21 - 7y$$
$$23 - 7y$$

A similar type of problem to the previous example, which also causes frequent errors, is when the term needing to be distributed is being *subtracted* from a constant. In the case of $10 - 2(w + 6)$, it's not uncommon for a student to forget to distribute the minus sign to *both* terms within the parentheses. Carefully follow the steps below to see how the subtraction is first turned into addition through the *keep-switch-switch* technique presented in Chapter 4. Using this method will help ensure that you distribute the negative sign to *both* terms inside the parentheses:

$$10 - 2(w + 6) =$$
$$10 + -2(w + 6) = 10 + -2(w + 6)$$
$$10 + -2(w) + -2(6)$$
$$10 + -2w + -12$$
$$\underline{-2 + -2w}$$

Adding and Subtracting Polynomial Expressions

When adding and subtracting terms in polynomial expressions, only *like terms* may be added and subtracted. *Like terms* are terms that have the same exact variables and exponents. Look at the following lists of *like* and *unlike* terms:

Like Terms:	Unlike Terms:
$3x$ and $-40x$	x and x^2
$10m^4$ and $\frac{1}{3}m^4$	$10m^4$ and $\frac{1}{3}m^5$
$2rb$ and $0.5rb$	$2rb$ and $0.5b$
x^3y and $7x^3y$	x^3y and $7x^3y^2$

> When combining like terms, add or subtract the coefficients and keep the variables and their exponents exactly the same:
> $$3x + -0x = -37x$$
> $$10m^4 + \frac{1}{3}m^4 = 10\frac{1}{3}m4$$
> $$2rb \text{ and } 0.5rb$$
> $$7x^3y - x^3y = 6x^3y$$

You will be expected to be able to add or subtract more complex expressions on the GED® test:

Example
Simplify $(6x^2 + 2xy - 9) - (4x^3 + 2x^2 - 5xy + 8)$.

This looks complicated, but really it is just adding and subtracting coefficients—the numbers in front of the variables—of like terms. One thing important to note in this problem is that we are subtracting a *quantity*. This means that the minus sign needs to be distributed to each of the terms in parentheses after it. The minus sign will make each of the terms in parentheses its opposite. The first step in simplifying this problem is to rewrite it with the distributed negative:

$$(6x^2 + 2xy - 9) - (4x^3 + 2x^2 - 5xy + 8)$$

The second step in simplifying is to combine *like* terms.

$$6x^2 + \mathbf{2xy} - 9 - 4x^3 - 2x^2 + \mathbf{5xy} - \mathbf{8}$$
$$6x^2 - 2x^2 = 4x^2$$
$$2xy + 5xy = 7xy$$
$$-9 - 8 = -17$$

$-4x^3$ has no other term like it, so it stays the same.

The last step is to rewrite the expression with the combined terms:

$$-4x^3 + 4x^2 + 7xy - 17$$

(*Note:* It's helpful to write the terms so that the value of the exponents goes from greatest to least as you read from left to right. Also, remember that positive numbers will have a plus sign in front while negative numbers will have a minus sign.)

Multiplying Expressions

When multiplying expressions, you don't have to worry about like terms. To multiply two expressions, follow these steps:

Step 1: Multiply the coefficients.

Step 2: Multiply all pairs of like variables together by adding their exponents.

Step 3: Combine the product of the coefficients with the products of the variables as one single term.

Here are two examples:

$$(3v)(8v) = (3 \times 8)(v \times v) = 24v^2$$
$$(5wy)(4y^2) = (5 \times 4)(w)(y \times y^2) = 20wy^3$$

DON'T DO THIS!

It can be easy to forget to pay attention to the exponents when multiplying two terms that don't have exponents greater than 1. In the case of a question such as $(4a)(9a)$, students tend to make the mistake of multiplying the coefficients but not the variables:

NO! $(4a)(9a) \neq 36a$
YES . . . $(4a)(9a) = 36a^2$

Dividing Expressions

When dividing polynomial expressions, we are looking for ways to reduce their coefficients and cancel out some of their exponents to arrive at a simplified answer. Let's review how to divide like bases with exponents:

RULE: DIVIDING LIKE BASES WITH EXPONENTS

When dividing like bases with exponents, subtract the exponents:

$$\frac{x^7}{x^4} = x^3$$

If the difference of the exponents is a negative exponent, we can move that base and exponent into the denominator of the fraction and write the exponent as positive. (Review Chapter 4 for clarification and practice with exponents.)

$$\frac{w^3x^6}{w^7x} = w^{(3-7)}x^{(6-1)} = w^{-4}x^5 = \frac{x^5}{w^4}$$

Using this information, let's take a look at the process used to simplify the following expression:

$$\frac{4y^3x^2}{2yx}$$

We need to call to mind our knowledge about reducing fractions as well as our knowledge about dividing exponents. To simplify this expression, let's look at

the numbers first. Can we reduce at all? Yes! We can divide 4 by 2, and then we are left with a 2 in the numerator only:

$$\frac{4y^3x^2}{2yx} = \frac{2y^3x^2}{yx}$$

Is there anything else we can simplify? There are x's and y's in both the numerator and the denominator, so we can divide the denominator into the numerator. Let's take the terms one at a time:

$$\frac{y^3}{y} = y^2$$

$$\frac{x^2}{x} = x$$

Our complete answer is $2y^2x$.

Multiplying Binomials with FOIL

A *binomial* is an algebraic expression with two terms that are added or subtracted. Examples of binomials are:

$$9 + f$$
$$x - 7$$
$$3y^2 + 4x$$

When two binomials are written directly next to each other in two sets of parentheses, it indicates multiplication. *The product of x + 2 and x − 4 is written as* $(x + 2)(x - 4)$. In order to perform this multiplication, the acronym FOIL is used to keep track of which parts must be multiplied. FOIL stands for the multiplication of:

F: First terms in each binomial
O: Outside terms in each binomial
I: Inside terms in each binomial
L: Last terms in each binomial

Let's use FOIL to guide us through the multiplication of $(x + 2)(x - 4)$:

Multiply Firsts:
$(\underline{x} + 2)(\underline{x} - 4) = \underline{x^2}$

Multiply Outsides:
$(\underline{x} + 2)(x \underline{- 4}) = x^2 \underline{- 4x}$

Multiply Insides:
$(x + \underline{2})(\underline{x} - 4) = x^2 - 4x + \underline{2x}$

Multiply Lasts:
$(x + \underline{2})(x \underline{- 4}) = x^2 - 4x + 2x \underline{- 8}$

We get the final answer after combining the two like terms, $-4x$ and $2x$:

$$x^2 - 2x - 8$$

Dividing Expressions through Factoring

Similar to how *multiplication* is the opposite operation of *division*, *factoring* is the opposite of *distributing*. While distributing requires us to *multiply* a common factor to two or more terms of an expression, *factoring* requires us to divide out the *greatest common factor* from two or more terms in an expression. Remember that the **greatest common factor**, or **GCF**, is the largest number that divides evenly into all terms.

Example

Use factoring to rewrite $40m + 32$ as the product of two factors.

Starting with $40m + 32$, identify the GFC as 8. Divide both $40m$ and 32 by the GCF: $40m \div 8 = 5m$ and $32 \div 8 = 4$.

Now reverse the distributive property by pulling the GCF outside of a single set of parentheses and put the two quotients inside the parentheses:

$$40m + 32 = 8(5m) + 8(4) = 8(5m + 4)$$

You can check your work by distributing, which should return your original expression:

$$8(5m + 4) = 8(5m) + 8(4) = 40m + 32$$

Practice

Simplify the following expressions:

15. $40 - 8(9 - c)$

16. $(7xy^2 + 8xy - 4) - (11x^2y - 12xy + 10)$

17. $(16a^3b^5c)(\frac{1}{2}ab^2c^3)$

18. $(24a^8b) \div (6a^5b^4)$

19. $(5 - x)(9 + x)$

20. $(y^2 - 3)(y^2 + 3)$

Write the following expression as a product of two factors:

21. $12y + 40x - 4$

22. $60f^4 - 18f$

Working with Linear Equations

In this section you will learn how to solve linear equations. A linear equation is an equation with one or more variables to the first power. Examples include:

$$3x + 7 = -5$$
$$y = mx + b$$
$$4z - 3 + n = 2$$

GED® QUESTION SNEAK PREVIEW!

On the GED® test you will be asked to solve for the value of variables in linear equations and this section will show you how to answer questions like this.

- Solve for x: $\frac{5}{2}x = -40$

- Solve for m in terms of n and p: $5 - 20n + 6m = p$

Solving Linear Equations

To solve linear equations with one variable, we need to get the variable by itself on one side of the equation. For instance, to find what x is in the equation $3x + 7 = -5$, we need to get x by itself. The goal is to get a mathematical sentence that reads "x = a number."

How do we do this? By stripping away the other numbers through performing opposite operations. In the following example, what is on the same side of the equation as x?

$$3x + 7 = -5$$

3 and 7: x is being multiplied by 3 and then added to 7. To undo these operations, we need to use opposite operations. *Opposite operations* are pairs of operations that undo each other. Addition and subtraction are opposite operations and multiplication and division are also opposite operations.

One other *very* important thing to keep in mind when solving linear equations: Whatever you do to one side of the equation, you *must* do to the other. This is so that you maintain a balance on each side of the equal sign.

The third critical step to keep in mind when solving linear equations is that we always undo equations in the *opposite order* of PEMDAS. That means that in order to get the variable alone, we perform addition or subtraction *first*, and then we will move on to the multiplication or division. Basically, what this looks like is moving the *farthest* number from x first, using opposite operations. These are the three cardinal rules for solving linear equations:

THREE RULES: SOLVING LINEAR EQUATIONS

1. Use opposite operations to move numbers away from the variable.
2. Whatever operation you do to one side of the equal sign, you must do the same to the other.
3. Reverse PEMDAS when isolating the variable in linear equations. Do +/− first and then perform ×/÷ to get the variable alone.

So, looking at $3x + 7 = -5$, let's perform opposite operations to get x by itself. Start from the number furthest from x on the same side and work your way to x.

$$3x + 7 = -5$$
$$\underline{-7 \quad -7}$$
$$3x + 0 = -12$$
$$\frac{3x}{3} = \frac{-12}{3}$$
$$x = -4$$

Equations with Multiple X-Terms

You may be asked to solve an equation that has more than one x-term:

$$4x + 10 = 2x - 20 + 8x$$

When an equation has multiple variable terms on one or both sides of the equal sign, there will just be one or two additional steps to solving your equation. Follow these steps:

Step 1: Combine any like terms that are on the same side of the equation by using the operations associated with them. (Do not use *opposite operations*.)

Step 2: Move the variable terms to one side of the equation by using opposite operations to combine them. (It doesn't matter if you move the variable terms to the left side or the right side of the equal sign.)

Step 3: Isolate the variable by using opposite operations in the reverse order of PEMDAS.

DON'T DO THIS!

Do *not* use opposite operations to combine like terms on the *same side* of the equation. Use opposite operations *only* to move the variable term *to the other side of the equation*. Students get confused and start using opposite operations on the same side of an equation once they start seeing more than one variable. Don't do that!

Example: *Given 10x + 9 + 2x = 4x + 5, what is the first step?*

   NO! Don't subtract the 2x from 10x to write 8x + 9 = 4x + 5

   YES . . . Instead, add the 2x to 10x to write 12x + 9 = 4x + 5

Example
What value of x makes the equation true: 4x + 10 = 5x – 20 – 3x

$4x + 10 = 5x - 20 - 3x$ (underline like terms on right side)

$4x + 10 = 2x + {-20}$ (combine $5x - 3x$ on right side)

$\underline{-2x \qquad -2x}$ (move the x terms to the left side)

$2x + 10 = -20$

$\underline{-10 \quad -10}$ (move the constants to the right side)

$\dfrac{2x}{2} = \dfrac{-30}{2}$ (divide both sides by 2 to get x alone)

$x = -15$ (arrive at final answer)

Solving Equations with Parentheses
Some linear equations will have parentheses that must be expanded before solving:

Example
Solve for x: 2(x – 6) = 4x + 20

In this case it is necessary to distribute the 2 before proceeding with the question. Follow along in the solution below:

$2(x - 6) = 4x + 20$

$2(x) - 2(6) = 4x + 20$ (distribute the 2)

$2x - 12 = 4x + 20$

$\underline{-2x \qquad -2x}$ (move the x terms to the right side)

$-12 = 2x + 20$

$\underline{-20 \qquad -20}$ (move the constants to the left side)

$-32 = 2x$

$\div 2 \quad \div 2$ (divide by 2 to get x alone)

$-16 = x$ (arrive at final answer)

Writing and Solving Equations from Word Problems

You practiced translating English into algebraic expressions earlier in this chapter. Now you're ready to write and solve algebraic equations from word problems that represent real-world situations. The most helpful tip when tackling word problems is to first use words to model the mathematical relationship that exists between the working parts of the word problem. The example below illustrates the 4-step process for translating word problems into algebraic equations.

Example
Jenna bought four identically priced nail polishes at the local pharmacy and paid with a $20 bill. She remembers receiving $2.80 in change but forgets the cost of each individual nail polish. Write an algebraic equation that could be used to determine how much each nail polish costs.

Step 1: Read the question, underline the relevant parts, and circle what you are being asked to solve for.

Step 2: Determine how the parts of the problem relate to one another and write out the relationship in words and operations:

[Money paid] – [Cost of 4 nail polishes] = Change received

Step 3: Define your variables and given information:
Money paid = $20
n = **cost of 1 nail polish**
$4n$ = **cost of 4 nail polishes**
Change received = $2.80

Step 4: Replace the words in your equation from Step 2 with the information you compiled in Step 3:
$20 – 4n = $2.80

Now we have an algebraic equation that can be solved using the techniques already presented. Sometimes the GED® test will want you to come up with an equation that represents the situation and other times you'll be expected to solve that equation for a final answer.

Practice

23. Solve for y: $2y - 4 = 21$

24. If $\frac{3}{4}x = 72$, then $x =$ _____

25. Solve for x: $7x + 20 = 13x - 4$

26. Solve for x in terms of y, w, and v: $xy + w = v$

27. Find the value of w that makes the following equation true: $\frac{2}{3}(w - 4) = 26$

28. Twice the sum of a number and ten is 42. Find the number.

29. The Free My Music store pays its sales associates a base rate of $525 per week plus an 8% commission on any sales the employee makes. If an employee makes d dollars in sales one week, write an expression in terms of d to represent her total paycheck for that week.

Summary

In this chapter you have built a solid foundation in algebra. You now know how to use variables to write expressions and to model real-world equations. You can evaluate expressions and solve many different types of linear equations. The following questions will give you a good idea of how you will use these new skills on test day!

Algebra Part I Review

1. Which algebraic expression represents each description? (Drag and drop question)

7 less than twice a number y: _____

Twice the sum of 7 and a number y: _____

$7 - 2y$

$(7 + y)2$

$2y + 7$

$2 \times 7 + y$

$2(7y)$

$7 + 2y$

$2y - 7$

$(7 + y)^2$

$2(7 - y)$

2. If n is any negative integer, complete the following statements: (Note: This would be a drop-down menu question on the GED test—to complete this practice question choose from *sometimes/always/never*.)

A. The expression $\frac{(-n)^4}{n}$ will *sometimes/always/ never* be positive.

B. The expression $\frac{-(n)^4}{n}$ will *sometimes/always/ never* be positive.

3. What is the value of $4x^2 + 3(1 - x)$, when $x = -3$?

a. 48

b. 156

c. −12

d. 30

4. Simplify the expression $5x + 3(x - 4)^2$

5. Expand and simplify the following expression: $7(x + 2y - 3) - 3(2x - 4y + 1)$

a. $x + 2y - 18$

b. $13x - 2y - 2$

c. $x + 26y - 24$

d. $x + 6y - 4$

6. If the sum of two polynomials is $8p^2 + 4p + 1$ and one of the polynomials is $8p^2 - 2p + 6$, what is the other polynomial?

a. $6p - 5$

b. $2p + 7$

c. $16p^2 - 2p + 7$

d. $16p^2 + 2p + 7$

7. Which of the following is equivalent to $2x(3xy + y)$?

a. $6x^2y + 2xy$

b. $6xy + 2xy$

c. $5x^2y + 2x + y$

d. $3xy + 2x + y$

8. Which expression is the equivalent of $32x^2 + 4x - 8$?

a. $32(x^2 + 4x - 8)$

b. $4x(x + x - 8)$

c. $4(x^2 + x - 2)$

d. $4(8x^2 + x - 2)$

9. Which of the following is a factored form of $10x^4y^6 - 5x^3y$?

a. $5xy^5$

b. $5x^3y$

c. $5x^3y(2xy^5 - y)$

d. $5x^3y(2xy^5 - 1)$

10. A host for a party decides to buy three balloons for every guest, plus 20 balloons to decorate the hall. If g represents the number of guests invited to the party and b represents the total number of balloons to be purchased, which equation shows the relationship between the number of balloons (b) and the number of guests (g)?

a. $b = 3(g + 20)$

b. $b = 3g + 20$

c. $b = 60g$

d. $b = 23g$

11. Farhiyo and Jen sold T-shirts for a campus club last Saturday. The club made $550 from selling these T-shirts. After donating some of the money to a local shelter, the club made $100 more than it donated. How much money did the club donate? _____

12. Aaron owns a pretzel stand. After observing sales patterns for a few months, he realizes that he needs to have three times as much cheese as he does ranch dressing to fulfill customers' orders. For every 48 ounces of cheese Aaron buys, how much ranch dressing should he buy?

a. 144 oz.

b. 24 oz.

c. 12 oz.

d. 16 oz.

13. Johanna and Paolo just finished a three-day promotional event for their new business. They distributed flyers to businesses and homes in the neighborhood to let the public know about their new shop. They printed a total of 1,000 flyers for this promotional effort and distributed them over the course of three days. They have x flyers left over. If they are expecting a 15% response rate—meaning that, of the flyers handed out, 15% will bring in one person—which expression illustrates how many more customers they are expecting in the near future as a result of this promotional effort?

a. $15(1,000 - x)$

b. $15(1,000x)$

c. $15 + 1,000 - x$

d. $0.15(1,000 - x)$

14. The product of 16 and one-half of a number is 136. Find the number. _____

Answers and Explanations

Chapter Practice

1. **$5 + 2w$.** Since *sum* means addition, and *twice* means multiplication by 2, "the sum of 5 and twice a number *w*" translates to $5 + 2w$.

2. **$\frac{1}{3}(6-x)$.** The word *difference* indicates to subtract the two terms in a set of parentheses before multiplying it by one-third: $\frac{1}{3}(6-x)$.

3. **$30 + x^2$.** *30 more than* indicates "30 +" and *a number squared* indicates x^2: $30 + x^2$.

4. **$3(x-13) + y$.** The term *the quantity* indicates to use parentheses around the information that follows. *13 less than a number* indicates subtraction in the opposite order: $x - 13$. Next, *is tripled* means to multiply $(x - 13)$ by 3: $3(x - 13)$. Lastly, add *y* (or any variable other than the first variable used) to the expression. $3(x - 13) + y$.

5. **($\$48.90 + \$20.20 + n) \div 2$.** *Combine* means to add, and *cut it in half* means to multiply it by one-half or divide it by 2: $(\$48.90 + \$20.20 + n) \div 2$.

6. **$x^3 - 12$.** *A dozen fewer than* means $- 12$ and *a cubed number* translates to x^3: $x^3 - 12$

7. **2.** Starting with $\frac{-10 + 3c}{4c}$, sub in -2 for both c values: $\frac{-10 + 3(-2)}{4(-2)}$. Then do the multiplication in the numerator and denominator: $\frac{-10 - 6}{-8}$. Combine terms in the numerator: $\frac{-16}{-8}$. Divide to get a final answer of 2.

8. **628.** The expression $3.14r^2h$ at $r = 10$ and $h = 2$ will be $3.14(10)^2(2)$ after 10 and 2 are subbed in. Perform the exponent first: $3.14(100)(2)$. Then multiplication yields 628.

9. **88.** Substitute $l = 6$, $w = 4$, and $h = 2$ into the expression $2(lw + wh + hl)$:
$$2[6(4) + 4(2) + 2(6)]$$
Then perform all of the multiplications within the brackets:
$$2[24 + 8 + 12]$$
Now add all of the terms in the brackets and multiply the sum by 2: $2[44] = 88$.

10. **Always.** The expression $-w^2$ will always be negative for non-zero values of *w*. The even exponent will guarantee that w^2 will be positive for all non-zero values of *w*, but the coefficient of -1 will always make $-w^2$ negative.

11. **Sometimes.** The expression $-v^3$ will be negative when *v* is positive. The expression $-v^3$ will be positive when *v* is negative.

12. **-36.** Starting with $-v^2 + v^3$, sub in -3 for both *v* variables:
$$-(-3)^2 + (-3)^3$$
Now evaluate both of the variables:
$$-(9) + (-27)$$
Adding these two negatives gives -36.

13. Marco's cube: $6s^2$ for $s = 2$: $6(2)^2 = 6(4) = 24$ square feet.
Polo's cube: $6s^2$ for $s = 3$: $6(3)^2 = 6(9) = 54$ square feet.
Polo's cube would have a surface area 30 square feet bigger Marco's cube. (It would be more than double.)

14. **$\$12,155$.** Starting with $C(1 + r)^t$, replace *C* with $\$10,000$, *r* with 5%, and *t* with 4:
$$\$10,000(1 + 0.05)^4$$
First add the number in the parentheses:
$$\$10,000(1.05)^4$$
Then raise 1.05 to the power of 4:
$$\$10,000(1.2155)$$
Then multiply:
$$\$12,155$$

15. **$-32 + 8c$.** Starting with $40 - 8(9 - c)$, use *keep-switch-switch* to turn the subtraction into addition: $40 + -8(9 - c)$. Next distribute the -8: $40 + (-8)(9) - (-8)(c)$. Perform the multiplication: $40 + (-72) - (-8c)$. Simplify: $-32 + 8c$.

16. $-4x^2y + 20xy - 14$. Distribute the minus sign to all of the terms in the second set of parentheses:

$(7xy^2 + 8xy - 4) - 11x^2y + 12xy - 10$

Now rewrite the expression with like terms next to each other:

$7xy^2 - 11x^2y + 8xy + 12xy - 4 - 10$

Lastly, combine like terms:

$-4x^2y + 20xy - 14$

17. $8a^4b^7c^4$. Multiply the coefficients of $(16a^3b^5c)(\frac{1}{2}ab^2c^3)$ and multiply the like variables by adding their exponents:

$(16)(\frac{1}{2})(a^3a)(b^5b^2)(cc^3) = 8a^4b^7c^4$

18. Divide the coefficients of $(24a^8b) \div (6a^5b^4)$ and divide the like variables by subtracting their exponents: $(24 \div 6) \times a^{(8-5)} \times b^{(1-4)} = 4a^3b^{-3}$. Now remember that a term with a negative exponent can get moved to the bottom of a fraction, and then the exponent will be positive: $\frac{4a^3}{b^3}$.

19. $-x^2 - 4x + 45$. Use FOIL to multiply $(5 - x)(9 + x)$:

    Firsts: $5 \times 9 = 45$

    Outsides: $5 \times x = 5x$

    Insides: $-x \times 9 = -9x$

    Lasts: $-x \times x = -x^2$

Now combine the terms together:

$45 + 5x - 9x - x^2 = -x^2 - 4x + 45$

20. $y^4 - 9$. Use FOIL to multiply $(y^2 - 3)(y^2 + 3)$:

    Firsts: $y^2 \times y^2 = y^4$

    Outsides: $y^2 \times 3 = 3y^2$

    Insides: $-3 \times y^2 = -3y^2$

    Lasts: $-3 \times 3 = -9$

Now combine the terms together:

$y^4 + 3y^2 - 3y^2 - 9 = y^4 - 9$

21. $4(3y + 10x - 1)$. 4 is the greatest common factor of all three terms in this expression. In order to factor out a 4, put a 4 on the outside of a set of parentheses and put the quotients from 4 and each of the 3 terms inside the parentheses:

$12y + 40x - 4 = 4(3y + 10x - 1)$

22. $6f(10f^3 - 3)$. $6f$ is the greatest common factor for both terms in this expression. In order to factor out $6f$, put $6f$ on the outside of a set of parentheses and write the quotients from $6f$ and each of the 2 terms inside the parentheses:

$60f^4 - 18f = 6f(10f^3 - 3)$

23. $y = 12.5$. Remember, reverse PEMDAS and use opposite operations to get the variable alone. To move the -4 away from $2y$, add 4 to each side of the equation:

$$2y - 4 = 21$$
$$\underline{\quad +4 \quad +4}$$
$$2y + 0 = 25$$

Next, divide each side of the equation by 2 to isolate y:

$$\frac{2y}{2} = \frac{25}{2}$$
$$y = 12.5$$

24. 96. Given $\frac{3}{4}x = 72$, in order to get x alone, we can multiply $\frac{3}{4}$ by its reciprocal, $\frac{4}{3}$, since they will cancel out to just $1x$:

$$(\frac{4}{3})(\frac{3}{4}x) = (\frac{4}{3})72$$
$$1x = \frac{72}{1} \times \frac{4}{3}$$

Conversely, you could choose to divide both sides by $\frac{3}{4}$. Since dividing by a fraction results in multiplying by that fraction's reciprocal, the answer would be the same.

25. $x = 4$. The first step is to move all of the variables onto the same side of the equation by subtracting $7x$ from both sides:

$$7x + 20 = 13x - 4$$
$$\underline{-7x \qquad\quad -7x}$$
$$20 = 6x - 4$$

Next, add 4 to both sides to get $6x$ alone:

$$20 = 6x - 4$$
$$\underline{+4 \qquad\quad +4}$$
$$24 = 6x$$

Lastly, divide both sides by 6 to arrive at the final answer.

$$24 = 6x$$
$$\underline{\div 6 \quad \div 6}$$
$$4 = x$$

26. $x = \frac{v-w}{y}$. When a question asks you to solve for a variable *in terms of* other variables, it simply means to isolate the first variable on one side of the equation. The first step to getting x alone in $xy + w = v$ is to subtract the w:

$$xy + w = v$$
$$\underline{\quad -w \quad -w \quad}$$
$$xy = v - w$$

Then, divide both sides by y:

$$xy = v - w$$
$$\frac{xy}{y} = \frac{v-w}{y}$$
$$x = \frac{v-w}{y}$$

27. $w = 43$. The first step in this problem is to distribute the $\frac{2}{3}$:

$$\frac{2}{3}(w - 4) = 26$$
$$\frac{2}{3}w - \frac{2}{3}(4) = 26$$
$$\frac{2}{3}w - \frac{8}{3} = 26$$

Now, add $\frac{8}{3}$ to both sides of the equation:

$$\frac{2}{3}w - \frac{8}{3} = 26$$
$$\underline{\quad + \frac{8}{3} \quad + \frac{8}{3} \quad}$$
$$\frac{2}{3}w = \frac{78}{3} + \frac{8}{3}$$
$$\frac{2}{3}w = \frac{86}{3}$$

Next, divide both sides by $\frac{2}{3}$:

$$\frac{2}{3}w = \frac{86}{3}$$
$$\div \frac{2}{3} \quad \div \frac{2}{3}$$
$$w = \frac{86}{3} \times \frac{3}{2}$$
$$w = 43.$$

28. 11. Let the number $= n$. Twice the sum of this number and 10 is represented as $2(n + 10)$. Set this equal to 42 and solve it by distributing the 2 and then using opposite operations to solve for n.

$$2(n + 10) = 42$$
$$2n + 20 = 42$$
$$\underline{\quad -20 \quad -20 \quad}$$
$$2n = 22$$
$$n = 11$$

29. **$\$525 + 0.08d$.** First, write the relationship out in words. The employee's commission will be 8% *of* her sales, so multiply 8% by the sales:

Total paycheck = [Base Rate] +
                 [8%][Weekly Sales]

Next sub in the given information, remembering to convert the percentage into a decimal. The base rate is $525, the commission is 8%, and the weekly sales is d:

Total paycheck = $\$525 + 0.08d$

Algebra Part I Review

1. **$2y - 7$ and $(7 + y)2$.** *Less than* means subtraction in the reverse order from that stated and *twice a number y* means $2y$, so the first expression, *7 less than twice a number y* is represented by $2y - 7$. In the second expression, the phrase *sum of 7 and a number y* indicates that $7 + y$ should be put inside a set of parentheses before being multiplied by 2. Therefore, the expression that represents *twice the sum of 7 and a number y* is represented by the expression $(7 + y)2$. The expression $2(7 + y)$ would also have worked, but this option was not on the list.

2. **never and always.** Think about the rules for how negative numbers are influenced by exponents and parentheses. For statement A, $\frac{(-n)^4}{n}$, the numerator will always be positive since the negative n will get canceled out by the negative sign that is within the parentheses. The denominator will always be negative. The quotient of a positive divided by a negative is never positive. For statement B, $\frac{-(n)^4}{n}$, the numerator will always be negative since n^4 will also yield a positive value and then the negative sign on the outside of the parentheses will make the numerator negative. The denominator will always be negative. The quotient of a negative divided by a negative is **always** positive.

3. a. We cannot multiply 4×-3 and then square the answer because exponents come before multiplication in the order of operations. Plus, there are parentheses in the second half of the problem, and PEMDAS indicates we do that first.

$$4(-3)^2 + 3(1 - -3) =$$
$$4(-3)(-3) + 3(1 - -3) =$$
$$4 \times 9 + 3(1 + 3) =$$
$$36 + 3(4) =$$
$$36 + 12 = 48.$$

Choice **b** is not the correct answer because 156 is the final answer received when 4 is multiplied to the -3 and *then* squared, rather than doing the squaring first. Choice **c** is not the correct answer because -12 is the answer when you mistake $(-3)^2$ for -6 instead of 9. Choice **d** is not the correct answer because 30 is the result of mistaking $(1 - -3)$ as -2 instead of as 4.

4. $3x^2 - 19x + 48$. To simplify $5x + 3(x - 4)^2$ we must first think about what $(x - 4)^2$ means:

$$5x + 3(x - 4)^2 = 5x + 3(x - 4)(x - 4)$$

Now use FOIL to expand $(x - 4)(x - 4)$ to be $(x^2 - 8x + 16)$ and plug that into the equation:

$$5x + 3(x^2 - 8x + 16)$$

Now distribute the 3 to all the terms inside the parentheses using multiplication:

$$5x + 3x^2 - 24x + 48$$

Lastly, combine the two x terms.

$$3x^2 - 19x + 48$$

5. c. This problem requires us to use the distributive property for two parts of the expression. First, we need to distribute 7 to each of the factors in the quantity after it: x, $2y$, and -3. This gives us $7x + 14y - 21$. Next, we need to distribute the -3 to each of the terms in the quantity after it: $2x$, $-4y$, and 1. This gives us $-6x + 12y - 3$. Now, we need to combine like terms to simplify the expression: $7x + 14y - 21 - 6x + 12y - 3 = x + 26y - 24$. Choice **a** did not distribute the negative with the 3 in the second half of the problem. Choice **b** reflects incorrectly distributing the coefficients and negatives to the other terms. Choice **d** did not distribute the coefficient to each term.

6. a. Deciding whether to add or subtract is the trick to answering this question.

Sum = first polynomial + second polynomial
Since the sum is already given, do not add. Instead, subtract the polynomial given from the sum to find the other polynomial. Be sure to combine like terms, distribute the subtraction, and be careful with negatives.

$$(8p^2 + 4p + 1) - (8p^2 - 2p + 6)$$
$$= (8p^2 - 8p^2) + (4p - (-2p)) + (1 - 6)$$
$$= 0 + (4p + 2p) + (-5)$$
$$= 6p - 5$$

7. a. $2x(3xy + y) = 2x(3xy) + 2x(y) = 6x^2y + 2xy$.

8. d. This answer is equivalent to the original because each of the terms was divided by 4, and then accurately written as a product of 4 and the quantity $8x^2 + x - 2$. This, in effect, is the un-distribution of a 4 from each term. Choices **a** and **b** incorrectly factor out 32 and $4x$, respectively, which leaves the remaining terms incorrect. Choice **c** looks very similar to choice **d**, but the 4 is not correctly factored out of the term $32x^2$.

9. d. To factor means to divide out the largest factor that all of the terms have in common. First, consider the coefficients: 5 is a factor of both coefficients, so divide the 5 out. Next, consider the variable x: x^3 is a factor of both terms, so divide out the x^3. Finally, consider the variable y: The second term has y raised to only the first power, so y is the largest factor.

After determining the largest factor, rewrite the expression by dividing each term by the factor:

$$5x^3y(2xy^5 - 1)$$

10. b. The party host must buy three balloons for each guest, so $3g$ represents the correct number of balloons for all the guests. The host must also buy 20 more balloons for the hall, so the total number of balloons is the number needed for the guests plus 20 more. This is the equation $b = 3g + 20$.

11. $225. A system of equations is needed to solve this problem. If C = the amount of money the club profits and D = the amount of money donated, the following two equations are true:

$C + D = 550$

$C - 100 = D$

When $C - 100$ is substituted into the first equation for D, the equation reads

$C + C - 100 = 550$.

$2C - 100 = 550$

$2C = 650$

$C = 325$

When this value is substituted for C in the second equation, the equation reads $325 - 100 = 225$.

12. d. Since we know that Aaron needs three times as much cheese as ranch dressing, we know that the 48 ounces of cheese are three times the needed ranch dressing. Either multiply 48 by $\frac{1}{3}$ or divide 48 by 3. They are essentially doing the same thing. The answer is 16 ounces of ranch. Choice **a** multiplies 48 by 3 instead of dividing 48 by 3. Choices **b** and **c** are factors of 48 and demonstrate a lack of understanding of how to calculate the answer to the problem.

13. d. In order to find out how many flyers Johanna and Paolo passed out, we need to subtract x, the amount left over, from the total, 1,000. Once we get that value, we multiply by 15% by changing 15% to a decimal, 0.15. Multiply 0.15 by $(1,000 - x)$ to get the number of new customers they will anticipate. Choices **a** and **b** do not convert the percentage to an equivalent decimal before multiplying. In addition, choice **b** multiplies the total number of flyers by the number left over instead of subtracting it. Choice **c** reflects a lack of understanding of how to calculate the anticipated response rate.

14. 17. Let x equal the number sought. The word *product* tells us to multiply 16 by one-half x, or $(16)(0.5x)$, which we set equal to 136. Therefore, $(16)(0.5x) = 136$, which reduces to $8x = 136$, resulting in $x = 17$.

ALGEBRA PART II: GRAPHS OF LINEAR EQUATIONS AND INEQUALITIES

Now that you have become familiar with using linear equations, you'll learn how to represent them and interpret them in a coordinate plane. This is an important skill because it will help you become familiar with representing information visually as well as understanding some key aspects when interpreting visual relationships. You will also be introduced to inequalities, which allow for a range of answers. Inequalities are valuable because they are used to model many real-world situations that don't have just a single correct value. Answers and explanations for all practice questions are at the end of the chapter.

This chapter covers:

- Understanding slope as a rate of change
- Calculating the slope from graphs, tables, and coordinate pairs
- Writing linear equations in slope-intercept form: $y = mx + b$
- Graphing linear equations
- Working with parallel and perpendicular lines in the coordinate plane
- Solving systems of linear equations
- Writing linear inequalities to represent real-world situations

- Solving linear inequalities
- Graphing linear inequalities on number lines

Writing Linear Equations

Graphs are a useful tool for understanding and comparing relationships between two different variables. When the value of one variable (such as time) determines the value of another variable (such as pay), that information can be represented in a linear equation and displayed on a graph. Here are some examples of the different relationships that can be represented in a graph:

- How *hours worked* determine *money earned*
- How *speed* determines *distance traveled*
- How *minutes of exercise* determine *calories burned*

In this section we will learn how to take information that is presented in a graph or table and represent it with a linear equation.

GED® QUESTION SNEAK PREVIEW!

In order to succeed on the GED® test, you must be able to determine the equation of a line when given a graph:

- *What is the equation that represents the line in the graph below:*

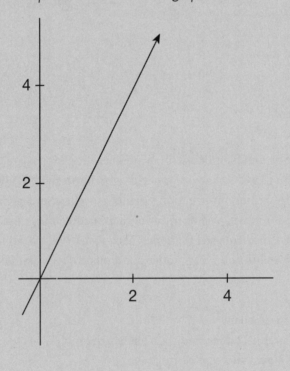

Graphing Points

Let's discuss how to graph (x,y) points on a coordinate plane. Graphs are made up of a horizontal number line called the x-axis and a vertical number line called the y-axis. The point of intersection between the x- and y-axis is called the **origin**. The origin has an x value of 0 and a y value of 0 and is written as the coordinate pair (0,0). There are four different quadrants that make up the coordinate plane. As you can see from the following illustration, any y value below the x-axis is negative. Any x value to the left of the y-axis is also negative.

a runner travels over 4 hours versus the second graph, which illustrates the distance a biker travels over 4 hours. The graph for the biker has a steeper slope because the biker has a greater speed, or rate of change:

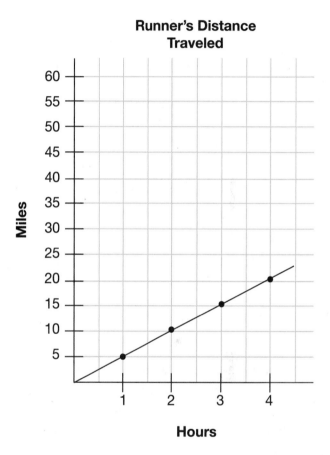

What Is Slope?

The slope of a line is a visual representation of the rate of change between the two different variables, such as speed and distance. The steeper a line is, the greater its rate of change is. A line with a moderate slope is showing a slow rate of change. The following two graphs are showing the different slopes for two different situations. The first graph plots the distance

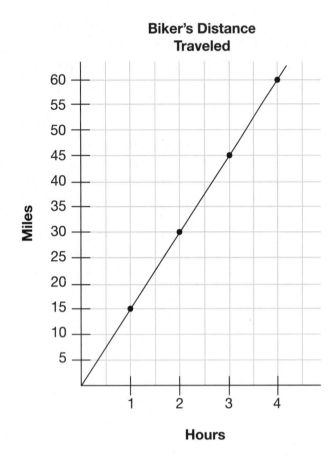

Biker's Distance Traveled

miles. Notice how the mapping between the two different variables is done: Starting at a point on the x-axis, move vertically up to a point on the line; then from that point, move horizontally to the left to a point on the y-axis. Be prepared to extract information from graphs like this on your GED® test.

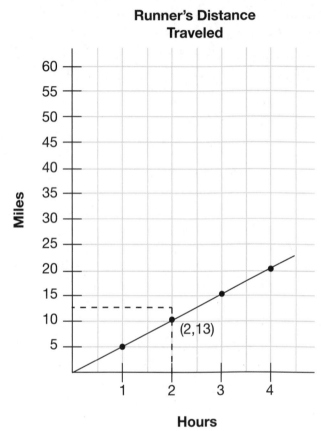

Runner's Distance Traveled

Interpreting Points on Graphs

In the previous graphs, *Hours* are on the x-axis and *Miles* are on the y-axis. It is important to notice that the information on the x-axis *determines* the information on the y-axis. For example, the *number of hours* that someone runs determines the *number of miles she travels*. Each point on a line is a coordinate pair in the form (x,y) and gives information about the relationship between the two variables in the graph. Looking at the runner's graph, let's interpret the coordinate pair (2,10). 2 is the x-value, representing 2 hours, and 10 is the y-value, representing 10 miles. Therefore (2,10) tells us that after 2 hours, the runner has traveled 10 miles. Similarly, the coordinate pair (2,30) on the biker's graph shows us that after 2 hours of biking, the distance traveled is 30

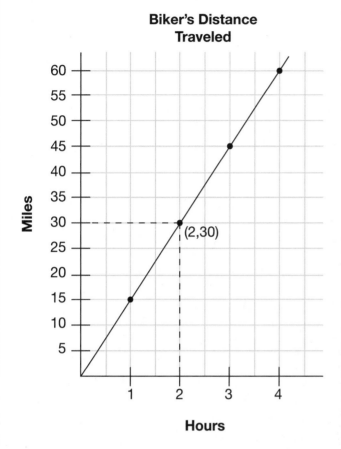

Biker's Distance Traveled

Miles / Hours

(2,30)

Formula: Slope

$$\text{Slope } \frac{\text{change in } y}{\text{change in } x} = \frac{y_2 - y_1}{x_2 - x_1}$$

This formula illustrates that as long as you can determine two different (x,y) coordinate pairs in a relationship, you can calculate the slope, or rate of change, of that relationship.

DON'T DO THIS!

When calculating slope, it is all too common for students to subtract the x-coordinates in the numerator and to put the y-coordinates in the denominator. We guarantee that you will make this easy mistake at least once, but if you know to look out for it and be careful, perhaps you'll make this mistake *just* once! Watch how easy it is to make a mistake when finding the slope between (1,2) and (10,20):

NO! $\frac{10 - 1}{20 - 2}$

YES . . . $\frac{20 - 2}{10 - 1}$

Calculating Slope from a Graph

Now that we know how to use a graph to determine coordinate pairs on the line, let's look at how to use a graph to determine a slope. Since slope is a measure of the rate of change, it is calculated by comparing the change in two y-coordinates to the change in the two corresponding x-coordinates. There is a formula used to find the slope between *any* two ordered pairs. We will write the pairs as (x_1, y_1) and (x_2, y_2). (This subscript notation of the tiny 1's and 2's is just a method for indicating which x-coordinate or y-coordinate is being referred to.) Here's the conventional slope formula:

Example

Find the slope of the following line:

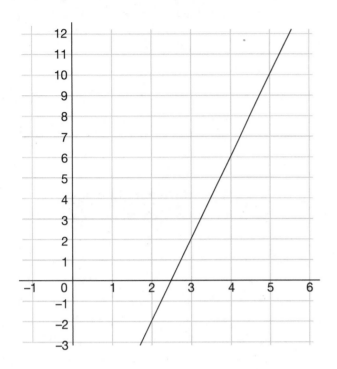

Step 1: The first step is to identify two coordinate pairs that sit on the line. We have identified (3,2) and (5,10).

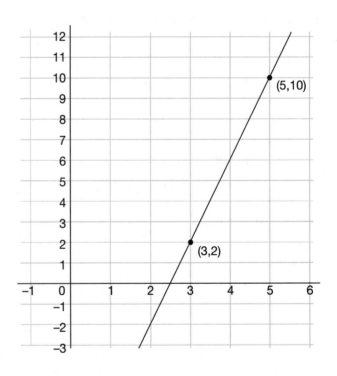

Step 2: Put those two coordinate pairs into the slope formula. Make sure the y-coordinates are subtracted in the numerator and the x-coordinates are subtracted in the denominator:

$$\textbf{Slope} = \frac{\text{change in } y}{\text{change in } x} = \frac{y_2 - y_1}{x_2 - x_1} = \frac{10 - 2}{5 - 3} = \frac{8}{2} = \frac{4}{1} \text{ or } 4$$

Therefore, the slope of the line in the given graph is 4 or $\frac{4}{1}$.

Calculating Slope from a Table

Sometimes you will be asked to compare the rate of change between a relationship shown in a table and another relationship shown in a graph.

Example

Mimi is a baker and on holidays she rents a booth at a local shopping center to sell her delicious treats. Her sales and profits are shown in the following table. Determine the rate of change displayed in the table and explain what the slope represents in real-world terms.

SALES	PROFIT
$1,000	$300
$1,800	$940
$2,500	$1,500

Step 1: Identify two coordinate pairs in the table. We will use (1,000, 300) and (2,500, 1,500) but any two coordinate pairs could be used.

Step 2: Put those two coordinate pairs into the slope formula. Make sure the y-coordinates are subtracted in the numerator and the x-coordinates are subtracted in the denominator:

$$\textbf{Slope} = \frac{\text{change in } y}{\text{change in } x} = \frac{y_2 - y_1}{x_2 - x_1} = \frac{1,500 - 300}{2,500 - 1,000} = \frac{1,200}{1,500} = \frac{4}{5}$$

Step 3: Since the slope is $\frac{4}{5}$, this means that for every $5 increase in sales, Mimi's profit increases $4.

Slope-Intercept Form: $y = mx + b$

The slope-intercept form of a line is $y = mx + b$, where y always has a coefficient of 1. The variable m will be a number that represents the slope of the line. The variable b will be a number representing the y-intercept. The *y-intercept* is the y-value at which the line crosses the y-axis. (The y-intercept is also sometimes referred to as the *starting point* since it represents the value of the relationship when $x = 0$.) The x and y in $y = mx + b$ are always kept as variables since they represent all the different (x, y) coordinate pairs that sit on the line. Here are examples of linear equations and their associated slopes and y-intercepts:

> $y = 3x - 8$: This has a slope of 3 and a
> y-intercept of –8.
> $\frac{1}{2}x + 20 = y$: This has a slope of $\frac{1}{2}$ and a
> y-intercept of 20.
> $y = 14 - 5x$: This has a slope of –5 and a
> y-intercept of 14.
> $5y = -6x + 8$: This is not in $y = mx + b$ form
> since the y is being multiplied by 5. In the next
> section you will learn how to deal with equa-
> tions presented like this.

Notice that in all the equations above, y must be by itself on one side of the equation, and the slope is always the value that is multiplied by x.

Manipulating Equations into $y = mx + b$

You probably noticed in the examples above that sometimes you will get a linear equation that is not in slope-intercept form. When dealing with lines that are *not* in the $y = mx + b$ format, isolate the y using opposite operations to get it into the form $y = mx + b$. This is required to answer a question such as this:

Example

What is the slope of the line $3x + 4y = 12$?

Use opposite operations to get y alone:

$$3x + 4y = 20$$
$$\underline{-3x \qquad -3x}$$
$$\frac{4y}{4} = \frac{-3x + 20}{4}$$
$$y = -\frac{3}{4}x + 5, \text{ so the slope of the line is } -\frac{3}{4}$$

Writing Equations in Slope-Intercept Form

You may be required to write the equation of a line in slope-intercept form when given a table, graph, or two coordinate pairs. You already know how to do the first two steps, so this process just includes two extra steps:

FINDING THE EQUATION OF A LINE

Step 1: Identify two coordinate pairs and write them in (x_1, y_1) and (x_2, y_2) form.

Step 2: Use those two coordinate pairs to calculate the slope, or **m**, using the slope formula:

$$\textbf{Slope} = \textbf{m} = \frac{y_2 - y_1}{x_2 - x_1}$$

Step 3: Starting with $y = mx + b$, substitute the slope you arrived at in Step 2 in for m, and use one of the coordinate pairs to plug in values for x and y. Then you will have an equation where b is the only unknown. Solve for b.

Step 4: Rewrite the equation $y = mx + b$ by using your found values for m and b, but keep x and y as variables.

Example

What is the equation of the line represented as follows?

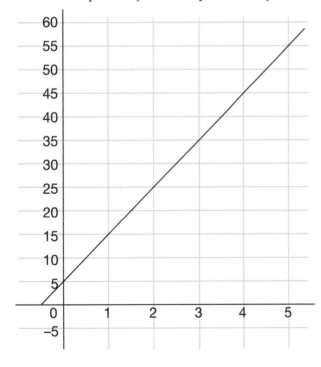

Step 1: First, identify two coordinate pairs that sit on this line. We will use $(3,35)$ and $(5,55)$, which you should be able to verify by looking at the graph:

Step 2: Find the slope:

$$\textbf{Slope} = \textbf{m} = \frac{\text{change in } y}{\text{change in } x} = \frac{y_2 - y_1}{x_2 - x_1} = \frac{55 - 35}{5 - 3} = \frac{20}{2},$$
$$\text{so } m = 10$$

Step 3: Starting with $y = mx + b$, use the coordinate pair $(3,35)$ to sub in $x = 3$, $y = 35$, along with $m = 10$ and then solve for b:

$$y = mx + b$$
$$35 = 10(3) + b$$
$$35 = 30 + b$$
$$\underline{-30 \quad -30}$$
$$5 = b$$

Step 4: Starting with $y = mx + b$, plug in $m = 10$ and $b = 5$ to get $y = 10x + 5$.

Note: When you have a graph, you can often simplify Step 3 by just looking at the graph to see where the line crosses the y-axis.

Finding $y = mx + b$ from Other Formats

Now that you know how to write an equation in slope-intercept form from a graph, it is simple to tackle the other types of questions you may encounter on the GED® test. Take a look at these three cases and how you'd use the steps outlined earlier to answer each question:

Case 1: You are given two points.

Example

What is the equation of the line that connects (8,–2) and (6,10)?

Since you already know two coordinate pairs, start at Step 2 and continue through Step 4.

Case 2: You are given a table.

Example

Write an equation that models the data in this table:

x	y
2	$24
4.5	$52
8	$96

Use that table to select any two coordinate pairs and then start at Step 1.

Case 3: You are given the slope and one point.

Example

What will the equation be of a line that has a slope of $\frac{2}{3}$ and goes through the point (12,5)?

Since you already know m and a coordinate pair, you get to skip Steps 1 and 2 and start at Step 3!

Parallel and Perpendicular Lines

Sometimes the GED® test will not give you either of the 3 previous cases, but instead will give you information about a line being *parallel* or *perpendicular* to another line. Two lines are **parallel** if they have the *same* slope. For instance, $y = 7x + 5$ and $y = 7x - 34$ are parallel. The slope of each line is 7.

Two lines are **perpendicular** if their slopes are *opposite reciprocals*. For instance, if the slope of a line A is 2, then the slope of its perpendicular line B is $-\frac{1}{2}$.

An infinite number of lines could be parallel and perpendicular to a given line when you look only at the slope as the determining factor. The only thing that changes with each of these lines is the y-intercept—where it crosses the y-axis.

However, what if we wanted to find a *particular* line that is parallel or perpendicular to a given line? As long as we know the slope and a point through which the line passes, we can find a particular parallel or perpendicular line.

Example

Find the equation of the line that is parallel to $3y - 6 = 18x$ and passes through the point (0,–3).

First, we need to get the given line into slope-intercept form: $y = mx + b$:

$$3y - 6 = 18x$$
$$\underline{ +6 \qquad +6}$$
$$3y \quad = 18x + 6$$
$$\frac{3y}{3} \quad = \frac{18x}{3} + 6$$
$$y \quad = 6x + 2$$

Our slope is 6, so the slope of the parallel line is also 6. Since we know an x and a y value for this parallel line, we can substitute these values into the slope-intercept form to find b, the y-intercept.

$$y = mx + b$$
$$-3 = 6(0) + b$$
$$-3 = b$$

So, the equation of the parallel line to $3y - 6 = 18x$ that passes through $(0,-3)$ is:

$$y = mx + b$$
$$y = 6x - 3$$

RULE: PARALLEL AND PERPENDICULAR LINES

When two lines are *parallel*, they have identical slopes.

> Example: $y = 6x + 2$ and $y = 6x - 7$ are parallel

When two lines are *perpendicular*, their slopes are opposite reciprocals. (The slopes are reciprocals of each other with opposite signs.)

> Example: $y = -\frac{3}{4}x + 5$ and $y = \frac{4}{3}x + 9$ are perpendicular.

Graphing Linear Equations

Graphing linear equations is actually much more simple than writing their equations. There are three different cases you may encounter:

Case 1: You are given two distinct points. These might be as coordinate pairs, in a table, in the context of a word problem. In this case, simply plot the two (x,y) coordinate pairs and draw a line through them extending in both directions.

Case 2: You are given the slope and one distinct point. Note that this may be in the context of a word problem where you will be given the rate of change and enough information to make a coordinate pair. In this case, first plot the distinct point on your graph. Then write the slope as a fraction, and set it equal to $\frac{rise}{run}$. Starting at your given point, move *up* ("rise") the number of units in the numerator, and then move *right* ("run") the number of units in the denominator. (Note: if your slope is negative, your first move will be *down* and your second move will still be to the *right*.)

For instance, you are asked to graph the line that has a slope of $\frac{4}{3}$ and passes through the point (2,0). First, plot the point (2,0):

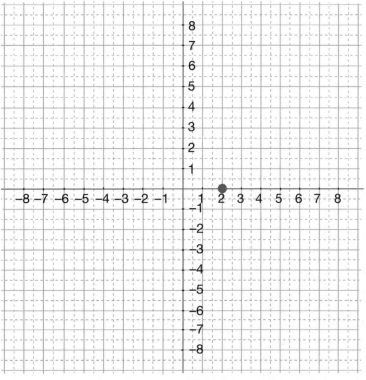

Now that the point is graphed, we need to find another point to draw a line. Since we know the slope is $\frac{4}{3}$, write $\frac{4}{3} = \frac{rise}{run}$. Next, start at the plotted point (2,0) and go up 4 and to the right 3:

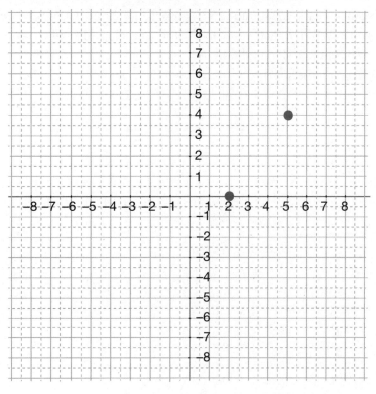

Last, draw a line that goes through both points:

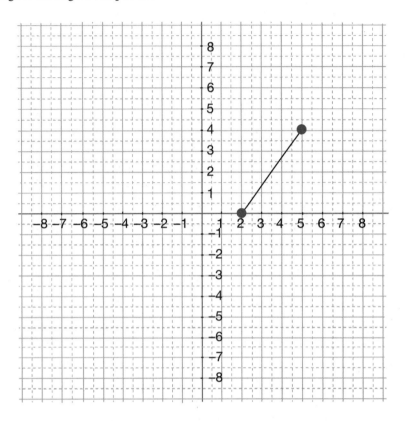

Case 3: You are given the equation of a line. First, use opposite operations to maneuver the equation into $y = mx + b$ form. Once you have done that, you can graph it by using the y-intercept and slope values.

For instance, to graph the line $y = 2x - 1$, first plot the y-intercept:

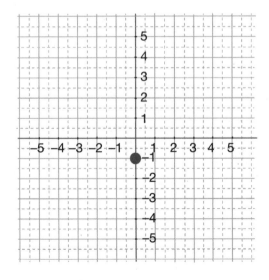

Since we know the slope is 2, we can follow the same procedure as in the previous example to graph the line: start at $(0,-1)$ and go up 2 and over 1:

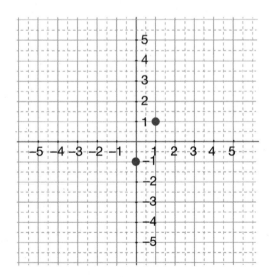

Last, draw a line that goes through both points:

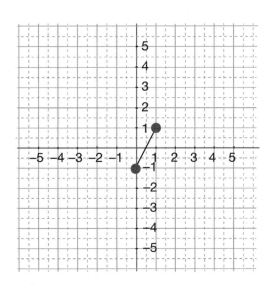

6. The figure represents the cumulative number of packages loaded onto trucks over the course of 8 hours at a small warehouse. When the day began, there were already 50 packages loaded. Based on this graph, how many packages were loaded each hour?

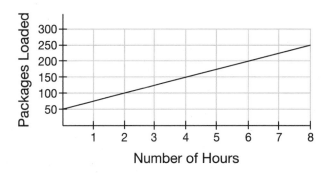

Practice

1. What is the slope of a line that goes through (8,−3) and (−2,2)?

2. What is the equation of a line that has a y-intercept of 4 and a slope of $\frac{2}{3}$?

3. The slope of line v is $\frac{2}{5}$. If line v goes through points (−4,7) and (6,x), find the value of x.

4. Write an equation that represents a line that crosses the y-axis at 8 and contains the point (2,4).

5.

x	0	2	4	6
y	1	4	7	10

The table above shows four points in the x-y coordinate plane that lie on the graph of a line $y = mx + b$. Based on this information, what is the value m?

7. What is the slope of the line represented by the equation $10x - 4y = 2$?

8. Find the equation of the line that passes through (9,−5) and has a slope of 0.5.

_____

9. Find the equation of the line that is perpendicular to $y = \frac{1}{4}x + 6$ that passes through the point (−2,8). _____

10. Determine the slope of this line:

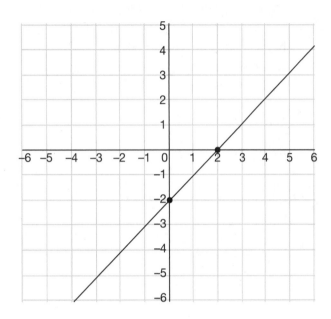

11. Make a graph for the equation $8x + 10y = 40$.

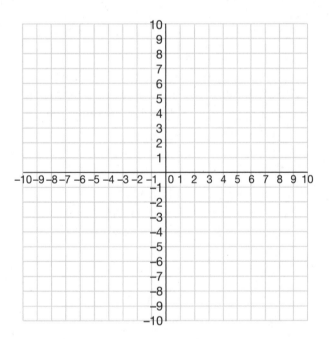

Systems of Linear Equations

Now that you are familiar with linear equations we are going to learn about systems of equations. A *system of equations* is when two linear equations are considered at the same time. In order to find the *solution* to the system of equations, we are looking for the coordinate pair (x,y) that works in both equations at the same time.

For example, look to see how the point $(4,8)$ will work in both of these equations:

$$y = 2x$$

$(4,8)$ works in this equation since when we plug in $x = 4$ and $y = 8$ we get the true statement $8 = 2(4)$.

$$12 = x + y$$

$(4,8)$ also works in this equation since when we plug in $x = 4$ and $y = 8$ we get the true statement $12 = 4 + 8$.

We could therefore say that *(4,8) is the solution to the system of equations $y = 2x$ and $12 = x + y$.*

GED® QUESTION SNEAK PREVIEW!

There are three different methods used to solve systems of equations. In this section we will illustrate how each method can be used to solve this problem:

- *What is the solution to the following system of equations:*

    $y = 2x - 4$

    $4y = 6x + 2$

Before we move on to the three methods for solving systems of equations, it must be understood that in order for a coordinate pair to be a *solution* to a linear equation, it must create a true statement when subbed into the equation. For example, (1,3) is a solution to the equation $4 = x + y$, since $4 = 3 + 1$. However, (1,3) is *not* a solution to $10 = x + y$, since $10 \neq 1 + 3$. So whenever you are asked if a coordinate pair is a *solution* to a system of equations, you can check by plugging each of the coordinates into the equations to see if they make both equations into true statements.

Method #1: Substitution

In order to find the solution for this system of equations using substitution, we first need to isolate one of the variables in one of the equations in order to substitute an equivalent value in the other equation. Luckily, one of the equations already has isolated y: $y = 2x - 4$. So, the next step is to use $2x - 4$ in place of y in the second equation so we can solve for x:

$$4(2x - 4) = 6x + 2$$

Distribute the 4 to each of the terms in the quantity $2x - 4$:

$$8x - 16 = 6x + 2$$

Next, get all the numbers on one side of the equation and the x quantity on the other. Add 16 to both sides and subtract $6x$ from both sides:

$$
\begin{array}{r}
8x - 16 = 6x + 2 \\
+ 16 + 16 \\
\hline
8x = 6x + 18 \\
-6x -6x \\
\hline
2x = 18
\end{array}
$$

To isolate x, we need to divide each side of the equation by 2.

$$\frac{2x}{2} = \frac{18}{2}$$
$$x = 9$$

So, if $x = 9$, what is the y-coordinate that corresponds with that x-coordinate? To find y, we substitute 9 for x into one of the original equations.

$$y = 2x - 4$$
$$y = 2(9) - 4$$
$$y = 18 - 4$$
$$y = 14$$

The solution to this system of equations is (9,14). Always write the x-coordinate first.

Method #2: Linear Combination

The method of linear combination is just what it sounds like: We are going to combine the two linear equations.

$$y = 2x - 4$$
$$4y = 6x + 2$$

The goal of combining the two equations is to eliminate one of the variables. We do this by adding the equations together. However, sometimes just adding the equations together as they are written will not cancel either variable out. Can we add y and $4y$ to get zero? No. Can we add $2x$ and $6x$ to get zero? No. So we need to do some manipulation.

Let's focus on eliminating the x's. If we have $6x$ in one equation, then we need $-6x$ in the other equation so that we get a sum of zero when they are added together. Is there a way to make the $2x$ into a $-6x$? Could we multiply by -3? Yes! If we multiply $2x$ by -3, then we *must* multiply the rest of the terms in that equation by -3:

$$(-3)y = -3(2x - 4)$$

Once the -3 is distributed to, or multiplied by, each term, we have

$$-3y = -6x + 12$$

How does this help us? Well, let's put the two equations on top of each other again, this time using the new, manipulated equation:

$$-3y = -6x + 12$$
$$+4y = 6x + 2$$

Notice that when we proceed to add each term together, we add $6x$ and $-6x$, which equals zero. That is what we want! Then, we can solve for y since it will be the only variable:

$$-3y = -6x + 12$$
$$+4y = 6x + 2$$
$$y = 0 + 14$$
$$y = 14$$

Now that we know that $y = 14$, we can solve for x by substituting 14 for y into one of the original equations:

$$y = 2x - 4$$
$$14 = 2x - 4$$

Add 4 to each side to get all the numbers on one side and all the x's on the other.

$$14 = 2x - 4$$
$$\underline{+4 \quad +4}$$
$$18 = 2x$$

Divide each side of the equation by 2 to isolate x.

$$\frac{18}{2} = \frac{2x}{2}$$
$$9 = x$$

The solution to this system of equations is $(9,14)$. Again, we always write the x-coordinate first.

Method #3: Graphing

$$y = 2x - 4$$
$$4y = 6x + 2$$

To solve this system of equations by graphing, we need to graph each of these lines. The point where these two lines intersect is the solution.

How do we plot these lines? First, we need each line to be in **slope-intercept form**. That is, we need each line to mirror the format $y = mx + b$.

The first equation is already in slope-intercept form, so we do not need to change it. However, we need to isolate y in the second equation to get it into slope-intercept form.

$$4y = 6x + 2$$

To get rid of the coefficient of 4, we need to divide each side of the equation by 4.

$$\frac{4y}{4} = \frac{6x+2}{4}$$
$$y = \frac{6}{4}x + \frac{2}{4}$$

Notice that both of the fractions are not in lowest form. We can reduce both of them by taking a factor of 2 out of each equation:

$$y = \frac{3}{2}x + \frac{1}{2}$$

This is now in slope-intercept form and can be graphed. When you graph the two lines, you see that the one solution that works for both is (9,14)—this is the one place where the lines cross.

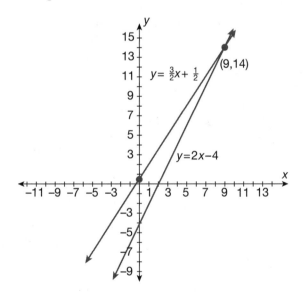

Practice

12. For which of the following systems of equations is (2,–3) a solution? (There may be more than one answer.)
    A. $4x - 3y = 17$ and $x - y = -1$
    B. $-5x - y = 7$ and $y = 7x - 17$
    C. $(y + 5) = \frac{1}{2}(x + 2)$ and $4x - 2y = 14$

13. Solve the following system of equations using substitution:
    $$4x + 2y = 20 \text{ and } x = 2 + y$$

14. Solve the following system of equations using combination:
    $$y = 2x + 6 \text{ and } y = x + 8$$

15. Use the coordinate plane provided to find the solution to the system of equations:
    $$y = 3x - 2$$
    $$-3x + 6y = 18$$

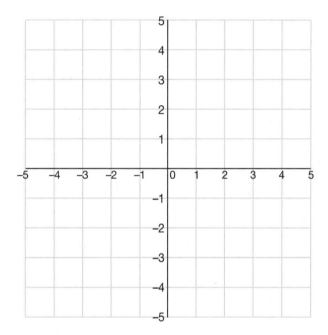

Inequalities

You now know that "14 less than $2y$" is represented as $2y - 14$. But what if the problem said instead, "14 *is* less than $2y$"? That one word "is" changes everything into an inequality. A **mathematical inequality** is what it sounds like—a mathematical statement where the two quantities are *not* equal. Instead, one quantity is greater than (>) or less than (<) the other. The inequality "14 is less than $2y$" is translated into $14 < 2y$, where the open side faces the larger quantity. In this section we will learn how to write, solve, and graph inequalities.

GED® QUESTION SNEAK PREVIEW!

Tes wants her average in Organic Chemistry to be between a 70 and an 80. Her teacher told her that in order to know what her 4th test score needs to be to achieve this, she should solve the following inequality. Find the acceptable range of test scores for Tes's 4th test.

$$70 < \frac{75 + 35 + 80 + 50 + x}{4} < 80$$

Writing Inequalities

Inequality symbols are used to model problems when there is not just one precise answer but instead, a range of answers is acceptable. You should be able to recognize inequalities in the context of word problems by keeping your eyes out for the following phrases. Notice that the verb "is" from the first column can be replaced with any other verb such as *weighs*, *earns*, *costs*, *eats*, etc. when expressing an inequality:

PHRASE	REAL WORLD	INEQUALITY
is at least	Maya is at least 29	$m \geq 29$
is at most	Chris weights at most 180	$c \leq 180$
is greater/more than	Hercules earned more than $20	$h > 20$
is no greater/more than	Hercules earned no more than $50	$h \leq 50$
between	Hercules earned between $20 and $50	$20 < h \leq 50$

Notice in the table above, some of the inequality symbols are underlined. This symbolizes "or equal to." Close attention must be paid to when the number highlight *is* or *is not* included in the inequality. For example, if "Hercules earned more than $20" then he could not have earned $20 so the inequality is not underlined. However if "Hercules earned no more than $50," then it is possible that he could have earned $50 so the inequality symbol is underlined. It is a good idea to re-read inequality descriptions carefully and ask yourself if the end number can or cannot be included, based on the context of the question.

Two-Sided Inequalities

When a situation has an upper limit as well as a lower limit, a 2-sided inequality is used to represent it.

Suppose Izzy wants to buy a wedding gift for a friend that is at least $75 but no more than $150. The first step to represent this is to put the smaller number on the left, the larger number on the right, and the variable representing the gift, *g*, in the middle:

$75 ____ *g* ____ $150

Then the inequality symbols are added to signify whether the outside numbers are included in the solution set or excluded. In this case, Izzy would be comfortable spending $75 or $150, so the "or equal to" symbols are used:

$75 ____ *g* ____ $150

Solving One-Sided Inequalities

To solve most inequalities you will follow the same exact steps used to solve linear equations. Let's work through a problem:

Example
Solve $2x + 4 \leq 0$.

Just like when solving linear equations (i.e., $2x + 4 = 0$), we isolate x on one side of the equation:

$$
\begin{array}{rl}
2x + 4 \leq & 0 \\
\underline{-4 \qquad} & \underline{-4} \\
2x \quad \leq & -4 \\
\frac{2x}{2} \quad \leq & \frac{-4}{2} \\
x \leq & -2
\end{array}
$$

What does this number sentence mean? It means that to keep $2x + 4 \leq 0$ a true statement, we can substitute *any* value of x that is *less than or equal to –2*.

Watch Out—Inequality Curve Ball!

There is one tricky thing to remember about solving inequalities: Whenever dividing or multiplying both sides *by a negative number*, you must **switch the direction of the inequality symbol**. This does not hold true if you add a negative number, or if your answer itself ends up being negative—the direction of the inequality symbol is *only* switched if you divide or multiply by a negative.

Example

Solve $10 - 5x > -40$.

The first step is going to be the same as the previous problem—we are going to subtract 10 from both sides to get the $-5x$ alone:

$$
\begin{array}{rl}
10 - 5x > & -40 \\
\underline{-10 \qquad} & \underline{-10} \\
-5x > & -50
\end{array}
$$

Now, we must divide both sides by –5 in order to get the x alone. Because of this step, when we carry the inequality symbol down, we will have to switch its direction:

$$
\frac{-5x}{-5} > \frac{-50}{-5}
$$
$$
x < 10
$$

This means that for any value of x less than 10, the original inequality, $10 - 5x > -40$ should be true. We can sub in 9 for x to test it:

$$
\begin{array}{l}
10 - 5x > -40; \; x = 9 \\
10 - 5(9) > -40 \\
10 - 45 > -40 \\
-35 > -40
\end{array}
$$

This true statement indicates that our answer, $x < 10$, is correct.

Solving Compound Inequalities

Solving compound inequalities, like $7 < 5x - 3 < 22$, is not as tricky as you might fear. The goal is to isolate the variable in the middle of the inequality symbols. When you perform an operation to the center of the inequality to get x alone, perform that same operation to both the left side and the right side of the compound inequality.

Example

Solve $7 < 5x - 3 < 22$.

Our first step to getting x alone is to add 3 to all three parts of the inequality:

$$
\begin{array}{ccc}
7 < & 5x - 3 & < 22 \\
\underline{+3} & \underline{+3} & \underline{+3} \\
10 < & 5x & < 25
\end{array}
$$

Our next step is to divide all three parts of the inequality:

$$\frac{10}{5} < \frac{5x}{-5} < 25$$

$2 < x < 5$ is your final answer.

Graphing Inequalities

You may be asked to graph the solution to an inequality on a number line. Let's use the example $c > 3$ to illustrate how this is done. Here are the steps for making an inequality number line:

Example

Graph the solution to $c > 3$.

Solution

1. Make a number line that has your solution in the middle and counts three units in both directions.

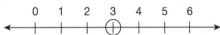

2. Circle your numerical solution on the number line. If the symbol in your solution is ≤ or ≥, **shade in your circle** to show that this number is part of the solution set. If the symbol is < or >, **keep your circle open** like an "o" to show that, NO, this number is *not* part of the solution set:

3. The last step is to shade the number line so that it correctly indicates your solution set. If your solution is "greater than" the variable, you will shade to the right, and if it is "less than," you will shade to the left. Since $c > 3$, we shade to the right:

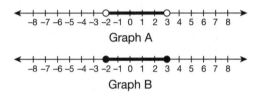

Graphing Compound Inequalities

The only difference with graphing compound inequalities is that your number line will not have an arrow on one side and it will instead show a maximum and a minimum. The compound inequality $-2 < x < 3$ is represented by Graph A below, and Graph B is an illustration of $-2 \leq x \leq 3$.

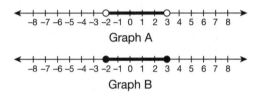

Graph A

Graph B

Practice

16. Write an inequality to represent "When Jennifer wasn't looking, Kai ate at least 7 Oreos."

17. Write an inequality to represent "Mika's boss asked her to pick up a gift for her client that was no more than $100."

18. Charlotte is on the track team and it's meet day. She really wants to run her 400m race faster than her time from last week, which was 70 seconds. However, her coach told her that he didn't want her running it any faster than 65 seconds, since she also has to run the 1-mile race at the end of the track meet. Write an inequality to represent the time that Charlotte is aiming for.

19. What is the solution set of the inequality $-x + 2 > 5$?

20. Solve the compound inequality: $-15 < 3x - 6 < 18$

21. A factory is able to produce at least 16 items, but no more than 20 items, for every hour the factory is open. If the factory is open for 8 hours a day, write an inequality to represent the possible range of numbers of items produced by the factory over a seven-day work period. Then solve the inequality and represent the solution set on a number line.

2. A specimen is removed from an arctic dig and placed in a heating chamber where the temperature is increased steadily over a period of hours. The temperature of the chamber over time is represented on the following graph. What is the temperature in degrees Fahrenheit after 2 hours? _____

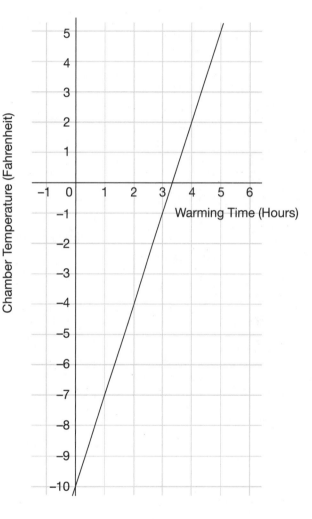

Summary

You now have a solid foundation in graphing and interpreting linear equations and inequalities. The following questions will test your ability to perform a wide array of skills, so make sure you go back and review any topics that you feel a bit uncertain of.

Algebra Part II Review

1. What is the slope of the following line?

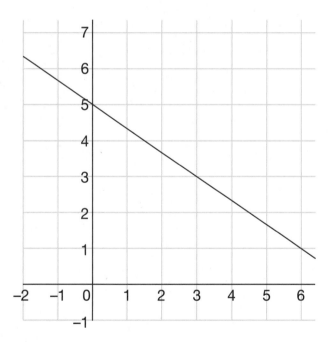

   a. $\frac{2}{3}$

   b. $-\frac{2}{3}$

   c. $-\frac{3}{2}$

   d. 5

3. Identify the rate of change from the following table:

x	−2	1	7
y	−5	0	10

   a. $\frac{5}{3}$

   b. $-\frac{5}{3}$

   c. $-\frac{3}{5}$

   d. $\frac{3}{5}$

4. Which of the following equations has a slope of $\frac{1}{2}$?

   a. $2y = \frac{1}{2}x + 10$

   b. $y = \frac{1}{2} + 10x$

   c. $3x + 6y = 10$

   d. $3x - 6y = 10$

5. What is the equation of the line illustrated in the following graph?

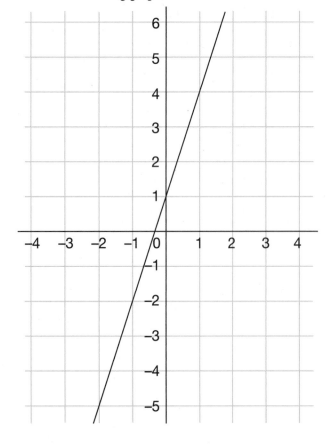

a. $y = 1x + 3$

b. $y = \frac{1}{3}x + 1$

c. $y = 3x - 1$

d. $y = 3x + 1$

6. What line is parallel to the line $y - 2 = 3x$?

   a. $y = 2x - 1$

   b. $y = 3x + 3$

   c. $y = -2x - 6$

   d. $y = \frac{-1}{3}x + 9$

7. What is the slope of a line perpendicular to $y + \frac{3}{4}x = 1$?

   a. $\frac{-4}{3}$

   b. -1

   c. 1

   d. $\frac{4}{3}$

8. What is an equation of the line that passes through $(-4,3)$ and has a slope of $\frac{1}{2}$?

   a. $x - 2y + 10 = 0$

   b. $2x - 4y - 6 = 0$

   c. $-4x - 3y - 7 = 0$

   d. $-4x + 3y + \frac{1}{2} = 0$

9. Which graph represents two relationships that have the same rate of change?

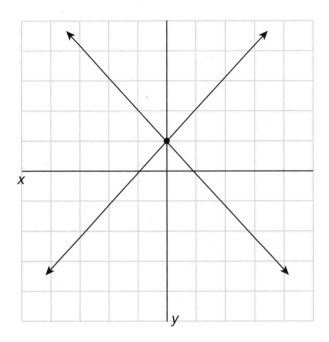

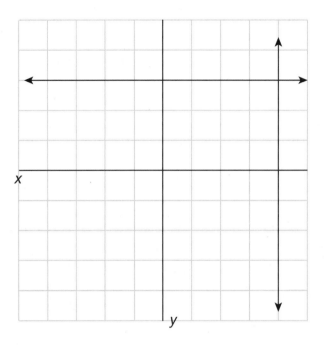

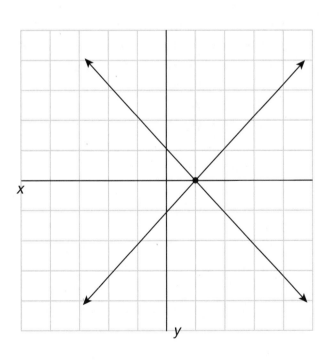

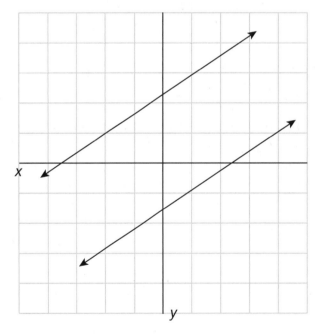

10. What is the solution to the following system of equations? _____

$y = 3x - 5$ and $2y + 2x = 14$

11. Which number line represents the solution set to the inequality $2x < 24 + 8x$?

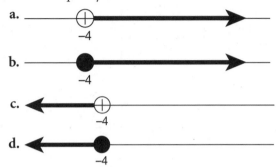

a.
-4

b.
-4

c.
-4

d.
-4

12. Enya makes $1,500 a month after taxes. She has $1,000 of expenses, including rent, utilities, and food. She wants to put at least $325 in savings each month so that she can buy a used car in a year or two. Which inequality accurately represents how much spending money, m, Enya can potentially have each month while still achieving her saving goal?

a. $m \geq \$175$

b. $m \geq \$325$

c. $m \leq \$325$

d. $m \leq \$175$

13. Find the solution set to the compound inequality: $3 < 4x - 9 < 23$

a. $x < 8$

b. $x > 8$ or $x < 3$

c. $3 > x > 8$

d. $3 < x < 8$

Answers and Explanations

Chapter Practice

1. $-\frac{1}{2}$. Use the two coordinate pairs in the slope formula:

$$m = \frac{2 - -3}{-2 - 8} = \frac{5}{-10} = \frac{-1}{2}$$

So the slope is $-\frac{1}{2}$.

2. $y = \frac{2}{3}x + 4$. Since you are given the y-intercept and the slope, plug both of these values into the $y = mx + b$ equation. Putting 4 in for b and $\frac{2}{3}$ in for m gives $y = \frac{2}{3}x + 4$.

3. $x = 11$. Since the slope is given, and 3 out of the 4 coordinates are also provided, plug all of these values into the slope formula and solve for the missing x-coordinate:

$$m = \frac{y_2 - y_1}{x_2 - x_1}$$

$$\frac{2}{5} = \frac{x - 7}{6 - -4}$$

$$\frac{2}{5} = \frac{x - 7}{10}$$

At this point, use cross products to solve for x, making sure you put the quantity $x - 7$ in parentheses so that the 5 gets distributed:

$$5(x - 7) = 2(10)$$

$$5x - 35 = 20$$

$$\underline{\quad +35 \quad +35 \quad}$$

$$5x \quad = 55$$

$$x \quad = \frac{55}{5}$$

$$x \quad = 11$$

4. $y = -2x + 8$. Start with the equation $y = mx + b$. Since the line crosses the y-axis at 8, plug 8 in for b:

$$y = mx + 8$$

Since we're given the point (2, 4), replace the x with 2 and the y with 4. Now there's enough information to solve for m:

$$4 = m(2) + 8$$

$$\underline{-8 \qquad -8}$$

$$-4 = 2m$$

$$-2 = m$$

Lastly, rewrite the equation $y = mx + b$ with the values for m and b: $y = -2x + 8$

5. $m = \frac{3}{2}$. To answer this question you may use any two coordinate pairs in the slope formula. We will use the first two points (0,1) and (2,4):

$m = \frac{y_2 - y_1}{x_2 - x_1} = \frac{4-1}{2-0} = \frac{3}{2}$

6. 25 packages per hour. The slope of the line will represent the number of packages loaded per hour. Use the starting point (0,50) and the end point (8, 250) in the slope formula:

$m = \frac{y_2 - y_1}{x_2 - x_1}$

$m = \frac{250 - 50}{8 - 0} = \frac{200}{8} = 25$ packages per hour

7. $\frac{5}{2}$. To find the slope of the line with this equation, isolate the y-variable and put the equation in the form $y = mx + b$, where m is the slope:

$10x - 4y = 2$

$\underline{-10x \qquad -10x}$

$-4y = -10x + 2$

$\frac{-4y}{-4} = \frac{-10x + 2}{-4}$

$y = \frac{-10}{-4}x + \frac{2}{-4}$

$y = \frac{5}{2}x + \frac{1}{2}$

8. $y = 0.5x - 9.5$. Substitute the known values into the equation $y = mx + b$ and solve for b.

$y \quad = mx + b$

$-5 \ = 0.5(9) + b$

$-5 \ = 4.5 + b$

$\underline{-4.5 \quad -4.5}$

$-9.5 = b$

The equation of this line, then, is $y = 0.5x - 9.5$.

9. $y = -4x$. If the slope of the given line is $\frac{1}{4}$, what is the slope of any line perpendicular to it? The opposite reciprocal: –4. Now that we have identified the slope, let's substitute the given x and y values into the slope-intercept equation to find the y-intercept of this particular line:

$y = mx + b$

$8 = -4(-2) + b$

$8 = 8 + b$

$\underline{-8 \ -8}$

$0 = b$

The equation of the line perpendicular to $y = \frac{1}{4}x + 6$ that passes through (–2,8) is $y = -4x + 0$, or just $y = -4x$.

10. $m = 1$. In order to find the slope, we must identify two coordinate pairs that sit on the line. (0,–2) and (2,0) are the points we will use in the slope formula:

$slope = \frac{y_2 - y_1}{x_2 - x_1} = \frac{0 - (-2)}{2 - 0} = \frac{2}{2} = 1$

So the slope of the line is 1.

11. See the following graph. First we must manipulate $8x + 10y = 40$ so that it is in $y = mx + b$ form:

$8x + 10y = 40$

$\underline{-8x \qquad -8x}$

$\frac{10y}{10} = \frac{-8x + 40}{10}$

$y = \frac{-8}{10}x + \frac{40}{10}$

$y = -\frac{4}{5}x + 4$

Now we can see that the y-intercept is 4 and that the slope, or $\frac{rise}{run}. = -\frac{4}{5}$. Begin by plotting the y-intercept on the y-axis at 4. Then, starting at this point, go *down* –4 and *right* 5 and plot a second point at (5,0). Connect these points to get:

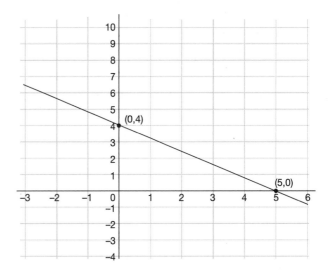

12. A. (2,–3) is a solution for $4x - 3y = 17$, but it does not work in $x - y = -1$, so it is not a solution for this system of equations.

B. (2,–3) is not a solution for $-5x - y = 7$, but it is a solution for $y = 7x - 17$, so it is not a solution for this system of equations.

C. (2,–3) is a solution to both $(y + 5) = \frac{1}{2}(x + 2)$ and $4x - 2y = 14$ so it is a solution to this system of equations.

13. (4,2). The substitution method isolates one variable in one of the equations, and substitutes its equivalent value $(2 + y)$ into the other equation. When this is done, only one variable exists in the new equation and it can be solved for that variable. Notice that in the second equation, x is already isolated, so we can replace the x in the first equation with the $(2 + y)$ value from the second equation:

$\underline{4x} + 2y = 20$ and $x = \underline{2 + y}$,

Replace the x in the first equation with $(2 + y)$ from the second equation:

$4\underline{(2 + y)} + 2y = 20$

Begin to solve $4\underline{(2 + y)} + 2y = 20$ for y by distributing the 4:

$8 + 4y + 2y = 20$

Combine like y terms and move the 8 to the right side to get, $6y = 12$. This ends with $y = 2$. Now that we have a value for y, solve for x by substituting $y = 2$ into one of the original equations:

$x = 2 + y$, and we know that $y = 2$.

So $x = 2 + 2$

And $x = 4$.

Therefore, the coordinate pair (4,2) is the solution to the system of equations.

14. (2,10). The combination method is easiest to use when both equations are in the same form and when either x or y have the opposite coefficient in both equations, like $5x$ and $-5x$.

We are given $y = 2x + 6$ and $y = x + 8$, so we will multiply one of the equations by -1 so that either y will have the opposite coefficients.

$-1(y) = -1(2x + 6)$, so $-y = -2x - 6$. Now we can add both of the equations together, so that the y's will cancel out:

$\begin{array}{r} -y = -2x - 6 \\ \underline{y = x + 8} \\ 0 = -1x + 2 \end{array}$

Since y has canceled out, we can solve for the remaining variable, x:

$\begin{array}{r} 0 = -1x + 2, \\ \underline{-2 -2} \\ -2 = -1x \end{array}$

so $x = 2$.

Now that we have a value for x, plug $x = 2$ back into one of the equations and solve for the y:

$y = x + 8$, and $x = 2$, so $y = 10$.

So (2,10) is the solution to the system of equations.

15. **(2,4).** The equation $y = 3x - 2$ is already in slope-intercept form so it can be easily graphed, but we must alter the second equation so that it is in the form $y = mx + b$:

$$-3x + 6y = 18$$
$$\underline{+3x \qquad +3x}$$
$$\frac{6y}{6} = \frac{3x + 18}{6}$$
$$y = \frac{1}{2}x + 3$$

Now we can graph each equation by plotting the y-intercept and using the slope's $\frac{rise}{run}$ instructions to plot additional points.

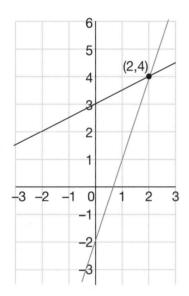

The lines cross at (2,4), which is the solution.

16. **$k \geq 7$.** Since Kai ate at least 7 Oreos, that means he could have eaten 7, 8, or more! The important thing is to realize that 7 is part of the solution set so your inequality symbol must indicate that. Represent this with $k \geq 7$.

17. **$g \leq \$100$.** Since the gift was to be no more than $100, this means it could have been $100 or less. It is important to realize that $100 is part of the solution set so the inequality symbol must indicate that. Represent this as $g \leq \$100$.

18. **$65 \leq c < 70$.** Since Charlotte wants her time to be under 70 seconds, 70 will not be included in her solution. Her coach doesn't want her to go any faster than 65 seconds, but 65 can be included in the solution: $65 \leq c < 70$

19. **$x < -3$.** First, subtract 2 from both sides:

$$2 - x > 5$$
$$\underline{-2 \qquad -2}$$
$$-x > 3$$

Now to get x alone, divide both sides by -1. Since we are dividing by a negative, we must switch the direction of the inequality sign:

$$x < -3$$

20. **$-3 < x < 8$.** The goal is to isolate x in the middle of the two inequalities. Start to get x alone by adding 6 to all three parts of the compound inequality:

$$-15 < 3x - 6 < 18$$
$$\underline{+6 \qquad +6 \quad +6}$$
$$-9 < 3x < 24$$

Now, divide all three sides by 3 to get the x alone:

$$-9 < 3x < 24$$
$$\frac{-9}{3} < \frac{3x}{3} < \frac{24}{3}$$
$$-3 < x < 8$$

21. **$896 < w < 1,120$.** The inequality that would represent the number of items produced in 1 hour would be $16 \leq h \leq 20$, where $h = $ hours. Since the factory is open for 8 hours each day, multiply each term in the compound inequality by 8:

$$(8)16 \leq (8)h \leq (8)20.$$

This simplifies to $128 \leq 8h \leq 160$.

Since 8 hours is equal to a single day, replace $8h$ with d:

$128 \leq d \leq 160$, where $d = $ days.

In order to look at the production over 7 days, multiply each part of the new inequality by 7:

$(7)128 \leq (7)d \leq (7)160$. This translates to $896 \leq w \leq 1,120$, where w is the production per week. The factory will produce anywhere from 896 to 1,120 items in a 7-day week of 8 hours per day.

Algebra Part II Review

1. b. First, select two coordinate pairs that sit on the line. We selected (3,3) and (6,1):

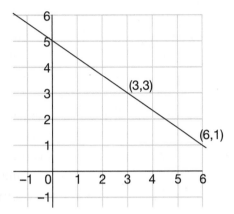

Now put these two coordinates into the slope formula:

Slope $= \dfrac{y_2 - y_1}{x_2 - x_1} = \dfrac{1 - 3}{6 - 3} = \dfrac{-2}{3}$

So the slope of this line is $-\frac{2}{3}$, so **b** is the correct answer. Choice **a** is not correct since this shows a positive slope but the line is clearly sloping downward from left to right. Choice **c** is the incorrect solution to arrive at when the x-values are used in the numerator of the slope formula instead of in the denominator. Choice **d** shows the y-intercept and not the slope and is therefore incorrect.

2. –4 degrees. Looking at the graph, we can see that when $x = 2$ hours, the line has a y-value of –4 degrees:

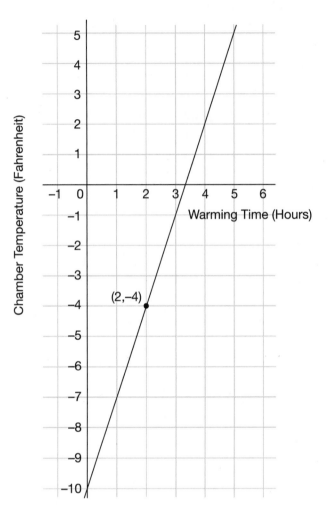

3. a. The rate of change is the slope of the relationship. Use the coordinate pairs $(1,0)$ and $(7,10)$ in the slope formula to calculate the rate of change:

$$\textbf{Slope} = \frac{y_2 - y_1}{x_2 - x_1} = \frac{10 - 0}{7 - 1} = \frac{10}{6} = \frac{5}{3}$$

So the rate of change is $\frac{5}{3}$. Choice **b** is not correct because the slope should be positive. Choice **d** is the incorrect answer found when the x coordinates are put in the numerator of the slope formula and choice **c** is also a result of that type of error.

4. d. When an equation is in the form $y = mx + b$, the coefficient of x, which is m, always represents the slope. Choice **a** is incorrect because the equation is not yet in $y = mx + b$ form since it begins with $2y$. When everything is divided by 2, the coefficient of x will no longer be $\frac{1}{2}$. The slope in choice **b** is 10 because that is the coefficient x. In choices **c** and **d**, manipulate the equations so that y is by itself. Here we isolate y in choice **d**:

$$\begin{aligned} 3x - 6y &= 10 \\ \underline{-3x \qquad\quad -3x} & \\ -6y &= -3x + 10 \\ \frac{-6y}{-6} &= \frac{-3x + 10}{-6} \\ y &= \frac{1}{2}x - \frac{10}{6} \end{aligned}$$

So choice **d** gives a slope of $\frac{1}{2}$. Choice **c** is not correct because that will yield a slope of $-\frac{1}{2}$.

5. d. First, recognize that this line has a y-intercept of 1. That will be the b in $y = mx + b$. Next, you can see that from the point $(0,1)$, you must move 3 spaces *up* and 1 space *over* to reach the point $(1,4)$ on the graph. Since slope is the $\frac{rise}{run}$ of a line we can record this information as slope $= \frac{3}{1}$. So the

slope, or m, in the equation will be 3. The final equation will be $y = 3x + 1$ and **d** is the correct answer. Choice **a** is not the correct answer because here the slope and y-intercept have been written in the wrong places. Choice **b** is incorrect since the slope is not equal to $\frac{1}{3}$, but is instead 3. Choice **c** is not the correct answer because that has a y intercept of -1.

6. b. The slope of the given line is 3, and the slope of the line in option **b** is also 3. Parallel lines have the same slope. Choices **a** and **c** mistakenly use the y-intercept value of 2, and choice **d** has a slope that renders it perpendicular to the given line.

7. d. To accurately identify the slope of a line perpendicular to the given one when the x term is on the other side of the equation, manipulate the equation to put it in $y = mx + b$ form.

$$\begin{aligned} y + \tfrac{3}{4}x &= 1 \\ \underline{-\tfrac{3}{4}x \qquad\quad -\tfrac{3}{4}x} & \\ y &= \tfrac{-3}{4}x + 1 \end{aligned}$$

The slope is $\frac{-3}{4}$, so the perpendicular slope must be the opposite reciprocal—a positive $\frac{4}{3}$. Choices **b** and **c** confuse the y-intercept term for the slope. Choice **a** has the wrong sign because the x term was not moved to the other side of the equation before identifying the slope.

An infinite number of lines could be parallel and perpendicular to a given line when we look only at the slope as the determining factor. The only thing that changes with each of these lines is the y-intercept—where it crosses the y-axis.

8. a. Use the point-slope form of an equation and the information given to answer the question: $y - y_1 = m(x - x_1)$.

Given:

$$x_1 = -4$$
$$y_1 = 3$$
$$m = \frac{1}{2}$$

Equation: $y - y_1 = m(x - x_1)$

Substitute: $y - 3 = \frac{1}{2}[x - (-4)]$

Simplify: $y - 3 = \frac{1}{2}(x + 4)$

Multiply by 2 to clear fractions: $2y - 6 = x + 4$

Add 6 to both sides: $2y = x + 10$

Rearrange terms to look like choices:

$0 = x - 2y + 10$

9. d. Graph **a** shows two relationships that have the same y-intercept, but one rate of change is positive and the other is negative so their rates of change are not equal. Graph **b** shows two relationships that have the same x-intercept, but one rate of change is positive and the other is negative so their rates of change are also not equal. Graph **c** shows two relationships that are perpendicular but their rates of change are not equal. Graph **d** shows two parallel lines and parallel lines always have an equal rate of change so this is the correct answer.

10. (3,4). Since one of the variables is already isolated in this equation, it can be solved most easily through substitution.

$y = \mathbf{3x - 5}$ and $2\mathbf{y} + 2x = 14$.

First, replace the y in the second equation with "$3x - 5$" from the first equation:

$2(\mathbf{3x - 5}) + 2x = 14$.

Next, solve $2(\mathbf{3x - 5}) + 2x = 14$ for x by distributing the 2 and then using the rules of opposite operations to get x alone:

$$6x - 10 + 2x = 14$$
$$\underline{+10 \qquad +10}$$
$$8x = 24$$
$$x = 3$$

Lastly, solve for y by substituting $x = 3$ into one of the original equations:

$y = 3x - 5$, and $x = 3$, so

$y = 3(3) - 5 = 4$.

So (3,4) is the solution to the system of equations.

11. a. Given $2x < 24 + 8x$, isolate x by using opposite operations.

Subtract $8x$ from both sides to move all the x terms to the left:

$-6x < 24$

Divide by -6 to get x alone, and switch the direction of the inequality sign:

$x > -4$

The graph of this inequality must have an open circle at -4 to show that -4 is not part of the solution set and it must be shaded to the right to include values greater than -4, so choice **a** is correct. Number line b shows the inequality $x \geq -4$. The number lines in graphs c and d shows the inequality $x < -4$ and $x \leq -4$. In this case, it was forgotten to switch the direction of the inequality symbol when dividing by a negative.

12. d. This scenario indicates that you want to save *at least* $325 per month. That means that after starting with $1,500 of income, and subtracting $1,000 for your expenses and also subtracting m dollars for your spending money, you want to have at least $325 left over. This can be represented as follows:

> $1,500 – $1,000 – $m \geq$ $325,
> where m = spending money
> Simplifying the left side yields
> $500 – $m \geq$ $325

Now move the m over to the right side and bring the $325 over to the left side for a final inequality of $175 \geq m$, which can also be written as $m \leq$ $175. This means that your monthly spending money must be $175 or less in order to meet your long-term goal of purchasing a car. Answer choice **a** doesn't make sense because if she spends more than $175 per month her savings will go below her $325/month goal. This would be the answer for a student who divided by a –1 to get m alone and then forgot to change the direction of the inequality sign. Answer choices **b** and **c** don't work because here the "saving money" is being used as the "spending money."

13. d. The goal is to isolate x in the middle of the two inequalities. What you do to the middle of the inequality, you must do to the left and right sides as well. The first step is to add 9 to all three parts of the compound inequality. Then divide all three parts by 4 to get x fully alone:

$$3 < 4x - 9 < 23$$
$$\underline{+9 \qquad +9 \quad +9}$$
$$12 < 4x < 32$$
$$\frac{12}{4} < \frac{4x}{4} < \frac{32}{4}$$
$$3 < x < 8$$

x is the set of all numbers greater than 3 and less than 8. Answer choices **b** and **c** all have aspects of the correct solution, but mistakes have been made with the directions of their inequality symbols. Choice **a** only has half of the solution, $x < 8$, but this must be paired with $x > 3$ as well.

C H A P T E R

8 ▶ ALGEBRA PART III: QUADRATICS AND FUNCTIONS

In the previous chapter you learned about linear equations and now you will study quadratic equations. Quadratics are important because they are used to model and solve many real-world problems that linear equations cannot handle. Quadratic equations are used in problems involving finance, gravity, and area. You will also learn about functions, which are special types of relationships that have their own unique notation. Answers and explanations for all practice questions are at the end of the chapter.

This chapter covers:

- The standard form of quadratic equations
- Factoring quadratic equations
- The four methods to solve quadratic equations
- Using the quadratic equation
- Interpreting vertices and intercepts of real-world graphs

- Recognizing functions
- Working with function notation
- Comparing functions

Quadratic Equations

A quadratic equation is an equation that has one variable to the second power, most commonly, x^2. The standard form of a quadratic equation is $y = ax^2 + bx + c$, where a, b, and c are numerical coefficients.

GED® QUESTION SNEAK PREVIEW!

When trying to solve a quadratic equation for the value of its unknown, there are often more steps involved than when solving a linear equation.

- *Find two values of x that satisfy the following equation: $x^2 + 6x = 16$*

If you try to do the above question in your head, you will find that it is extremely difficult. In this section you will learn the techniques for solving quadratics.

Standard Form of Quadratic Equations

Similarly to how all linear equations can be written in the form $y = mx + b$, where m and b are coefficients, quadratic equations can all be written in the form $ax^2 + bx + c = y$, where a, b, and c are coefficients. When there is no y in the equation, it is best to represent quadratics as an equation equal to 0: $ax^2 + bx + c = 0$. For example, the previous equation, $x^2 + 6x = 16$, should be rewritten as $x^2 + 6x - 16 = 0$. It is important to always make sure that the a, the coefficient of the x^2, is positive.

QUADRATIC EQUATION STANDARD FORM

When a quadratic equation contains y, its standard form will be:
$$ax^2 + bx + c = y$$
When a quadratic equation does not contain y, move everything over to one side, keeping a positive and set it equal to 0:
$$ax^2 + bx + c = 0$$

Factoring Quadratic Equations

It is likely that you will be asked to *factor* a quadratic equation on your GED® test. You probably remember from an earlier chapter that polynomials are factored by pulling the greatest common factor outside a set of parentheses. This process was like "undoing" the distributive property.

Recall how the expression $10x^3 + 5xy + 30x$ is factored by dividing everything by the GCF, $5x$:

$$10x^3 + 5xy^2 + 30xz = 5x(2x^2 + y^2 + 6z)$$

Factoring quadratic equations is done very differently because there normally isn't a greatest common factor that divides into all the terms. Instead, when factoring a quadratic $x^2 + bx + c$, the quadratic will be broken down into the product of two binomials, $(x + m)(x + n)$, for two real numbers m and n. When the coefficient of the x^2 term is 1, there are two easy tricks to finding the values of m and n:

1. m and n must multiply to c
2. m and n must add to b

RULE: FACTORING QUADRATIC EQUATIONS WHEN $a = 1$

When $a = 1$, a quadratic in the form $1x^2 + bx + c$ will be factored into the product $(x + m)(x + n)$ for two real numbers m and n. To determine m and n:

1. m and n must multiply to c

2. m and n must add to b

Example
Factor $x^2 + 2x - 15$.

First, set up a product of binomials for the factored form of a quadratic:

$$(x + m)(x + n)$$

Next, make a list of factors that satisfy the first criterion, that m and n must multiply to c. So in this case, $m \times n = -15$:

$$\{1, -15\}, \quad \{-15, 1\}, \quad \{3, -5\}, \quad \{-3, 5\}$$

(Note: these are not coordinate pairs, but just factor pairs that multiply to –15.)

Next, determine which of the pairs also satisfies the second criterion that m and n must add to b. In this case $m + n = 2$. Since –3 and 5 add to 2 we know that our two factors must be $\{-3, 5\}$. The final step is to write them in factored notation: $(x - 3)(x + 5)$.

Working Backward: Checking Factored Form

We can always check our factored form by working backward. If we apply FOIL to a factored answer, we should arrive at the original quadratic. (You can actually use this method to find the correct answer to a factoring question on the GED® test if it is a multiple choice question.) Let's check our factored form of $x^2 + 2x - 15$ by applying FOIL to $(x - 3)(x + 5)$:

Multiply Firsts:
$(\underline{x} - 3)(\underline{x} + 5) = \underline{x^2}$

Multiply Outsides:
$(\underline{x} - 3)(x \underline{+ 5}) = \underline{5x}$

Multiply Insides:
$(x \underline{- 3})(\underline{x} + 5) = x^2 + 5x \underline{- 3x}$

Multiply Lasts:
$(x \underline{- 3})(x \underline{+ 5}) = x^2 + 5x - 3x \underline{- 15}$

Combine the x terms to simplify:

$$x^2 + 5x - 3x - 15 = x^2 + 2x - 15$$

Since FOIL brought us back to our original quadratic, we know that our factored form $(x - 3)(x + 5)$ is correct.

Special Case Factoring

Sometimes you will be asked to factor a quadratic that does not seem to fit into the $x^2 + bx + c$. For example, how would you approach $x^2 - 4$? In this case, it is important to recognize that the b coefficient in this equation is equal to zero: $x^2 - 4$ is the same as $x^2 + 0x - 4$.

Example
Factor $x^2 - 4$.

First, rewrite $x^2 - 4$ as $x^2 + 0x - 4$, so that you can clearly see that $b = 0$.

Then, set up a product of binomials for the factored form of a quadratic:

$$(x + m)(x + n)$$

Next, m and n must multiply to c, which in this case equals -4:

$$\{1, -4\}, \quad \{-4, 1\}, \quad \{-2, 2\}$$

Next, determine which of the pairs above also satisfies the second criterion that m and n must add to b, which in this case is 0. Since -2 and 2 add to 0, our two factors must be $\{-2, 2\}$. The final step is to write them in factored notation: $(x - 2)(x + 2)$.

QUICK FACTORING TIPS

You should now feel confident that many quadratics in the form $1x^2 + bx + c$ can be factored into the form $(x + m)(x + n)$, where $m \times n = c$ and $m + n = b$. The signs of your factors will change when the coefficients b and c are not both positive. Here are the 4 different cases for the signs of your factors. Use these as you work through the practice problems. Your understanding of this will deepen as you get more practice and by test day, you should be comfortable with recognizing these cases:

Case 1: $ax^2 + bx + c \Rightarrow m$ and n will both be positive

Case 2: $ax^2 - bx + c \Rightarrow m$ and n will both be negative (since they must multiply to a positive c and add to a negative b)

Case 3: $ax^2 + bx - c \Rightarrow m$ and n will be different signs and the larger factor will be positive (since they must multiply to a negative c and add to a positive b)

Case 4: $ax^2 - bx - c \Rightarrow m$ and n will be different signs and the larger factor will be negative (since they must multiply to a negative c and add to a negative b)

Solving Quadratics

Aside from factoring quadratic equations, it is critical that you know how to *solve* quadratic equations. Linear equations are solved by isolating the variable through opposite operations. Solving quadratic equations normally requires a much different technique. Next, we will investigate the 4 different ways to solve a quadratic equation:

- Method 1: Square Root Technique
- Method 2: Factoring
- Method 3: Quadratic Formula
- Method 4: Completing the Square

Method 1: Square Root Technique

When you are asked to solve a quadratic that does not have an x-term, the process is quite straightforward. For example, if given $x^2 + 20 = 56$, we can use the square root technique.

Example

Solve $x^2 + 20 = 56$.

To use the square root technique, the first step is to get the x^2 term alone so that we can then take the square root of both sides of the equation:

$$x^2 + 20 = 56$$
$$\underline{-20 \quad -20}$$
$$x^2 = 36$$

Now, we can easily get x by itself by taking the square root of both sides of the equation:

$$\sqrt{x^2} = \sqrt{36}$$

Remember, since $(-6)(-6) = 36$, we have to account for a potential negative value of x. So don't forget the $\pm$ sign when you write your answer:

$$x = \sqrt{36} = \pm 6$$

Therefore, $x = 6$ and $x = -6$ are the two solutions to the equation $x^2 + 20 = 56$.

RULE: TAKING THE SQUARE ROOT

It is important to remember that when taking the square root of a number there will always be two answers: a negative root and a positive root.

$\sqrt{x^2} = \pm x$, since $(x)(x) = x^2$ and $(-x)(-x) = x^2$

Example: $\sqrt{16} = 4$ and -4, since $(4)(4) = 16$ and $(-4)(-4) = 16$

Example: $\sqrt{7} = \pm\sqrt{7}$, since $(\sqrt{7})(\sqrt{7}) = 7$ and $(-\sqrt{7})(-\sqrt{7}) = 7$

Method 2: Factoring

Most of the time you will be asked to solve a quadratic that *does* have an *x*-term. In this case, you will not be able to just isolate *x* and you must instead go through a longer sequence of steps. If asked to solve a quadratic that can be easily factored into $(x + m)(x + n)$, then factoring is the best method to also arrive at a numerical solution. Let's work through the Sneak Preview problem from above to see how to solve a quadratic equation through factoring.

Example

Find two values of x that satisfy *the following equation:*
$x^2 + 6x = 16.$

The first step is to rearrange the original problem so that all the numbers are on one side and the equation is set to 0:

$$x^2 + 6x = 16$$
$$\underline{ -16 \quad -16}$$
$$x^2 + 6x - 16 = 0$$

Now we will factor it by first writing out all the factors that *multiply* to –16:

$$\{-1,16\} \quad \{1,-16\} \quad \{4,-4\} \quad \{2,-8\} \quad \{-2,8\}$$

Next, determine which of those pair of numbers also *add* to 6. We see that –2 and 8 will satisfy that requirement so we can rewrite our equation in factored form:

$$x^2 + 6x - 16 = 0$$
$$(x - 2)(x + 8) = 0$$

Since $(x - 2)(x + 8) = 0$, either the $(x - 2)$ *or* the $(x + 8)$ term must have a value of zero. They don't both need to be equal to zero at the same time. As long as one of them equals zero, their product will equal zero. Therefore, our two solutions can be found by considering the equations:

$$x - 2 = 0, \text{ and}$$
$$x + 8 = 0$$

Our solutions are $x = 2$ and $x = -8$.

We can check these solutions by inputting each of them into the original equation, $x^2 + 6x = 16$.

First investigate what happens when $x = 2$:

$$x^2 + 6x = 16$$
$$2^2 + 6 \times 2 = 16$$

$4 + 12 = 16$, which is a true statement, so this solution must be correct.

Next, test the equation when $x = -8$:

$$x^2 + 6x = 16$$
$$(-8)^2 + 6 \times (-8) = 16$$

$64 + (-48) = 16$, which is also a true statement, so this solution is the correct second solution.

THREE STEPS FOR SOLVING QUADRATICS WITH FACTORING

When $a = 1$ use these three steps to solve for *x* through factoring:

Step 1: Get the equation into the form $x^2 + bx + c = 0$
Step 2: Factor it into $(x + m)(x + n) = 0$, so that $mn = c$ and $m + n = b$
Step 3: Set $(x + m) = 0$ and $(x + n) = 0$ and solve for *m* and *n*.

Method 3: Quadratic Formula

Although factoring is a great method to use when $a = 1$, factoring becomes considerably more difficult when a doesn't equal 1. Therefore, whenever $a \neq 1$, consider using the quadratic formula. Although the quadratic formula looks very confusing, don't panic—this formula will be on your GED® test reference sheet on test day:

$$x = \frac{-b \pm \sqrt{b^2 - 4ac}}{2a}$$

To use the quadratic formula:

Step 1. Identify the values of a, b, and c in your quadratic equation

Step 2. Substitute these values into the quadratic formula

Step 3. Evaluate the expression by following the order of operations in PEMDAS

Example

Find two values of x that satisfy the following equation: $2x^2 + 11x = -12$.

In order to identify the values of a, b, and c in $2x^2 + 11x = -12$, we must first set the equation equal to zero. Add 12 to both sides to do this:

$$2x^2 + 11x = -12$$
$$\underline{ +12 \quad +12}$$
$$2x^2 + 11x + 12 = 0$$

Now we can see that $a = 2$, $b = 11$, and $c = 12$. Put these values into the quadratic formula:

$$x = \frac{-b \pm \sqrt{b^2 - 4ac}}{2a}$$

$$x = \frac{-11 \pm \sqrt{11^2 - 4(2)(12)}}{2(2)}$$

$$x = \frac{-11 \pm \sqrt{121 - 96}}{4}$$

$$x = \frac{-11 \pm \sqrt{25}}{4}$$

$$x = \frac{-11 \pm 5}{4}$$

At this point, we need to perform two separate equations—one for addition in the numerator and another for subtraction in the numerator:

$$x = \frac{-11 + 5}{4} = \frac{-6}{4} = -\frac{3}{2}$$
$$x = \frac{-11 - 5}{4} = \frac{-16}{4} = -4$$

Our two solutions are $x = -\frac{3}{2}$ and $x = -4$. That means that both of these values work in the original equation, $2x^2 + 11x = -12$.

QUADRATIC FORMULA

To use the quadratic formula, put your quadratic equation into the form $ax^2 + bx + c = 0$. Then plug the values of a, b, and c into the formula, paying close attention to their signs, and evaluate it for two solutions.

$$x = \frac{-b \pm \sqrt{b^2 - 4ac}}{2a}$$

Beware, the quadratic formula will *not* always give you two solutions! Why is that? Because the quadratic formula contains the square root $\sqrt{b^2 - 4ac}$. Look at these three different cases you might encounter when using the quadratic formula:

- Case 1: If $b^2 - 4ac$ equals a positive number, you'll have two different solutions.
- Case 2: If $b^2 - 4ac$ equals a negative number, you'll have zero solutions since it is impossible to take the square root of a negative number.
- Case 3: If $b^2 - 4ac$ equals zero, you'll have just one solution since adding and subtracting 0 to your $-b$ term in the numerator will yield the same answer.

Method 4: Completing the Square

We saved this method for last since this might be the least common method required on the GED® test. In fact, you will not have to use this method to *solve* a quadratic for its answer; it is most commonly used to rewrite quadratic equations in a different format. Nonetheless, it *can* be used to solve a quadratic so let's solve $x^2 + 6x - 16 = 0$ by completing the square:

Step 1: Get the x^2 and bx terms on one side of the equation with the constant on the other side: $x^2 + bx - c = 0$ becomes $x^2 + bx = c$

$$x^2 + 6x - 16 = 0$$
$$\underline{ +16 \qquad +16}$$
$$x^2 + 6x = 16$$

Step 2: Then find half of b and square it to get $(\frac{1}{2}b)^2$

In this case, $b = 6$, so $(\frac{1}{2}b)^2 = (\frac{1}{2} \times 6)^2 = 3^2 = 9$

Step 3: Next add your found value of $(\frac{1}{2})^2 =$ to both sides of the equation:

$$x^2 + 6x = 16$$
$$x^2 + 6x \underline{+9} = 16 \underline{+9}$$

Step 4: Now the left side of the equation can be written as $(x + \frac{1}{2}b)^2$:

$$x^2 + 6x + 9 = 25$$
$$(x + 3)^2 = 25$$

Step 5: Now this equation can be solved by taking the square root of both sides. Remember that when you take the square root of the right side, there will be a negative and positive answer:

$$(x + 3)^2 = 25$$
$$\sqrt{(x+3)^2} = \sqrt{25}$$
$$x + 3 = \pm 5$$

Now perform two separate calculations to get your final answers:

$$x + 3 = 5, \text{ so } x = 2$$
$$x + 3 = -5, \text{ so } x = -8$$

The values of $x = 2$ and $x = -8$ will both work in the original equation, $x^2 + 6x = 16$

Real-World Context

There are times when real-world problems cannot be modeled with linear equations and instead we must model them with quadratic equations. Some common situations requiring quadratics are problems involving area, volume, and gravity. For instance, let's consider the problem that Terry the mason has to tackle.

Example

Terry is given instructions to create a tile patio so that the length is twice as long as the width. The budget for the project only pays for 72 square feet of tile, so he's trying to determine the exact dimensions of the tiled area. Write and solve a quadratic to determine the dimensions of the patio.

Let's start by letting the width of the patio equal w and the length of the patio equal twice that, or $2w$. Here's a picture to illustrate:

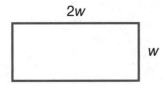

The area of this rectangle is length × width, which is $(2w)(w) = 2w^2$. Set this expression equal to 72 square feet:

$$2w^2 = 72$$

Since this quadratic doesn't have a b term, this is an ideal opportunity to use the square root technique. Get w^2 alone and then take the square root of both sides:

$$2w^2 = 72$$
$$\frac{2w^2}{2} = \frac{72}{2}$$
$$w^2 = 36$$
$$\sqrt{w^2} = \sqrt{36}$$
$$w = \pm 6$$

$w = 6$ and $w = -6$ are solutions to this equation. However, since we are talking about dimensions of a tiled area, it does not make sense to have a negative solution. Therefore, $w = 6$.

If the width is 6, we simply multiply that by 2 to get the length.

Thus, the dimensions of the tile patio are going to be 12 feet by 6 feet and the patio will have an area of 72 square feet.

Practice

1. Factor the following expression: $x^2 + 6x + 5$.

2. Factor $x^2 - 11x + 24$.

3. Factor $x^2 - 81$.

4. Determine whether $(2x + 2)(x - 8)$ is the correct factored form of $2x^2 - 6x - 16$.

5. Solve $x^2 + 40 = 45$. _____

6. Use factoring to find the solution to $x^2 = 24 - 2x$.

7. What is the largest possible value of x if $x^2 - 14x + 35 = -10$?

8. Solve the following equation by using the quadratic formula: $3x^2 - 11x = 20$.

9. Theo has a square garden plot in his front yard with side lengths of x feet. He has asked his parents if he can extend the length by 5 feet and the width by 2 feet. His parents are unsure because if he does this expansion his garden will cover 100 square feet of their yard. Write a quadratic equation that could be used to solve for the current dimensions of Theo's garden plot.

Graphs of Quadratics

Now that you have learned how to factor and solve quadratics, let's take a look at the graphs of quadratics in the coordinate plane.

GED® QUESTION SNEAK PREVIEW!

Although you don't need to know all the specifics of graphing quadratic equations, you do need to be familiar with their shape.

- *Which of the following graphs could represent $y = x^2 + 2x + 4$?*

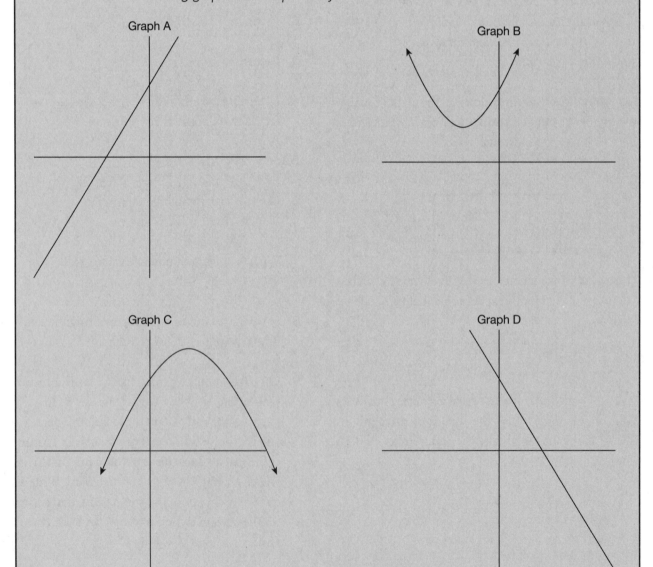

Graph A

Graph B

Graph C

Graph D

Decoding Quadratic Equations

When graphed, quadratic equations make the shape of a parabola, which is a bell-shaped curve. Parabolas can open upward and look like a smile, or downward and look like a frown. Parabolas can be wide or narrow.

Once a quadratic equation is in the standard form, $ax^2 + bx + c = y$, the variables a and c reveal important characteristics about the appearance of the graph:

The coefficient "a" determines the direction and steepness of the parabola:
- When a is positive, the parabola opens upward and looks like a smile.
- When a is negative the parabola opens downward and looks like a frown.

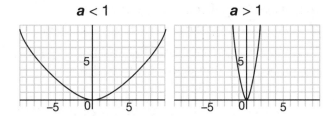

a is positive   *a* is negative

opens upward   *opens downward*

- When a is a larger number ($a > 1$), the walls of the parabola are steep and it makes a narrow bell shape.
- When a has a smaller value ($a < 1$), the walls of the parabola are gradual and it is a wider bell shape.

a < 1   *a* > 1

The constant "c" will always represent the y-intercept of the parabola, or where the parabola crosses the y-axis.

The following is a graph of $y = 3x^2 + 4x + 2$:

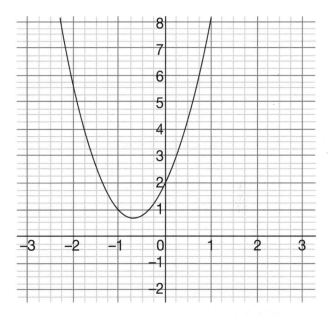

Vertex: The Maximum or Minimum

The vertex of a parabola is the point at which the slope of a parabola changes from negative to positive or vice versa. The vertex in an upward facing parabola is where the parabola has a **minimum**, meaning it is the lowest point in the entire parabola. The following illustration shows a parabola with a vertex at $(-1,1)$, which is the minimum of the parabola:

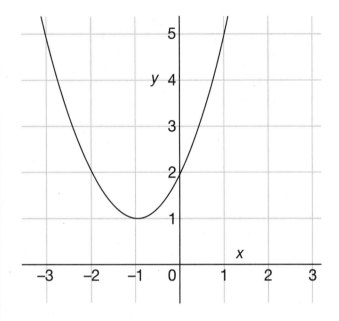

If the parabola is downward facing, its vertex represents the **maximum**, or highest point on the parabola. The following illustration shows a parabola with a vertex at (3,1), which represents the maximum of the parabola:

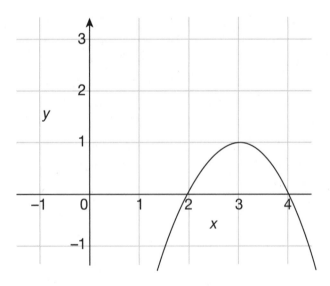

Interpreting Intercepts

Parabolas can be used to represent situations involving force and gravity. For example, if you were standing on a second story deck and you threw a ball upward, but off the deck, the following parabola

could represent the trajectory, or path, of the ball over time:

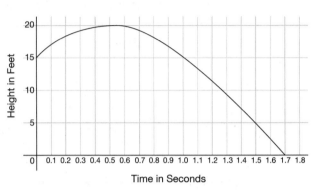

Let's consider the rea-world context of what the intercepts and vertex mean:

- The **y-intercept** is (0,15). Since the *x*-axis is showing Time in Seconds and the *y*-axis is representing Height in Feet, we can interpret the point (0,15) to mean that at 0 seconds (the time the ball was thrown), the ball was 15 feet high. Therefore, we can identify that the deck from which the ball was thrown was 15 feet off the ground.
- Similarly, we get information by observing the **vertex**, which is approximately (0.55,20). This tells us the ball reached a maximum height of 20 feet, 0.55 seconds after it was thrown.
- Lastly, the **x-intercept** can also be decoded. The point (1.7,0) tells us that at 1.7 seconds, the ball was 0 feet off the ground, meaning that it landed on the ground 1.7 seconds after it was thrown.

Interpreting Increasing and Decreasing Intervals

Notice that the vertex represents the highest point of the ball's path. From 0 seconds to 0.55 seconds, the ball was getting higher, and the function was **increasing**. You can recognize an *increasing interval* because the slope of the curve will be going upward from left to right. Around 0.55 seconds the ball stopped moving for a split second, as gravity stopped the ball's upward motion, and then the ball began falling toward the ground. From 0.55 seconds until 1.7 seconds, the function was **decreasing**. You can recognize a *decreasing interval* because the slope of the curve will be going down from left to right. At 0.55 seconds, the ball was still for a moment, so at 0.55 seconds the ball was neither increasing nor decreasing. (We will discuss the specific notation we use with increasing and decreasing intervals in the next chapter.)

Identifying Intercepts from an Equation

Parabolas will always have one *y*-**intercept**, which can be easily found by identifying the c variable in the quadratic equation. (Note that sometimes you won't be able to find c because it will be equal to 0. Two such examples of that are $y = x^2$ and $y = 3x^2 + x$. Both of these parabolas will have a *y*-intercept of 0.

All parabolas are not guaranteed to have *x*-**intercepts**. Depending on where a parabola's vertex is, and if the bell curve opens upward or downward, quadratics can have 0, 1, or 2 *x*-intercepts:

1 *x*-intercept

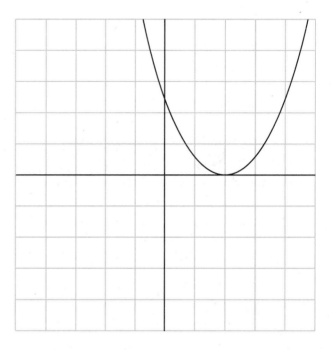

2 *x*-intercepts

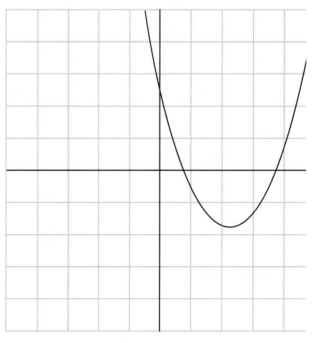

0 *x*-intercepts

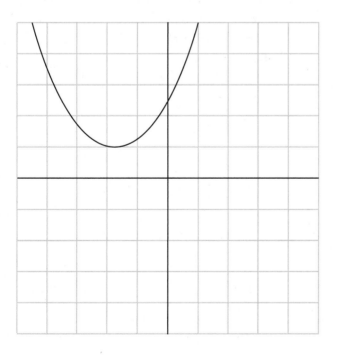

It's important to understand that whenever the parabola hits the *x*-axis, the *y*-coordinate will have a value of 0. This is because the curve does not have any vertical movement off the *x*-axis. Therefore, to solve for the *x*-intercepts when given an equation, set $y = 0$ and solve the quadratic equation by one of the 4 methods discussed.

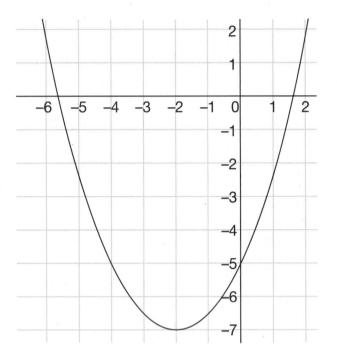

RULE: SOLVING FOR INTERCEPTS

When given a graph, it's easy to identify the *x*-intercept and *y*-intercept by seeing where the curve crosses the line. But if working from a quadratic equation:

- Find the **y-intercept** by identifying the *c* when the equation is in standard form.

- Find the **x-intercept** by setting $y = 0$ and then use one of the 4 methods discussed earlier to solve a quadratic equation.

Practice

10. If the quadratic equation $10x - 5x^2 + 7 = y$ is graphed on the coordinate plane, which direction will the parabola open?

11. What is the *y*-intercept of the quadratic $y + 7 = 10x - 5x^2$?

12. What are the *x*-intercepts of $y = x^2 + 8x + 16$?

13. Identify the vertex of the following quadratic:

14. The following illustration shows the flight path of a beanbag that Amara threw from the top of a slide. Use the graph to answer the following questions:
   a. From what height was the bean bag thrown?
   b. After how many seconds was the bean bag at its peak and how high was it from the ground?
   c. After how many seconds did the beanbag hit the ground?

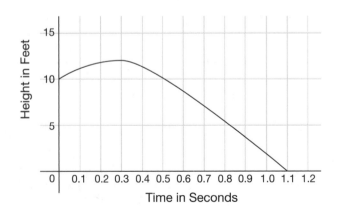

Functions

A function is a mathematic relationship where every *x* input corresponds to a unique *y* output. One example of a function is how *hours worked* correspond with *pay received*. In this section you will come to see that functions are actually used in everyday life more than you realize.

GED® QUESTION SNEAK PREVIEW!

Although functions are commonly used to solve real-world problems, their notation is often initially confusing to students. You will need to understand how to work with function notation on the GED® test:

- If given the function f(x) = 4x + 10, what is the value of f(5)?

Definition of a Function

You are already familiar with a very common type of function: linear equations. In the equation $y = 2x + 3$, the *x* variable is the *input* or the value for which you substitute a number. After you plug a number in for x, the corresponding *y-value* you get after multiplying that number by 2 and adding 3 is the *output*. An equation or relationship is a function if each input value has only one possible output value.

The relationship *Distance* = 50(*time*) is a function that relates the *time* a train has been moving (the input) to the *distance* it has traveled (the output). Any group of variables can be considered a function as long as every *x* input has one, and only one, corresponding *y* output. If the same *x*-value is paired with two different *y*-values, that relation is *not* a function. You may be be asked a question like this:

Example
Name all of the following relations that represent a function:
A. *(1,3), (3,1), (2,3), (4,1)*
B. *(1,3), (3,1), (2,3), (3,1)*
C. *(1,3), (3,1), (2,3), (3,4)*

In order for a relation to *not* be a function, the same *x*-coordinate must correspond to two different *y*-values.

Relation A is a function because there are four different *x*-coordinates.

Relation B is a function because although two of the points have the same *x*-coordinate, those coordinate pairs also have the same *y*-coordinate. This satisfies the rule that every *x* has one, and only one, corresponding *y*-value.

Relation C is not a function since the points (3,1) and (3,4) do not abide by the rule that every *x* has one, and only one, corresponding *y*-value.

VOCABULARY ALERT! FUNCTIONS

An equation or relationship is a **function** if each *input* value has only one possible *output* value. As long as every unique *x* has one and only one *y*, then a relation is a function. If the same *x* values have two different *y*-values associated with it, then the relation is *not* a function.

Working with Function Notation

Functions are written using a notation, $f(x)$. $f(x)$ is read "*f* of *x*," and this notation represents the *y*-value of a function for a given *x-value*. Let's consider $f(x) = 2x + 5$. The notation $f(x) = 2x + 5$ is simply another way to write $y = 2x + 5$. The $f(x)$ is used to show that in this mathematical relationship, the input values for *x* are determining the output values for y. $f(4)$ means *the y-value of a function when x = 4*. So $f(4)$ is asking, "What is the value of *y* when *x* = 4?" In order to calculate the value of $f(4)$, replace all of the *x-values* in an equation with 4 and evaluate the expression as is done below:

Example

Given the function $f(x) = 2x + 5$, *find the value of* $f(4)$.

Start with $f(x) = 2x + 5$, and plug in 4 for the *x*-coordinate. Then evaluate:

$$f(\underline{4}) = 2(\underline{4}) + 5$$
$$f(\underline{4}) = 8 + 5 = 13$$

Sometimes you will need to substitute the value for *x* into more than place. Since all quadratic equations are functions, we'll use a quadratic as our focus of the next example:

Example

Given the function $f(x) = 2x^2 - 5x + 10$, *determine the value of* $f(-3)$.

This equation is asking what the value of the function is when *x* = –3. Therefore, we must substitute –3 in for all the *x*'s in the equation:

$$f(x) = 2x^2 - 5x + 10$$
$$f(-3) = 2(-3)^2 - 5(-3) + 10$$

Now we need to carefully follow the correct order of operations:

$$f(-3) = 2(9) - (-15) + 10$$
$$f(-3) = 18 + 15 + 10$$
$$f(-3) = 43$$

The answer, $f(-3) = 43$, is read "*f* of –3 is 43" and it means that when *x* is –3, the value of the function, or *y*, equals 43. (Notice that the phrase "value of the function" means the *y*-value.)

Comparing Functions

You may be asked to compare the rate of change or the starting points of two functions presented in two different ways. If one function is represented as a table of points and another function is displayed as a graph or an equation, how can you compare their rates of change or *y*-intercepts? Don't let the function notation or language of the questions confuse you—you already have the skills to do this!

Equation: If you're given an equation, put it into $y = mx + b$ form and the rate of change is equal to *m*. The *y*-intercept will be the value of *b*.

Table: If you're given a table, use any two points to calculate the rate of change with the slope formula: $slope = \frac{y_2 - y_1}{x_2 - x_1}$. If one of the points in the table has $x = 0$, its corresponding y-value will be the y-intercept. (You can also solve for b by putting the slope and one of the coordinates in the $y = mx + b$ equation.)

Graph: If you're given a graph, the y-intercept is easy to identify. The slope can be calculated by counting the *rise* over the *run* between any two points or by plugging any two coordinate pairs on the line in the slope formula: $slope = \frac{y_2 - y_1}{x_2 - x_1}$.

Example

Three linear functions are represented below. Order the functions by their rates of change, from smallest to largest.

Function A: $f(x) = 10 - 3x$
Function B:

x	f(x)
4	7
10	10
18	14

Function C:

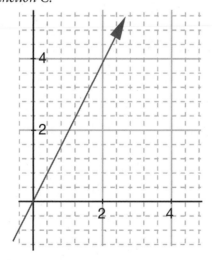

After rewriting Function A as $f(x) = -3x + 10$, we can see that the rate of change of this function is -3.

Using the slope formula for the points $(4,7)$ and $(10,10)$ we calculate that the rate of change for Function B is $\frac{1}{2}$: $slope = \frac{y_2 - y_1}{x_2 - x_1} = \frac{10 - 7}{10 - 4} = \frac{3}{6} = \frac{1}{2}$

We see that the line passes through the origin $(0,0)$ as well as the point $(2,4)$. We can use these two points to determine the slope, or rate of change, by calculating $\frac{y_2 - y_1}{x_2 - x_1}$:

$$\frac{4 - 0}{2 - 0} = \frac{4}{2} = 2$$

The rate of change of this line is 2.

Therefore, the correct order of their slopes is:

Function A, at $m = -3$
Function B, at $m = \frac{1}{2}$
Function C: at $m = 2$

Practice

15. Determine whether tables A, B, and C represent functions:

TABLE A:		TABLE B:		TABLE C:	
m	**n**	**p**	**q**	**t**	**s**
2	5	1	5	5	1
3	10	2	5	5	2
1	1	3	5	5	3
0	2	4	5	5	4
3	10	5	5	5	5

16. If given the function $f(x) = 4x + 10$, what is the value of f(5)?

17. What is the value of $f(-1)$ if $f(x) = 3x^2 - 6x + 8$?

18. For input k, the function f is defined as $f(k) = -2k^2 + 1$. What is the value of $f(-8)$?

19. Given the following equation, fill in the chart for all values of $f(x)$.

$f(x) = 3x^3 - 12$

x	f(x)
1	
3	
5	
7	

20. Evaluate the function $f(x) = 2x^2 + 5x$ when $x = 3v$.

21. Write a function to represent the following situation:

Greg is paid an hourly rate as well as a commission for the number of refrigerators he sells in one day. He gets $13 per hour and works 8-hour days. For every refrigerator he sells, he gets $40. What function represents the amount of money Greg earns on a given day?

_____

Summary

Congratulations—you have just wrapped up your third chapter on Algebra and have accumulated a rich variety of new skills. Now you know how to recognize, factor, solve, write, and interpret quadratic equations. You also understand how to tell if a grouping of coordinates is a function and you can work with function notation. Test your quadratic and function knowledge with these that closely model what you'll see on test day!

Quadratics and Functions Review

Note: Several of these questions are examples of drag and drop questions you might see on your GED® test.

1. Factor $x^2 - 12x + 32$ by dragging and dropping numbers and operations from the list below. (You may use each number or sign more than once.)

$(x \_\_ \_\_\_\_\_)(x \_\_ \_\_\_\_\_)$

+	–	1	2	3	4	5	6	7	8	9	16

2. Factor $w^2 - 36$ by dragging and dropping numbers and operations from the list below. (You may use each number or sign more than once.)

$(w \_\_ \_\_\_\_\_)(w \_\_ \_\_\_\_\_)$

+	–	1	2	3	4	5	6	7	8	9	16

3. Which of the following functions will have a bell-shaped curve when graphed?
a. $y = \frac{1}{x^2}$
b. $x^3 + 2x^2 + 8 = y$
c. $y = 8x - 3$
d. $(x - 8)^2 = 3x + y$

4. What are the solutions to the equation $17 + x^2 = 81$?
a. 9 and 9
b. $\pm\sqrt{98}$
c. 8 and −8
d. 9 and −9

5. What is the smallest solution to $x^2 - 15x = 100$?

6. Find the two solutions to the equation
$x^2 - 5x = -6$.
a. 2, −3
b. 2, 3
c. −2, −3
d. −2, 3

7. Without repeating one of the existing coordinate pairs, select two numbers that would make the following a function:

x	f(x)
6	4
5	3
2	8
1	9

1	2	3	4	5	6

8. What function represents the information in the following table?

x	f(x)
−3	−23
0	4
3	−23
6	−104

a. $f(x) = 3x^2 - 4$
b. $f(x) = -2x^2 - 4$
c. $f(x) = 2x^2 - 4$
d. $f(x) = -3x^2 + 4$

9. The graph shown here represents a function $y = g(x)$. What is the vertex of $g(x)$?

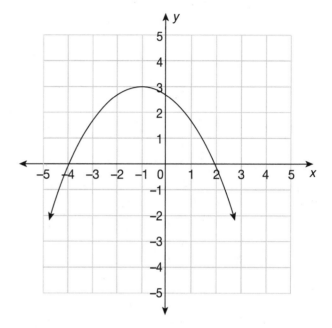

10. Find the two solutions to $2x^2 - 9x - 18 = 0$.

11. Which of the following is an equivalent expression of $2y^2 - yp - p^2$?
a. $(2y + p)(y - p)$
b. $(y + p)(y - p)$
c. $2(y^2 - yp - p^2)$
d. $(2y - p)(y + p)$

12. Where does the function $f(x) = 5x^2 - 25$ intersect the x-axis?
a. $x = 5, x = -5$
b. $y = 5, y = -5$
c. $x = \sqrt{5}, x = -\sqrt{5}$
d. $y = \sqrt{5}, y = -\sqrt{5}$

Answers and Explanations

Chapter Practice

1. **$(x + 5)(x + 1)$.** The factored form of $x^2 + 6x + 5$ will be $(x + m)(x + n)$ where $mn = c$ and $m + n = b$. Identify that $c = 5$ and $b = 6$ in the given quadratic. The only factors of 5 are 5 and 1 and they will multiply to 5 and add to 6, so substitute 5 and 1 into $(x + m)(x + n)$: $(x + 5)(x + 1)$.

2. **$(x - 8)(x - 3)$.** The factored form of $x^2 - 11x + 24$ will be $(x + m)(x + n)$ where $mn = c$ and $m + n = b$. Identify that $c = 24$ and $b = -11$ in the given quadratic. Since the two factors must multiply to a positive 24 and add to a negative 11, we can identify that both factors must be negative. Come up with a list of factor pairs: $\{-1, -24\}$, $\{-2, -12\}$, $\{-3, -8\}$, and $\{-4, -6\}$. The factors -8 and -3 will multiply to 24 and add to -11, so substitute -8 and -3 into $(x + m)(x + n)$: $(x - 8)(x - 3)$.

3. **$(x + 9)(x - 9)$.** The factored form of $x^2 - 81$ will be $(x + m)(x + n)$ where $mn = c$ and $m + n = b$. Identify that $c = -81$ and $b = 0$ in the given quadratic. The factors 9 and -9 will multiply to -81 and add to 0, so substitute 9 and -9 into $(x + m)(x + n)$: $(x + 9)(x - 9)$.

4. **No.** In order to determine whether $(2x + 2)(x - 8)$ is the correct factored form of $2x^2 - 6x - 16$, multiply the binomial by using FOIL:

   Firsts: $(2x)(x) = 2x^2$
   Outsides: $(2x)(-8) = -16x$
   Insides: $(2)(x) = 2x$
   Lasts: $(2)(-8) = -16$

   Now combine all the terms from above and simplify:

   $2x^2 - 16x + 2x - 16 = 2x^2 - 14x - 16$. Since $(2x + 2)(x - 8)$ does not simplify to $2x^2 - 6x - 16$, it must not be the correct factorization of the quadratic.

5. **$x = \pm\sqrt{5}$.** Since the equation $x^2 + 40 = 45$ only has an x^2 and does not have an x term, use the square root method. Isolate the x^2 and take the square root of both sides:

   $x^2 + 40 = 45$
   $x^2 = 5$
   $x^2 = \sqrt{x^2} = \sqrt{5}$
   $x = \sqrt{5}$ and $x = -\sqrt{5}$

6. **$x = 4$ and $x = -6$.** First rearrange $x^2 = 24 - 2x$ so that a is positive, all the terms are on one side of the equation, and it looks like $ax^2 + bx + c = 0$

   $x^2 = 24 - 2x$
   $\underline{-24 \quad -24}$
   $x^2 - 24 = -2x$
   $\underline{+2x \quad +2x}$
   $x^2 + 2x - 24 = 0$

   The factored form of this will be $(x + m)(x + n) = 0$ where $mn = c$ and $m + n = b$. Identify that $c = -24$ and $b = 2$. Since the two factors must multiply to a -24 and add to a positive 2, we can identify that one factor will be negative and another factor must be positive. Create a list of factor pairs where the larger factor is positive (that way they will add to a positive b): $\{-1, 24\}$, $\{-2, 12\}$, $\{-3, 8\}$, and $\{-4, 6\}$. The factors -4 and 6 will multiply to -24 and add to 2, so substitute -4 and 6 into $(x + m)(x + n)$: $(x - 4)(x + 6) = 0$. Now solve for $(x - 4) = 0$ and $(x + 6) = 0$ to arrive at the two solutions of $x = 4$ and $x = -6$.

7. 9. This question requires you to solve $x^2 - 14x + 35 = -10$ and identify the largest solution. First rearrange $x^2 - 14x + 35 = -10$ so that a is positive, all the terms are on one side of the equation, and it looks like $ax^2 + bx + c = 0$.

$$x^2 - 14x + 35 = -10$$
$$\underline{ +10 \quad +10}$$
$$x^2 - 14x + 45 = 0$$

The factored form of this will be $(x + m)(x + n) = 0$ where $mn = c$ and $m + n = b$. Identify that $c = 45$ and $b = -14$. Since the two factors must multiply to a positive 45 and add to a -14, we can identify that both factors must be negative. Create a list of factor pairs that multiply to 45: $\{-1,-45\}$, $\{-3,-15\}$, and $\{-5,-9\}$. The factors -5 and -9 will multiply to 45 and add to -14, so substitute -5 and -9 into $(x + m)(x + n)$: $(x - 5)(x - 9) = 0$. Now solve for $(x - 5) = 0$ and $(x - 9) = 0$ to arrive at the two solutions of $x = 5$ and $x = 9$. Since the question asked for the *largest possible value of x*, the correct answer will be $x = 9$.

8. $x = 5$ **and** $-\frac{4}{3}$. First rearrange $3x^2 - 11x = 20$ so that a is positive, all the terms are on one side of the equation, it looks like $ax^2 + bx + c = 0$:

$$3x^2 - 11x = 20$$
$$\underline{ -20 \quad -20}$$
$$3x^2 - 11x - 20 = 0$$

Now identify that $a = 3$, $b = -11$, and $c = -20$. Plug these values into the quadratic formula:

$$x = \frac{-b \pm \sqrt{b^2 - 4ac}}{2a}$$

$$x = \frac{-(-11) \pm \sqrt{(-11)^2 - 4(3)(-20)}}{2(3)}$$

$$x = \frac{11 \pm \sqrt{121 + 240}}{6}$$

$$x = \frac{11 \pm \sqrt{361}}{6}$$

$$x = \frac{11 \pm 19}{6}$$

Now solve for $x = \frac{11 + 19}{6}$ and $x = \frac{11 - 19}{6}$:

$$x = \frac{11 + 19}{6} = \frac{30}{6} = 5$$
$$x = \frac{11 - 19}{6} = \frac{-8}{6} = -\frac{4}{3}$$

So, the two solutions are $x = 5$ and $x = -\frac{4}{3}$.

9. $100 = x^2 + 7x + 10$. Theo's current garden plot is a square with side lengths of x feet. Since he wants to extend the length by 5 feet and the width by 2 feet, we can write:

new length $= x + 5$

new width $= x + 2$

With these dimensions, the new garden plot would have an area of 100 square feet. Use this information in the area formula to write a quadratic equation:

Area $=$ length $\times$ width

$$100 = (x + 5)(x + 2)$$

Use FOIL to multiply the right side of the equation to get $x^2 + 7x + 10$:

$$100 = x^2 + 7x + 10$$

This equation could be solved to find the current dimensions of Theo's square garden plot with side length x.

10. Parabola will open downward. First, get $10x - 5x^2 + 7 = y$ in standard form, $y = ax^2 + bx + c$, by rearranging the terms: $y = -5x^2 + 10x + 7$. Since a determines the direction that the parabola opens, identify a as -5. This tells us that the parabola will open downward and have steep walls and a narrow bell shape.

11. $y = -7$. To identify the y-intercept of a quadratic from its equation, move it into standard form, $y = ax^2 + bx + c$, and identify c.

$$y + 7 = 10x - 5x^2$$
$$\underline{ -7 \qquad\qquad -7}$$
$$y = -5x^2 + 10x - 7$$

Since $c = -7$, the y-intercept of the quadratic is -7.

12. $x = -4$. To find the x-intercepts of $y = x^2 + 8x + 16$, set $y = 0$ and use one of the 4 techniques to solve quadratic equations. The factored form of $0 = x^2 + 8x + 16$ will be $0 = (x + m)(x + n)$ where $mn = c$ and $m + n = b$. Identify that $c = 16$ and $b = 8$ in the given quadratic. Two factors that will multiply to 16 and add to 8 are 4 and 4, so substitute 4 and 4 into $0 = (x + m)(x + n)$: $(x + 4)(x + 4)$. Solving for $(x + 4) = 0$ gives the answer $x = -4$. There is only 1 unique x-intercept for this quadratic since the solution $(x + 4) = 0$ repeats.

13. $(-2,-7)$. The vertex of a parabola is its minimum or maximum and is the turning point. This parabola has a minimum of $(-2,-7)$.

14. a. 10 feet; b. 0.3 seconds; 12 feet; c. 1.1 seconds. In order to determine the height that the beanbag was thrown from, look at the y-intercept. The y-intercept is at $(0,10)$, which means that at 0 seconds the beanbag was 10 feet off the ground. Therefore it was thrown from 10 feet. The vertex can be used to identify when the beanbag was at its peak and how high it was from the ground. The vertex is approximately $(0.3,12)$, which indicates that after 0.3 seconds, the beanbag reached a maximum height of 12 feet. The x-intercept, $(1.1,0)$, tells us that after 1.1 seconds, the beanbag was 0 feet from the ground, so this was the point at which it hit the ground.

15. A and B yes; C no. Table A represents a function since the only input values that repeat are 3 and both of these input values have the same output value, 10. Table B also represents a function. Even though all of the output values are the same at $q = 5$, every input value is unique and has one-and-only-one output value. Table C is not a function because there are repeated input values that all have different output values, so this violates the function definition that every input must have one and only one output.

16. $f(5) = 30$. Given the function $f(x) = 4x + 10$, $f(5)$ means the y-value of the function when $x = 5$. Therefore, plug 5 into the equation for the x variable and evaluate:

$$f(x) = 4x + 10$$
$$f(5) = 4(5) + 10$$
$$f(5) = 30, \text{ so } f(5) = 30$$

17. $f(-1) = 17$. In order to find the value of $f(-1)$ if $f(x) = 3x^2 - 6x + 8$, replace all of the x values with -1 and evaluate the expression:

$$f(x) = 3x^2 - 6x + 8$$
$$f(-1) = 3(-1)^2 - 6(-1) + 8$$
$$f(-1) = 3(1) - (-6) + 8$$
$$f(-1) = 3 + 6 + 8$$
$$f(-1) = 17$$

18. $f(-8) = -127$. In order to find the value of $f(-8)$ if $f(k) = -2k^2 + 1$, replace k with -8 and evaluate:

$$f(k) = -2k^2 + 1$$
$$f(-8) = -2(-8)^2 + 1$$
$$f(-8) = -2(-8)(-8) + 1$$
$$f(-8) = -2(64) + 1$$
$$f(-8) = -127$$

19.

x	f(x)
1	–9
3	69
5	363
7	1,017

To find the output values, we need to substitute our inputs into the function $f(x)$.

$$f(x) = 3x^3 - 12$$
$$f(1) = 3(1)^3 - 12$$
$$= 3 - 12$$
$$= -9$$
$$f(3) = 3(3)^3 - 12$$
$$= 3(27) - 12$$
$$= 81 - 12$$
$$= 69$$
$$f(5) = 3(5)^3 - 12$$
$$= 3(125) - 12$$
$$= 375 - 12$$
$$= 363$$
$$f(7) = 3(7)x^3 - 12$$
$$= 3(343) - 12$$
$$= 1,029 - 12$$
$$= 1,017$$

Notice that $f(x)$ is the y-coordinate. These points could be plotted on a graph to see this portion of the function.

20. $18v^2 + 15v$ **or** $3v(6v + 5)$. Notice that this question is not simply asking you to evaluate the function for a *numerical* value of x, but instead you will substitute in the algebraic term, $3v$, for both x's in the function and then simplify the function by performing the required operations:

$$f(x) = 2x^2 + 5x$$
$$f(3v) = 2(3v)^2 + 5(3v)$$
$$f(3v) = 2(3v)(3v) + 5(3v)$$
$$f(3v) = 2(9v^2) + 15v$$
$$f(3v) = 18v^2 + 15v$$
$$f(3v) = 3v(6v + 5)$$

21. $M = 104 + 40n$ **(variables will vary).** Let's use M for the total amount of money Greg earns on a given day. We know for sure that he gets paid $13 per hour and that he works 8 hours per day. So far,

$$M = (13)(8)$$

In addition, though, Greg gets a $40 commission for every refrigerator he sells. Let's let n stand for the number of refrigerators Greg sells. This probably changes from day to day. When we put this into the equation, we multiply it by $40, since Greg gets $40 for each refrigerator he sells.

$$M = (13)(8) + 40n$$

Simplified, the function is

$$M = 104 + 40n$$

This is a function because the value M will change depending on the value, n, that is substituted into the equation. Each input n will yield a different output, M.

Quadratics and Functions Review

1. $(x-8)(x-4)$. The factored form of $x^2 - 12x + 32$ will be $(x + m)(x + n)$ where $mn = c$ and $m + n = b$. Identify that $c = 32$ and $b = -12$ in the given quadratic. Since the two factors must multiply to a positive 32 and add to a negative 12, we can identify that both factors must be negative. Come up with a list of factor pairs: $\{-1,-21\}$, $\{-2,-16\}$, and $\{-4,-8\}$. The factors -8 and -4 will multiply to 32 and add to -12, so substitute -8 and -4 into $(x + m)(x + n)$: $(x - 8)(x - 4)$.

2. $(w-6)(w+6)$. The factored form of $w^2 - 36$ will be $(w + m)(w + n)$ where $mn = c$ and $m + n = b$. Since there is no w term, this means that b must equal 0: $w^2 + 0w - 36$. However, $c = -36$. The two factors that multiply to -36 and add to 0 are -6 and 6, so substitute -6 and 6 into $(w + m)(w + n)$: $(w - 6)(w + 6)$.

3. **d.** Since quadratics have bell-shaped curves, identify which of the following equations is a quadratic. The equation in choice **a** has an x^2 term in it; however, it is in the bottom of a fraction, so this is not a quadratic. The equation in choice **b** has a leading term of x^3 so this is not a quadratic and is instead a cubic. The equation in choice **c** is in $y = mx + b$ form, so it is therefore a linear equation and will not have a bell-shaped curve when graphed. The equation in choice **d** will have an x^2 term in it on the left-hand side, after $(x - 8)^2$ is expanded through FOIL multiplication. This equation is a quadratic that will have a bell-shaped curve.

4. **c.** Since there are no x terms in the equation $17 + x^2 = 81$, this is a great opportunity to use the square root technique. Get x^2 alone and then take the square root of both sides:

$$17 + x^2 = 81$$
$$\underline{-17 \qquad -17}$$
$$x^2 = 64$$

Take the square root of both sides:

$$x^2 = 64$$
$$\sqrt{x^2} = \sqrt{64}$$

so $x = 8$ and -8. Incorrect answer choices **a** and **d** were gotten by taking the square root of 81 instead of solving the equation for x. Incorrect answer choice **b** would be the answer arrived at if 81 and 17 were added instead of subtracted.

5. $x = -5$. This question requires you to solve $x^2 - 15x = 100$ and identify the larger solution. First rearrange $x^2 - 15x = 100$ so that a is positive and all the terms are on one side of the equation:

$$x^2 - 15x = 100$$
$$\underline{-100 \quad -100}$$
$$x^2 - 15x - 100 = 0$$

The factored form of this will be $(x + m)(x + n) = 0$, where $mn = c$ and $m + n = b$. Identify that $c = -100$ and $b = -15$. Since the two factors must multiply to a negative and add to a negative, we can identify that one factor must be negative and the other must be positive. Create a list of factor pairs that multiply to -100 with the larger factor being negative (that way they will add to a negative b): $\{1,-100\}$, $\{2,-50\}$, $\{3,-25\}$, $\{5,-20\}$, and $\{10,-10\}$. The factors 5 and -20 will multiply to -100 and add to -15, so substitute 5 and -20 into $(x + m)(x + n)$: $(x + 5)(x - 20) = 0$. Now solve for $(x + 5) = 0$ and $(x - 20) = 0$ to arrive at the two solutions of $x = -5$ and $x = 20$. Since the question asked for the *smallest solution*, the correct answer will be $x = -5$.

6. b. This is a quadratic equation and can be solved in several ways: factoring, completing the square, or using the quadratic formula. However, looking at the terms $-5x$ and -6, it is apparent that factors of 6 can add to 5, so we will factor this quadratic to get the solutions. First, we set the equation equal to 0: $x^2 - 5x + 6 = 0$. We want to find the two values of x where the equation is equal to 0. By factoring, we get $(x - 2)(x - 3)$. Multiply it out if necessary to check that it in fact yields the original equation. Anything multiplied by 0 is 0, so for what values of x would we get an answer of 0? When $x = 2$ and when $x = 3$. Choices **a**, **c**, and **d** have incorrectly placed positive and negative signs.

7. Since you are not permitted to repeat one of the existing coordinate pairs, you cannot use 6, 5, 2, or 1 as x-values since those are the existing x-values in unique pairings. Only the coordinates 3 or 4 could be chosen for the x value and then any of other terms could work for the corresponding y-values.

8. d. By plugging the values from the table into each of the equations, it is clear that $-3x^2 + 4$ is the only equation that satisfies the relationships between the inputs and outputs. Without even substituting all of the inputs to check the outputs, the input 0 makes it obvious that **d** is the only function that satisfies the relationship.

9. **(1,3).** The vertex of a parabola is its minimum or maximum point. $g(x)$ has a maximum at $(-1,3)$.

10. $x = 6$ **and** $x = -\frac{3}{2}$. Since $a \neq 1$ in $2x^2 - 9x - 18 = 0$, we will solve this using the quadratic formula. First, identify that $a = 2$, $b = -9$, and $c = -18$. Plug these values into the quadratic formula:

$$x = \frac{-b \pm \sqrt{b^2 - 4ac}}{2a}$$

$$x = \frac{-(-9) \pm \sqrt{(-9)^2 - 4(2)(-18)}}{2(2)}$$

$$x = \frac{9 \pm \sqrt{81 + 144}}{4}$$

$$x = \frac{9 \pm \sqrt{225}}{4}$$

$$x = \frac{9 \pm 15}{4}$$

Now solve for $x = \frac{9 + 15}{4}$ and $x = \frac{9 - 15}{4}$:

$$x = \frac{9 + 15}{4} = \frac{24}{4} = 6$$
$$x = \frac{9 - 15}{4} = \frac{-6}{4} = -\frac{3}{2}$$

So, the two solutions are $x = 6$ and $x = -\frac{3}{2}$.

11. a. Looking at the answer options, we can deduce that we need to factor $2y^2 - yp - p^2$. Keeping in mind how to FOIL backwards, we get the two factors $(2y + p)(y - p)$. When these two binomials are multiplied, or FOILed, we get the original expression. Choice **b** does not have the necessary factor of 2 to get $2y^2$. Choice **c** incorrectly factors out a 2 from the first term only. Choice **c** has the addition and subtraction signs incorrectly placed. The way **d** is written, we would get $+yp$ instead of $-yp$ when multiplied out.

12. c. In order to determine where a function hits the x-axis, set $y = 0$ and solve for x:

$$f(x) = 5x^2 - 25$$
$$0 = 5x^2 - 25$$

Since this quadratic doesn't have a b term, solve this equation with the square root technique. To do this, isolate the b^2 and then take the square root of both sides:

$$0 = 5x^2 - 25$$
$$\underline{+25 \qquad +25}$$
$$\frac{25}{5} = \frac{5x^2}{5}$$
$$5 = x^2$$

Now put the x^2 on the left and take the square root of both sides:

$$\sqrt{x^2} = \sqrt{5}$$
$$x = \sqrt{5} \text{ and } x = -\sqrt{5}$$

So **c** is the correct answer. Choice **d** mistakenly sets the x-intercept equal to y, but y must have a value of 0 at the point where the curve hits the x-axis. Choices **a** and **b** came about by somehow dropping a 5 and taking the square root of 25.

9 ▶ INTERPRETING DATA IN GRAPHS AND TABLES

Graphs and tables allow us to present information visually on a wide range of subjects: the rising cost of healthcare, historical fluctuations of the stock market, the number and types of people who live in a community, and much more. Graphic information is everywhere—television commercials, newspaper reports, and web pages, to name just a few sources.

This chapter shows you how to interpret graphs with precise language as well as how to manipulate data to create tables that accurately portray key information. Answers and explanations for all practice questions are at the end of the chapter.

This chapter covers:

- Increasing and decreasing intervals
- Positive and negative intervals
- Relative maximums and minimums
- Graph symmetry
- End behavior of functions
- Bar graphs and histograms

- Pie charts
- Dot plots, box plots, and scatter plots

Key Features of Graphs

Every graph tells a story of the data it is representing. Graphs have many features that can be used to describe what is happening in a real-world situation. Key features can also help identify the equation of the function being represented. In this section we are going to take a closer look at intercepts, increasing and decreasing intervals, positive and negative intervals, relative maximums and minimums, symmetries, and end behavior.

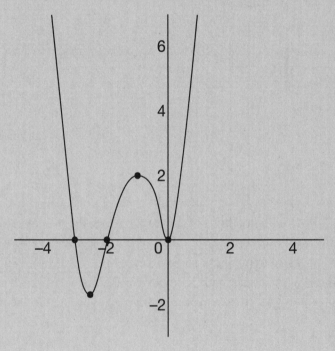

Finding Intercepts on Graphs

There are **x-intercepts** and **y-intercepts**, which are points at which the graph line intersects an axis. As you would imagine, *x*-intercepts intercept, or cross over, the *x*-axis, and *y*-intercepts intercept, or cross over, the *y*-axis.

Look at the following graph of $y = x + 4$.

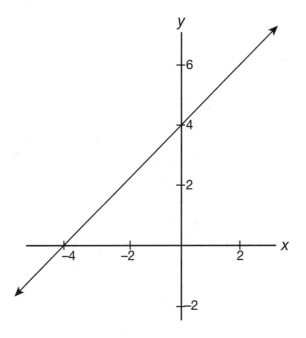

At which point does the line cross the *x*-axis?

$(-4,0)$

The *x*-intercept of this function is –4. What do you notice about the *y*-value? It is 0. If a function crosses the *x*-axis, then at that exact point there is no height—upward or downward movement—of the function. Therefore, the *y*-value must be 0.

At which point does the line cross the *y*-axis?

$(0,4)$

The *y*-intercept is 4. What do you notice about the *x*-value? It is 0. If a function crosses the *y*-axis at that exact point, there is no width—left or right movement—of the function. Therefore, the value of *x* must be 0.

Sometimes functions have more than one *x*-intercept and/or *y*-intercept. Look at the following graph.

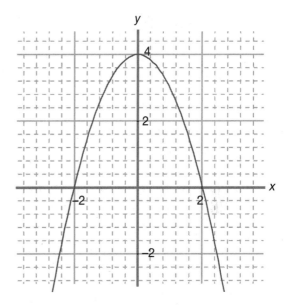

How many *y*-intercepts does this parabola have?

One: When $x = 0$, $y = 4$.

How many *x*-intercepts does this parabola have?

Two: When $y = 0$, $x = 2$ and –2.

Finding Intercepts from Equations

You should now be familiar with these two facts:

- *x*-intercepts will always have a *y*-value of 0
- *y*-intercepts will always have an *x*-value of 0

Therefore, if you are asked to determine the intercepts from an equation instead of a graph, follow these steps:

RULE: CALCULATING INTERCEPTS

When finding the intercepts of a function from an equation:

- Find the x-intercept by setting $y = 0$ and then solve the equation for x.
- Find the y-intercept by setting $x = 0$ and then solve the equation for y.

Example

Find the x-intercepts and y-intercepts of the function $f(x) = x^2 + 10x + 9$.

The notation $f(x)$ is the same as "y." So find the x-intercept by replacing $f(x)$ with 0 and then solve for x:

$$0 = x^2 + 10x + 9$$

Let's use factoring to solve this quadratic. Since 9 and 1 multiply to 9 and add to 10, we can factor this into:

$$0 = (x + 9)(x + 1)$$

Now, set each binomial factor equal to zero and solve for x:

$$x + 9 = 0$$
$$x = -9$$

$$x + 1 = 0$$
$$x = -1$$

So the two x-intercepts are at $x = -1$, and $x = -9$.

Next, solve for the y-intercept by setting $x = 0$ and solving for y:

$$f(x) = (0)^2 + 10(0) + 9$$
$$y = 0 + 0 + 9$$
$$y = 9$$

So the y-intercept occurs at $y = 9$.

Increasing and Decreasing Intervals

A way to think about the concept of increasing and decreasing intervals is to observe whether the graph is rising or falling from left to right. It is important to remember that graphs are read like words, from left to right, and not the other way around! A function is **increasing** during intervals over which the graph rises from left to right. Functions have a **positive slope** during increasing intervals. Conversely, a function is **decreasing** during intervals over which the graph falls from left to right. Functions have a **negative slope** during decreasing intervals. It is important to recognize that the points where the function changes from increasing to decreasing (or vice versa) are points where the function is *neither* increasing *nor* decreasing. In graphs, these non-increasing and non-decreasing points looks like the tops of peaks or the bottoms of valleys.

When discussing intervals, we name the x-values over which a certain behavior exists. For instance, the function graphed next is increasing from before we can even see the graph (from the negative x values) until it reaches a peak when $x = 0$. Since it appears that this graph goes on forever, we use $-\infty$ to represent infinite negative x-values. We say that this function is increasing over the interval $(-\infty, 0)$.

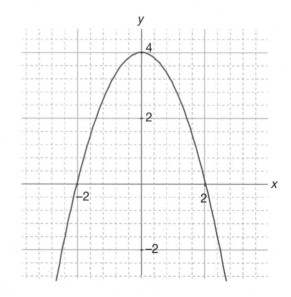

Looking at the previous illustration, we see that this graph has a downward slope from $x = 0$ until what appears to be infinity, so we say that this function is decreasing over the interval $(0, +\infty)$, where it has a negative slope. It is very important to notice that we are using parentheses ( ) instead of brackets [ ]. Since the function is neither increasing nor decreasing at $x = 0$, 0 must *not be* included in either the increasing or decreasing intervals. Parentheses indicate that the value is *not* included in the interval, whereas brackets *do* include the number in the interval. Since ∞ and $-\infty$ are not exact numbers, parentheses are always used with these symbols.

RULE: INTERVAL NOTATION

Intervals represent the *x*-values over which a function is exhibiting a certain behavior (increasing, deceasing, constant). The point at which the behavior changes should *not* be included in the interval and parentheses are used to show when a point is *not* included in an interval.

$(-\infty, 8)$ signifies the interval from which *x* begins at negative infinity up until (but not including) $x = 8$.

$[-2, \infty)$ signifies the interval from which *x* begins at –2 up until (but not including) $x = \infty$. Note that –2 is included in this interval.

Let's look at another function to illustrate increasing and decreasing intervals:

Example
Over which interval(s) is the $f(x)$ increasing?
Over which interval(s) is the $f(x)$ decreasing?

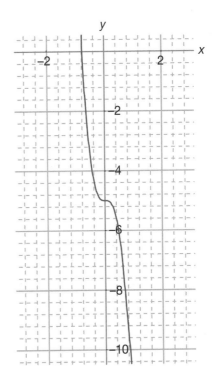

Notice that this function is sloped downward to the right and never curves upward. Therefore, there are no intervals where $f(x)$ is increasing. However, another important feature to notice is where the function crosses the *y*-axis. At this point, $f(x)$ flattens out momentarily and it is neither increasing nor decreasing. With the exception of this point $(0, -5)$, where the graph is neither rising nor falling, the graph is decreasing. In order to exclude $x = 0$ from the decreasing interval, we need to describe the decreasing intervals as a union of the two separate decreasing intervals $(-\infty, 0)$ and $(0, +\infty)$. We write these two decreasing intervals joined with a $\cup$ to illustrate this concept:

The function $f(x)$ decreases $(-\infty, 0) \cup (0, +\infty)$.

Positive and Negative

Functions are considered positive or negative based on the *y* values. That is, we can tell during which interval(s) the function is positive or negative by looking for portions of the graph that are above or below the *x*-axis. Any part of the function above the *x*-axis means the *y* value is **positive**. Any part of the function below the *x*-axis means the *y*-value is **negative**.

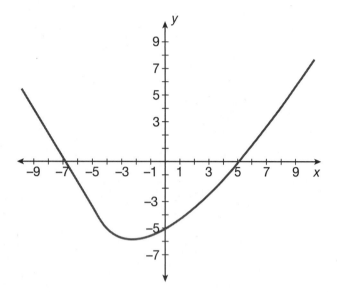

This function is positive on the intervals (∞,–7) ∪ (5,∞) and is *negative* on the interval (–7,5). Notice that parentheses are used here to show that –7 and 5 are *not* included in these intervals. This is because when *x* = –7 and *x* = 5, the value of *y* is 0, so the value of the function is neither positive nor negative at these two points.

Relative Maximums and Minimums

In the previous chapter you learned that the maximum or minimum in a parabola is its peak or valley. Other types of functions can have *relative maximums* and *relative minimums*. The word *relative* refers to the region of the graph where a peak or valley is located. For example, if you were the tallest person in your class, but not the tallest person in the school, we would say that *relative to your class, you are the tallest.*

Relative maximums and relative minimums occur where the slope of the function changes direction; they're easy to recognize since they form a peak or valley. There can be more than one relative maximum and/or relative minimum in a function. The

Sneak Preview question from earlier in this chapter is one illustration of this that we'll come back to later. For now, work through the following example:

Example

Identify the relative maximums and relative minimums in the function f(x):

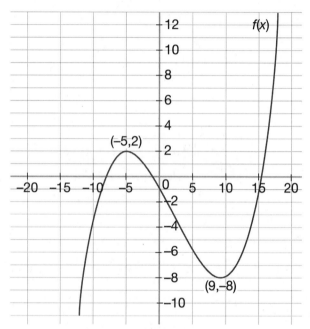

Since the point (–5,2) is relatively higher than all the points immediately surrounding it, (–5,2) is a relative maximum. Notice that it is at a peak in the graph.

Since the point (9,–8) is relatively lower than all the points immediately surrounding it, this point is a relative minimum. Notice that it is at the bottom of a valley in the graph.

Symmetries

Some graphs are **symmetrical** about the *x*-axis or *y*-axis. Creating symmetry is like looking in a mirror. If you were given half of the information of a symmetrical function, you would be able to complete the graph. For instance, look at this graph:

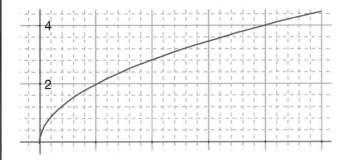

If this function is symmetrical about the *x*-axis, you can mirror the relationship and sketch the rest of the graph.

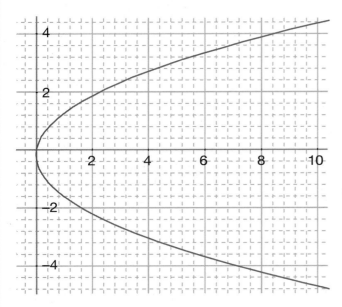

If the same original graph had symmetry about the *y*-axis, it would be mirrored horizontally and look like this:

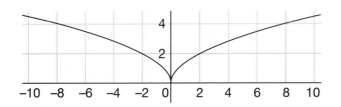

Consider this next graph:

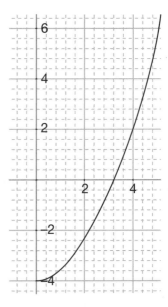

If you were told it is symmetrical about the *y*-axis, how would you complete the graph?

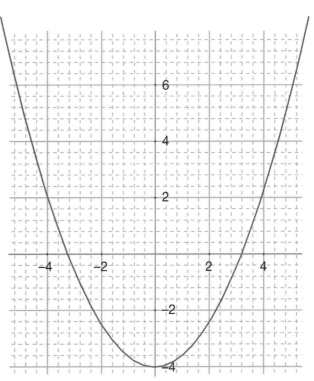

End Behavior

End behavior refers to what the function is doing as the *x*-values approach +∞ and –∞. Generally, you will be concerned with determining if the *y*-values are going to +∞ and –∞ as *x* gets infinitely large or small. If you look at a graph, it is easy to tell what is happening to the *y*-values as the *x*-values approach +∞ or –∞. However, what if you do not have a graph, but are only given a functional equation?

There are two features that are used to determine a function's end behavior. Let's define *degree* and *leading coefficient*:

> The **degree** of a function is the largest exponent in a function.
> The **leading coefficient** is the number that is being multiplied to the term with the largest exponent.

For instance, $y = -4x^3 + 2x - 7$ is a third degree function with a leading coefficient of –4. There are two different sets of rules to follow for functions with even degrees and functions with odd degrees:

Even Degree Functions

All functions that have an even degree (x^2, x^4, x^8, etc.) will have a parabolic shape with identical end behavior occurring in each direction.

- **Even functions with a positive leading coefficient will open upward.** The value of *y* will approach +∞ as *x* approaches +∞ or –∞. This is written as $x \rightarrow +\infty$, $y \rightarrow +\infty$, and also *as* $x \rightarrow -\infty$, $y \rightarrow +\infty$.
- **Even functions with a negative leading coefficient will open downward.** The value of *y* will approach –∞ as *x* approaches +∞ or –∞. Therefore, as $x \rightarrow +\infty$, $y \rightarrow -\infty$ and as $x \rightarrow -\infty$, $y \rightarrow -\infty$.

The following two examples illustrate the behavior of even degree functions:

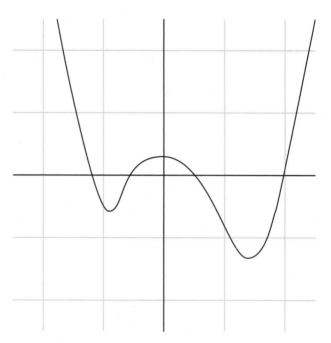

Positive Leading Coefficient of a
Function with an Even Degree

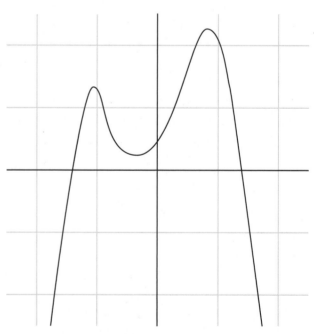

Negative Leading Coefficient of a
Function with an Odd Degree

Odd Degree Functions

All functions that have an odd degree (x^3, x^5, x^7, etc.) will have a *cubic* shape with opposite end behavior occurring in each direction.

- **Odd functions with a positive leading coefficient** will start from the bottom left of the graph and go up toward the right. The value of y will approach $+\infty$ as x approaches $+\infty$. The value of y approaches $-\infty$ as x approaches $-\infty$. This is written as $x \to +\infty$, $y \to +\infty$, and also as $x \to -\infty$, $y \to -\infty$.

Here is an illustration of an odd degree function with a positive leading coefficient:

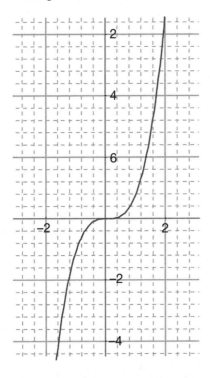

- **Odd functions with a negative leading coefficient** will start from the top left of the graph and go down toward the right. The value of y approaches $-\infty$ as x approaches $+\infty$. The value of y approaches $+\infty$ as x approaches $-\infty$. Therefore, as $x \to +\infty$, $y \to -\infty$ and as $x \to -\infty$, $y \to +\infty$.

Here is an illustration of an odd degree function with a negative leading coefficient:

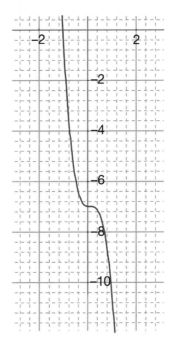

Practice

1. Identify the x-intercept and y-intercept of the function $f(x) = 3x + 4$.

2. Where will the function $g(x) = 10x^3 - 5x^2 - 15x + 20$ cross the y-axis?

Use the following illustration to answer questions 3–9:

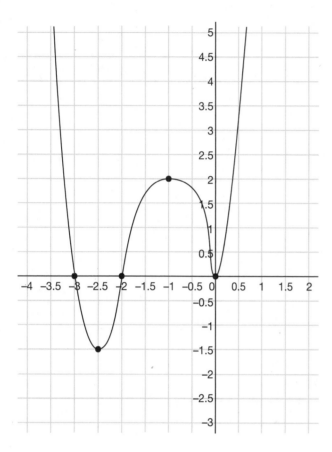

3. Name the coordinates of all of the relative maximums.

4. Name the coordinates of all of the relative minimums.

5. Name the coordinates of the x-intercepts.

6. Name the coordinates of the y-intercepts.

7. Over what intervals is this function increasing?

8. Over what intervals is this function decreasing?

9. Name the intervals for which the function is positive and the intervals for which the function is negative.

10. What is the end behavior of the function $x^4 + 3x^3 - 2x$ as $x \rightarrow -\infty$? _____

11. What is the end behavior of the function $-2x^5 + 3x^3 + x^2$ as $x \rightarrow +\infty$? _____

Representing Data with Different Types of Graphs

One set of data can be represented in many different graphical formats. The GED® test will ask you to answer questions based on information presented in bar graphs, circle graphs/pie charts, dot plots, box plots, histograms, and scatter plots.

Bar Graphs

Bar graphs are used to represent and display data with differing values for each category. The differing heights of the bars offer a quick-glance comparison of data. There are two types of bar graphs: vertical and horizontal.

Vertical bar graphs display the categories along the x-axis and the values along the y-axis.

For example, the following bar graph shows the average number of children per household for Carolyn Dexter's family. The data includes the past four generations in addition to the current generation of the Dexter clan.

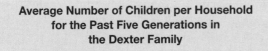

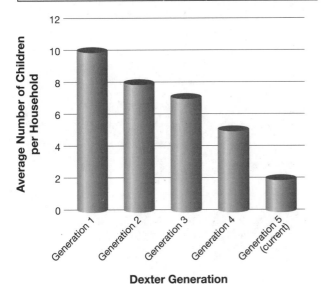

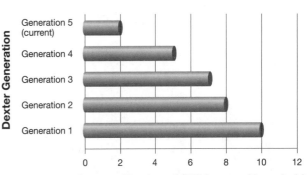

As you can see, the categories—Generation 1, Generation 2, Generation 3, Generation 4, and Generation 5 (current)—are placed along the *x*-axis. The data values—the average number of children per household—are placed along the *y*-axis at equal intervals. At a quick glance, you can see that the average number of children per household has decreased from generation to generation.

Horizontal bar graphs display the categories along the *y*-axis and the data values along the *x*-axis. Using the same data as before, we can also make a horizontal bar graph. It would look like the following:

Here, you can see, the categories—Generation 1, Generation 2, Generation 3, Generation 4, and Generation 5 (current)—are now placed along the *y*-axis. The data values—the average number of children per household—are now placed along the *x*-axis. Still, it is easy to see at a quick glance that the average number of children per household has decreased from generation to generation.

On the GED® test, you may be asked to interpret information presented in bar graphs or finish constructing a bar graph by dragging and dropping the correct bar height to complete the graph according to a given set of data.

Practice

12. On average, how many more children did households have in the first generation than the current Dexter generation, according to the graphs? _____

13. If the current trend in family size continues for the Dexter family, which is the least likely number of children for the 6th generation?
   a. 0
   b. 1
   c. 2
   d. 3

There are five different categories of books at the Everdale Library. Use the following bar graph to answer questions 14 and 15:

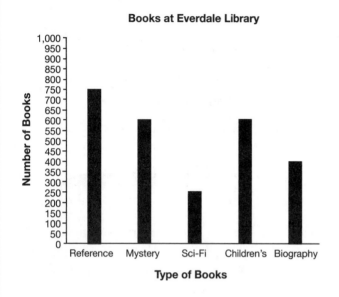

14. Everdale Library seems to have about the same number of which two categories of books?

15. Complete the following statement from the choices that follow: "The number of Sci-Fi books at the Everdale Library seems to be about _____ the number of Reference books."
   a. twice as many as
   b. half as many as
   c. three times as many as
   d. one-third as many as

Circle Graphs/Pie Charts

Circle graphs, or **pie charts**, are used to express data that collectively makes a whole. This is best used when looking at percentages out of 100%. It's good for getting a comparison of a particular piece of information against the whole. For instance, if 80% of all children in developing countries are malnourished, a circle graph could easily display this data.

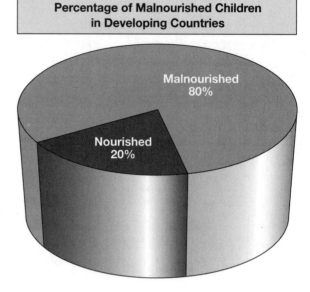

The 80% of malnourished children in developing countries plus the 20% of nourished children under five years old in developing countries equals a whole 100% of children. The circle graph provides a visual representation of the statistic.

On the test, you may have to identify the correct piece of the circle to complete a graph, similar to the bar graph example. Or you may have to find percentages of data to correctly construct the circle graph, or at least recognize the correct graph.

Practice

16. Based on the values in the table, which circle graph accurately represents this data?

U.S. Census Bureau Statistics, 2012

SINGLE MOTHERS WITH CHILDREN UNDER 18	SINGLE FATHERS WITH CHILDREN UNDER 18
10.322 million	1.956 million

a.

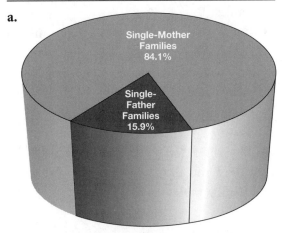

b.

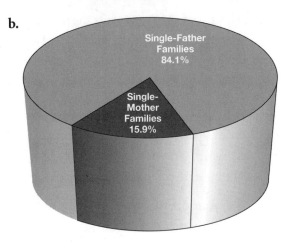

c.

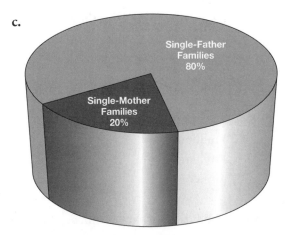

d.

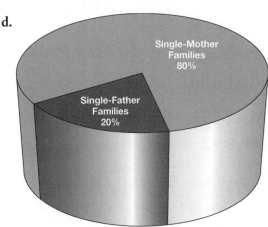

Use the pie chart below to answer questions 17 and 18:

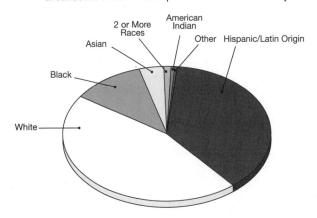

Breakdown of Ethnic Groups in Undisclosed Country

17. If the pie chart represents the breakdown of ethnic groups in a country of 10 million people, what is the best estimate for the number of people of Hispanic/Latin origin in that country?
   a. 5 million
   b. 3 million
   c. 2 million
   d. 1 million

18. Approximately what percentage of the population is white in this country?
   a. 30% – 40%
   b. 40% – 50%
   c. 50% – 60%
   d. 60% – 70%

Dot Plots

Dot plots are used to display numerical or categorical data along a horizontal line. Numerical data placed along the horizontal line might represent "the number of minutes students commute to school," while categorical data could show "favorite flavor of ice cream." The number of dots or x's above each category represents the frequency of the data being represented. Dot plots are a great way to quickly see how data is distributed. The following dot plot represents the number of miles teachers from Windmere Academy biked to school during Bike to Work Week:

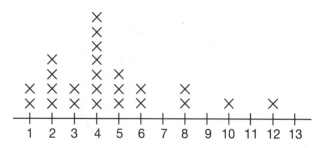

Windmere Teacher *Bike to Work Week* Participation

It doesn't take long to get a variety of information by looking at this dot plot:

- The fewest number of miles biked was 1 mile, which was the commute of 2 teachers.
- The longest commute was 12 miles, which was done by one teacher.
- The most common distance biked to work was 4 miles.
- The range of miles biked was from 1 mile to 12 miles
- If we count all the x's we can see that 24 teachers participated in Bike to Work Week at Windmere Academy.

On the GED® test, be prepared to create dot plots with drag and drop questions as well as interpret information presented in dot plots.

Practice

19. This list of data represents the number of disposable coffee cups the members of a local police force reported using in a given week. Make a dot plot to accurately represent this data: 7, 5, 7, 2, 10, 0, 7, 5, 12, 0, 7, 5, 1, 14, 8

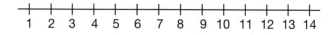

20. Use your dot plot from question 19 to determine whether each of the following statements is true, false, or cannot be determined:
   A. The majority of the police force averages at least one disposable coffee cup per day.
   B. Two people on the police force do not drink coffee.
   C. Three people on the police force use three or fewer disposable coffee cups per week.

Box Plots

Box plots are similar to dot plots in that they also display data along a horizontal line. However, box plots are more useful for summarizing a large amount of data. Once data is organized in a box plot, it is easy to see all the *quartiles*, or numbers that divide the data into quarters. At a glance, box plots show us where the top 25% of the data sits, where the top (and bottom) 50% of the data sits, and where the lowest 25% of the data sits. Let's take a look at the recent test scores in Miss Betty's class of 25 students:

25 Scores from Miss Betty's Class Test:
55, 65, 67, 69, 75, 76, 78, 79, 82, 83, 84, 85, 86, 87, 87, 89, 90, 91, 91, 91, 92, 93, 93, 93, 100

Note: Miss Betty's student's scores are already listed in chronological order here. If data is given that is *not* listed from least to greatest, you *must* order the data before making a box plot.

Even though there are 25 numbers in the data set, a box plot offers a *summary* of the data where only five numbers will be plotted:
  1. Median of the entire data set
  2. Lower quartile (i.e., the median of the lower half of the data set)
  3. Upper quartile (i.e., the median of the upper half of the data set)
  4. Minimum (i.e., the lowest point of the data set)
  5. Maximum (i.e., the highest point of the data set)

So, how do we find these five numbers? Let's start with the median of the entire data set. (We will discuss the median more in the next chapter, but for now, know that the median of a data set is the *middle number* when that data is listed in chronological order.) Looking at our chronological list of data, what is the *median*, or very middle number?

55, 65, 67, 69, 75, 76, 78, 79, 82, 83, 84, 85, **86**, 87, 87, 89, 90, 91, 91, 91, 92, 93, 93, 93, 100

The number 86 is the median because there is an even 12 numbers on each side of it in the data set.

Next, let's find the lower quartile, the median of the lower half of the data set. The first 12 values are:

55, 65, 67, 69, 75, **76, 78**, 79, 82, 83, 84, 85. . . .

There is an even number of data points, so we need to find the average of the two middle numbers to get our lower quartile:

Average of Middle 2 Numbers: $\frac{76 + 78}{2} = 77$

The number 77 is the lower quartile, the median of the lower half of the data set.

To find the upper quartile, find the median of the upper half of the data set:

. . . 87, 87, 89, 90, 91, **91, 91**, 92, 93, 93, 93, 100

Again, there are 12 numbers, but the two middle numbers are the same, so it is easy to take the average of them to get the upper quartile:

Average of Middle 2 Numbers: $\frac{91 + 91}{2} = 91$

The number 91 is the upper quartile, the median of the upper half of the data set.

The minimum and maximum are easy to find. They are simply the lowest number and the highest number in the data set—in this case, 55 and 100.

Now that we have our five points, let's plot them on the number line.

Minimum: 55
Lower quartile: 77
Median: 86
Upper quartile: 91
Maximum: 100

The bolded numbers are going to become lines to make a box. The extremes are simply going to be dots.

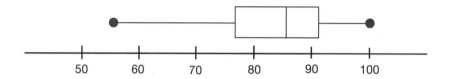

What does this visual tell us? It is actually a summary of some pretty useful information! We'll break it down into its key parts:

The box: Do you see how the box contains three vertical lines? The lines at the left end, middle, and right end of the box represent the values of 77, 86, and 91. The box lets Miss Betty see that the middle 50% of her students fall within the range of the boxed values, from 77 to 91.

The endpoints: The outermost points of 55 and 100 let Miss Betty see the extremes of her data set. She can quickly see how far above and below her highest and lowest students scored with respect to the 50% of the grades in the box.

The spread: Since the line inside the box at 77 represents the median score of all the data, we can quickly determine how consolidated, or

similar, the scores were in the top half of the class versus the bottom half of the class. Miss Betty can see that the lower half of the class's scores are more spread out, while the upper half of the class's scores are closer together. This means that the top performers are more similar in their performance than the bottom performers, who have larger differences in their abilities.

The quartiles: The last terminology you must know for box plots involves quartiles. The *quartiles* are the three central measurements that divide the data set up into quarters, or sections of 25% of the data. The first, second, and third quartiles are shown in the following data set, named Q_1, Q_2, and Q_3, respectively. Notice how they split the data up into four quarters. We can see that the top 75% of the grades had a spread, or range, that is very similar to just the lower 25% of the grades:

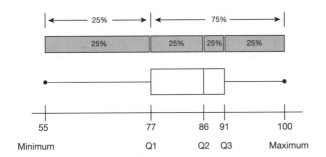

On your GED® test you may be asked to interpret information from a single box plot, compare data sets represented by two different box plots, or determine which box plot accurately represents a data set.

DON'T DO THIS!

Remember: To make a box plot your data must first be listed out in chronological order. Do not try to make a box plot without organizing your data from smallest to greatest!

Although making a box plot is a more intensive process than constructing any of the earlier tables we have discussed in this section, hopefully you can see how useful box plots are for evaluating large data sets.

Practice

21. The two box plots below show the data for daily high temperatures for every day of the fall in Minnesota and Alaska. Which state has a more consistent temperature in the fall?

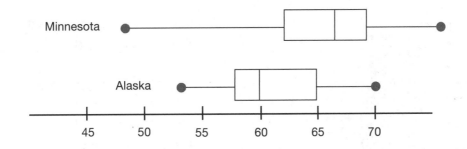

22. What is the median of the data displayed here? _____

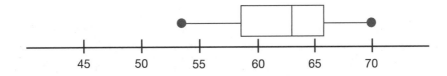

Histograms

Histograms look a lot like bar graphs, in that the *x*-axis contains data and the *y*-axis shows the frequency of that data. The important difference between bar graphs and histograms is that bar graphs can present categorical data or precise numerical data on the *x*-axis, while histograms are used to represent *consecutive ranges of data* along the *x*-axis. This makes histograms a better choice for large sets of data or data that has a wider range of numbers.

The following histogram displays the age range of students enrolled in Mr. Duvall's *Retirement for Rookies* class at a local community college. Notice in the following graph that the bars are plotted side by side, rather than having a gap between them as bar graphs do:

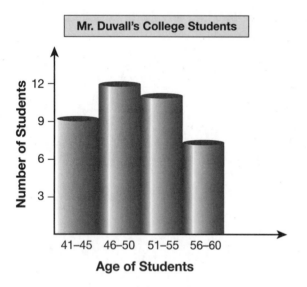

On the GED® test, you may be asked to drag and drop the appropriate bar to complete a set of data, or you may be asked to provide answers based on reading the histogram.

Example

How many students are in Mr. Duvall's class?

A. 50
B. 44
C. 39
D. 35

The correct answer is choice **c**. Add up how many students are in each of the age ranges:

   9 41- to 45-year-olds
12 46- to 50-year-olds
11 51- to 55-year-olds
+7 56- to 60-year-olds
39 students

Practice

Use the previous graph of Mr. Duvall's students to answer questions 23 and 24.

23. According to the graph, what percentage of students are ages 46 to 50? _____

24. According to the graph, what is the percentage difference between the age group with the highest number of students and the age group with the lowest number of students? _____

Scatter Plots

Data that is **bivariate** compares two different variables. For example, the bivariate data we are going to look at later in this section compares the number of hours a student studied each week to the number of weeks it took that student to pass the GED® test. **Scatter plots** allow us to interpret the relationship between the two variables in bivariate data in order to recognize trends and make predictions about data not contained in the graph.

Here are some terms to know with respect to scatter plots:

Cluster: A cluster of points is where most of the plotted points are located. It can also refer to the direction of the plotted points as a whole.

Outlier: This is a point that is not with the cluster. It is either significantly larger or smaller or a point that does not correlate with the rest of the data.

Linear association: A graph has linear association if the plotted points resemble a line.

Nonlinear association: A graph has nonlinear association if the plotted points resemble a curve.

Positive association: Positive association of bivariate data means that as one variable increases, the other increases as well.

Negative association: Negative association of bivariate data means that as one variable increases, the other decreases.

Now, let's use these terms to describe the following scatter plot, which compares time driven in minutes on a freeway to distance driven in miles.

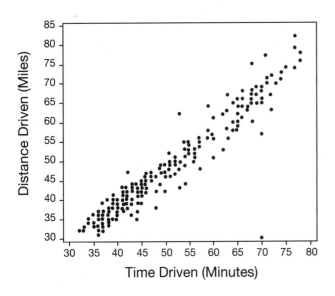

- The largest **cluster** of points is from 35 minutes to 47 minutes.
- The point (70,30) is an **outlier**. It might represent someone who had something wrong with her car or was an overly cautious driver.
- This scatter plot shows **a positive linear association**: As the number of minutes increases, so does the number of miles.

Creating a Scatter Plot

Here is a table of bivariate data: the number of hours each student studied each week compared to the number of weeks it took each to pass his or her GED® test.

HOURS OF STUDYING	NUMBER OF WEEKS TO PASS GED
1	30
3	25
4	24
6	21
8	19
10	27
11	17
12	16
14	14
17	13
20	10

Using this data, let the left column of "Study Hours" represent the x-coordinates. Let the corresponding data of "Weeks to Pass the GED" in the right column represent the y-coordinates. Then plot each of these 11 coordinate pairs in the following scatter plot:

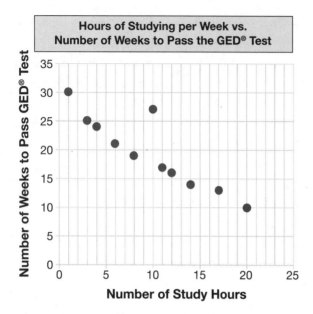

Hours of Studying per Week vs. Number of Weeks to Pass the GED® Test

At this point, it might be helpful for you to review slope and linear equations in Chapter 7 to recall how to calculate slope, how to calculate the *y*-intercept, and how to interpret the intercepts of a graph. On the GED® test you may be asked to perform these tasks from a scatter plot as well as to use a scatter plot to make predictions about data points that are not on the graph. For example, looking at this graph, how many weeks would you predict it would take someone to pass the GED® test if she studied for 25 hours a week? You should be able to look at the graph and make a prediction of 5–7 weeks based on the trend pictured. Practice your scatter plot interpretations with the following practice questions.

Practice

Use the preceding scatter plot comparing hours studies to weeks needed to pass the GED® test to answer questions 25 through 27.

25. Does this data show a positive or negative association? _____

26. Which point would be considered an outlier?
   a. (14,14)
   b. (3,25)
   c. (10,27)
   d. (17,13)

27. Which statement is NOT true about this graph?
   a. The data shows negative linear association.
   b. The data shows that the more hours one studies each week, the more quickly one passes the GED® test.
   c. The data shows negative nonlinear association.
   d. One can quite confidently predict that a student who studies 19 hours a week will pass the GED® test in roughly 11 weeks.

Summary

Now you have a rich repertoire of techniques to display, interpret, and discuss data. You are probably noticing that as you learn more and more math skills, you are incorporating previous skills into the new material. Practice your skills here and get ready to move into applying all of your algebra skills to the geometry topics in the next chapter!

Interpreting Data in Graphs and Tables Review

1. Which graph has a *y*-intercept at –5 and increases during the interval $(-\infty, -5) \cup (-5, \infty)$?

a.

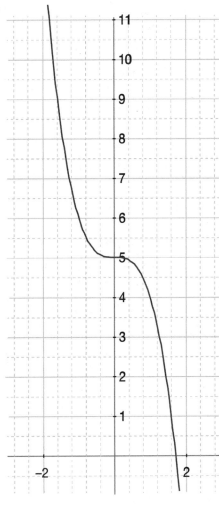

b.

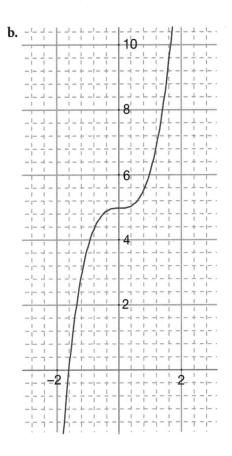

c.

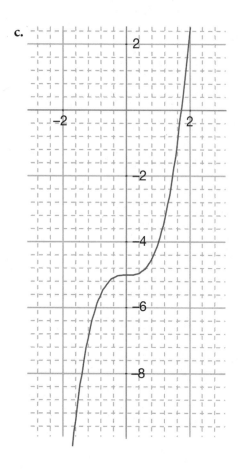

d.

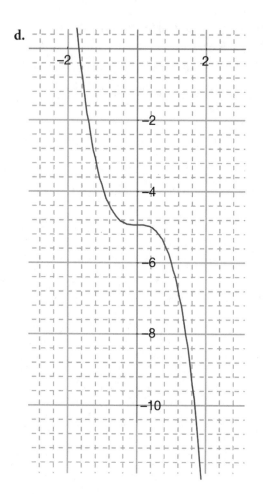

Use the following graph of the function g(x) to answer questions 2 through 5:

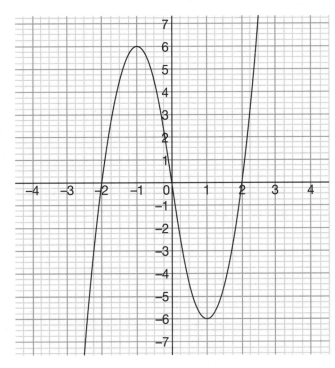

2. On what interval is g(x) decreasing?
   a. [−2,0]
   b. (0,2)
   c. (−1,1)
   d. (6,−6)

3. Which of the following functions could be the general form of the equation that represents this function, for real coefficients a, b, c, d, and m?
   a. $y = ax^2 + bx + c$
   b. $y = ax^3 + bx^2 + cx + d$
   c. $y = mx + b$
   d. $y = \frac{1}{x}$

4. What is the best approximation of the relative minimum of g(x)?
   a. (−1,6)
   b. (0,0)
   c. (1,−6)
   d. (−2.4,−7.5)

5. Over which interval or intervals is g(x) positive?
   a. (0,6)
   b. (−2,0)
   c. (−∞,−1) and (1,+∞)
   d. (−2,0) and (2,+∞)

Use the following bar graph to answer questions 6 and 7:

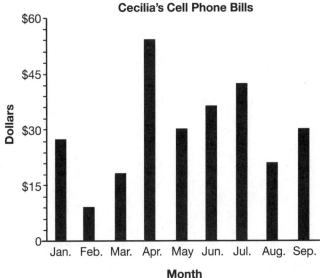

6. Cecilia plots on a bar graph the cost of her cell phone bill for each month from January through September. How much did Cecilia spend on her cell phone in April and May combined? _____

7. Which answer best approximates the average cost of Cecilia's cell phone bill each month?
   a. $15
   b. $20
   c. $30
   d. $40

Use the following box plot to answer questions 8 and 9:

8. This box plot shows the prices of textbooks at a local high school. What range describes the middle 50% of the prices (*p*) of the textbooks?
   a. $30 < p < $85
   b. $50 < p < $85
   c. $50 < p < $90
   d. $85 < p < $90

9. What percentage of books cost between $85 and $90?
   a. 25%
   b. 50%
   c. 75%
   d. It cannot be determined from this graph.

Use the following pie chart to answer questions 10 and 11:

Johnson Family Budget

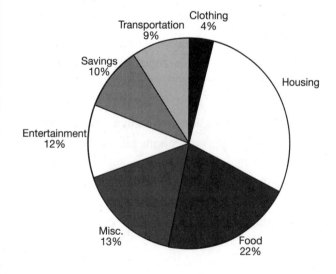

10. The graph shows the Johnson family budget for one month.

In percentage of overall expenses, how much more money is spent on food than on transportation and clothing combined?

_____

11. What percentage does the Johnson Family have budgeted for their housing? _____

12. Which of the following statements best describes the relationship between the data points shown on the scatter plot?

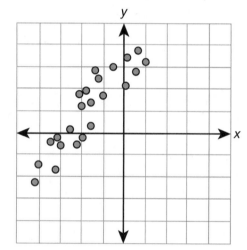

   a. There is a positive correlation.
   b. There is a negative correlation.
   c. There does not appear to be any correlation.
   d. It cannot be determined without knowing the values of the data points.

Answers and Explanations

Chapter Practice

1. $y = 4$ **and** $x = -\frac{4}{3}$. Since the linear equation $f(x) = 3x + 4$ is in the form $y = mx + b$, we know that b or 4 is the y-intercept. To find the x-intercept, replace y with 0 and solve for x:

$$f(x) = 3x + 4$$
$$0 = 3x + 4$$
$$\underline{-4 \qquad\quad -4}$$
$$\frac{-4}{3} = \frac{3x}{3}$$
$$x = -\frac{4}{3}$$

2. $y = 20$. The x-value will be 0 at the point where a function crosses the y-axis. Therefore, replace all of the x variables with 0 and solve for y:

$$g(x) = 10x^3 - 5x^2 - 15x + 20$$
$$y = 10(0)^3 - 5(0)^2 - 15(0) + 20$$
$$y = 20$$

3. **(–1,2).** There is only one relative maximum at (–1,2), which makes a peak.

4. **(–2.5,–1.5) and (0,0).** There are two relative minimums that occur at the two valleys: (–2.5,–1.5) and (0,0).

5. **(–3,0), (–2,0), and (0,0).** The function touches the x-axis in three different places: (–3,0), (–2,0), and (0,0).

6. **(0,0).** There is only one y-intercept at (0,0).

7. **(–2.5,–1) and (0,+∞).** Functions are increasing over the intervals where their slope is positive, or going up from left to right. Intervals are defined by the x-values over which a behavior is being exhibited. In this function, the slope is positive from when $x = -2.5$ until $x = -1$. Then the slope is again positive from $x = 0$ until what appears to be $x = \infty$. Exclude the endpoints by writing these intervals with parentheses. This function is increasing over the intervals (–2.5,–1) and (0, +∞).

8. **(–2.5,–1) and (0, +∞).** Functions are decreasing over the intervals where their slope is negative, or going down from left to right. Intervals are defined by the x-values over which a behavior is being exhibited. In this function the slope is negative from what appears to be $x = -\infty$ until $x = -2.5$. Then the slope is again negative from $x = -1$ until $x = 0$. Exclude the endpoints by writing these intervals with parentheses. This function is increasing over the intervals (–2.5,–1) and (0, +∞).

9. **Positive: (–∞,–3) ∪ (–2,0) ∪ (0,∞). Negative: (–3,–2).** Intervals are expressed in terms of the x-values for which a certain behavior is exhibited. A function is positive when its y-value is positive and its graph is above the x-axis. This function is positive over (–∞,–3) ∪ (–2,0) ∪ (0,∞). A function is negative when it is located below the x-axis and its y-values are negative. This function is negative over (–3,–2). Note that the points at which the function hits the x-axis are neither positive nor negative, so these must be excluded from the intervals by using parentheses instead of brackets.

10. **as $x \to -\infty, f(x) \to +\infty$.** We are concerned about only the first term. It has an even power of x and a positive coefficient. Therefore, it will behave like a parabola with a positive coefficient. The parabolic shape will be upright, so as $x \to -\infty, f(x) \to +\infty$.

11. **as $x \to +\infty, f(x) \to -\infty$.** Again, we are concerned with only the first term. It has an odd power of x and a negative coefficient. Therefore, it will behave like a cubic function with a negative coefficient. The function will generally decrease from the left of the graph to the right of the graph. As $x \to +\infty, f(x) \to -\infty$.

12. 8. The first generation displayed is Generation 1. The height of the bar for Generation 1 is 10, which means each household had an average of 10 children. The height of the bar for the current generation, Generation 5, is 2, which means that each household in the Dexter family today has an average of 2 children. On average, the difference between the first generation displayed and the current Dexter generation is 8 children per household.

13. d. The 5th (current) generation in the Dexter family has 2 children. Since the number of children has gone down from each generation to the next, it would be least likely for the number of children in the 6th generation to *increase* to 3 children. Answer choice **c**, 2 children, is also not incredibly likely, since the trend has been for the number of children to *decrease*, but 3 children is more unlikely since increasing the number of children is the opposite of decreasing the number of children in a generation.

14. Mystery and Children's. According to the bar graph, the height of the bar representing the mystery books is about equal to the height of the bar of the children's books. Everdale Library has about the same number of mystery and children's books.

15. d. According to the bar graph, the height of the sci-fi bar is at approximately 250 books, while the height of the reference bar shows about 750 books. Therefore, there are about $\frac{1}{3}$ the number of sci-fi books as reference books. Choice **c** is an easy mistake to make because this reverses the relationship: there are *three times* as many reference books as there are sci-fi books.

16. a. To represent information in a circle graph, we have to first find the percentage of the whole for each statistic, since the circle represents a whole. First, we need to find the total number of single parents by adding 10.322 million and 1.956 million:

$$\begin{array}{r} 10.322 \text{ million} \\ + 1.956 \text{ million} \\ \hline 12.278 \text{ million} \end{array}$$

Now that we know the total number of families, we can find the percentage of single-mother families and single-father families by doing division problems:

$$\frac{\text{\# of single-mother families}}{\text{Total number of families}} = \frac{10.322 \text{ million}}{12.278 \text{ million}} = 0.8406$$
$$= 84.1\% \text{ (when rounded)}$$

$$\frac{\text{\# of single-father families}}{\text{Total number of families}} = \frac{1.956 \text{ million}}{12.278 \text{ million}} = 0.1593 =$$
$$15.9\% \text{ (when rounded)}$$

Choice **b** has the statistics for single fathers and single mothers reversed. Choice **d** is a rounded answer, but with choice **a** available, choice **d** is not as accurate. Choice **c** is similar to choice **d**, but the statistics are reversed.

17. b. Looking at the pie chart, the number of Hispanic/Latin origin people make up about one-third of the population. If the pie chart represents a total of 10 million people, then one-third of 10 million would be 3.3 million, so **b** is the best answer. Choice **a** is incorrect because 5 million Hispanic/Latin origin people out of a total of 10 million would be 50% of the population and the graph does not show Hispanic/Latin origin people taking up half the circle chart. Similarly, choices **c** and **d** represent one-fifth and one-tenth of the population, but by looking at the graph, we can see that the Hispanic/Latin origin people make up more the one-fifth of the circle graph.

18. Looking at the circle graph, we can see that just under 50% of the population in this country is white, so answer choice **b** is the correct answer. Answer choices **c** and **d** would require the section representing whites to take up more than half the graph, which it doesn't. Choice **a** is way too low to be correct.

19. Since the range of data went from 0 to 14, make a number line that is evenly spaced from 0 to 14. Each time a data point appears in the set, put an *x* above that data label:

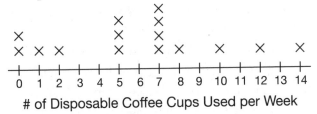

# of Disposable Coffee Cups Used per Week

20. **A: true; B: cannot be determined; C: false.** Counting all the data points, we see that there are 15 people being represented in this dot plot. Statement A, "The majority of the police force averages at least one disposable coffee cup per day," is true because only 2 out of the 15 people do not use at least one disposable cup per day. Statement B, "Two people on the police force do not drink coffee," might be true since two people don't use disposable coffee cups, but we don't know if they drink their coffee at home or use reusable coffee cups instead, so this cannot be determined. Statement C, "three people on the police force use three or fewer disposable coffee cups per week," is false since there are four people who use three or fewer disposable coffee cups per week.

21. **Alaska.** The span of the extreme temperatures is not quite as long in Alaska as the span of the extreme temperatures in Minnesota. Therefore, if you were trying to decide where to go for vacation in the fall and you wanted to pack rather lightly, you would want to go to Alaska since you would not need to bring as many clothes to allow for changing weather.

22. **63.** To find the median of the data displayed, look for the value of the central line in the box.

23. **31%.** To find the percentage of students ages 46 to 50, you first have to find the total number of students. In the first example, we calculated 39 total students. Reading the graph, we can see that the number of students ages 46 to 50 is 12. To find the percentage, we simply divide 12 by 39 and then move the decimal point two spaces to the right.

$\frac{12}{39} = 0.307 = 30.7 = 31\%$ (when rounded)

So, 31% of Mr. Duvall's students are ages 46 to 50.

24. **13%.** We found the percentage of the age group with the highest number of students in the previous example. Next, we need to find the percentage of students in the age group with the lowest number of students. The lowest number of students in an age group is 7, in the 56 to 60 age range. Find the percentage by dividing 7 by the total number of students, and then move the decimal place.

$\frac{7}{39} = 0.179 = 17.9 = 18\%$ (when rounded)

The percentage difference is then

$$\begin{array}{r} 31\% \\ -18\% \\ \hline 13\% \end{array}$$

So, the percentage difference between the age groups with the highest number of students and the lowest number of students in Mr. Duvall's class is 13%.

25. **negative association.** Look back at the six terms defined earlier. Negative association means that as one variable increases, the other decreases. In this graph, as the number of hours of studying increases, the amount of time it takes to pass the GED® test decreases.

26. **c.** This point on the graph is located away from the cluster that is trending downward. There must be other reasons that this student did not pass his or her GED® test in fewer weeks, because it does not follow the trend.

27. c. The graph does show a linear association, so choice **c** is not true. The graph has a negative association: as the number of hours of studying increases, the number of weeks it takes to pass the GED® test decreases. Since the graph does have a linear association, one can predict values not plotted that follow the linear progression.

Interpreting Data in Graphs and Tables Review

1. c. This graph intercepts the y-axis at –5. It also increases from $(-\infty,-5) \cup (-5,\infty)$.

2. c. Functions are decreasing over the intervals where their slope is negative, or going down from left to right. Intervals are defined by the x-values over which a behavior is being exhibited. In this function, the slope is negative from when $x = -1$ until $x = 1$. So this function is decreasing over the intervals $(-1,1)$. Answer choice **d** names the *y-values* over which the function is decreased, but this is not the correct convention for discussing intervals. Choices **a** and **b** show the intervals over which the function is *positive* and *negative*, respectively (parentheses and brackets should be used in choice **a**).

3. b. Even degree functions have similar end behavior in both directions, while odd degree functions have opposite behavior in both directions. Since this function is going in two opposite directions as x approaches ∞ and as x approaches $-\infty$, it must be an odd degree function. This rules out choice **a**. Choice **c** does not make sense since that is a linear equation and this graph is curved. Choice **d** does not make sense since x is in the bottom of a fraction. Choice **b** is the correct answer because it shows a cubic function, and cubic functions always have opposite behavior in both directions.

4. c. The relative minimum of $g(x)$ will be where it hits a valley and the slope has changed directions. Choice **d** shows the lowest point on the graph, but this is not by definition the *relative minimum*. Choice **b** shows the origin, which is not in a valley. Choice **a** shows the relative maximum, which is at a peak. Choice **c** is the relative minimum and the valley is at $(1,-6)$.

5. A function is positive when its y-value is positive and its graph is above the x-axis. Intervals are expressed in terms of the x-values for which a certain behavior is exhibited. The function $g(x)$ is positive as x goes from –2 to 0 and then again as x goes from 2 to ∞. This is written as $(-2,0)$ and $(2,+\infty)$ so **d** is the correct answer. Choice **c** is incorrect because it is naming the intervals of the function where it is *increasing* rather than naming where it is *positive*. Choice **b** is naming just one interval where the function is positive but it is forgetting the interval $(2,+\infty)$. Choice **a** is listing the height range of the function in the second quadrant, which has nothing to do with the interval of the function being positive.

6. $84. Use the bar graph to find how much Cecilia spent on her cell phone in April and how much she spent on her cell phone in May. Then add those two values to find how much she spent in the two months combined.
Each tick mark on the vertical axis of the graph represents $3. Cecilia spent $54 in April and $30 in May.

$54 + $30 = $84

Cecilia spent $84 on her cell phone in April and May combined.

7. c. Looking at the graph we can consider each answer choice to see which one best approximates the average cost of Cecilia's cell phone bill each month. Choice **a** doesn't make sense since February is the only bill that is less than $15 and the rest of the months are considerably higher than that. Choice **b** doesn't make much sense either since only three of the nine months are $20 or less and the remaining six months are nearly $30 or above. Choice **d** doesn't seem like the best answer since only two out of the nine months are $40 or above; this average seems too high. After eliminating these three choices, it is clear that choice **c** is the best approximation since all but three of the nine months are reasonably close to $30.

8. c. Each point on a box plot represents the beginning and/or end of a quartile. The left-most point represents the beginning of the first quartile, the next point represents the end of the first quartile and the beginning of the second quartile, and so on. Each quartile accounts for 25% of the data. Since there are four quartiles in a data set, the middle two quartiles (the second and third quartiles) represent the middle 50% of the data. For this data set, the beginning of the second quartile is $50 and the end of the third quartile is $90. So, the middle 50% of the data is between $50 and $90.

9. a. Since $85 represents the median and $90 represents the upper quartile, we can conclude that 25% of the data falls between $85 and $90. Choice **b** is not correct because 50% of the data is either the range demonstrated by the box ($50 to $90), or the range from the median to the maximum ($85 to $110). Choice **c** is incorrect because 75% of the books are *lower than* $90 but higher than $30, but the books between $85 and $90 are not 75% of the data.

10. 9%. To find the difference between food and the combined total of transportation and clothing expenses, look at the numbers on the graph. Food expense is 22%, transportation is 9%, and clothing is 4%; $22 - (9 + 4) = 9\%$.

11. 30%. In a pie chart, all of the percentages must sum to 100%. When adding all the other given percentages together, we get 70%, so this means that 30% is left for housing.

12. a. When looking at a scatter plot of data points, a correlation exists if there is a relationship between x and y that holds true for the majority of the points. For example, if the y-values get larger as the x-values get larger, there is a positive correlation. In other words, if the points seem to rise as you move from left to right on the graph, there is a positive correlation. Similarly, if the y-values get smaller as the x-values get larger, there is a negative correlation; the values are behaving in an opposite way to each other. According to this scatter plot, there is a distinct relationship. As the x-values get larger, so do the y-values. Therefore, there is a positive correlation.

10 ▶ GEOMETRY FOUNDATIONS

Geometry is the study of shapes and spatial relationships. The geometry skills that you are required to have for the GED® test are also important life skills that will benefit you in the real world: working with perimeter, area, volume, and surface area of shapes. Whether you're buying carpeting for your home, grass seed for your lawn, or fencing to protect your dog, you will find these geometry skills useful in your everyday life. Answers and explanations for all practice questions are at the end of the chapter.

This chapter covers:

- Perimeter
- Using the Pythagorean theorem with right triangles
- Circumference
- Area
- Surface area of prisms
- Volume of prisms
- Applying scale factors to geometric shapes

GED® TEST MATHEMATICS FORMULA SHEET

You will not need to memorize the formulas for perimeter, area, volume, or surface area in order to succeed on the GED® test. On test day, you will have access to a formula sheet, which will contain all the formulas you need. What you *must* be familiar with is:

- *when* you will need to use each formula,
- *what* the different variables stand for in each formula, and
- *how* to correctly calculate the values to input into the formula.

For example, consider a question that requires you to use the surface area formula for a right prism: $SA = ph + 2B$.

You must know that p = perimeter of the front face, h = height of the prism, and B = area of the base. The formula reference sheet on page 191 contains the formulas you'll have access to on test day. As you work through the practice questions in this chapter, use this reference sheet in order to simulate your testing conditions.

Area

Parallelogram: $A = bh$

Trapezoid: $A = \frac{1}{2}h(b_1 + b_2)$

Surface Area and Volume

Rectangular/right prism:	$SA = ph + 2B$	$V = Bh$
Cylinder:	$SA = 2\pi rh + 2\pi r^2$	$V = \pi r^2 h$
Pyramid:	$SA = \frac{1}{2}ps + B$	$V = \frac{1}{3}Bh$
Cone:	$SA = \pi rs + \pi r^2$	$V = \frac{1}{3}\pi r^2 h$
Sphere:	$SA = 4\pi r^2$	$V = \frac{4}{3}\pi r^3$

(p = perimeter of base B; $\pi \approx 3.14$)

Algebra

Slope of a line: $m = \frac{y_2 - y_1}{x_2 - x_1}$

Slope-intercept form of the equation of a line: $y = mx + b$

Point-slope form of the equation of a line: $y - y_1 = m(x - x_1)$

Standard form of a quadratic equation: $y = ax^2 + bx + c$

Quadratic formula: $x = \frac{-b \pm \sqrt{b^2 - 4ac}}{2a}$

Pythagorean theorem: $a^2 + b^2 = c^2$

Simple interest: $I = prt$

(I = interest, p = principal, r = rate, t = time)

WORKING BACKWARD WITH FORMULAS

In the following sections you will be asked not only to calculate perimeter, area, and volume, by using the formulas, but you will also be asked to work backwards. For example, you may be required to solve for a missing dimension, such as *height*, when the volume, length, and width of a prism are known. You already have the skills needed for working backward: Plug in all the given information and use your algebra skills to isolate the unknown variable.

Perimeter

Peri means "around" and *meter* means "measure." So, the **perimeter** of any figure is simply the measure around the figure. A soccer coach might have his team run laps around the perimeter of the soccer field or a contractor might put up a temporary fence around a work site so that pedestrians don't enter it by mistake and get injured. Since a word problem won't necessarily ask you to find the *perimeter* of a given shape, it's important that you be able to recognize that questions concerning the distance around the outside of a shape are referring to that shape's perimeter.

GED® QUESTION SNEAK PREVIEW!

On the GED® test you must be prepared to work backward to solve for a missing measurement when the distance around a shape is given:

- *What is the radius of a circle with a circumference of 16π?*

Rectangles and Squares

To find the perimeter of a rectangle or square, simply find the sum of the measurements of each side of the figure. It's helpful to use the following formulas when given the perimeter and being asked to determine the side length of a square.

Perimeter of a Rectangle $= l + l + w + w$

$\mathbf{P = 2l + 2w}$

l = length and w = width

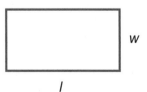

Example

How much fencing will be needed to enclose a rectangular garden that is 9 feet long and 5.5 feet wide?

First, you need to recognize that this question requires perimeter since it needs you to determine the distance *around* a rectangle. Since you are given a length of 9 and a width of 5.5, put both of these measurements into the formula:

$$P = 2l + 2w$$
$$P = 2(9) + 2(5.5)$$
$$P = 18 + 11$$
$$P = 29$$

29 feet of fencing is needed to enclose this garden.

Perimeter of a Square = $s + s + s + s$

P = 4s

s = side length (all 4 sides of a square are equal in length)

s

Example

Fernando has 30 feet of decorative tile left to create a border around an outside patio. If he wants the patio to be square, what is the side length of the largest patio he could use this boarder tile on?

The word "border" indicates that this question requires us to work with perimeter since a border goes *around* a shape. Notice that you are given the perimeter here (30 feet) and solving for the side length. This is a *working backward* question! 30 feet must be inputted as the perimeter in the formula and then the side length can be solved for:

$P = 4s$

$30 = 4s$

$\frac{30}{4} = s$

$s = 7.5$

The maximum side length of a square patio that can be enclosed with 30 feet of decorative tile is 7.5 feet.

Triangles

There is no formula for finding the perimeter of a triangle. To find the perimeter of a **triangle**, simply sum the measurements of the three sides.

For example, let's find the perimeter of the following triangle:

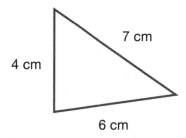

Perimeter = 4 cm + 6 cm + 7 cm = 17 cm

Pythagorean Theorem

One skill you may need to find the perimeter of a right triangle is the Pythagorean theorem. This theorem is used to find the missing side length of **right triangles**. In order to use the formula correctly, it's important to know the parts that make up right triangles:

Legs: The two sides that form the right angle are called the *legs* of the triangle.

Hypotenuse: The longest side of right triangles is always opposite the right angle and it is called the *hypotenuse*.

Here is an illustration of a right triangle with legs a and b and a hypotenuse c:

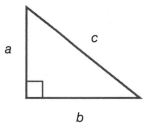

The **Pythagorean theorem** states that:

$$(\text{Leg 1})^2 + (\text{Leg 2})^2 = (\text{Hypotenuse})^2$$

Instead of using words to represent the formula, it is usually abbreviated with the variables *a*, *b*, and *c*:

$$a^2 + b^2 = c^2$$

In order to use the formula correctly, it is not extremely important that you pay attention to the exact variables. It is, however, *very* important that you make sure that the hypotenuse is by itself and the legs are together. Look at the following example where the hypotenuse is labeled *b* and notice how this is handled:

Example
What is the length of side *b*?

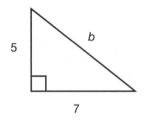

Even though *b* is the unknown side in this triangle, this is not the same *b* as is given in the Pythagorean theorem $a^2 + b^2 = c^2$. It is important to remember that the hypotenuse must be by itself. In this given triangle, *b* is the hypotenuse and the two given sides are legs. Starting with the formula, fill in the information for the legs and solve for the hypotenuse:

$$a^2 + b^2 = c^2$$
$$5^2 + 7^2 = b^2$$
$$25 + 49 = b^2$$
$$74 = b^2$$
$$\sqrt{74} = \sqrt{b^2}$$
$$8.60 = b$$

It is a tendency for students to want to put the unknown variable by itself and solve for the hypotenuse when working with the Pythagorean theorem. It's important to recognize when the question is asking you to solve for a leg. Look at this common error when setting up the Pythagorean theorem to solve for the missing side in the following triangle:

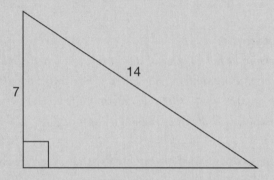

NO! $7^2 + 14^2 = c^2$ (The missing side is *not* the hypotenuse.)
YES . . . $7^2 + b^2 = 14^2$ (The missing side *is* the leg.)

Polygons
A **polygon** is a two-dimensional figure with at least three straight sides. To find the perimeter of a polygon, find the sum of the measurements of all the sides. One thing to look out for in polygons are hash marks on the sides indicating congruence. If two sides both have a single hash mark going through them, this means they are **congruent**, or equal in length. The same goes for a double hash mark or triple hash marks in two or more sides. For example, in the following figure, notice that the small sides all have a single hash mark—this indicates that they are all 1.5 yards long. The double hash marks in the two horizontal sides on top and bottom indicate that

these two sides are also congruent. Find the perimeter of the following figure:

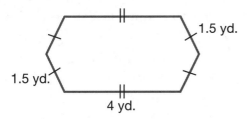

Perimeter = 4 yd. + 4 yd. + 1.5 yd. + 1.5 yd. +
            1.5 yd. + 1.5 yd.
          = 2(4 yd.) + 4(1.5 yd.)
          = 8 yd. + 6 yd.
          = 14 yd.

Circumference

The **circumference** of a circle measures the distance around the circle. This concept is similar to finding the perimeter of a straight-sided figure. However, since a circle does not have any straight sides, the distance around the circle—the circumference—needs to be calculated differently.

Before you can calculate the circumference of a circle, there are a few terms you need to know.

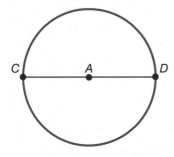

Center: In the figure, the center is at point *A*.
Radius: Any line that is drawn from the center, *A*, to the outside of the circle is called a radius. Thus, the line from *A* to *D*, $\overline{AD}$, is a radius, and the distance from *A* to *C*, $\overline{CA}$, is a radius. Therefore, $\overline{AD} = \overline{CA}$.

Diameter: Any line that is drawn from one end of the circle to the other end *and* passes through the center of the circle is called a diameter. Thus, the line is a diameter because it passes through the center of the circle, *A*.

Notice that $\overline{CA} + \overline{AD} = \overline{CD}$. The length of the diameter of a circle is equivalent to two times the radius: $d = 2r$.

π (pi—sounds like "pie") = 3.14159265359 . . .

For the purposes of equations involving circles, you can round to 3.14.

Whenever you need to find the distance around a circle, use the circumference formula. You just learned that the diameter is equal to two times the radius: $d = 2r$. This is why there are two different ways for the circumference formula to be written:

Circumference = $2\pi r$ **Circumference = πd**
r = radius   *d* = diameter

Example

What is the circumference of the following circle if $\overline{AB} = 4$ cm?

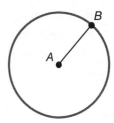

To find the circumference of the circle, use the formula $2\pi r$. In this problem, the radius, *r*, is 4 cm:

$C = 2\pi r$
$\quad = 2\pi(4 \text{ cm})$
$\quad = 8(3.14) \text{ cm}$
$\quad = 25.12 \text{ cm}$

Practice

1. Find the perimeter of the following rectangle:

_____

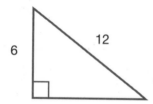

3 in.

5 in.

2. Lizzy used 64 inches of ribbon to go around a square box. What was the side length of the box?

3. What is the missing side length of the following triangle? _____

6

12

4. Reggie bikes to work every day, going 10 miles north from his house on Robert Street and then going 8 miles east on Dodd Road. He can bike 18 mph. How much time would Reggie save if he used the bike path that cuts straight through the park? _____

5. One side of a regular octagon has a length of 4 cm. What is the perimeter of the octagon?
   a. 8 cm
   b. 24 cm
   c. 36 cm
   d. 32 cm

6. Rusty needs to order enough wood to fence in the community garden grounds, which are in the shape of a regular pentagon—a pentagon with five congruent sides. If the fencing costs $12.50 per foot, how much will it cost to fence in the community garden? _____

15 ft.

7. Emma works for a catering company and her boss asked her to line the edges of the serving dishes with a bright red ribbon for Valentine's Day. How much ribbon will Emma need to wrap around a circular pan that can hold a pizza that has a 14-inch diameter? Round your answer to the nearest inch.

8. If the circumference of a circle is 62.8 mm, what is its diameter? _____

Area

Whereas the perimeter refers to the measurement *around* a figure, **area** refers to the space *inside* a figure. If a gardener wants to know how much grass seed is needed to plant a new lawn or a homeowner wants to order fabric to cover his pool at night, both of these people will need to perform *area* calculations. In general, to find the area of figures such as rectangles, squares, triangles, and circles, you will use multiplication.

GED® QUESTION SNEAK PREVIEW!

Not only will you be expected to find the areas of standard shapes on your GED® test, but you will also need to be able to calculate the area of composite shapes, which are forms made up of various shapes put together.

■ *What is the area of the following figure?*

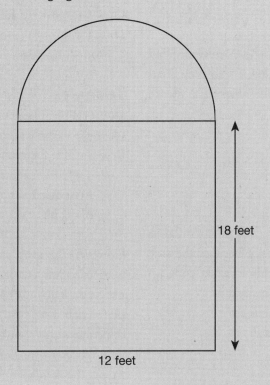

18 feet

12 feet

Rectangles and Squares

To find the perimeter of a rectangle or square, simply multiply any two adjacent sides together. If you are required to work backward to find a missing dimension, it's helpful to use the area formula for rectangles or squares.

> **Area of a Rectangle = length × width**
> **A = *l* × *w***

RULE: INDICATING AREA

Since area represents a two-dimensional space, it is necessary to use *units squared* when expressing an area measurement. An area of 10 ft² is read "ten square feet" and it means the space taken up by 10 squares, each measuring 1 foot by 1 foot. If no unit of measurement is given, write *units²* following an area measurement.

Example

What is the area of this figure?

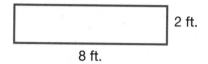

8 ft.

2 ft.

Since the area of a rectangle is *length × width* and you are given both of these dimensions, simply plug them into the formula and write your answer in square feet:

$$A = l \times w$$
$$A = (8 \text{ ft.})(2 \text{ ft.})$$
$$A = 16 \text{ ft.}^2$$

The way to calculate the area of a square is similar to finding the area of a rectangle, but because the side lengths are equal, notice that this formula ends up being the square of one of the side lengths:

Area of a Square = side × side
$$A = s \times s$$
$$A = s^2$$

Questions concerning the area of a square will most commonly ask you to work backward:

Example

Odessa wants to build a square planter box. She has enough seeds to cover an area of 20 square feet. What should the side length of her planter box be?

Use the area formula for a square, plug in the area as 20 square feet, and solve for the side length:

$$A = s^2$$
$$20 = s^2$$

Remember that since s is squared, you need to take the square root of both sides to isolate s:

$$\sqrt{20} = \sqrt{s^2}$$
$$\pm 4.5 \approx s$$

Only the positive solution of 4.5 makes real-world sense for this problem, so the planter box should have 4.5-foot-long sides.

Triangles

Upon a brief inspection, the formula for the area of triangles doesn't seem too much more complicated than the area formula for rectangles:

Area of a Triangle = $\frac{1}{2}$(base × height)
$$A = \frac{1}{2}bh$$

However, the most important aspect when working with triangles is selecting the correct dimension to use as the height. The **height** of a triangle is the perpendicular line that extends from the base to the opposite vertex. Looking at the triangle below, if we let b represent the **base** of the triangle, h would have to be the height, since it extends perpendicularly from base b to the opposite vertex.

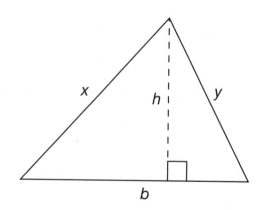

RULE: HEIGHT OF A TRIANGLE

The **height** of a triangle is the perpendicular line extending from the base to the opposite vertex. Two sides can only be considered perpendicular if there is a small square drawn where the sides meet or if this symbol is used in the text of the problem: ⊥. In every triangle, each side can be considered the base, but the height must always be perpendicular to that side and extend to the opposite vertex. The following illustration shows how the height changes as the base changes:

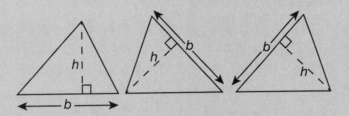

Example
What is the area of the following triangle?

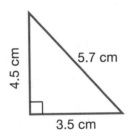

Although you are given all three sides of this triangle, you must be careful as you select the two sides to use as your base and your height. Even though 5.7 looks like it's the bottom or *base* of the triangle, it does not have a perpendicular line extending to the opposite vertex. Since the side labeled 4.5 cm is perpendicular to the side labeled 3.5 cm, use these as your base and height:

$$A = \frac{1}{2}bh$$
$$= (\tfrac{1}{2})(3.5 \text{ cm})(4.5 \text{ cm})$$
$$= (\tfrac{1}{2})(15.75 \text{ cm}^2)$$
$$= 7.875 \text{ cm}^2 \approx 7.88 \text{ cm}^2$$

Trapezoids
A **trapezoid** is a four-sided polygon with one pair of parallel sides. The parallel sides are called *bases* and the *height* of a trapezoid is the perpendicular line that connects the bases. In the following illustration, the two bases are labeled b_1 and b_2 and the height is labeled h:

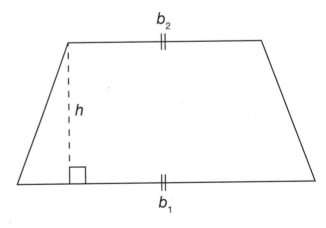

Area of a Trapezoid = $\frac{1}{2}$(height)(base$_1$ + base$_2$)
$A = \frac{1}{2}h(b_1 + b_2)$

The non-parallel sides of a trapezoid are called its *legs*. Sometimes one of the legs will be perpendicular to both the bases and in this case it can be used as the height. (But be careful not to use a non-perpendicular leg of a trapezoid as its height!)

Example

What is the area of the trapezoid pictured below?

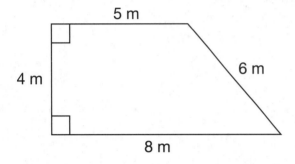

Since the parallel bases measure 8 m and 5 m, these will be our values for b_1 and b_2. Notice that the left side is perpendicular to the base. Use its dimension of 4 m as the height:

$$A = \frac{1}{2}h(b_1 + b_2)$$
$$A = \frac{1}{2}4(5 + 8)$$
$$A = \frac{1}{2}4(13)$$
$$A = 26\ m^2$$

Parallelograms

A **parallelogram** is a four-sided polygon with two pairs of parallel sides. The height of a parallelogram is the perpendicular line that connects the pairs of the sides, called bases. Notice in the illustration that instead of hash marks in the sides, there are arrow markings. These arrow markings indicate that two sides are parallel. The top and bottom sides have just one arrow marking, showing that they are parallel. The left and right sides have two arrow markings indicating that they create another parallel pair.

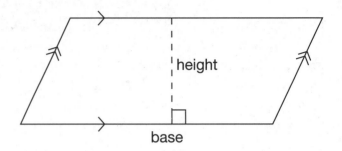

Area of a Parallelogram = (base)(height)
$A = bh$

Circles

The area formula for circles is sometimes confused with the circumference formula, but if you keep in mind that area is always written in *squared units*, that should help you remember that the area formula for circles contains r^2:

Area of a Circle = π(radius)²
$A = \pi r^2$

When using this formula it's important to remember that you must square the radius first, before multiplying it by π. It's also helpful to keep in mind that sometimes you may be given the diameter and you will need to convert that into the radius before using this formula.

Example

Find the area of the following circle if line AB measures 2.75 inches.

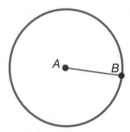

$A = \pi r^2$
$A = \pi(2.75\ \text{in.})^2$
$\quad = 7.5625\ \text{in.}^2$
$\quad = 23.74625\ \text{in.}^2 \approx 23.75\ \text{in.}^2$

Practice

9. The board members of an apartment complex decide that they want to designate 200 ft² of the common space to make a rectangular picnic area with a grill and some tables. If one of the board members suggests that the length of this space be 25 feet long, how wide would the area be?

10. 32 feet of fencing is needed to enclose a square chicken coop. What is the area of this chicken coop?

11. Calculate the area of the triangle:

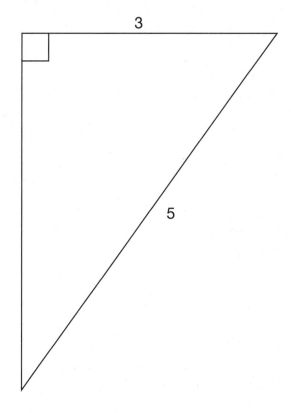

12. What is the area of this circle? _____

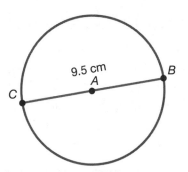

13. Brenda has hired a landscaper to turn her soil-covered backyard into a unique hangout spot. She would like to have a circular deck with a diameter of 10 feet built in the middle of her rectangular backyard, which is 25 feet by 18 feet. Since the yard is soil right now, she is going to purchase sod to go around the deck. If the contractor charges $1.20 per square foot of sod installed, how much will the purchase of the sod cost Brenda? _____

14. Find the missing value in the given trapezoid if its area is 45 cm².

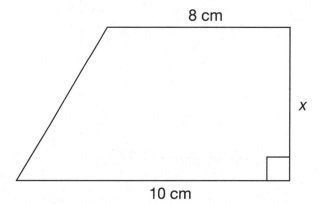

Volume

Volume measures the space within a three-dimensional object. Volume is measured in terms of how many equal sized cubes are needed to completely fill a space. Imagine how many wooden cubes with a side length of 1 inch it would take to fill a shoebox if they were stacked neatly next to each other without gaps. That number of cubes would be the volume of that box in cubic inches, written in^3. The 3 indicates that there are 3 dimensions being considered: length, width, and height, so make sure to always express volume in units *cubed*. Although the formulas for calculating volume will be available to you during the GED® test, in this section you should work on becoming comfortable using them.

GED® QUESTION SNEAK PREVIEW!

Volume questions are likely to appear in the form of word problems:

- *How many cubic feet of water are needed to completely fill a pond that is 18 feet long, 3 feet wide, and 2 feet deep?*

Rectangular and Right Prisms

A prism is a solid three-dimensional object. It has two congruent ends and polygon faces that intersect with the ends at 90-degree angles. The ends, or **bases**, of **rectangular prisms** are rectangles. These are examples of rectangular prisms:

A **right prism** can have bases that are triangles, parallelograms, trapezoids, or any shape of polygon. As long as the two polygon bases are congruent and the other faces are all rectangular, a prism is considered a right prism. Here are some examples:

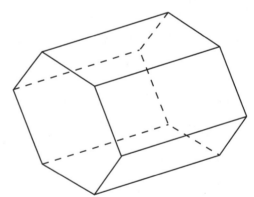

Hexagonal Prism

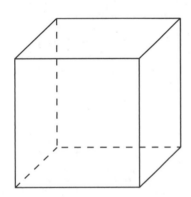

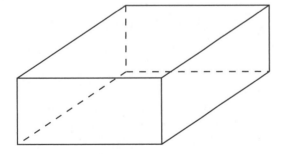

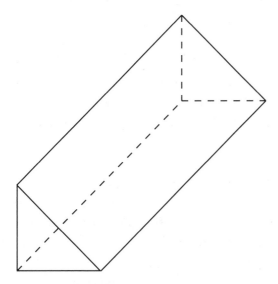

Triangular Prism

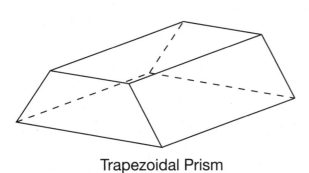

Trapezoidal Prism

Rectangular prisms and right prisms are grouped together in this section because they both use the same formula to calculate volume. To find the volume of these types of prisms, multiply the area of the polygon base by the height of the rectangular face. Pay close attention to the formula you will have access to on test day:

> **Volume of a Rectangular/Right Prism = *Bh***
> *B* = area of the base, *h* = height

Notice that the single variable, *B*, is used to indicate the *area of the base*. Depending on whether the base is a rectangle, triangle, or trapezoid, the formula you will need to first use to calculate *B* will change. Let's take a look at how we'd use this formula with the following rectangular prism.

Example

Find the volume of the rectangular prism pictured:

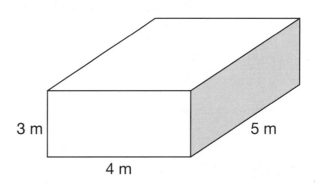

In this case, the two identical bases are the front face and the back face, which are both 4 meters long by 3 meters wide. The height of this prism is 5 meters. Input all of this information into the formula and solve for the volume:

$$\text{Volume} = Bh$$
$$B = \text{area of the base} = length \times width$$
$$B = 4\ m \times 3\ m = 12\ m^2, h = 5\ m$$
$$V = Bh = 12\ m^2 \times 5\ m$$
$$V = 60\ m^3$$

Sometimes you will need to use the volume formula to work backward to solve for a missing dimension:

Example

If the height of a rectangular prism is 3 cm and the length of the prism is 8 cm, find the width in cm if the volume is 96 cm³.

First, write the formula for the volume of a rectangular prism:

$$V = Bh$$

Since this is a rectangular prism, rewrite *B* as *lw* since that is the formula for the area of the rectangular base:

$$V = (lw)h$$

Now we are ready to plug in the given values:

$$96 \text{ cm}^3 = (8 \text{ cm})(3 \text{ cm})w$$
$$96 \text{ cm}^3 = (24 \text{ cm}^2)w$$
$$\frac{96 \text{ cm}^3}{24 \text{ cm}^2} = \frac{(24 \text{ cm}^2)w}{24 \text{ cm}^2}$$
$$4 \text{ cm} = w$$

So, the unknown width of the rectangular prism is 4 cm.

Cylinders

A cylinder is a three-dimensional shape that has two circles as its bases. An empty toilet paper roll is a perfect example of a cylinder. Finding the volume of a cylinder is similar to finding the volume of a prism in that you are multiplying the area of the base by the height. However, in a cylinder, the area of the base is the area of a circle, πr^2.

Volume of a Cylinder $= \pi r^2 h$
r = radius, h = height

If you are given the diameter you will need to divide it by 2, to find the radius before using the formula.

Example

Ari is designing a cylindrical fish tank that will be 1 foot tall. If he wants this tank to hold 3 cubic feet of water, how wide should the tank be?

This is a case where we know what the volume is, but we are asked to find the diameter. Therefore, we must work backward to solve for the only unknown in the formula, the radius, and then double it to answer the question.

$$V = \pi r^2 h$$
$$3 \text{ ft}^3 = \pi r^2 (1 \text{ ft})$$
$$\frac{3 \text{ ft}^3}{3.14 \text{ ft}} = \frac{(3.14 \text{ ft})r^2}{3.14 \text{ ft}}$$
$$0.96 \text{ ft} \approx r^2$$
$$\sqrt{0.96} = \sqrt{r^2}$$

$$\pm 0.98 = r$$
$$\pm 1 \text{ ft} \approx r$$

The negative solution does not make real-world sense in this question, so the radius should be 1 foot wide. This means that the diameter should be 2 feet wide.

Right Circular Cone

In the last section, we pictured an empty toilet paper roll as our example of a cylinder. Now for our right circular cone, let's picture a pointy ice cream cone that has the same height and width as the empty toilet paper roll:

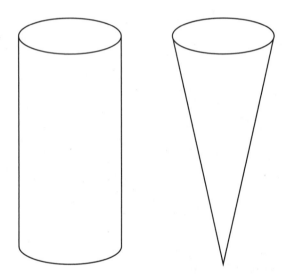

Can you imagine that the cone would hold about $\frac{1}{3}$ the amount of liquid or ice cream as the cylinder would hold? Notice that the following formula for the volume of a right circular cone is $\frac{1}{3}$ the volume of a cylinder, which was $\pi r^2 h$.

Volume of a Right Circular Cone $= \frac{1}{3}\pi r^2 h$
r = radius, h = height

The *height* in a cone is the line that goes from the tip of the cone to the *center* of the circle on top. Read the information in the following box carefully to make sure you don't use the wrong information in this volume formula!

DON'T DO THIS!

Sometimes the GED® test will give you information that you do not need, which makes the question more challenging. With right circular cones, you might be tempted to use the slant height of the cone in the volume formula, but make sure the height you are selecting goes from the tip of the cone to the *center* of the circle. Let's look at how to set up the volume calculations for the following cone using the formula $V = \frac{1}{3}\pi r^2 h$.

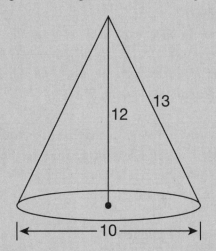

NO! Volume $\neq \frac{1}{3}\pi(10)^2(13)$. This is incorrect because the *diameter* is 10 and not the radius. This is also incorrect because 13 is the *slant height* of the cone and not the *height*.

YES . . . Volume $= \frac{1}{3}\pi(5)^2(12)$. This is correct since the diameter was cut in half to get a radius of 5, and the correct height of 12 was used.

Right Pyramids

You just learned that the formula for the volume for a cone is $\frac{1}{3}$ of the formula for the volume of a cylinder. You might not be entirely surprised now to hear that the volume for a right pyramid is $\frac{1}{3}$ the volume of a right prism! Look at this illustration of a pyramid inside a right prism to gain a visual understanding of how a pyramid's volume relates to a prism's volume:

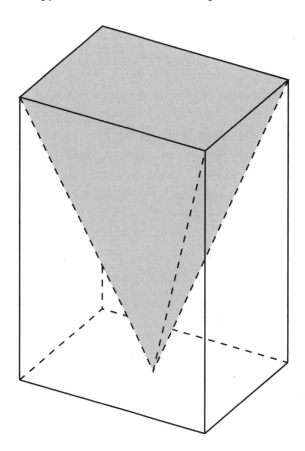

Volume of a Right Pyramid $= \frac{1}{3}Bh$
B = area of the base, h = height

Example

Find the height of this pyramid if the volume is 54 mm³.

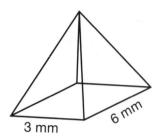

3 mm   6 mm

We know the volume is 54 mm³. We can find B by multiplying the length × width of the rectangular base:

$$B = (6 \text{ mm})(3 \text{ mm})$$
$$= 18 \text{ mm}^2$$

Return to the formula and substitute the known values to find the height:

$$V = \tfrac{1}{3}Bh$$
$$54 \text{ mm}^3 = \tfrac{1}{3}(18 \text{ mm}^2)(h)$$
$$(3)(54 \text{ mm}^3) = (3)\tfrac{1}{3}(18 \text{ mm}^2)(h)$$
$$162 \text{ mm}^3 = (18 \text{ mm}^2)h$$
$$9 \text{ mm} = h$$

Spheres

The formula for the volume of spheres also involves a fractional factor, but the factor is $\tfrac{4}{3}$ instead of $\tfrac{1}{3}$:

Volume of a Sphere $= \tfrac{4}{3}\pi r^3$
r = radius

NOTE: WORKING WITH π

You may see questions on the GED® test that ask you to express your answer "in terms of π." This means that instead of using 3.14 as the value for π in your calculations, you can simply leave π as part of your final answer. Sometimes you might not receive this explicit instruction, but all the answer choices will have π in them. Therefore, it's a good idea to skim the answer choices before beginning a question that requires the use of π.

Example

Mia received a huge round helium balloon that is 3 feet wide—it almost lifts her off the ground! How many cubic feet of helium were needed to fill this balloon? Express your answer in terms of π.

First, we need to recognize that the information provided refers to the diameter and not to the radius. Since the diameter is 3 feet, use a radius of $\tfrac{3}{2}$ foot in the volume formula for spheres.

Volume of a Sphere $= \tfrac{4}{3}\pi r^3$
$$V = \tfrac{4}{3}\pi(\tfrac{3}{2})^3$$

Although it looks odd to have a fraction cubed, cubing $\tfrac{3}{2}$ is actually a lot easier to calculate than cubing 1.5:

$$V = \tfrac{4}{3}\pi(\tfrac{3}{2})(\tfrac{3}{2})(\tfrac{3}{2})$$
$$V = \tfrac{4}{3}\pi(\tfrac{27}{8})$$
$$V = \tfrac{9}{2}\pi$$

So, the balloon needed $\tfrac{9}{2}\pi$ cubic feet of helium.

In a question like this, notice that it is also a good idea to check to see if your answers are in decimal or fraction form, since cubing $\frac{3}{2}$ in this question was much easier than cubing its decimal equivalent.

Practice

15. What is the volume of the following right prism in terms of x?

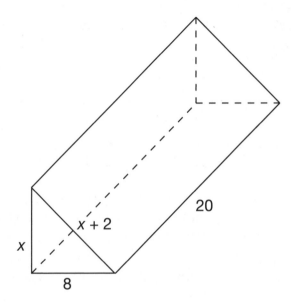

16. Find the volume of the cylinder shown here.

_____

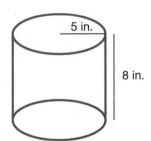

17. An empty cylindrical can has a height of 4 inches and a base with a radius of 1.5 inches. Melanie fills the can with water. What is the volume of the water Melanie pours into the can?
   a. 5.5π cubic inches
   b. 6π cubic inches
   c. 6.5π cubic inches
   d. 9π cubic inches

18. Find the radius of the cone if the volume is 148 cm³ and the height is 7 cm. Round your answer to the nearest tenth of a centimeter.

_____

19. The Great Pyramid at Giza has a square base with a side length of approximately 750 feet. The height of the pyramid is approximately 450 feet tall. How many cubic feet of stone were used to build this pyramid?

20. Find the volume of a sphere with a diameter of 11 inches. Round your final answer to the nearest whole inch.

21. These two boxes have the same volume
($V = l \times w \times h$). Find the length of the missing
side on box B.

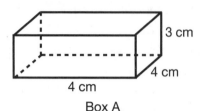

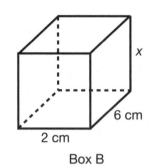

Box A

Box B

a. 3
b. 4
c. 5
d. 6

Surface Area

You learned earlier that **area** refers to the measurement inside a two-dimensional figure, such as how much paint would be needed to cover a single wall. Now you will learn how to calculate the area of the entire surface of a three-dimensional figure, such as how much paint would be needed to paint all the sides of a cube. When we measure the combined areas of all the sides of a three-dimensional object, we are finding its **surface area**. You will have access to the following surface area formulas provided, so spend your time here learning how to use them.

Rectangular and Right Prisms

You will notice some new variables in the formulas for surface area. For example, the formula for calculating the surface area of rectangular and right prisms requires you to find the perimeter of the base, which is represented by p:

**Surface Area of Rectangular/Right Prisms =
$ph + 2B$**
B = Area of base, p = perimeter of base,
h = height of prism

Example
Calculate the surface area of the following rectangular prism:

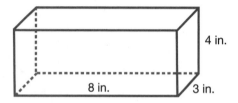

There are three unknown values you need to find in order to solve for the surface area: p, h, and B.

p = the perimeter of the base = 8 in. + 8 in. +
   3 in. + 3 in. = 22 in.
h = the height of the prism = 4 in.
B = the area of the base = (8 in.)(3 in.) = 24 in.^{2}

Substitute these values into the formula to get

$SA = (22 \text{ in.})(4 \text{ in.}) + 2(24 \text{ in.}^2)$
$= 88 \text{ in.}^2 + 48 \text{ in.}^2$
$= 136 \text{ in.}^2$

So, the surface area of the figure is 136 square inches.

Cylinders
The formula for the surface area of cylinders might look complicated, but it is more straightforward than the right prism surface area formula since it just requires you to plug in the height and radius.

Surface Area of a Cylinder = $2\pi rh + 2\pi r^2$
r = radius, h = height of prism

Example

Find the height of a cylinder that is 20 cm wide if it has a surface area of 1,256 cm².

Since the surface area is given, this will be a problem that requires us to work backward. First determine that since the cylinder is 20 cm wide, its radius is 10 cm. Plug this into r in the equation and use 1,256 cm² as the surface area:

Surface Area of a Cylinder = $2\pi rh + 2\pi r^2$

$1{,}256 = 2\pi 10h + 2\pi 10^2$

$1{,}256 = 20\pi h + 200\pi$

$1{,}256 = 62.8h + 628$

$\underline{-628 \qquad\qquad -628}$

$\frac{628}{62.8} = \frac{62.8h}{62.8}$

$10 = h$

So, the height of this cylinder is 10 cm.

Right Circular Cones

Recall that when learning how to calculate the volume of right circular cones earlier in this chapter, we warned against mistakenly using *slant height* as the *height*. When determining the surface area of right circular cones the slant height is used instead of the height. In the following illustration, s represents the slant height:

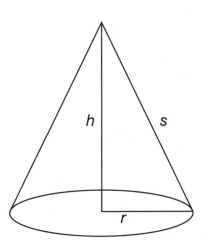

Surface Area of a Cone = $\pi rs + \pi r^2$

r = radius, s = slant height

Example

Represent the surface area of the following cone in terms of π.

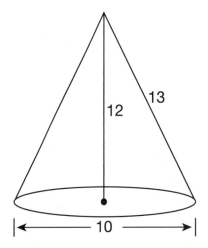

Identify that $r = 5$ and $s = 13$ and use these values in the surface area formula:

Surface Area of a Cone = $\pi rs + \pi r^2$

$SA = \pi(5)(13) + \pi(5)^2$

$SA = 65\pi + 25\pi$

$SA = 90\pi$

So, the surface area of this cone in terms of π is 90π units².

Right Pyramid

Since the perimeter of the base is required to find the surface area of a right prism, it might not surprise you to learn that you will also need to find the perimeter of the base to calculate the surface area of a pyramid. Notice also, that similar to cones, the *slant height* is used in calculating the surface area of pyramids, rather than the *height*:

Surface Area of a Pyramid = $\frac{1}{2}ps + B$

p = perimeter of the base, s = slant height,

B = area of the base

Note: You will only be working with right pyramids on the GED® test. In right pyramids all the slant heights are congruent, so you just need to be given one of these dimensions.

Example

Calculate the surface area of the following pyramid to the nearest tenth:

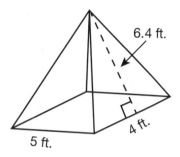

6.4 ft.

4 ft.

5 ft.

We can see that the slant length, *s*, is 6.4 ft. To find *p* and *B*, we need to do a few calculations.

p = the perimeter of base B = 5 ft. + 5 ft. + 4 ft. + 4 ft. = 18 ft.

B = the area of the base = (5 ft.)(4 ft.) = 20 ft.^{2}

Substitute these values into the formula:

$SA = \frac{1}{2}ps + B$

$SA = \frac{1}{2}(18 \text{ ft.})(6.4 \text{ ft.}) + 20 \text{ ft.}^2$

$\quad = 57.6 \text{ ft.}^2 + 20 \text{ ft.}^2$

$\quad = 77.6 \text{ ft.}^2$

So, the surface area of the pyramid is 77.6 square feet.

Spheres

Notice that the formula for the surface area of a sphere is 4 times the area of a circle:

Surface Area of a Sphere = $4\pi r^2$

r = radius

Example

If the surface area of a bouncy ball is 113.04 *square inches, what is the radius of the bouncy ball?*

In this problem, the surface area is given, and we need to solve for the radius. Substitute the value of the surface area into the formula and solve for *r*.

$SA = 4\pi r^2$

$113.04 \text{ in.}^2 = 4\pi r^2$

$\frac{113.04 \text{ in.}^2}{4(3.14)} = \frac{4(3.14)r^2}{4(3.14)}$

$9 \text{ in.}^2 = r^2$

$\sqrt{9 \text{ in.}^2} = \sqrt{r^2}$

$3 \text{ in.} = r$

So, the radius of the sphere is 3 in.

Practice

22. Find the surface area of the following prism:

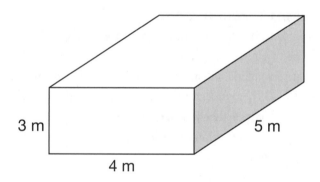

3 m

4 m

5 m

23. Find the surface area of a cylinder that has a diameter of 12 cm and a height of 20 cm.

_____

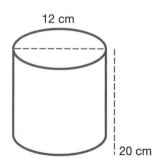

12 cm

20 cm

24. Find the surface area of the cone. Represent your answer in terms of π.

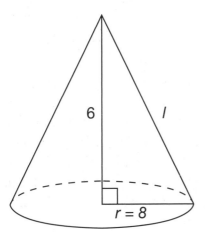

25. The Great Pyramid at Giza has a square base with a side length of approximately 750 feet. The height of the pyramid is approximately 450 feet tall and the slant height is approximately 783 feet. What is the surface area of the sides of the Great Pyramid that are exposed to sunlight and oxygen (excluding the base)?

26. Calculate the surface area of a marble that has a diameter of 14 mm. Round your answer to the nearest tenth.

Composite Shapes

You have so far been working with a set body of basic shapes—rectangles, squares, circles, etc. **Composite shapes** are shapes that can be broken down into two or more basic shapes.

Calculating with Composite Shapes
The GED® test may ask you to find the perimeter, area, volume, and surface area of composite shapes. In order to tackle these types of problems, you will not be able to simply apply a single formula. Instead,

you will need to think analytically about how to break the composite shape down into basic shapes, or parts of basic shapes, and how to apply the correct formulas.

Example
John James High School is making a basketball court in its outdoor playground. The following is a picture of the key they wish to make in front of each net. If Beto needs to tape around the perimeter of the key so that he can paint it accurately, how many feet of tape does he need?

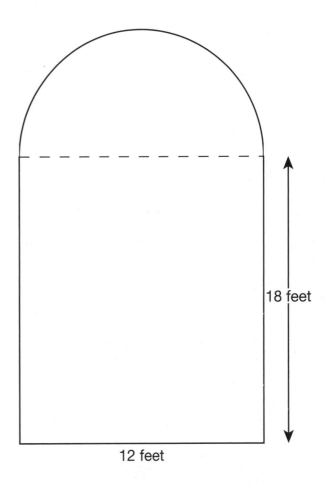

Since we are being asked to find the perimeter of this shape, we first need to identify that this is a rectangle on the bottom with half of a circle on top. We will not count the top part of the rectangle (where the dotted line is) so this dimension will need to be omitted from the calculations. Label all the sides carefully:

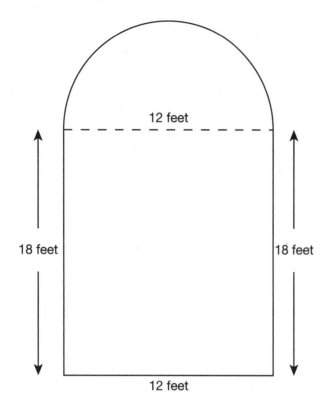

Calculate the partial perimeter of the rectangular base:

Partial Perimeter of Rectangular Base = 18 + 12 + 18 = 48 ft

Since the top of the rectangle has been labeled 12 feet, it should be apparent that the semicircle has a radius of 6 feet. Calculate the circumference of the circular top and then cut it in half to find the circumference of just half the circle:

Circumference of Circular Top = πr^2
$C = \pi 6^2$
$C = 36\pi \approx 113$ ft

The semicircle top of the figure has a circumference of $\frac{113}{2} = 56.5$ ft

Combine the partial perimeter and half circle circumference to get the complete perimeter of the

basketball key: 48 ft. + 56.5 ft. = 104.5 ft. Beto will need about 105 feet of tape to tape off the perimeter of the key.

Working with Negative Space

Negative space is the remaining space after part of a space has been removed. The GED® test may test your ability to find the area, volume, or surface area of negative space in a composite shape. In order to tackle a task like this, first calculate the area, volume, or surface area of the entire space. Then calculate the area, volume, or surface area for the space that is to be excluded and subtract that from the calculation for the entire space.

Example

The following is an illustration of the back patio being constructed at a restaurant. The patio will be 35 feet long by 15 feet wide and will have a round fountain with an 8-foot diameter. Determine the number of square feet of tile needed to cover the patio that is represented by the shaded area as follows:

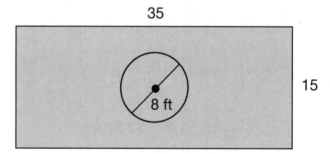

Since this illustration represents a circle within a rectangle, you will need to first find the area of the rectangle:

Area of Rectangle = lw
Area of Rectangle = (35)(15) = 525 ft.^{2}

Next, find the area of the circle, which has a diameter of 8 feet and a radius of 4 feet.

Area of Circle = πr^2

Area of Circle = $\pi(4^2) \approx 50$ ft.^{2}

Lastly, subtract the two areas:

Area to be tiled = (Area of Rectangle) –
(Area of Circle)

Area to be tiled = (525 ft.^{2}) – (50 ft.^{2}) = 475 ft.^{2}

So, this restaurant will need to buy 475 ft.^{2} of tile for the patio.

Scale Factor

Scale factors are used in a variety of settings: maps, floor plans, and building blueprints are a few examples. To reproduce the floor plan of an office building on a size of paper that is manageable, scale factors are necessary. If every shape and dimension of the floor plan is reduced by the same factor, the drawing will be an accurate reproduction of the spatial dimensions.

Reducing and Enlarging

A scale factor is a factor that multiplies a collection of terms by the same factor, in order to change all the values at a constant rate. For example, if 4 and $10x$ are increased by a scale factor of 3, the values would become 12 and $30x$. When we multiply things by a scale factor that is less than 1, we are shrinking the size of the original terms. For example, 4 and $10x$ would become 2 and $5x$ after being multiplied by a scale factor of $\frac{1}{2}$.

The most straightforward question you'll be asked to perform with scale factor is to reproduce a shape using a scale factor:

Example

What are the new dimensions of this triangle if it is increased by a scale factor of 4?

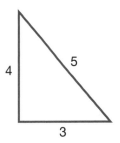

Multiply each side length by 4 to get the new dimensions:

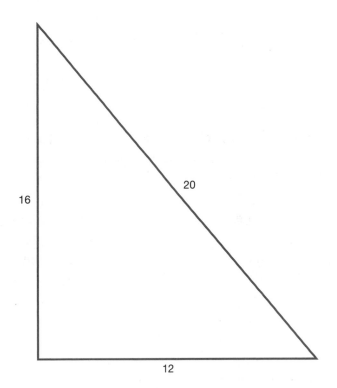

Solving for Scale Factors

Problems involving scale factor may require you to identify the scale factor that has been used by giving you an original and a scaled dimension:

Example

A map of the Grand Canyon shows a 2-mile road as 10 millimeters. What is the scale of the map?

Since the map is a scaled down version of the Grand Canyon, we are being asked to determine how much distance each mm represents on the map. In order to do this, set it up as a ratio comparing miles to mm:

$$\frac{\text{miles}}{\text{mm}} = \frac{2 \text{ miles}}{10 \text{ mm}}$$

Now simplify this ratio so that the denominator reads "1 mm." To do this, we will divide the numerator and denominator both by 10:

$$\frac{\text{miles}}{\text{mm}} = \frac{2 \text{ miles} \div 10}{10 \text{ mm} \div 10} = \frac{0.2 \text{ miles}}{1 \text{ mm}}$$

This means that the map is using a scale of 1 mm : 0.2 miles.

Using Proportions with Scale Factors

Other times you will be given a scale problem with 3 dimensions and you will have to solve for the missing fourth dimension. In order to do this, set up a proportion by carefully keeping like items in the same parts of your ratios. (For a review on setting up proportions and solving them with cross products, refer to Chapter 5.)

Example

A map is drawn such that 2.5 inches on the map represents a true distance of 10 miles. If two cities are 7.1 inches apart on the map, then to the nearest tenth of a mile, what is the true distance between the two cities?

Set up a proportion that shows two ratios that each compare inches to miles. If m is the number of miles between the two cities, then the following proportion represents the information given:

$$\frac{\text{inches}}{\text{miles}} = \frac{2.5 \text{ inches}}{10 \text{ miles}} = \frac{7.1 \text{ inches}}{m \text{ miles}}$$

Now use cross products to solve for m:

$$10(7.1) = 2.5(m)$$
$$71 = 2.5m$$
$$m = 28.4 \text{ miles}$$

Practice

27. On a given map, Grand Rapids, Michigan, is 27 centimeters from Akron, Ohio. If these two cities are 324 miles apart, what is the scale factor being used on this map?

Summary

After completing this chapter, you'll have a thorough understanding of how to work with perimeter, area, volume, and surface area for myriad shapes. You'll have also learned how to handle these types of calculations with compound shapes, as well as how to combine your geometry and algebra skills to working with scale. Use the given reference sheet as you practice the following questions, which are similar to what you will see on your GED® test, and see how well you understand the many formulas presented.

Geometry Foundations Review

1. The length of a side of square *A* is twice as long as a side of square *B*. How much larger is the area of square *A*?
a. 4 times larger
b. 2 times larger
c. 8 times larger
d. 0.5 times larger

2. The perimeter of a square is 24 inches. What is its area?
a. 144 in.^{2}
b. 576 in.^{2}
c. 16 in.^{2}
d. 36 in.^{2}

3. Find the area of the shaded region in this figure. Remember that the formula for the area of a circle is $A = \pi r^2$.

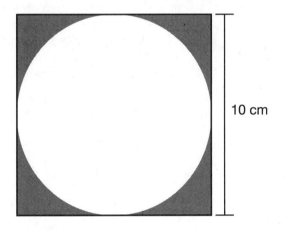

10 cm

a. 100 cm^2
b. 78.5 cm^2
c. 21.5 cm^2
d. 178.5 cm^2

4. The surface area of a cube is given by the expression $6s^2$, where *s* is the length of an edge. If a cube has a surface area of 54 square centimeters, what is the length of its edges?
a. 3 cm
b. 6 cm
c. 9 cm
d. 81 cm

5. If the edge of a cube is 10 cm and the edge of a second cube is 8 cm, what is the difference in the surface areas of the two cubes?
a. 216 cm^2
b. 384 cm^2
c. 488 cm^2
d. 600 cm^2

6. Find the area of the following shape.

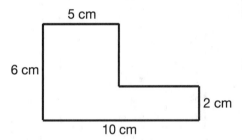

a. 60 cm^2
b. 23 cm^2
c. 50 cm^2
d. 40 cm^2

7. The distance between Hamden and Milford is 1.75 cm on a map. In real life, Hamden is 105 km from Milford. On the same map, Cheshire is 2 cm from Mystic. How far is Cheshire from Mystic in real life?
a. 210 km
b. 3.5 km
c. 120 km
d. 107 km

8. The following figure is a regular octagon. What is the perimeter of the figure? _____

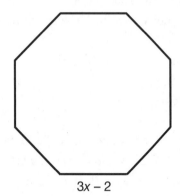

$3x - 2$

9. Jim works for a carpeting company. His next job is to recarpet an office space. According to the diagram, how many square feet of carpet does he need to complete this job?

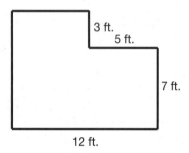

3 ft.
5 ft.
7 ft.
12 ft.

a. 44 ft.^{2}
b. 105 ft.^{2}
c. 120 ft.^{2}
d. 144 ft.^{2}

10. The perimeter of a rectangle is 64. The length of one of the sides of the rectangle is 8. Find the lengths of the other three sides.
a. 10, 23, 23
b. 8, 22, 22
c. 8, 24, 24
d. 12, 22, 22

11. If the following figure is increased by a scale factor of 4, what will the perimeter of the new shape be? _____

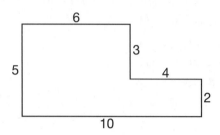

6
3
5
4
2
10

12. Keyonna is reading the plans for an apartment she is decorating. She uses her ruler to see that in the drawing the kitchen measures 2 inches wide by 3.5 inches long. What is the area in square feet of the kitchen?

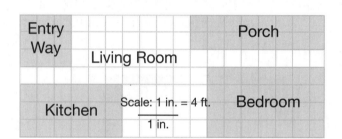

Entry Way
Porch
Living Room
Kitchen
Scale: 1 in. = 4 ft.
1 in.
Bedroom

Answers and Explanations

Chapter Practice

1. **16 in.**

   Perimeter = $2l + 2w$
   $$= 2(5 \text{ in.}) + 2(3 \text{ in.})$$
   $$= 10 \text{ in.} + 6 \text{ in.}$$
   $$= 16 \text{ in.}$$

2. **$s = 16$.** You are given the value for the perimeter of a square, so plug that into the square perimeter formula and solve for the side length:

   Perimeter = $4s$
   $$64 = 4s$$
   $$\frac{64}{4} = s, \text{ so } s = 16.$$

3. **10.4.** Again, substitute the given values into the Pythagorean theorem. Note that the missing side is *not* the hypotenuse, so let's use a as the missing side length.

   $$a^2 + 6^2 = 12^2$$
   $$a^2 + 36 = 144$$
   $$a^2 + 36 = 144$$
   $$\underline{\quad -36 \quad -36 \quad}$$
   $$\sqrt{a^2} = \sqrt{108}$$
   $$a \approx 10.4$$

4. **17 minutes.** First, let's find how long it takes Reggie to get to work using his normal route. He bikes 10 miles north and then 8 miles east for a total of 18 miles. If he bikes 18 mph, how long does it take him to get to work? Use the *distance* = *rate* × *time* formula and solve for time:

   $$d = rt$$
   $$18 = 18t$$
   $$\frac{18}{18} = \frac{18t}{18}$$
   $$1 \text{ hour} = t$$

   It takes Reggie 1 hour to get to work using his normal route. To find how long it would take him to get to work using the bike path, we need to find its distance using the Pythagorean theorem.

   $$a^2 + b^2 = c^2$$

   $$10^2 + 8^2 = c^2$$
   $$100 + 64 = c^2$$
   $$164 = c^2$$
   $$\sqrt{164} = \sqrt{c^2}$$
   $$12.8 = c$$

   The distance from Reggie's house to work using the bike path is 12.8 miles. Use the distance formula to find how long it will take Reggie to get to work using the bike path:

   $$d = rt$$
   $$12.8 = 18t$$
   $$0.71 \text{ hours} = t$$

   To find how much faster Reggie would get to work using the bike path versus his normal route, subtract the two times.

   0.71 of an hour = $(0.71)(60) = 42.6 \approx 43$ minutes

   60 minutes − 43 minutes = 17 minutes

   So, if Reggie uses the bike path to get to work, he will get to work 17 minutes faster than by taking his normal route.

5. **d.** A regular octagon has eight sides, all of which are the same length. The perimeter is the length around the outside of a figure. If all eight sides of 4 cm each are added up, the perimeter is 32 cm.

6. **\$937.50.** Since the garden is in the shape of a regular pentagon, the side lengths are equivalent. Therefore, the perimeter is

   $$p = 5(15 \text{ ft.})$$
   $$= 75 \text{ ft.}$$

   The cost of the fencing is \$12.50 per foot, so the total cost to fence in the community garden is

   $$C = (75 \text{ ft.})(\$12.50)$$
   $$= \$937.50$$

7. Use the circumference formula with diameter since that is the dimension provided:

   Circumference = πd
   $$C = \pi(14)$$
   $$C = 43.96, \text{ which rounds to 44 inches of ribbon.}$$

8. **20 mm.** Remember, the equation for circumference is $C = 2\pi r$ or $C = \pi d$. Since we need to find the diameter to solve this problem, let's use $C = \pi d$.

$$C = \pi d$$
$$62.8 \text{ mm} = (3.14)d$$
$$20 \text{ mm} = d$$

9. **8 feet.** Since this is going to be a rectangular picnic area, use the area formula for a rectangle, plug in the given dimensions for the area and the length, and work backward to see what the width would be:

$$\text{Area} = length \times width$$
$$200 = 25 \times w$$
$$\frac{200}{25} = w, \text{ so the width would be 8 feet. That}$$
would be a pretty narrow picnic area!

10. **64 ft².** The first piece of information is the perimeter of the coop, since 32 feet *encloses* the coop. Once we find the side length, we can use that in the area formula for a square. Since we are working with a square coop, use the perimeter formula for a square, plug in the perimeter of 32 feet, and work backward to obtain the side length:

$$\text{Perimeter} = 4s$$
$$32 = 4s$$

So, $s = 8$. Now, plug this into the area formula:

$$\text{Area} = s^2$$
$$\text{Area} = 8^2 = 64 \text{ ft}^2$$

11. **6 units².** In order to calculate the area of any triangle, you must have the dimensions of its *base* and *height*, which are perpendicular to one another. You have two perpendicular sides in this triangle, but do not know both of their dimensions. You are given the hypotenuse of 5 and one of the legs of 3, so use this information to solve for the missing leg in the Pythagorean theorem:

$$a^2 + b^2 = c^2$$
$$(3)^2 + b^2 = (5)^2$$
$$9 + b^2 = 25$$
$$b^2 = 16$$
$$b = 4$$

Now that you know that the two perpendicular sides measure 3 units and 4 units, you can put them into the area formula for triangles:

$$\text{A} = \tfrac{1}{2}bh = \tfrac{1}{2}(4)(3) = 6 \text{ units}^2$$

12. **70.85 cm².** The equation for the area of a circle requires the value of the radius, r. However, in this problem we have been given the diameter. Remember, $d = 2r$, so $\frac{d}{2} = r$.

$$\frac{9.5 \text{ cm}}{2} = 4.75 \text{ cm} = r$$

Now, use the equation for area:

$$A = \pi r^2$$
$$= \pi \,(4.75 \text{ cm})^2$$
$$= 22.5626\pi \text{ cm}^2$$
$$= 70.84625 \text{ cm}^2 \approx 70.85 \text{ cm}^2$$

13. **$445.80.** To find the cost of the sod, we need to find the area of the rectangular yard and then subtract the area of the circular deck.

$$A_{\text{yard}} = \text{length} \times \text{width}$$
$$= (25 \text{ ft.})(18 \text{ ft.})$$
$$= 450 \text{ ft.}^2$$
$$A_{\text{deck}} = \pi r^2$$
$$= (3.14)(5 \text{ ft.})^2$$
$$= 78.5 \text{ ft.}^2$$
$$A_{\text{sod}} = 450 \text{ ft.}^2 - 78.5 \text{ ft.}^2$$
$$= 371.5 \text{ ft.}^2$$

Last, multiply the sodded area by the cost per square foot to get the total cost of installation of sod.

$$\text{Cost} = (371.5)(\$1.20)$$
$$= \$445.80$$

14. **5 cm.** Since we are given the area of both the bases, we can put these into the trapezoid area formula and work backward to find the height, x:

$$A = \tfrac{1}{2}h(b_1 + b_2)$$
$$45 = \tfrac{1}{2}h(10 + 8)$$
$$45 = \tfrac{1}{2}h(18)$$
$$45 = h(9), \text{ so } h = 5 \text{ cm}$$

15. **$80x$ cm^3.** Starting with the formula for the volume of a right prism $V = Bh$, we see that we have to first find the area of the base, B. Since this is a triangular prism, find B by using the formula for the area of a triangle:

Area of Triangle Base $= \tfrac{1}{2}bh$

The base and height must be perpendicular to each other, so we will use the triangle's side lengths of 8 and x in the formula:

Area of Triangle Base $= \tfrac{1}{2}(8 \text{ cm})(x \text{ cm}) = 4x \text{ cm}^2$

Use $4x$ cm^2 as the B in the volume formula and use 20 cm as the height of the prism, h:

$$V = Bh$$
$$V = (4x \text{ cm}^2)(20 \text{ cm})$$
$$V = 80x \text{ cm}^3$$

16. **628 in^3.** The formula for the volume of a cylinder is $V = \pi r^2 h$. From the diagram, we can see that the height of the cylinder is 8 inches and the radius is 5 inches. Substitute these values into the formula to solve for the volume.

$$V = \pi r^2 h$$
$$= \pi(5 \text{ in.})^2(8 \text{ in.})$$
$$= \pi(25 \text{ in.}^2)(8 \text{ in.})$$
$$= (3.14)(200 \text{ in.}^3)$$
$$= 628 \text{ in.}^3$$

17. **d.** Use the formula $V = \pi r^2 h$, where r is the radius of the base and h is the height of the cylinder: $\pi(1.5^2)4 = \pi \times 2.25 \times 4$, which equals 9π.

18. **4.5 cm.** The formula for the volume of a cone is $V = \tfrac{1}{3}r^2 h$. We have values for V and h:

$$V = 148 \text{ cm}^3$$
$$h = 7 \text{ cm}$$

We then substitute these values into the formula, giving us the following equation with r as the only unknown:

$$V = \tfrac{1}{3}r^2 h$$
$$148 \text{ cm}^3 = \tfrac{1}{3}\pi r^2(7 \text{ cm})$$
$$(3)148 \text{ cm}^3 = (3)\tfrac{1}{3}\pi r^2(7 \text{ cm})$$
$$444 \text{ cm}^3 = (3.14)(7 \text{ cm})r^2$$
$$\frac{444 \text{ cm}^3}{(3.14)(7 \text{ cm})} = \frac{(3.14)(7 \text{ cm})r^2}{(3.14)(7 \text{ cm})}$$
$$20.2 \text{ cm}^2 = r^2$$
$$\sqrt{20.2 \text{ cm}^2} = \sqrt{r^2}$$
$$4.5 \text{ cm} = r \text{ (rounded to 10th)}$$

Rounded to the nearest tenth of a centimeter, the volume is 4.5 cm.

19. **84,375,000 ft^3.** The volume formula for the area of a right pyramid requires that we first find the area of the rectangular base of the pyramid. Since the Great Pyramid at Giza has a square base with a side length of approximately 750, multiply 750 by itself to get the area of the square base: $750 \times 750 = 562{,}500$ ft^2. Since we know the height of the Great Pyramid is approximately 450 feet, we are ready to use the volume formula for pyramids:

Volume of a Right Pyramid $= \tfrac{1}{3}Bh$

Volume $= \tfrac{1}{3}(562{,}500 \text{ ft}^2)(450 \text{ ft})$

$$V = 84{,}375{,}000 \text{ ft}^3$$

So, the equivalent of over 84 million 1-foot cubes were used to construct the Great Pyramid!

20. 697 in³. The diameter of 11 inches informs us that the radius is half of 11 inches; the radius is, therefore, 5.5 inches. Substitute this value back into the formula to find the volume of the sphere:

$V = \frac{4}{3}\pi r^3$

$V = \frac{4}{3}\pi(5.5 \text{ in.})^3$

$V = \frac{4}{3}\pi(166.375 \text{ in.}^3)$

$V = \frac{4}{3}(522.4175 \text{ in.}^3)$

$V = 696.5566 \text{ in.}^3$

$V \approx 697 \text{ in.}^3$

21. b. The volume of box A is 48 cm³ ($4 \times 4 \times 3 = 48$). The volume of box B must also be 48 cm³, so the three dimensions of box B will multiply to 48. Solve the equation for x:

$2 \times 6 \times x = 48$

$12x = 48$

$x = 4$

22. 94 m². Start with the formula for the surface area of a rectangular prism: $ph + 2B$.

First calculate B, the area of the base, by multiplying the length by the width: $(3 \text{ m})(4 \text{ m}) = 12$ m². $B = 12$ m². Next, calculate, p = perimeter of base. Perimeter = $2l + 2w = 2(4 \text{ m}) + 2(3 \text{ m}) = 14$ m. The height of the prism is 5 m. Plug these three measurements into the surface area formula:

$SA = ph + 2B$

$SA = (14 \text{ m})(5 \text{ m}) + 2(12 \text{ m}^2)$

$SA = 70 \text{ m}^2 + 24 \text{ m}^2$

$SA = 94 \text{ m}^2$

23. 979.68 cm³. To substitute values into the formula $SA = 2\pi rh + 2\pi r^2$, we first need to identify the radius. The problem states that the diameter is 12 cm. The radius is half of the diameter, so the radius = 6 cm.

Now, substitute values into the formula for the surface area of a cylinder:

$SA = 2\pi rh + 2\pi r^2$

$= 2\pi(6 \text{ cm})(20 \text{ cm}) + 2\pi(6 \text{ cm})^2$

$= 2\pi(120 \text{ cm}^2) + 2\pi(36 \text{ cm}^2)$

$= 2(3.14)(120 \text{ cm}^2) + 2(3.14)(36 \text{ cm}^2)$

$= 753.6 \text{ cm}^2 + 226.08 \text{ cm}^2$

$= 979.68 \text{ cm}^2$

So, the surface area of the cylinder is 979.68 cm².

24. 144π cm². Remember that the surface area for a cone requires the slant height of the cone. Here, the slant height is labeled as l but we can solve for l by using 6 and 8 as the legs in the Pythagorean theorem:

$a^2 + b^2 = c^2$

$6^2 + 8^2 = c^2$

$36 + 64 = c^2$

$100 = c^2$

$c = 10$, so we now know that the slant height = 10.

Now use the surface area formula, keeping the final answer in terms of π:

Surface Area of a Cone = $\pi rs + \pi r^2$

$SA = \pi(8 \text{ cm})(10 \text{ cm}) + \pi(8 \text{ cm})^2$

$SA = 80\pi \text{ cm}^2 + 64\pi \text{ cm}^2$

$SA = 144\pi \text{ cm}^2$

25. **1,174,500 ft².** Consider the formula for the surface area of a pyramid: $\frac{1}{2}ps + B$. Since this question asks for the surface area of the sides of the Great Pyramid that are exposed to sunlight and oxygen, excluding the base, that means that we can just ignore the final part of the formula, the "$+ B$," since that represents the area of the base. Since the side lengths of the square base are 750 feet, we can determine that the perimeter of the base = 4(750 ft) = 3,000 ft. Put this and the slant height of 783 feet into the shortened formula:

Surface Area without the base = $\frac{1}{2}ps$

SA = $\frac{1}{2}$(3,000)(783) = 1,174,500 ft²

26. **615.4 mm².** First, cut the diameter in half to get a radius of 7 to use in the surface area formula:

SA = $4\pi r^2$

SA = $4\pi(7)^2$

SA = 196π mm² = 615.44 mm²

27. **1 cm : 12 miles.** We are being asked to determine how many miles each cm represents on the map. In order to do this, set it up as a ratio that compares miles to centimeters:

$$\frac{\text{miles}}{\text{cm}} = \frac{324\text{ miles}}{27\text{ cm}}$$

Now, simplify the ratio we created so the denominator reads "1 cm." To do this, divide the numerator and denominator both by 27:

$$\frac{\text{miles}}{\text{cm}} = \frac{324\text{ miles} \div 27}{10\text{ cm} \div 27} = \frac{12\text{ miles}}{1\text{ cm}}$$

This scale can be written 1 cm : 12 miles.

Geometry Foundation Review

1. a. *Method 1:*

Choose a few examples of the given situation and analyze the results.

Example: If square A has sides of length 10, square B will have sides of length 5.

Then, the area of A is 100, and the area of B is 25.

The area of square A is 4 times the area of square B.

Example: If square A has sides of length 6, square B will have sides of length 3.

Then, the area of A is 36, and the area of B is 9.

The area of square A is 4 times the area of square B.

If you continue to try other situations, the results will be the same. The area of the larger square is always 4 times the area of the smaller square.

Method 2:

The situation can be analyzed algebraically.

Length of side of square $B = x$

Length of side of square $A = 2x$

Area of square $B = x^2$

Area of square $A = (2x)^2 = 4x^2$

$4x^2$ is 4 times x^2.

2. d. All sides of a square are the same length. The perimeter is the distance around the outside of a figure. You can divide the perimeter of a square by 4 to determine the length of a side: $24 \div 4 = 6$. Therefore, the length of a side of the square is 6 inches. To find the area, multiply the length by the width. In a square, the length and the width are the same. In this case, they are both 6 inches, and $6 \times 6 = 36$. The area of the square is 36 square inches.

3. c. To find the area of the shaded region, subtract the area of the circle from the area of the square. Notice that the radius of the circle is half the length of one side of the square. Therefore, the radius is 5 cm.

Area of square: $10 \times 10 = 100$ cm^2

Area of circle: $3.14 \times 5^2 = 3.14 \times 25 = 78.5$ cm^2

Area of shaded region: square − circle

$100 - 78.5 = 21.5$ cm^2

The area of the shaded region is 21.5 cm^2.

4. a. The surface area of the cube is the product of 6 and a number squared. So, you can write the equation $6s^2 = 54$ and solve it for s:

$6s^2 = 54$

$s^2 = 9$

Because $s^2 = 9$, each edge measures 3 cm.

5. a. Since each edge of a cube has the same length, the area of each face is s^2. There are six faces on every cube, so the surface area of a cube is $6s^2$.

The surface area of the first cube is:

$6(10^2) = 6(100) = 600$

The surface area of the second cube is:

$6(8^2) = 6(64) = 384$

The difference between the two surface areas is:

$600 - 384 = 216$

6. d. Find the lengths of the two missing sides. The horizontal missing side can be found by subtracting the 5 cm side from the 10 cm side. Therefore, the horizontal missing side is 5 cm.

The vertical missing side can be found by subtracting the 2 cm side from the 6 cm side across from it. Therefore, the vertical missing side is 4 cm.

The following drawing shows all of the sides.

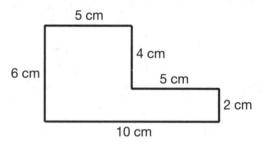

The shape can be broken into two rectangles (two possible ways are shown).

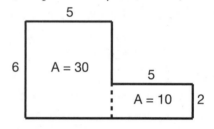

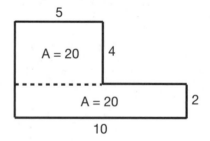

In the first figure, the area of the larger rectangle is 30 cm^2, and the smaller rectangle is 10 cm^2. The total area is 40 cm^2 (30 + 10). In the second figure, the area of the top rectangle is 20 cm^2, and the area of the bottom rectangle is 20 cm^2. The total area is 40 cm^2 (20 + 20).

7. c.

Method 1:

Set up a proportion comparing the distance in real life and the distance on the map:

$$\frac{\text{map Hamden to Milford}}{\text{real-life Hamden to Milford}} = \frac{\text{map Cheshire to Mystic}}{\text{real-life Cheshire to Mystic}}$$

$$\frac{1.75x}{105} = \frac{2}{x}$$

$$1.75x = 210$$

$$x = 120$$

The distance between Cheshire and Mystic is 120 km.

Method 2:

Determine the number of kilometers represented by 1 cm on the map: $105 \div 1.75 = 60$.

Each centimeter on the map is 60 km in real life.

The distance from Cheshire to Mystic on the map is 2 cm. Since $2 \times 60 = 120$, the distance from Cheshire to Mystic in real life is 120 km.

8. **$24x - 16$.** The perimeter of a figure is the distance around it. For a regular octagon (whose sides all have equal lengths), the perimeter can be found by multiplying the length of one side times the total number of sides. According to the diagram, the length of each side of the octagon is $3x - 2$, so the perimeter is $8(3x - 2)$. Be sure to distribute the 8 to both terms inside the parentheses so as not to arrive at $24x - 2$, which is incorrect.

When the 8 is distributed correctly,

$$P = 8(3x) - 8(2)$$
$$= 24x - 16$$

9. b. There are two ways to solve this problem. The first is to divide the room into two rectangles, calculate the area of each, and add the areas together. There are two ways to divide the room into two rectangles:

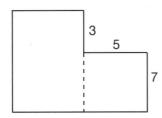 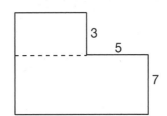

In the diagram on the left, one rectangle has a length of 5 feet and a width of 7 feet and the other has a length of 10 feet, resulting from $7 + 3$, and a width of 7, resulting from $12 - 5$. To find the area of the room, set up the following equation: (5 ft.)(7 ft.) + (10 ft.)(7 ft.). This yields 105 ft.^{2} as the area of the room.

In the diagram on the right, one rectangle has a length of 12 feet and a width of 7 feet and the other has a length of 7 feet, resulting from $12 - 5$, and a width of 3 feet. To find the area of the room, set up the following equation: (12 ft.)(7 ft.) + (7 ft.)(3 ft.). This also yields 105 ft.^{2} as the area of the room.

The second method is to calculate the area of the big rectangle—(12 ft.)(10 ft.)—and subtract the area of the part of the room that is missing—(5 ft.)(3 ft.). This equation reads 120 ft.^{2} – 15 ft.^{2} = 105 square feet.

10. c. The perimeter of a figure is the distance around the figure. Since the opposite sides of a rectangle are equal, and one side of this rectangle has a length of 8, another side also has a length of 8. The set of numbers whose sum is 64 when added to 8 is 8 + 8 + 24 + 24 = 64.

11. 120 units. The perimeter of the original compound shape will be the sum of all of its sides: 5 + 6 + 3 + 4 + 2 + 10 = 30 units. When a figure is increased by a scale factor, all of its individual sides are multiplied by that factor. Therefore, all of the sides here would be multiplied by 4 in order to determine the side lengths and associated perimeter of the new figure: 5(4) + 6(4) + 3(4) + 4(4) + 2(4) + 10(4) = 120 units.

A shortcut to finding the new perimeter after using a scale factor of 4 is to simply multiply the original perimeter by 4: 30 units × 4 = 120 units.

12. 112 ft². Since each inch in the drawing represents 4 feet in real life, multiply the scaled dimensions by 4 to get their real-life dimensions:

2 inch width × 4 feet = 8 feet wide

3.5 inch length × 4 feet = 14 feet long

Since the kitchen is 8 feet wide by 14 feet long, multiply these two dimensions to get the area: 8 feet × 14 feet = 112 ft.²

11 ▶ STATISTICS AND PROBABILITY

The field of statistics revolves around data—how it is collected, organized, and manipulated so that we can interpret information to make predictions. Understanding measures of central tendency, like mean, median, and mode, are important for being able to summarize a "typical" number from of a body of information. Probability is an application of statistics aimed at predicting the likelihood of events happening. Lastly, counting methods help us calculate the number of different groupings that are possible from a given set of options. Answers and explanations for all practice questions are at the end of the chapter.

This chapter covers:

- Mean, median, and mode of data sets
- Weighted averages
- Simple probability
- Compound probability
- Permutations
- Combinations

Measures of Central Tendencies

Measures of central tendencies are a way to talk about a data set using one number to summarize the data. As you will see throughout this book, many sections of the GED® test will require you to understand how to both find and interpret these measurements

in order to understand data presented, whether it be something like scientific experiment data, information in a social studies population table, or a straightforward math problem. There are four different measures of central tendencies that you will need to know how to calculate: mean, median, mode, and weighted average.

GED® QUESTION SNEAK PREVIEW!

With measures of central tendency, it is critical that you keep all the different definitions straight so that you can accurately respond to questions:

■ *List the mean, median, and mode of the data set:*

{3, 9, 6, 4, 8, 3, 6, 4, 7, 10, 1, 20, 4}

Calculating Mean

The **mean** is the same as the *average* of a data set. To find the mean, add up all the numbers in the data set and then divide by the total number of data values. For instance, if there are five numbers in a set of data, add up the five numbers and then divide by 5. If there are 12 numbers in a set of data, add up the 12 numbers and then divide by 12.

$$\frac{\text{sum of data values}}{\text{total \# of data values}} = \text{average (mean)}$$

Take the following scenario as an example.

Example
Bobbi buys groceries every two weeks. Her last four grocery bills were $75.30, $59.65, $72.92, and $67.20. What is the average amount of money Bobbi spends every two weeks on groceries?

To find the average amount Bobbi spends on groceries, add up the four grocery bills and then divide by 4:

$$\$75.30 + \$59.65 + \$72.92 + \$67.20 = \$275.07$$
$$\frac{\$275.07}{4} \approx \$68.77$$

So on average, Bobbi spent $68.77 every two weeks on groceries.

Working Backward with a Given Mean
Sometimes you will be given the mean and asked to work backward to determine the value of one or some of the data points. In this case, you will need to assign algebraic expressions such as x or $2x$ to the unknowns that you can solve for after substituting all the given information into an equation. These are popular questions on the GED® test, so make sure you understand the methods used in the following problem:

Example

Ms. Reba keeps track of how many students drop in Monday through Thursday to study for their GED® test. Usually, students come in groups. Here is a chart of last week's numbers:

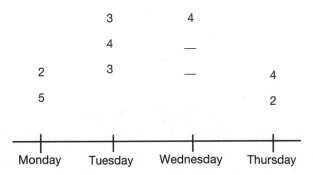

Ms. Reba forgot to write down two numbers for Wednesday. If the average number of students per group was 3.2, and one of the unknown groups had one more student than the other unknown group, what is the average number of students who came to see Ms. Reba each day?

First, interpret the words into math. We know that one of the Wednesday groups had one more student than the other. Assign x to one of the groups and $x + 1$ to the other.

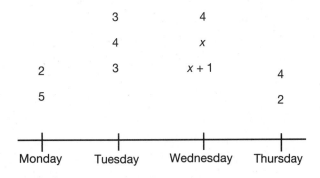

Next, add up all the numbers, divide by 10, and set it equal to the known average of 3.2:

$$\frac{2 + 5 + 3 + 4 + 3 + 4 + x + x + 1 + 4 + 2}{10} = 3.2$$

$$\frac{28 + 2x}{10} = 3.2$$

$$\frac{10(28 + 2x)}{10} = (3.2)10$$

$$28 + 2x = 32$$

$$\underline{-28 \qquad -28}$$

$$2x = 4$$

$$\frac{2x}{2} = \frac{4}{2}$$

$$x = 2$$

So now we know that one of the Wednesday groups had 2 students (x) and the other had 3 students ($x + 1$).

Finally, we can calculate the average number of students Ms. Reba saw per day:

Monday: $2 + 5 = 7$
Tuesday: $3 + 4 + 3 = 10$
Wednesday: $4 + 2 + 3 = 9$
Thursday: $4 + 2 = 6$

$$\frac{7 + 10 + 9 + 6}{4} = 8 \text{ students per day}$$

Median

The **median** of a data set is the middle value of a chronological set of data. To understand the concept, consider this question:

What is the median of the following data values?
63, 72, 54, 69, 66

To find the median, first rewrite the numbers in chronological order:

54, 63, 66, 69, 72

The median is 66 because there are two numbers to the left and two numbers to the right of it.

54, 63, $\boxed{66}$, 69, 72

Finding the median is very simple when there is an odd number of values. However, what if there is an even number of values? In that case, take the average of the middle two numbers.

What is the median of the following data values?

23, 10, 31, 5, 39, 33

First, rewrite the values in chronological order:

5, 10, 23, 31, 33, 39

The two middle numbers are 23 and 31:

5, 10, $\boxed{23, 31,}$ 33, 39

The median of this data set is the average of 23 and 31:

$$\frac{23 + 31}{2} = 27$$

GED® TEST MATHEMATICS FORMULA SHEET

The definitions for mean and median will be on the formula sheet on test day. Although this might make it tempting to not learn how to calculate these measures by heart, it will be important to not waste valuable testing time looking for these definitions.

- **mean** is equal to the total of the values of a data set, divided by the number of elements in the data set
- **median** is the middle value in an odd number of ordered values of a data set, or the mean of the two middle values in an even number of ordered values in a data set

---

Mode

The **mode** of a data set is the number that appears most often. It is important to know that a data set does not always have one and only one mode. Here are the three different possibilities for the mode of a data set:

One mode: A set of numbers has just one mode if only one number appears more often than all the others.

Example: 9, 3, 4, 2, 9, 8, 9, 2, 9, 4
Solution: The mode of the data set is 9, since it appears more than any other number in the data set.

No mode: If there is no number that appears more than the other numbers, then the data set has no mode.

Example: 3, 4, 2, 9, 8, 11, 2, 1, 5, 4
Solution: This data has no mode since no number occurs more than the rest of the numbers.

More than one mode: If more than one number appears more frequently than the remainder of the data, then there can be multiple modes.

Example: 3, 4, 7, 9, 8, 5, 2, 8, 9, 4, 3, 9, 4, 8
Solution: The modes of the data set are 4, 8, and 9 since each of these numbers appear equally more than the rest. (Notice that even though 3 occurs twice, it is not a mode, since the 4, 8, and 9 each occurred three times.)

VOCABULARY: MEAN, MEDIAN, MODE

Use these simple tricks to keep the definitions of *mean*, *median*, and *mode* straight!

Mean: "I can't believe that *mean* teacher gave me such a bad average in his class."

Median: This word sounds like medium, which is in the middle of sizes small and large. "I'd like to order a size *median*, please . . . I mean a *medium*!"

Mode: This word sounds most similar to the word *most*, so remember that the *mode* of a data set is the one that happens the *most*.

Weighted Average

A weighted average is the average found with terms that have different "weight" or importance within a data set. For example, a teacher might count the final exam score more than a quiz score. There are two cases when you will calculate a weighted average instead of a standard average, or mean. We will explain each case separately.

Case 1: Quantities of different values

Data presented in tables or graphics often requires a weighted average. This is because each of the values in the table is not just occurring once, but is occurring a different number of times than other values. For example, the following table shows the number of times Brooke ran a given number of miles over the course of a month:

NUMBER OF MILES RUN	FREQUENCY OVER A MONTH
2	9
4	8
6	5
8	3

How do we calculate the average number of miles Brooke ran each day? First, figure out how many times she went running that month by adding the values in the frequency column: Brooke ran 25 times over the course of the month ($9 + 8 + 5 + 3 = 25$).

Next, since Brooke ran 2 miles 9 times, 4 miles 8 times, 6 miles 5 times, and 8 miles 3 times, it's helpful to understand that we could write her 25 different run mileages out as such:

2, 2, 2, 2, 2, 2, 2, 2, 2, 4, 4, 4, 4, 4, 4, 4, 4, 6, 6, 6, 6, 6, 8, 8, and 8

9 runs of 2 miles   8 runs of 4 miles   5 runs of 6 miles   3 runs of 8 miles

While you could find the average by summing these 25 mileages and dividing that by 25, it's more efficient to find the weighted average by multiplying the number of runs by the miles run to obtain subtotals:

- Add a third column to the table, and label it "Miles Subtotal."
- Fill it in with the products of (# of miles) × (frequency):

NUMBER OF MILES RUN	FREQUENCY OVER A MONTH	MILES SUBTOTAL (# OF MILES) × (FREQUENCY):
2	9	$2 \times 9 = 18$ miles
4	8	$4 \times 8 = 32$ miles
6	5	$6 \times 5 = 30$ miles
8	3	$8 \times 3 = 24$ miles
	Total # of Runs = 25	Total Miles = 104

- Add the four products in the right column to get a total mileage for the month of 104 miles.
- Since Brooke ran 25 days, divide this by 25 to find the weighted average:

Average Mileage: $\frac{104}{25} = 4.16$ miles per run.

Sometimes you will get questions that present data that involves frequency in a word problem format. For instance, "In June, Brooke ran 2 miles on 9 days, 4 miles on 8 days, 6 miles on 5 days, and 8 miles on 3 days. Determine the average distance Brooke covered each day she ran." In this case, the solution would still involve a weighted average by first multiplying the *frequencies* by the *values*.

DON'T DO THIS!

When students see tables of numbers, they are always tempted to just add up values in the left column (or right column) and divide by the number of rows in the table. This is almost always wrong because data expressed in tables or charts is often presenting the frequency that each value is occurring. Since *frequency* means the *number of times*, you need to find a weighted average, and not just the mean whenever frequency information is given.

Case 2: Weighting Values with Percentages

Final grade scores for classes are often computed using a weighted average, since a teacher may want to count certain types of assignments (like tests), more than other types of assignments (like homework). Let's work through this question step by step to illustrate how to calculate weighted averages when data is weighted with percents:

Myrna teaches at a university. When assigning final grades, she gives each type of assignment a different level of importance. The collection of Myrna's assignments are worth a total of 100 points.

ASSIGNMENT	NUMBER	PERCENTAGE
Tests	4	70%
Homework	6	10%
Final exam	1	20%

Chad's scores are shown in the next table. What is his final grade for the course?

ASSIGNMENT	SCORES
Tests	78, 85, 88, 90
Homework	87, 90, 83, 93, 91, 90
Final exam	82

Although all of the given information might make this question seem overwhelming at first, solving it isn't as bad as you might fear. There are just three steps to follow:

Step 1: Find the basic average for each of the three different types of assignments:

Test Average $= \frac{78 + 85 + 88 + 90}{4} = 85.25$

Homework Average $= \frac{87 + 90 + 83 + 93 + 91 + 90}{6} = 89$

Final Exam $= 82$ (only one score here)

Step 2: Multiply the percentage weight associated with each type of assignment by the average for that assignment. This will determine how many points each assignment type will contribute to Chad's final grade. (Remember to turn the weighting percentages into decimals before multiplying)!

Test Average (70%) $= 85.25 \times 0.70 = 59.675$

Homework Average (10%) $= 89 \times 0.10 = 8.9$

Final Exam (20%) $= 82 \times 0.20 = 16.4$

Step 3: Add the values together from Step 2 to get Chad's final grade for the course.

Final Grade = 59.675 + 8.9 + 16.4 = 84.975

So, Chad's final grade was 85%.

Practice

1. Mr. Carlo's class is learning about frogs. He took his class to the pond to observe them in their environment. One of the assignments was for each of the 14 students to measure one frog in order to calculate an average length. The average length was 2.35 inches. Using the following data, calculate the length of the 14th frog.

FROG	LENGTH (IN.)
1	2.3
2	1.9
3	2.0
4	2.4
5	2.5
6	3.0
7	2.7
8	2.6
9	2.5
10	2.4
11	2.3
12	2.1
13	2.4
14	x

2. Holly is competing in 4 different gymnastics events and wants to get an average score of 9.2. Her vault score was 8.9, her uneven bar score was 8.6, and her balance beam score was 9.5. What must she score on her floor routine to achieve her goal of a 9.2 average for the meet?

3. Ash is a real estate agent trying to sell a home in a neighborhood she's not familiar with. She wants to be able to tell the family she's representing what the median home price is for the local sales that have occurred over the past month. The past month, housing sold for the following prices: $280,000, $200,000, $424,000, $390,000, $280,000, and $320,000. Find the median house price.

For questions 4 and 5, identify the modes of the data sets.

4. 45, 56, 23, 45, 12, 56, 38 _____

5. 100, 96, 94, 101, 106 _____

For questions 6–7, use the following bar graph, which illustrates the number of pencils students had in their bags when arriving to an art class.

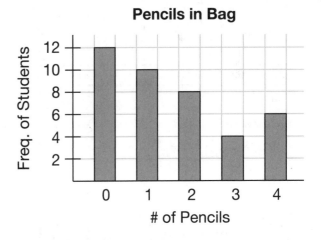

Pencils in Bag

6. What was the median number of pencils that students had in their bags when they arrived to art class?

7. What number of pencils represents the mode?

8. The following table illustrates the number of miles each student travels one way to get to Ms. Bradley's viola class. Find the average number of miles that Ms. Bradley's students travel one way:

NUMBER OF MILES TRAVELED ONE WAY	NUMBER OF STUDENTS
1	4
2	3
3	5
4	6
5	3

9. Stephanie owns a bakery and is purchasing supplies. If she buys 20 cans of peaches for $6.50 each, and 28 cans of cherries for $9 each, what is the average price per can of fruit?

10. Mr. Gallespie is a high-school science teacher. The weight he gives each assignment is listed in the following table.

ASSIGNMENT	NUMBER	PERCENTAGE
Tests	5	60%
Homework	5	15%
Experiments	4	25%

Looking at Katie's scores, calculate her final grade for the semester to the nearest hundredth of a percentage point. _____

ASSIGNMENT	SCORES (OUT OF 100)
Tests	93, 97, 88, 91, 95
Homework	90, 99, 100, 95, 96
Experiments	89, 90, 85, 92

Probability

Chances are, you've heard someone exclaim, "What is the probability of that happening?" The **probability** of something happening is the likelihood of an event happening. For example, if you live in the desert, the probability of it raining in June is very low. There are two types of probability: simple and compound. **Simple probability** refers to a single event happening, like rolling a 1 with a die on a single toss. **Compound probability** refers to the likelihood of more than one condition being met, like rolling a 1 with a die and then getting tails when flipping a coin.

GED® QUESTION SNEAK PREVIEW!

An understanding of probabilities will help you understand the likelihood of events in the real world happening, and will help you answer questions like this on the GED® test.

- *If there are 17 men and 23 women being considered to sit on a jury, what is the probability that all 12 jurors selected will be men?*

Simple Probability

Simple probability is the ratio of the number of desirable outcomes to the total number of possible outcomes. Probability is usually represented as a fraction in lowest terms or sometimes as a percentage. The notation used to express the probability of an event happening is $P(E)$, which means the probability of event E happening:

$$\text{Probability of Event Happening} = \frac{\text{\# of desirable events}}{\text{total \# of possible events}}$$

Notice that the numerator states a plural "# of desirable events" even though the probability is for a singular "Event Happening." There can sometimes be more than one outcome that would result in a "success." For example, if you wanted your birthday to fall on a weekend, there would be two desirable events that would satisfy that wish: Saturday and Sunday. Since the total number of possible events includes all 7 days of the week, we write the following:

$$P(\text{Weekend Birthday}) = \frac{\text{\# of weekend days}}{\text{total \# of days in week}} = \frac{2}{7}$$

The probability $\frac{2}{7}$ can also be converted to 29%. (For a review on converting fractions to percents, review Chapter 5.) Although you might hear the weather report say "there's a 40% chance of rain," the GED® test will generally ask for probability answers to be fractions in lowest terms.

RULE: SIMPLE PROBABILITY

The **probability** of an event happening is the ratio of the number of desirable outcomes to the total number of possible outcomes and is written in shorthand $P(E)$:

$$P(E) = \frac{\text{\# of desirable events}}{\text{total \# of possible events}}$$

Let's review a few common simple probabilities that might appear on test day. Being familiar with these probabilities will help you solve the compound probability questions presented in the next section.

Example

What is the probability of getting heads when you flip a coin?

There are 2 possibilities when flipping a coin: heads or tails:

$$P(\text{Heads}) = \frac{\text{\# of heads}}{\text{total \# of sides}} = \frac{1}{2}$$

Notice that the probability of getting tails with the single flip of a coin is also $\frac{1}{2}$. Now let's look at some probabilities involving a standard 6-sided die.

Example

What is the probability of getting a 5 when rolling one die?

There are 6 possibilities of all the faces of the die, and this probability is asking for just one of them, a 5:

$$P(\text{Rolling a 5}) = \frac{\text{\# of desirable events}}{\text{total \# of possible events}} = \frac{1}{6}$$

Just because there are 6 possible events when rolling a die, don't expect for the denominator to always be a 6 when answering probability questions. Remember to reduce your answer to lowest terms:

Example

What is the probability of getting a prime number when rolling one die?

There are still 6 possible events, but now we need to be more careful as we determine the number of desired events. There are 3 prime numbers up to 6: 2, 3, and 5 are all prime. (Recall that a *prime number* is any number *greater than* 1 that has no factors other than 1 and itself.) Now we'll represent our findings using the probability formula:

$$P(\text{Rolling a prime}) = \frac{\text{\# of desirable events}}{\text{total \# of possible events}} = \frac{3}{6}$$
$$= \frac{1}{2}$$

So, there is a $\frac{1}{2}$ probability that each time you roll the die you will get a prime number. This means that for every two rolls, it is likely that you will get a prime number once. Now that you have simple probability down, let's move on to compound probability.

Compound Probability

Compound probability refers to the likeliness of two unrelated events happening. The compound probability of two events happening is found by multiplying the probability of the first event by the probability of the second event. Compound probability is written like this:

$$P(A \text{ and } B) = P(A) \times P(B)$$

Let's answer a common compound probability question:

Example

What is the probability of flipping a coin two times and getting heads twice in a row?

Since the probability of getting heads is $\frac{1}{2}$, use this in the compound probability formula:

$$P(\text{Heads and Heads}) = P(\text{Heads}) \times P(\text{Heads})$$
$$P(\text{Heads and Heads}) = \frac{1}{2} \times \frac{1}{2} = \frac{1}{4}$$

So, the probability of getting two heads when a coin is flipped twice is $\frac{1}{4}$ or 25%.

The compound probability formula can be expanded to investigate the probability of more than two independent events happening:

Example

What is the probability of rolling a die three times and getting 1, 2, 3 in that order?

The probability of getting a single number on a die is $\frac{1}{6}$; use this in the compound probability formula:

$$P(1 \text{ then } 2 \text{ then } 3) = P(1) \times P(2) \times P(3)$$
$$P(1 \text{ then } 2 \text{ then } 3) = \frac{1}{6} \times \frac{1}{6} \times \frac{1}{6} = \frac{1}{216}$$

So, the probability of getting 1, 2, and 3 when rolling a die three times is $\frac{1}{216}$, which is less than a 1% chance!

RULE: COMPOUND PROBABILITY

The **compound probability** of two or more events happening is the product of each of the individual events' simple probabilities:

- $P(A, B, \text{ and } C) = P(A) \times P(B) \times P(C)$

Probability with and without Replacement

Sometimes in compound probability problems, the likeliness of a second event is influenced by the previous event. Let's say there are 5 Starburst candies in your pocket: pink, red, yellow, orange, and green. You really want the red one! The probability that the first Starburst you pick will be the red one is $\frac{1}{5}$. If instead you pick an orange one (and eat it), now there are just 4 Starbursts in your pocket. Therefore, the probability of the second candy you pick being the red one will be $\frac{1}{4}$. In math context, this method (of not putting the first item back) is usually referred to as "without replacement." On the GED® test, look for it to explicitly state in the question that an item is put back before the next event occurs (that's called "with replacement"). If it doesn't state that, be careful when determining the probability of the second event.

Calculated without Replacement Probabilities

In order to calculate the compound probability of the two events happening, always assume that the desired first event happened when you are reassessing the probability of the second event happening. Let's look at how to do this with the following question:

Example

Suppose there are 8 tennis balls in a container: 5 green and 3 red. What is the probability of pulling out a green ball on the first try and then a red ball on the second try, without adding the first ball back into the container?

First, we know that we are going to be answering the question with this formula:

$$P(\text{Green then Red}) = P(\text{Green}) \times P(\text{then Red})$$

Notice that we used the term "then Red" above instead of "and Red." This language is used to remind us that we need to consider the probability of the second event carefully since the first event is influencing its likelihood.

Since there are 5 green tennis balls and 8 total tennis balls, the probability of pulling a green tennis ball out first is $\frac{5}{8}$. So $P(\text{Green}) = \frac{5}{8}$.

Now $P(\text{then Red})$ must be calculated with the assumption that the first ball picked was green. Now there are still 3 red tennis balls, but there are only 7 tennis balls in total since the first ball wasn't replaced. Therefore, $P(\text{then Red}) = \frac{3}{7}$.

Put both of these probabilities into the compound probability formula:

$$P(\text{Green then Red}) = P(\text{Green}) \times P(\text{then Red})$$
$$P(\text{Green then Red}) = \frac{5}{8} \times \frac{3}{7} = \frac{15}{56}$$

$\frac{15}{56}$ is a little awkward to mentally make sense out of, so it can be helpful to also consider this as approximately 27% probability.

Practice

Use the following information to answer questions 11–13.

Every student in the senior class at Alexa Mae prep school gets assigned a unique 3-digit ID number between 000 and 999. All of the ID numbers have 3 digits, so ID number 7 is written 007 and ID number 16 is written 016. Once a number is assigned to a student, it cannot be assigned again.

11. Delilah is obsessed with π, so she is hoping to get the number 314. What is the probability that she'll get 314 as her ID number?

12. Skye loves triple repeating digits and doesn't care which number it is, as long as her ID number is three of the same number. What is the probability that Skye will get a repeating digit ID number?

13. Lulu has her heart set on any number with consecutive digits counting up or down, such as 123 and 876. What is the probability she'll get a number she wants?

Use the bar graph from questions 6 and 7 in the previous section to answer questions 14 and 15:

14. If a student is chosen at random from the class, what is the probability that he or she will have exactly 3 pencils?

15. If a student is chosen at random from the class, what is the probability that he or she will have at least 1 pencil?

16. The probability of pulling a fork out of a drawer is $\frac{4}{13}$. A utensil is removed and placed on the counter. Then another utensil is removed from the same drawer. What is the probability that both utensils drawn from the drawer were forks?

17. Wyeth would like to pick 3 students from his class of 30 students to be class leaders. His class has 16 girls and 14 boys. If Wyeth picks these students one at a time, without replacement, what is the probability that all three class leaders are boys? Express your answer as a percentage to the nearest whole number.

Counting Techniques

In the context of statistics and probability, the phrase "counting techniques" refers to the methods used to calculate the number of different groupings that can be made out of a given set of options. The counting techniques featured on the GED® test are permutations and combinations.

GED® QUESTION SNEAK PREVIEW!

You may find that counting techniques are useful skills to have outside of your GED® test.

- *Mara has packed 4 shirts, 3 skirts, and 2 pairs of shoes for her vacation. How many unique outfits, consisting of one skirt, one shirt, and one pair of shoes, can she wear with the clothing she packed?*

Fundamental Counting Principle

The fundamental counting principle gives us a way to compute the total number of ways different independent events can happen together. It states that if there are *m* possible outcomes for a first event and *n* possible outcomes for a second event, then the total number of possible outcomes for the two events together is the product of *m* × *n*. This principle holds true for as many number of different events there are. Let's look at how we apply this principle to solve the previous Sneak Preview question:

Example

Mara has packed 4 shirts, 3 skirts, and 2 pairs of shoes for her vacation. How many unique outfits, consisting of one skirt, one shirt, and one pair of shoes, can she wear with the clothing she packed?

A problem like this is straightforward to solve since the different number of outcomes for each event are clearly stated: Mara has 4 shirts, 3 shirts, and 2 pairs of shoes. Multiply these numbers together to calculate the total number or unique outfits she can make:

$$4 \times 3 \times 2 = 24 \text{ outfits}$$

It is sometimes helpful to draw out a counting problem with tree illustrations, like the following one. If you look at this diagram, you should be able to understand *why* this principle works. Notice that just with shirts and skirts alone, Mara has 12 different outfits she could make. Then each of those 12 outfits has 2 different shoe options to choose from, so the 12 shirt-and-skirt outfits will become 24 shirt-skirt-and-shoe outfits:

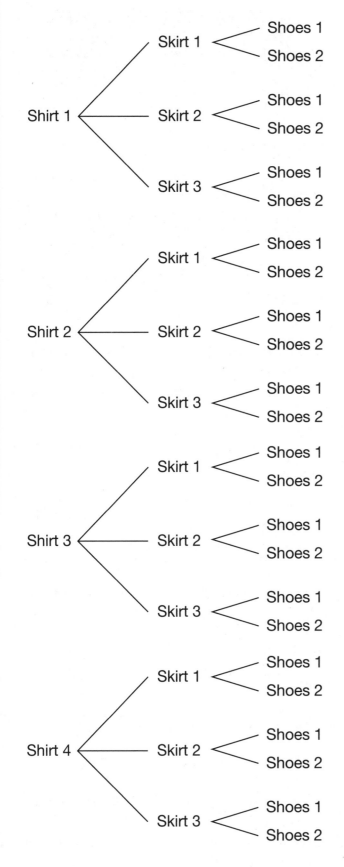

The previous problem illustrated the fundamental counting principle when the items were completely independent. Similar to the probability problems we did "without replacement," sometimes we use the fundamental counting principle when the first event impacts the number of possibilities for the second event, as you will see in the following example.

Example

There are 15 different teams competing in a science fair. How many different ways can 1st, 2nd, 3rd, and 4th place trophies be awarded?

There are 15 different teams and only four trophies. How many teams could win first place? 15

After the first place trophy is given out, how many teams could win second place? 14

After second place is handed out, how many teams could win third place? 13

After third place is handed out, how many teams could win fourth place? 12

Notice that after each event, the number of possibilities for the next event decreases by 1. So now we have 4 events happening and the number of possibilities for each event to occur is 15, 14, 13, and then 12. The fundamental principle of counting says to multiply these numbers together to determine the total number of possible combinations for the 15 teams to win the four trophies:

$$15 \times 14 \times 13 \times 12 = 32{,}760$$

Notice that in this final calculation we started with the total number of options and then reduced that option by one each time. We did this 4 times since there were 4 teams being chosen. This same technique can by applied to similar problems. For example, if 3 students out of 10 students were going to be selected at random to prepare a snack, prepare a beverage, and wash dishes, the number of possible ways students could be assigned these tasks would be found by multiplying $10 \times 9 \times 8$.

Factorials

Before moving on to the formulas for permutations and combinations, it is necessary that you know how to work with factorials. A **factorial** is a mathematical instruction to multiply a number n by every positive integer less than n. Factorials are indicated with an exclamation point and "$n!$" is said "n factorial." Here is the definition of $n!$:

$$n! = n(n-1)(n-2)(n-3)\ldots(1)$$

Although you will not get a question like "What is the value of 5!" on your GED® test, you need to understand factorial notation to use the formulas presented in the next two sections. You should feel comfortable converting 5! in the following way:

$$5! = 5 \times 4 \times 3 \times 2 \times 1 = 120$$

Permutations

Permutations are groupings where the *order matters*. Since getting a 1st place trophy is different from getting a 4th place trophy, our earlier exploration of the number of ways 1st, 2nd, 3rd, and 4th place trophies could be awarded to 15 teams is an example of permutation. However, if 4 prizes of equal value were to be given to 4 out of 15 teams, this would be an example of when order would *not* matter (we will discuss these types of questions in the following section).

Although we solved the permutation question above of the 4 trophies to 15 teams by using the fundamental counting principle, there is a formula that can be applied to any problem regarding permutation. Unfortunately, the permutation formula will not be provided to you on the GED® test, so you'll want to commit it to memory.

RULE: PERMUTATION FORMULA

When n items are to be put into groups of k and order is significant, the number of **permutations** can be calculated as such:

$$P(n,k) = \frac{n!}{(n-k)!}$$

Permutation will be used for situations that involve ranking or for events where one ordering of options is significantly different from another ordering of the same options. With permutations, A-B-C and C-B-A count as two separate groupings. These count as two different permutations.

Let's use the preceding problem of first, second, third, and fourth place teams being selected from a group of 15 teams to illustrate this formula. First, recognize that $n = 15$ and $k = 4$.

$$P(n,k) = \frac{n!}{(n-k)!}$$
$$P(15,4) = \frac{15!}{(15-4)!}$$
$$P(15,4) = \frac{15!}{11!}$$
$$P(15,4) =$$
$$\frac{15 \times 14 \times 13 \times 12 \times 11 \times 10 \times 9 \times 8 \times 7 \times 6 \times 5 \times 4 \times 3 \times 2 \times 1}{11 \times 10 \times 9 \times 8 \times 7 \times 6 \times 5 \times 4 \times 3 \times 2 \times 1}$$

Now, notice that all the factors in the numerator from 11 down to 1 can be canceled out with all the factors from 11 to 1 in the denominator. Making sure that you do this cancelation will significantly reduce the time it takes you to do questions like this!

$$P(15,4) =$$
$$\frac{15 \times 14 \times 13 \times 12 \times \cancel{11 \times 10 \times 9 \times 8 \times 7 \times 6 \times 5 \times 4 \times 3 \times 2 \times 1}}{\cancel{11 \times 10 \times 9 \times 8 \times 7 \times 6 \times 5 \times 4 \times 3 \times 2 \times 1}}$$
$$P(15,4) = 15 \times 14 \times 13 \times 12 = 32,760$$

Therefore, the number of permutations of 4 teams being ranked from 15 teams is 32,760, which is the same answer we got above using the fundamental counting principle.

Combinations

Order does not matter with **combinations**. For instance, the number of combinations of three different appetizers a group could order at a restaurant is an example of a combination. It does not matter what order the chosen appetizers are listed in: salad, soup, and flatbread is the same as soup, flatbread, and salad.

The formula for combinations is similar to the one for permutations; however, another factor is added to the denominator to reduce the number of possibilities. Again, if order does not matter, then 1, 2, 3 is the same as 3, 2, 1; thus, the combination is counted only once.

RULE: COMBINATION FORMULA

When *n* items are to be put into groups of *k* and order is *not* significant, the number of **combinations** can be calculated as such:

$$C(n,k) = \frac{n!}{k!(n-k)!}$$

With combinations, A-B-C does not count separately as C-B-A. These are counted as a single combination. That is why *n*! is divided by *k*!—this is to reduce the answer by the repeated combinations.

Notice that the only difference between the formula for permutation and combination is the *k*! in the denominator of the combination formula. Again, this is to eliminate repetitive combinations in the answer, since order does not matter.

Example

There are 13 different appetizers to choose from at a restaurant. Rafael and his friends want to order three appetizers for the table to share. How many different combinations of three appetizers could they order?

Since order does not matter for this problem, use the combinations formula. Set $n = 13$ and $k = 3$:

$$C(n,k) = \frac{n!}{(n-k)!}$$
$$C(13,3) = \frac{13!}{3!(13-3)!}$$
$$C(13,3) = \frac{13!}{3!(10)!}$$
$$C(13,3) = \frac{13 \times 12 \times 11 \times \cancel{10 \times 9 \times 8 \times 7 \times 6 \times 5 \times 4 \times 3 \times 2 \times 1}}{3 \times 2 \times 1 (\cancel{10 \times 9 \times 8 \times 7 \times 6 \times 5 \times 4 \times 3 \times 2 \times 1})}$$
$$C(13,3) = \frac{1,716}{6}$$
$$C(13,3) = 286$$

Rafael and his friends better choose carefully because there are 286 different combinations of three appetizers they could select from the different 13 options!

DON'T DO THIS!

One of the most difficult things to do when answering problems involving combinations and permutations is to sort out which type of problem it is. In order to decide which formula to use, switch up the order of the same grouping of items and ask yourself if that ordering is significantly different from the first ordering. Would getting *chips* and *guacamole* be the same thing as getting *guacamole* and *chips*? Would *1234* be the same password as *4321*?

Practice

18. If Odessa flips a coin and rolls a die, how many different outcomes are there?

19. Using your answer from the previous question, what is the probability that Odessa will get a tails when she flips the coin and a 3 when she rolls the die?

20. Maya loves to prepare tasty food and host dinners at her home. She has four favorite salads, five favorite entrées, and three favorite desserts that she likes to make. Using these recipes, how many unique combinations can Maya offer her guests of one salad, one entrée, and one dessert?

21. There are 20 athletes competing in a swim meet for first, second, and third places. How many different ways could the trophies be awarded? _____

22. There are 10 different colors of sticky notes in the supply closet at Zachary's office. Employees can choose four different colors to organize their materials. How many different color combinations could Zachary select when choosing four sticky notes? _____

Summary

You have now thoroughly surveyed the most fundamental and important topics in statistics and probability: measure of central tendency, probability, and counting methods. Test your ability to correctly recall and apply all the different definitions and formulas with the following comprehensive review questions.

Statistics and Probability Review

1. What is the mode of the following data set? {45, 56, 23, 36, 45, 79, 12, 12, 56, 38, 80}
 a. 79
 b. 45
 c. 12, 45, 56
 d. 80

2. Phoebe works part-time at the movie theater. Her schedule for the next three weeks, shown here, lists the number of hours Phoebe will work each day.

SUNDAY	MONDAY	TUESDAY	WEDNESDAY	THURSDAY	FRIDAY	SATURDAY
0	7	0	4	4	5	0
0	4	6	5	3	2	0
0	5	4	3	6	5	0

What is the median number of hours Phoebe will work in one day over the next three weeks?
 a. 0 hours
 b. 3 hours
 c. 4 hours
 d. 5 hours

3. Pat spends Friday night at the bowling alley. In his first four games, he bowls scores of 123, 165, 127, and 144. If the mean of Pat's five games is 146, what does Pat bowl in his fifth game?
 a. 140
 b. 141
 c. 146
 d. 171

4. Jackie plays a ring-finding game in her swimming pool. She has 30 seconds to retrieve as many rings as she can from the bottom of the pool. She plays the game nine times, and her scores are shown in the table. What is Jackie's median score?

GAME NUMBER	RING SCORE
1	4
2	3
3	5
4	8
5	6
6	3
7	9
8	3
9	4

a. 3
b. 4
c. 5
d. 6

5. A spinner is divided into ten equal sections, numbered 1 through 10. If the spinner is spun once, what is the probability that the spinner will land on a number less than 5?

a. $\frac{1}{5}$
b. $\frac{2}{5}$
c. $\frac{1}{2}$
d. $\frac{1}{10}$

6. A piggy bank contains three quarters, five pennies, two nickels, and six dimes. Evander picks a coin at random from the bank and pulls out a quarter. This quarter is NOT replaced. If Evander selects another coin, what is the probability that it will be a quarter?

a. $\frac{2}{15}$
b. $\frac{3}{15}$
c. $\frac{2}{16}$
d. $\frac{3}{16}$

7. Yolanda is playing a memory card game with her niece. They have a stack of 28 cards made up of 14 pairs of matching animals. Each player gets a turn to flip over two cards in hopes of finding a match. If Yolanda goes first, what is the probability that she will get a matching pair during her first turn?

a. $\frac{1}{27}$
b. $\frac{1}{28}$
c. $\frac{1}{378}$
d. $\frac{1}{756}$

8. How many different ways could the first-, second-, and third-place trophies be awarded to the Little League teams in the end-of-season tournament?

Panthers
Cougars
Sharks
Lions
Tigers
Blue Devils
Mariners

a. 5,040
b. 7
c. 210
d. 3

9. Joan has seven CDs she wants to pack in her suitcase, but only four will fit. How many different combinations of CDs could be packed in Joan's suitcase?

a. 28

b. 35

c. 210

d. 840

10. The graph shows how much homework Michael has done each night. What is the mean number of hours Michael has spent doing homework on the nights shown? _____

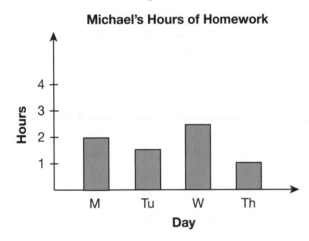

Michael's Hours of Homework

11. Mr. Kissam has the following seven final exam scores in his grade book for his Art History class: 92, 84, 79, 92, 84, 94, and 92. There were 8 students in the class, but he forgot to record the final exam grade for the eighth student before passing the exams back. Mr. Kissam sees this student a few days later at the pizza shop and asks what his final exam score was. The student couldn't recall exactly but he told Mr. Kissam that he did better than his friend who got an 84 but not as good as his roommate, who scored a 92. If Mr. Kissam recalls that the median of all eight scores was 90.5, find the missing student's grade. _____

12. A basketball coach has 9 players on her team. How many different 5-player lineups can she create for the starting team?

a. 15,120

b. 45

c. 126

d. 25

Answers and Explanations

Chapter Practice

1. **1.8 in.** Assign a variable to the missing length, x. Write an equation of the average, and then solve for x:

$$\text{average/mean} = \frac{\text{sum of data values}}{\text{\# of data values}}$$

$$2.35 = $$
$$\frac{2.3 + 1.9 + 2.0 + 2.4 + 2.5 + 3.0 + 2.7 + 2.6 + 2.5 + 2.4 + 2.3 + 2.1 + 2.4 + x}{14}$$

$$2.35 = \frac{31.1 + x}{14}$$

$$2.35(14) = \frac{14(31.1 + x)}{14}$$

$$32.9 = 31.1 + x$$

$$\underline{-31.1 \quad\quad -31.1}$$

$$1.8 = x$$

The length of the 14th frog is 1.8 inches.

2. **9.8.** Since Holly is competing in 4 events, the average will be calculated by adding the score from all four events and then dividing that sum by 4:

$$Average = \frac{vault + uneven + balance + floor}{4}$$

Fill in the given information, and use the variable f to represent her floor score. Work backward to find out what her floor event score must be to get an average of 9.2:

$$9.2 = \frac{8.9 + 8.6 + 9.5 + f}{4}$$

$$9.2 = \frac{27 + f}{4}$$

Here we multiply both sides by 4 to get $26.9 + f$ alone:

$$9.2(\times 4) = \frac{27 + f}{4}(\times 4)$$

$$36.8 = 27 + f$$

$$\underline{-27 \quad -27}$$

$$9.8 = f$$

So, in order to achieve her goal, Holly must get a 9.8 on floor today!

3. **$300,000.** In order to find the median of a set of data, they must first be put in chronological order and the *middle* piece of data will be the median.

   $200,000, $280,000, $\underline{280,000}$, $\underline{320,000}$, $390,000, $424,000

   In this case, there are two house prices that make up the *middle* of the data, so we must take the average of those: $\frac{280,000 + 320,000}{2} = 300,000$. So the median house price in this neighborhood is $300,000.

4. **45 and 56.** There are two modes in this data set, as both 45 and 56 appear twice.

5. **None.** Since no numbers appear more than once in this data set, we can say that there is no mode for this set of data.

6. **1.** To find the median number of pencils, we first need to find out the total number of students who were in class that day. Add the frequency for each bar: $12 + 10 + 8 + 4 + 6 = 40$ students. The median will be the piece of data that is right in the middle when the individual entries are in chronological order. Since this is an even number of data entries, the middle piece will be the average of the 20th and 21st piece of data. Use the bars to count the data points: since there are 12 students who brought 0 pencils and 10 students who brought 1 pencil, we know that the 20th and 21st pieces of data are both going to be in the column of students who brought 1 pencil, so the median is 1.

7. **0.** The mode is the most frequent piece of data and since the bar for 0 pencils is the tallest, we know that 0 is the mode.

8. **3 miles.** Since there are a different number of students in each category, it is necessary to find the weighted average. Begin by calculating the total number of miles traveled one way by *all* of Ms. Bradley's students by multiplying the number of miles in the first column by the number of students in the second column. Write these products in a third column:

NUMBER OF MILES TRAVELED ONE WAY	NUMBER OF STUDENTS	(# MILES)(# STUDENTS) = SUBTOTALS OF MILES
1	4	1(4) = 4
2	3	2(3) = 6
3	5	3(5) = 15
4	6	4(6) = 24
5	3	5(3) = 15

Total number of one-way miles: $4 + 6 + 15 + 24 + 15 = 64$. Then divide that by the number of total students in her viola class: $4 + 3 + 5 + 6 + 3 = 21$ students. So, the average miles driven will be total miles divided by number of students: $\frac{64}{21} \approx 3.05$. On average, Ms. Bradley's students travel about 3 miles each way to get to her viola class.

9. **$7.96.** Since the different cans of fruits have different prices, each type must get multiplied by the quantity that was purchased before the average can be found. Since Stephanie bought 20 cans at $6.50 each and 28 cans at $9 each, the total amount spent can be set up as $6.50(20) + $9.00(28) and the total number of cans will be found by adding 20 + 28:

Mean Price per Can = $\frac{\text{Total cost of all cans of fruit}}{\text{\# of cans of fruit}}$

Mean Price per Can = $\frac{\$6.50(20) + \$9.00(28)}{20 + 28}$

Mean Price per Can = $\frac{\$382}{48} = \$7.96$

So, the average price per can of fruit that Stephanie spent was $7.96/can.

10. **92.33%.** To find Katie's final grade, a weighted average must be calculated since Mr. Gallespie weights each type of assignment differently. Find the average score of each type of assignment, multiply it by its percentage weight, then add the percentages together to get Katie's final grade.

Final grade = $0.60(\frac{93 + 97 + 88 + 91 + 95}{5})$
$+ 0.15(\frac{90 + 99 + 100 + 95 + 96}{5})$
$+ 0.25(\frac{89 + 90 + 85 + 92}{4})$
$= 0.60(92.8) + 0.15(96) + 0.25(89)$
$= 55.68 + 14.4 + 22.25$
$= 92.33$

11. $\frac{1}{1,000}$. The probability of an event happening is $P(E) = \frac{\text{\# of desirable events}}{\text{total \# of possible events}}$. Since there are 1,000 possible 3-digit ID numbers from 000 to 999, and the only ID number that Delilah wants is 314, her chances of getting her π ID number are $\frac{1}{1,000}$.

12. $\frac{1}{100}$. There are 10 possible ID numbers that are triple repeating digits: 000, 111, 222, ... 999. There are 1,000 possible events of 3-digit numbers from 000 to 999. Since the probability of an event happening is $P(E) = \frac{\text{\# of desirable events}}{\text{total \# of possible events}}$, the probability that Skye will get a triple repeating digit ID number is $\frac{10}{1,000} = \frac{1}{100}$.

13. $\frac{2}{125}$. First, we will list out all of the ID numbers that have consecutive digits counting up: 012, 123, 234, 345, 456, 567, 678, and 789. Since there are 8 that count upward, that means there must be 8 that count down, so there are 16 ID numbers in total that Lulu would be happy to have. Since there are 1,000 possible 3-digit numbers from 000 to 999, the probability that she'll get one of these 16 numbers is $\frac{16}{1,000} = \frac{2}{125}$.

14. $\frac{1}{10}$. Looking at the graph, there are 4 students who had 3 pencils in their bags. Since there were 40 students in total (see explanation for question #6 for student total), the probability that a student chosen at random will have exactly 3 pencils is $\frac{4}{40} = \frac{1}{10}$.

15. $\frac{7}{10}$. Since we need to find the probability that a student has *at least 1 pencil*, this will include all of the students other than the students who had 0 pencils. Since there were 40 students in total, and 12 of them had 0 pencils in their bags, this means that 28 of them had 1 or more pencils in their bags. Therefore, the probability that a student chosen at random will have at least 1 pencil is $\frac{28}{40} = \frac{7}{10}$.

16. $\frac{1}{13}$. Since the first utensil removed is not returned to the drawer, the number of utensils in the drawer decreases to 13. When calculating compound probability, it is always assumed that the first event is a success, in order to determine the simple probability of the second event. This means that $P(\text{First utensil fork}) = \frac{4}{13}$ and $P(\text{Second utensil fork}) = \frac{3}{12}$. Multiply both of these simple probabilities together to find the compound probability of both events happening: $\frac{4}{13} \times \frac{3}{12} = \frac{12}{156} = \frac{1}{13}$.

17. 9%. Since these students are being picked without replacement, each time a student is picked, the class size will decrease by one. When calculating "without replacement" probability, you must assume that each event is a "success" so the number of boys available to pick from must also reduce by 1:

$P(\text{First student being a boy}) = \frac{14}{30}$

$P(\text{Second student being a boy}) = \frac{13}{29}$

$P(\text{Third student being a boy}) = \frac{12}{28}$

For compound probability, multiply all three of these probabilities together:

$P(\text{Boy then boy then boy}) \frac{14}{30} \times \frac{13}{29} \times \frac{12}{28} = \frac{2,184}{24,360} = 0.09 = 9\%$

So, the probability that all three students chosen at random will be boys is 9%.

18. 12. Since there are 2 possible outcomes with the coin toss and 6 possible outcomes with rolling a die, multiply these two numbers together to calculate the total number of possible combinations: $2 \times 6 = 12$.

19. $\frac{1}{12}$. There is only one way that Odessa can get a tails when she flips the coin *and* get a 3 when she rolls the die. But since there are 12 possible outcomes in total, the probability that she will arrive at this one specific outcome is $\frac{1}{12}$.

20. 60. The fundamental counting principle states that the total number of possible outcomes for the three separate events is the product of the numbers of possibilities for each event. Since Maya has four favorite salads, five favorite entrées, and three favorite desserts, multiply 4 by 5 by 3 to get 60 unique combinations.

21. 6,840. This is a problem of permutation (i.e., the order matters). Just by thinking about it, how many athletes can win first place? 20. How many can win second place after first place has been awarded? 19. How many can win third place after first and second places have been awarded? 18. So, the number of combinations the trophies could be awarded is $20 \times 19 \times 18 = 6,840$.

Using the formula, we will get the same answer:
$$P(20,3) = \frac{n!}{k!(n-k)!} = \frac{20!}{(20-3)!}$$

$$= \frac{20 \times 19 \times 18 \times 17 \times 16 \times 15 \times 14 \times 13 \times 12 \times 11 \times 10 \times 9 \times 8 \times 7 \times 6 \times 5 \times 4 \times 3 \times 2 \times 1}{17 \times 16 \times 15 \times 14 \times 13 \times 12 \times 11 \times 10 \times 9 \times 8 \times 7 \times 6 \times 5 \times 4 \times 3 \times 2 \times 1}$$

$$= \frac{20 \times 19 \times 18 \times \cancel{17 \times 16 \times 15 \times 14 \times 13 \times 12 \times 11 \times 10 \times 9 \times 8 \times 7 \times 6 \times 5 \times 4 \times 3 \times 2 \times 1}}{\cancel{17 \times 16 \times 15 \times 14 \times 13 \times 12 \times 11 \times 10 \times 9 \times 8 \times 7 \times 6 \times 5 \times 4 \times 3 \times 2 \times 1}}$$

$$= 20 \times 19 \times 18 = 6,840$$

22. 210. This is an example of combination, where the order does not matter. Use the formula for combinations to find how many color combinations of four sticky notes can result from ten different colors.
$$C(10,4) = \frac{10!}{4!(10-4)!}$$
$$= \frac{10 \times 9 \times 8 \times 7 \times 6 \times 5 \times 4 \times 3 \times 2 \times 1}{4 \times 3 \times 2 \times 1(6 \times 5 \times 4 \times 3 \times 2 \times 1)}$$
$$= \frac{10 \times 9 \times 8 \times 7 \times \cancel{6 \times 5 \times 4 \times 3 \times 2 \times 1}}{4 \times 3 \times 2 \times 1(\cancel{6 \times 5 \times 4 \times 3 \times 2 \times 1})} = \frac{10 \times 9 \times 8 \times 7}{4 \times 3 \times 2 \times 1}$$
$$= \frac{5,040}{24} = 210$$

Statistics and Probability Review

1. c. The *mode* is the number that appears most frequently. This data set has 3 modes because 12, 45, and 56 occur more than any of the other numbers. Choice **b** is the correct median of this data set, but not the mode. (It is the central piece of data when it is listed in chronological order.) Choice **a** is the incorrect median of this data set. (It's in the middle of the data set as the data is presented, but the data was not put into chronological order.) Choice **d** is the maximum of the data set but not the mode.

2. c. The median of a data set is the piece of data that occurs right in the middle after the data is put in order. To find the median number of hours Phoebe will work in one day over the next three weeks, put the number of hours she works each day in order and choose the number in the middle:

0, 0, 0, 0, 0, 0, 0, 2, 3, 3, **4**, 4, 4, 4, 5, 5, 5, 5, 6, 6, 7

There are 21 days on the schedule, so the middle number is the eleventh number shown above, 4. The median number of hours Phoebe will work is 4.

3. d. The mean, or average score, of Pat's five games is 146. That means that Pat scores a total of 5×146, or 730, over five games. Let x represent Pat's score in the fifth game. His total score over five games is equal to:

$123 + 165 + 127 + 144 + x = 559 + x$

Now, set that total equal to Pat's total score, 730:

$559 + x = 730$

Subtract 559 from both sides:

$x = 171$

Pat scores 171 in his fifth game.

To check your answer, add Pat's score in each of the five games and divide the sum by 5:

$123 + 165 + 127 + 144 + 171 = 730$

The dividend should be equal to Pat's mean, 146:

$730 \div 5 = 146$

4. b. Put the nine ring scores in order from least to greatest. The middle value (the fifth value) is the median score:

3, 3, 3, 4, **4**, 5, 6, 8, 9

The median score is 4.

5. b. The spinner has ten equal sections, so the probability of the spinner landing on any one number is $\frac{1}{10}$. There are four numbers on the spinner that are less than 5 (1, 2, 3, and 4). The probability of the spinner landing on a number less than 5 is $\frac{4}{10}$, or $\frac{2}{5}$.

6. a. Before Evander removes a coin, there are 16 coins in the bank:

3 quarters + 5 pennies + 2 nickels + 6 dimes = 16 coins

After Evander removes the first quarter, there are:

2 quarters + 5 pennies + 2 nickels + 6 dimes = 15 coins

There are only 15 coins in the bank now, and only two of them are quarters. If Evander selects another coin, the probability that it will be a quarter is $\frac{2}{15}$.

7. a. We are looking for the compound probability of P(Animal then matching animal). In order to calculate the compound probability of two related events, we multiply the simple probability of each event happening. Since Yolanda does not care what animal is on the first card she flips over, we use a probability of 1 for the first card. (Basically, the P(Animal) for the first card she flips over is $\frac{28}{28} = 1$, since it doesn't matter *what* animal is on the first card.) Now there are 27 cards remaining and Yolanda is hoping to flip over the *one* card that has the matching animal on it. Therefore, the P(then matching animal) is $\frac{1}{27}$. So multiply the two probabilities together to get the compound probability: P(Animal then matching animal) = $1 \times \frac{1}{27} = \frac{1}{27}$. Therefore, the probability that Yolanda gets any matching pair in the first two flips of cards is $\frac{1}{27}$. Choice **c** was the result of an error of thinking that Yolanda was looking

for a *specific* animal in the first flip of the card, and therefore started out with an incorrect probability of $\frac{2}{28}$ for the first card and $\frac{1}{27}$ for the second card. Choice **b** is an incorrect answer, due to forgetting to reduce the number of available cards by one for the second flip and therefore using $\frac{1}{28}$ for the second card. Choice **d** is the result of using $\frac{1}{28}$ and $\frac{1}{27}$ as the two simple probabilities.

8. c. This is a problem involving permutation, which requires the following formula: $\frac{n!}{(n-r)!}$, where n = the total number of options and r = the number of options chosen. Since there are seven teams that could win a trophy, $n = 7$. Only three teams will get trophies, so $r = 3$. When these values are substituted into the equation, we get $\frac{n!}{(n-r)!} = \frac{7!}{(7-3)!} = \frac{7 \cdot 6 \cdot 5 \cdot 4 \cdot 3 \cdot 2 \cdot 1}{4 \cdot 3 \cdot 2 \cdot 1} = 7 \cdot 6 \cdot 5 = 210$.

9. b. Joan can fit four of her seven CDs in her suitcase. It is important to understand that the order in which she chooses the CDs does not matter. The group of CDs A, B, C, and D is the same as the group A, B, D, and C, or D, C, A, and B.

This is a combination problem, so you must use the combination formula to find the answer:

$C(n,k) = \frac{n!}{k!(n-k)!}$, where n is the number of options and k is the number of choices made.

Joan has seven CDs and chooses four. Divide by 4! to ensure that you do not count the same group of four CDs more than once:

$$\frac{7 \times 6 \times 5 \times 4 \times 3 \times 2 \times 1}{(4 \times 3 \times 2 \times 1)(3 \times 2 \times 1)} = \frac{7 \times 6 \times 5 \times \cancel{4 \times 3 \times 2 \times 1}}{(4 \times 3 \times 2 \times 1)(3 \times 2 \times 1)}$$
$$= \frac{7 \times 6 \times 5}{3 \times 2 \times 1} = \frac{210}{6} = 35$$

10. 1.75 hours. The mean is the average. To find the average of four numbers, find the sum of the numbers and divide by 4. Michael spent 2 hours doing homework on Monday, 1.5 hours on Tuesday, 2.5 hours on Wednesday, and 1 hour on Thursday. The sum of this time is 7 hours $(2 + 1.5 + 2.5 + 1 = 7)$. Next, divide 7 by 4 $(7 \div 4 = 1.75)$. The mean is 1.75 hours.

11. The median of a data set is always the very middle number when they are arranged chronologically. With an odd number of data points, finding the median is easy. However, when you have an even number of data points, there are two middle numbers. The median is then the average of those two middle numbers.

To find the missing score, we first need to order the data points from least to greatest:

79, 84, 84, 92, 92, 92, 94

The problem states that the missing point in the data set is between 84 and 92. So, let's let x represent the missing score and add it to our chronological list:

79, 84, 84, x, 92, 92, 92, 94

The middle two numbers are x and 92.

The problem also states that the average of these two numbers is 90.5. Let's set up an equation and then solve for x:

$$\frac{x + 92}{2} = 90.5$$
$$2\left(\frac{x + 92}{2}\right) = (90.5) \times 2$$
$$x + 92 = 181$$
$$\underline{-92 \qquad -92}$$
$$x = 89$$

The missing point is 89.

12. c. The order in which the starting players are selected is not significant, so use combination to solve this problem. (Using the combination formula will keep from counting players A, B, C, D, and E as a different team lineup then A, B, C, E, and D.)

$$C(n,k) = \frac{n!}{k!(n-k)!}$$
$$C(9,5) = \frac{9!}{5!(9-5)!}$$
$$C(9,5) = \frac{9!}{5! \times 4!} = \frac{9 \times 8 \times 7 \times 6 \times 5!}{5! \times (4 \times 3 \times 2 \times 1)}$$
$$C(9,5) = 126$$

Choice **a** is incorrect because that is the answer from using the permutations formula. Choice **b** is just the product of the number of players on the team and the number of players in the starting lineup, which has nothing to do with the number of starting teams.

12 ▶ CALCULATOR SKILLS ON THE TI-30XS

I n this chapter you will learn how to use the TI-30XS MultiView Calculator by Texas Instruments. You should be able to purchase this calculator at an office supply store or online for under $20. Having this calculator in hand as you study for the GED® test will be a big advantage for you on test day. The better you understand how to use the calculator, the more help it will be to you. Students often input information into the calculator incorrectly, resulting in wrong answers, so it's important to learn how to use the calculator's different functions accurately. If you don't purchase this calculator for your test preparation, see if you can borrow one from your school or library.

The GED® Testing Service has put together a brief Calculator Tutorial. Although not required, you may find it helpful to watch before continuing with this chapter. It can be found here: http://www.gedtestingservice .com/ged_calc_en_web/

This chapter covers:

- Critical keys on the TI-30XS
- Working with radicals and exponents

- Using previous answers in current calculations
- Answer toggle key
- Working with percentages
- Working with scientific notation

THE TI-30XS: A DOUBLE-EDGED SWORD!

You may have heard teachers mention in the past that a calculator is not a replacement for common sense. It's easy to press the × instead of the +, and get a completely wrong answer, or to skip a digit when typing in a long number. Therefore, it's critical that you *think carefully* about your answers before making your final selection. The people who write the GED® TEST are trained to come up with false answer choices that represent the common mistakes students will make with their calculators. So just because an answer you calculated is there in choice **b**, that doesn't mean it's correct! For example, 7% sales tax on a $20 shirt should not be $14, but $14 will definitely be an answer choice because that is the result of a common calculator error!

Your TI-30XS is a double-edged sword: It helps students be efficient with myriad calculations, but it also gives a false sense of confidence that critical thinking can be bypassed. Make sure you use your head to estimate solutions before doing a problem on your calculator. Once you have an answer on your screen, use your mind to determine if it makes real-world sense before selecting your answer and moving forward.

Critical Keys

The TI-30XS is not your ordinary 4-operation calculator. It can calculate problems entered in as percents, fractions, and scientific notation. It can also convert between equivalent forms of values such as decimals and fractions; square roots and decimals; and π and decimals. Let's discuss some of the most important keys:

on: This key in the bottom left corner of the keypad turns your T1-30XS on.

enter: This bottom right key is equivalent to the = when you are doing calculations. It also functions as the enter/yes key when you are selecting modes or commands.

◄►: Just above the arrow key is the toggle key. This key will be used to move between

equivalent expressions of numbers, such as going from $\frac{1}{2}$ to 0.5. We will discuss how to use the toggle key later in this chapter.

⬤: In the top right corner of the keypad you will find a 4-way arrow button. Use this to move the curser left, right, up, and down. Throughout this chapter, rather than show this entire button each time we are instructing you to move the cursor, we will use the following symbols for moving left, right, up, and down with this button: ◄, ►, ▲, ▼. To change a character that you have already input, simply use the 4-way arrow button to move the cursor over the character you wish to change. Type the character you wish to have instead and it will replace the unwanted character with the new character.

2nd: The green key in the top left corner of the keypad allows you to access all the secondary functions that are written in green above many of the keys. Notice that when you press the 2nd key you see "2ND" appear in the top left portion of the screen. This means your TI-30XS is ready to access a secondary feature. When you press the 2nd key again, you will see "2ND" disappear from your screen, meaning it's back in primary mode.

[**off**]: Find the on key located at the bottom left corner of the keypad. Above it you will see the word "off" written in green. Any time you see text in green, this feature will be accessed by using it with the 2nd button. In this chapter, we will indicate secondary features by using brackets around them rather than a complete box around them. Practice accessing the 2nd feature now by turning your calculator on and off with these steps and notice how the same key is written with two different notations below:

on 2nd off

(−) **versus** −: Take the time now to notice that there are two keys with a "−" on them. The (−) key below 3 is a negative symbol, while the − to the right of 9 is used for subtraction. If you confuse these two keys you will get wrong calculations or error messages, so it is important to keep them straight.

clear: At the top right of the keypad, above ÷, sits clear. Use this key to clear all of the characters in an entry line at once. This key is also used to clear an error message.

delete: In the top row of keys, the rightmost key is delete. Unlike clear, which clears an entire row of data, delete is used to remove a single character. If you want to remove the last character you typed, simply hit delete. If you want to remove an earlier character, use the directional keys to move the cursor over the character you would like to remove and press delete.

KEY SYMBOLS IN THIS CHAPTER

As discussed, the 2nd key can be used to access all of the secondary features written in green on the TI-30XS. In this chapter, it will be important for you to be able to discern which types of keys we are referring to as you learn how to use the TI-30XS.

Primary keys have their functions directly on the faces of the keys. We will use a box around the function to indicate primary keys:

- Ex: on indicates the "on" key in the bottom left corner of your keypad.

Secondary keys have their functions written in green above the faces of the keys on the body of the calculator. We will use straight brackets around the function to indicate secondary keys:

- Ex: [off] indicates the secondary "off" function associated with the on key.

Note: When you see 2nd in the instructions, the next key will always be a secondary key in straight brackets, so remember to look for that next function in *green*!

Modes of the TI-30XS

Your TI-30XS has the ability to operate in several different modes, depending on the types of calculations you are doing. This is a particularly useful feature for trigonometry and for calculating in radians, but these are not topics covered on the GED® test. You can read your calculator's instruction manual or watch some online tutorials about working in these other modes, but for the most part, we will use the default mode of the calculator discussed in the following section.

Default Mode

The screens illustrated in this chapter are associated with your TI-30XS being in the default mode, *Math-Print*, unless stated otherwise. When you first turn on the calculator, press mode, which is to the right of the green 2nd. This should bring up the following screen:

```
                              DEG
DEG RAD GRAD
NORM SCI ENG
FLOAT 0123456789
CLASSIC MATHPRINT
```

In order to change the mode, use the 4-way arrow button and press enter once your cursor is on the mode you would like to select. You may want to use *SCI* mode for doing problems with scientific notation, but it is not necessary. (We will cover calculating in scientific notation later.)

Resetting Default Mode

If you get out of default mode and would like to reset your calculator to default mode, Press 2nd [reset] 2. This will bring back all of the default settings, but it will also clear the memory as well as all the entries in your history, so be careful there's nothing you need in your calculator's memory or history when you reset it.

Working with Radicals and Exponents

Recall that $\sqrt{x^2} = \pm x$. Taking the square root is the opposite operation of squaring a number, so it shouldn't surprise you that you will find [√] as the secondary function to x^2. Let's discuss how to perform some basic operations with square roots.

Calculating a Square Root

To find the square root of a number, press 2nd [√] and enter the number that is being square rooted. If you are trying to enter something like $\sqrt{5} + 2$, use ▶ to exit the radical sign before you type +2. If you don't use the arrow key, you will end up with $\sqrt{5 + 2}$, which is incorrect.

The default mode of the TI-30XS is to return answers to radical calculations in simplest radical form. For example, if you input $\sqrt{8}$ and press enter, the answer $2\sqrt{2}$ will appear on the right side of your screen, since $\sqrt{8} = 2\sqrt{2}$. If you want to see the decimal equivalent of $2\sqrt{2}$, simply press the toggle key, ◀▶. This will return the decimal 2.828427125. Press ◀▶ again to return to the radical form, $2\sqrt{2}$. Pretty cool, right?

Operations with Square Roots

As we mentioned, when working with radical expressions, like $\sqrt{35} - \sqrt{10}$, it is very important to keep the two radicals separate. It is easy to mistakenly input $\sqrt{35 - 10}$, which will result in the wrong answer. (If you are wondering why $\sqrt{35} - \sqrt{10}$ cannot equal $\sqrt{35 - 10}$, this is a great opportunity to review the Exponents section in Chapter 3.)

In order to correctly enter $\sqrt{35} - \sqrt{10}$, follow these steps:

$\boxed{\text{2nd}}\ [\sqrt{\ }]\ \boxed{3}\boxed{5}\ \blacktriangleright\ \boxed{-}\ \boxed{\text{2nd}}\ [\sqrt{\ }]\ \boxed{1}\boxed{0}\ \blacktriangleright\ \boxed{\text{enter}}$

You may be surprised to see that the answer returned after hitting $\boxed{\text{enter}}$ is simply $\sqrt{35} - \sqrt{10}$. This is because both $\sqrt{35}$ and $\sqrt{10}$ are in simplest form. In order to see what $\sqrt{35} - \sqrt{10}$ is in decimal, press the toggle key, $\boxed{\blacktriangleleft \blacktriangleright}$, which will return 2.753802123.

DON'T DO THIS!

Recall that $\sqrt{16}$ has two solutions: 4 and –4. There is something very important to keep in mind when you are working with square roots on your TI-30XS. Calculators only return a single positive solution when answering square root questions! It is imperative that you don't let your brain slip into *Calculator Autopilot* mode and choose that answer choice that lists *just the positive solution*. Beware of how easy it is to make this common mistake, and instead select the answer that shows both solutions! (Of course if it is a real-world context question, only the positive answer may make sense, but that is up to you to discern.)

NO! $\sqrt{16} = 4$ (This is what your TI-30XS will tell you, but it forgot "–4.")

YES . . . $\sqrt{16} = +4$ and –4 (This is what your brain should tell you!)

Raising a Number to a Power

Diagonal from $\boxed{7}$ is the carrot key, $\boxed{\wedge}$. This is used to raise a number to a power. In order to calculate 2^4, type $\boxed{2}\boxed{\wedge}\boxed{4}$ and you will see 2^4 on the left side of the screen. If you want to add more operations, use the right arrow key, $\blacktriangleright$, to get out of the exponent box. If

you simply want to calculate 2^4, just press $\boxed{\text{enter}}$ and 16 will appear on the right side of the screen.

DON'T DO THIS!

You need to be very careful when calculating exponents with negative bases on the TI-30XS. If you are trying to find the square of –12, you *must* put –12 in a set of parentheses when you enter it into the calculator. Work through the following two key sequences on your calculator and notice how they return different answers:

$\boxed{(}\ \boxed{(-)}\ \boxed{5}\ \boxed{)}\ \boxed{x^2}\ \boxed{\text{enter}}$: This will produce $(-5)^2$ on the left side of the screen and an answer of 25.

$\boxed{(-)}\ \boxed{5}\ \boxed{x^2}\ \boxed{\text{enter}}$: This will produce -5^2 on the left side of the screen and an answer of –25.

It is a great idea to always use parentheses when subbing a negative value into a variable expression on your calculator.

Taking the Cube Root of a Number

You can determine cube roots easily with the TI-30XS. The *nth root* button is the secondary function of the $\boxed{\wedge}$. Look for the green $[\sqrt[x]{\ }]$. Let's use this function to solve the following example:

Example

Find the value of $\sqrt[3]{-64}$.

In order to find the cube root of –64 first enter $\boxed{3}$ and then $\boxed{\text{2nd}}\ [\sqrt[x]{\ }]$. This will produce a radical sign with a small 3 in the upper left-hand root position. Since we want to enter –64 inside the radical sign, press $\boxed{(-)}$ $\boxed{6}\boxed{4}$ followed by $\boxed{\text{enter}}$. This should return –4 as the answer on the right side of the screen.

Using Previous Answers in Current Calculations

One of the most helpful features in the TI-30XS is that you can use the most recent answer to perform new calculations. This can be done two different ways:

1. You can use the previous answer at the start of a new calculation by pressing any operation key ($\boxed{+}$, $\boxed{-}$, $\boxed{\div}$, $\boxed{\times}$, $\boxed{x^2}$, etc.).
2. You can use the previous answer in the middle or end of a new calculation, by pressing $\boxed{2nd}$ [ans].

Let's learn how to do both of these tasks with three simple exercises. Beginning with a clear screen, perform the operation 12×2 on your calculator and hit $\boxed{enter}$. Once your screen reads "12*2" on the left and "24" on the right, work through these exercises without clearing your screen between the exercises:

Exercise 1. Press $\boxed{+}$ and you will see "ans +" appear on the left of your screen. This is indicating that the calculator is going to start with the previous answer, 24, and add that to your next input. Enter $\boxed{6}$ and press $\boxed{enter}$ and you will see 30 appear on the right.

Exercise 2. Now press $\boxed{3}$ $\boxed{9}$ $\boxed{-}$ followed by $\boxed{2nd}$ [ans] and you will see "39–ans" on the left side of your screen. This is indicating that the calculator is going to start with 39 and subtract the previous answer, 30. Press $\boxed{enter}$ and you will see "9" appear on the right.

Exercise 3. Now press $\boxed{2nd}$ [$\sqrt{\ }$] and a square root symbol with a cursor inside it will appear, looking like this: $\sqrt{\square}$. Now when you press $\boxed{2nd}$ [ans] you will see "ans" appear within the square root box: $\sqrt{ans}$. This is indicating that the calculator is going to take the square root of

the previous answer, 9. Press $\boxed{enter}$ and you will see "3" appear on the right since 3 is the square root of 9. (Remember that your calculator forgets to include the negative square root of 9. Get your brain in the habit of including the negative square root answer when working with square roots on the calculator.)

As you practice your calculator skills, use this "*ans*" feature as often as possible. Using the previous answer will keep you from making careless errors while retyping values into the calculator. Be aware that any time you see "*ans*" appear on your screen, you will be using the previous answer obtained for that entry.

Working with Fractions

Performing operations with fractions is easy on the TI-30XS.

Entering Fractions
There are two different methods to enter a fraction:

Method 1: Press the $\boxed{\frac{n}{d}}$ key. An empty fraction will appear. Enter your numerator on the top of the fraction, then use ▼ to move into the bottom of the fraction and enter the denominator.

Method 2: Enter your numerator first, and then press the $\boxed{\frac{n}{d}}$ key. This puts the first number you typed directly into the numerator and moves the curser to the denominator without you having to use the arrow key. Enter the denominator.

Reducing Fractions to Lowest Terms
In order to reduce a fraction to lowest terms, enter the fraction in the TI-30XS using one of the methods above and press $\boxed{enter}$. The answer that appears on the right-hand side will be an equivalent fraction in lowest terms. That's pretty helpful, isn't it!

Operations with Fractions

To perform operations with fractions, the most important step to remember is to press the ▶ key to get out of the fraction. Once that is done you can enter the operation or character desired. Follow these steps to add $\frac{5}{3} + \frac{7}{6}$.

1. Press 5 $\boxed{\frac{n}{d}}$ 3 ▶ $\boxed{+}$ 7 $\boxed{\frac{n}{d}}$ 6. You should see $\frac{5}{3} + \frac{7}{6}$ on the left of your screen.
2. Press $\boxed{\text{enter}}$ and the answer $\frac{17}{6}$ will appear on the right side of your screen.

Improper Fractions and Mixed Numbers Conversions

Let's say you work out some calculations by hand and get $\frac{172}{20}$ as your final answer. You feel good about your answer, but all the answer choices are in mixed number format and you don't have the time to covert $\frac{172}{20}$ to a mixed number by hand. There is an easy way to turn $\frac{172}{20}$ into a mixed number. The secondary key, $[\frac{n}{d} ◀ ▶ U\frac{n}{d}]$, is used to toggle from improper fractions to mixed numbers and vice versa. Practice using it below:

1. Enter 172 $\boxed{\frac{n}{d}}$ 20 ▶ to get $\frac{172}{20}$ on the left of your screen and the cursor out of the fraction.
2. Now press $\boxed{\text{2nd}}$ $[\frac{n}{d} ◀ ▶ U\frac{n}{d}]$ to add the conversion function to this line.
3. When you press $\boxed{\text{enter}}$ the mixed number $8\frac{3}{5}$ will appear on the right side of your screen.
4. Lastly, let's put this mixed number back into improper fraction form. Press $\boxed{\text{2nd}}$ $[\frac{n}{d} ◀ ▶ U\frac{n}{d}]$ to bring $8\frac{3}{5}$ ▶ $\frac{n}{d} ◀ ▶ U\frac{n}{d}$ to the left side of your screen. Next press $\boxed{\text{enter}}$ and the improper fraction $\frac{43}{5}$ will appear on the right of your screen. Why did $\frac{43}{5}$ appear instead of the original $\frac{172}{20}$? Your TI-30XS will *always* express fraction answers in *lowest terms*. This is very convenient since answers on the GED® test are always in lowest terms!

Inputting Mixed Numbers

Use the sequence $\boxed{\text{2nd}}$ $[U\frac{n}{d}]$ to input mixed numbers. Pressing $\boxed{\text{2nd}}$ $[U\frac{n}{d}]$ will bring up this blank mixed number template with 3 empty boxes: $\square\frac{\square}{\square}$. Use the 4-way arrow key to move into each box to input the correct values and press ▶ to move out of the mixed number when you are ready to enter your operation or following character.

To convert a mixed number to an improper fraction, input the mixed number and press $\boxed{\text{enter}}$.

Using Operations within Fractions

When the TI-30XS is in *MathPrint* mode, you will be able to enter operations or complex fractions within fractions.

Complex Numerators and Denominators

In order to enter multiple operations into fractions, simply enter the entire expression desired into the numerator before using ▼ to move to the denominator. Then, once you are in the denominator, enter the entire expression desired in the denominator and use ▶ to exit the fraction.

Entering Fractions within Fractions

Students often get confused when there are fractions within fractions, so this is a useful skill to be able to perform on your TI-30XS. To enter a fraction in the numerator or denominator of a fraction, simply press $\boxed{\frac{n}{d}}$ again when in the top or bottom of the fraction. Practice this in the following two exercises:

Exercise 1: Enter $\frac{\left(\frac{2}{3}\right)}{3}$ with these steps:

$\boxed{\frac{n}{d}}\boxed{\frac{n}{d}}\boxed{2}$ ▼ $\boxed{3}$ ▼ $\boxed{3}$ ▶. Now, when you hit $\boxed{\text{enter}}$, $\frac{2}{9}$ should appear on the right side of your screen.

Exercise 2: Enter $\frac{3}{\left(\frac{2}{3}\right)}$ with these steps:

$\boxed{\frac{n}{d}}\boxed{3}$ ▼ $\boxed{\frac{n}{d}}\boxed{2}$ ▼ $\boxed{3}$ ▶ ▶. Notice that you had to press ▶ *twice*: The first ▶ got you out of the fraction in the denominator, but you were still in the denominator of the primary fraction. The second ▶ got you out of the entire fraction. Now, when you hit ⎡enter⎤, $\frac{9}{2}$ should appear on the right side of your screen.

Using Radicals within Fractions

To enter a fraction like $\frac{\sqrt{5}}{3\sqrt{2}}$ into the TI-30XS, you must first press $\boxed{\frac{n}{d}}$ before putting the $\sqrt{5}$ in the numerator. Follow these keystrokes:

$\boxed{\frac{n}{d}}$ ⎡2nd⎤ [√] ⎡5⎤ ▼ ⎡3⎤ ⎡2nd⎤ [√] ⎡2⎤ ▶▶ ⎡enter⎤. This should simplify to $\frac{\sqrt{10}}{6}$ on the right side of your screen. Hit the toggle key, ⎡◀ ▶⎤, to see the decimal equivalent of this answer.

Answer Toggle Key

Above ⎡enter⎤, you will find what might become your favorite key: ⎡◀ ▶⎤. This is the toggle key, which switches a given answer to an equivalent form. There are three different kinds of conversions this key performs:

1. Decimal to Fraction Conversions

When you get an answer in decimal form on the right side of your screen, pressing ⎡◀ ▶⎤ once will show its fractional equivalent on the right side of the screen. If you want to convert a given decimal to a fraction, enter the value of the decimal, then press ⎡◀ ▶⎤ ⎡enter⎤.

Similarly, when you get an answer as a fraction, pressing ⎡◀ ▶⎤ once will show its decimal equivalent.

2. Radical to Decimal Conversions

As discussed earlier, ⎡◀ ▶⎤ will turn an answer returned in radical form into its decimal equivalent.

3. π to Decimal Conversions

If you put $16 \times \pi$ into your calculator, and press ⎡enter⎤, it will return 16π as the answer on the right-hand side. Pressing ⎡◀ ▶⎤ once will convert answers in terms of π into their decimal equivalents.

Working with Percentages

The TI-30XS can perform operations with percentages. It can also turn decimal answers into percentages.

Entering Percentages

When using the percentage feature to input percentages, you do not need to first convert the percentages into decimals as we did in an earlier chapter. You will find the percentage button as the secondary feature above the left parentheses: [%]. When entering a value as a percentage, simply enter the value, followed by [%], and the calculator will move the decimal place back two spaces for you when it does the calculation.

Example

If the local tax rate is 9.5% and Miguel buys a computer for $1,300, calculate the dollar amount of sales tax he will pay.

Since this question is asking you to find 9.5% of $1,300, enter the following into your TI-30XS:

9.5 ⎡2nd⎤ [%] ⎡×⎤ 1300 ⎡enter⎤

This will generate "9.5%∗1300" on the left of your screen and the answer "123.5" on the right of your screen. Therefore, the sales tax will be $123.50.

Converting Ratios into Percentages

Your TI-30XS can convert fractions and decimals into percentages. This can be useful when using a ratio to determine what percentage a part is of a whole.

Example

A local newscaster took a poll and found that 52 out of 65 people were in support of banning the sale of plastic water bottles in Summit County. What percentage of people supported this potential ban?

You can convert 52 out of 65 into a decimal by entering it as a fraction into your TI-30XS and using the secondary [→ %] feature:

$$52 \; \boxed{\tfrac{n}{d}} \; 65 \; \blacktriangleright \; \boxed{\text{2nd}} \; [\to \%] \; \boxed{\text{enter}}$$

This sequence will return "80%" as the answer on the right side of the screen.

Note: You can also use $\boxed{\text{2nd}}$ [→ %] $\boxed{\text{enter}}$ to convert a previous fractional or decimal answer into a percentage. When using this feature, the answer shown will be followed by a % symbol, indicating that it is a percentage.

Working with Scientific Notation

You can easily perform operations in scientific notation on the TI-30XS. To do so, locate the $\boxed{\times 10^{n}}$ key that is three keys above $\boxed{8}$. When the calculator is in the default *MathPrint* mode, all of the answers will be in standard form, rather than in scientific notation. In order to display answers in scientific notation, the calculator should be in Scientific mode, abbreviated *SCI*.

Entering Scientific Notation

Keep your calculator in *MathPrint* mode for now. Let's enter 2.8×10^{5} into your calculator using the scientific notation shortcut:

$$2.8 \; \boxed{\times 10^{n}} \; \boxed{5} \; \boxed{\text{enter}}$$

This sequence of steps will return 280,000 on the right side of the screen.

Using Scientific Notation Mode

Putting the calculator in scientific notation mode will guarantee that all the answers will be given in scientific notation. Press $\boxed{\text{mode}}$ and move the cursor over to the SCI on the second row and press $\boxed{\text{enter}}$. Next, press $\boxed{\text{clear}}$ to exit that screen and return to the main screen. Now we'll work through an exercise in SCI mode:

Example
What is the value of 8.8×10^{7} divided by 2.2×10^{3}?

Enter each of these scientific numbers in parentheses to ensure the correct order of operations:

$$\boxed{(} \; 8.8 \; \boxed{\times 10^{n}} \; \boxed{7} \; \blacktriangleright \; \boxed{)}$$

This should input $(8.8*10^{7})$ on the left on the screen. Press $\boxed{\div}$ and then use the following sequence to input the second number in scientific notation:

$$\boxed{(} \; 2.2 \; \boxed{\times 10^{n}} \; \boxed{3} \; \blacktriangleright \; \boxed{)}$$

Now you should have $(8.8*10^{7}) \div (2.2*10^{3})$ on your screen (you will have to use the right and left arrow keys to see the entire expression together). Press $\boxed{\text{enter}}$ and the answer will appear in scientific notation on the right side: $4*10^{4}$. If you'd like to see this number in standard notation, press $\boxed{\blacktriangleleft \blacktriangleright}$ once and 40,000 will appear below.

DON'T DO THIS!

If you put your calculator in scientific notation mode, make sure you return it to the default mode before moving on to other types of questions. If you forget to do this, just some simple division, like 1 ÷ 2, will return odd-looking answers like $5*10^{-1}$ instead of 0.5! In order to return your calculator to the default mode, follow this sequence:

Press mode, use the arrow key ▼ to select "*NORM*" on the second line, and press enter clear.

Calculator Skills Review

You now have a comprehensive set of calculator skills to apply to your problem solving on the GED® test. Use these skills carefully and accurately on the second GED® Mathematical Reasoning test provided in the following chapter, and remember to *think* about whether the answers on your calculator make sense before making your final selections!

13 ▶ GED® MATHEMATICAL REASONING PRACTICE TEST

This practice test is modeled on the format, content, and timing of the official GED® Mathematical Reasoning test. Like the official test, the questions focus on your quantitative and algebraic problem-solving skills.

You may refer to the formula sheet in the Appendix on page 277 as you take this exam. Answer questions 1–5 *without* using a calculator. You may use a scientific calculator (or a calculator of any kind) for the remaining exam questions.

Before you begin, it's important to know that you should work carefully but not spend too much time on any one question. Be sure you answer every question.

Set a timer for 115 minutes (1 hour and 55 minutes), and try to take this test uninterrupted, under quiet conditions.

Complete answer explanations for all of the test questions follow the exam. Good luck!

45 Questions
115 Minutes

1. Joseph owns v video games. Harry owns 10 fewer than two times the number of video games that Joseph owns. Which expression represents the number of video games that Harry owns in terms of v?
   a. $10v - 2$
   b. $2v - 10$
   c. $2(v - 10)$
   d. $10(v - 2)$

2. Which of the following is equivalent to $\frac{\sqrt[3]{9} \times \sqrt[3]{18}}{3}$?
   a. $\sqrt[3]{2}$
   b. $3\sqrt[3]{2}$
   c. $\sqrt[3]{6}$
   d. $\sqrt[3]{18}$

3. Write your answer on the line below. You may use numbers, symbols, and/or text in your response.

An expression is shown below. Simplify the expression completely. Be sure to leave your answer in radical form.

$\frac{\sqrt{72}}{\sqrt{36}}$

4. Draw a dot on the grid below to plot the point indicated by the ordered pair $(-2,1)$.

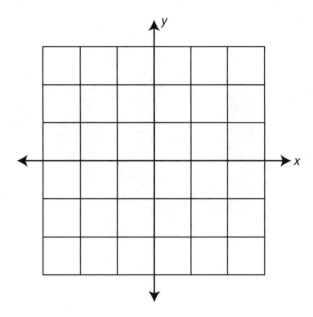

5. As part of a game, Gilbert must take a number and use a special procedure to come up with a new number. To come up with his new number, Gilbert takes the original number, cubes it, adds 5 to it, and finally multiplies it by 2. If the original number is represented by x, which of the following represents Gilbert's new number?
   a. $2(3x + 5)$
   b. $2(x^3 + 5)$
   c. $2x^3 + 5$
   d. $x^6 + 5$

6. The sum of a number n and 4 is less than 5 times the number m. If m is 6, which of the following is true?
   a. n is greater than 6
   b. $n + 4$ is less than 26
   c. n is less than 26
   d. n is equal to 26

7. A company pays its sales employees a base rate of $450 a week plus a 4% commission on any sales the employee makes. If an employee makes $1,020 in sales one week, what will be his total paycheck for that week? Write your answer in the box below.

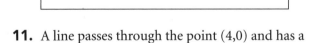

8. The diameter of a circle is 10 meters. In meters, which of the following is the circumference of this circle?
 a. 5π
 b. 10π
 c. 25π
 d. 100π

9. Which of the following is equivalent to $\left(\frac{3}{4}\right)^3$?
 a. $\frac{3^3}{4^3}$
 b. $\frac{3 \times 3}{4 \times 3}$
 c. $\frac{3^3}{4}$
 d. $\frac{3}{4 \times 3}$

10. The line n is parallel to the line $y = 3x - 7$ and passes through the point (5,1). At what point does the line n cross the y-axis? Write your answer in the box below.

11. A line passes through the point (4,0) and has a slope of $-\frac{1}{2}$. What is the equation of this line?
 a. $y = -\frac{1}{2}x + 2$
 b. $y = -\frac{1}{2}x - 2$
 c. $y = -\frac{1}{2}x + 4$
 d. $y = -\frac{1}{2}x - 4$

12. What is the value of $f(-1)$ if $f(x) = 3(x - 1)^2 + 5$?
 a. 8
 b. 11
 c. 15
 d. 17

13. What is the equation of the line that passes through the points (–2,1) and (4,5) in the Cartesian coordinate plane?
 a. $y = \frac{2}{3}x - \frac{4}{3}$
 b. $y = \frac{2}{3}x - \frac{1}{3}$
 c. $y = \frac{2}{3}x + \frac{7}{3}$
 d. $y = \frac{2}{3}x + 4$

14. A 9-foot-long ladder is placed against the side of a building such that the top of the ladder reaches a window that is 6 feet above the ground. To the nearest 10th of a foot, what is the distance from the bottom of the ladder to the building?
 a. 1.7
 b. 2.4
 c. 6.7
 d. 10.8

15. The figure below represents the rate of cooling for a particular material after it was placed in a super-cooled bath.

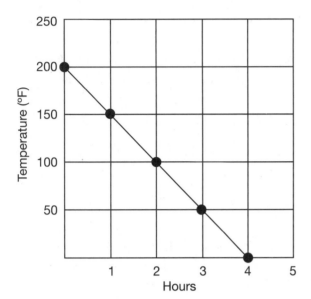

If the temperature, in Fahrenheit, is represented by T and the number of hours elapsed is represented by H, then which of the following would represent a situation where the rate of cooling was faster than the rate indicated in the graph?

a. $T = -25H + 150$
b. $T = -60H + 300$
c. $T = -10H + 200$
d. $T = -50H + 250$

16. In a study of its employees, a company found that about 50% spent more than 2 hours a day composing or reading e-mails. The overall distribution of time employees spent on these activities was skewed right with a mean time of about 2.5 hours. Complete the box plot below so that it matches the given information.

Draw as many vertical lines as needed on the graph to represent the data.

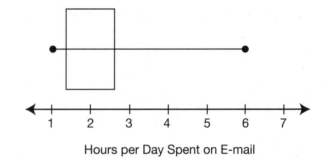

17. What is the equation of the line graphed in the figure below?

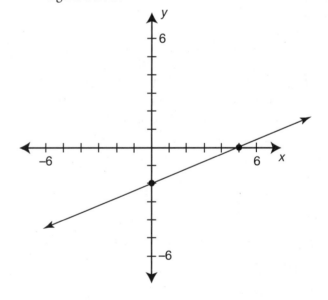

a. $y = \frac{2}{5}x - 2$
b. $y = -\frac{2}{5}x - 2$
c. $y = \frac{2}{5}x + 5$
d. $y = -\frac{2}{5}x - 5$

18. What is a positive solution to the equation $x^2 - 5x = 14$?

a. 2

b. 7

c. 5

d. 9

19. What is the slope of the line represented by the equation $10x - y = 2$?

a. 1

b. 2

c. 5

d. 10

20. Which of the following is equivalent to $5^{\frac{1}{2}} \times 5^2$?

a. $5^{-\frac{3}{2}}$

b. 5

c. $5^{\frac{5}{2}}$

d. $5^{\frac{1}{4}}$

21. A specialized part for a manufacturing process has a thickness of 1.2×10^{-3} inches. To the ten-thousandth of an inch, what would be the thickness of a stack of 10 of these parts?

a. 0.0001

b. 0.0012

c. 0.0120

d. 0.1200

22. A line is perpendicular to the line $y = \frac{5}{6}x + 1$ and has a y-intercept of $(0, -4)$. What is the equation of this line?

a. $y = -4x + 1$

b. $y = \frac{5}{6}x - 4$

c. $y = -\frac{6}{5}x + 1$

d. $y = -\frac{6}{5}x - 4$

23. Which of the following expressions is equivalent to $\frac{3}{x} \div \frac{5x}{2}$ for all nonzero x?

a. $\frac{6}{5x^2}$

b. $\frac{15x^2}{2}$

c. $\frac{3}{2}$

d. $\frac{15}{2}$

24. A factory is able to produce at least 16 items, but no more than 20 items, for every hour the factory is open. If the factory is open for 8 hours a day, which of the following are possibly the numbers of items produced by the factory over a 7-day work period?

Select all of the correct possibilities from the list and write them in the box below.

128

150

850

910

1,115

☐

25. A 32-ounce bag of potato chips has a retail cost of $3.45. To the nearest 10th of a cent, what is the price per ounce of this item (in cents)?

a. 9.3

b. 10.8

c. 28.5

d. 35.45

26.

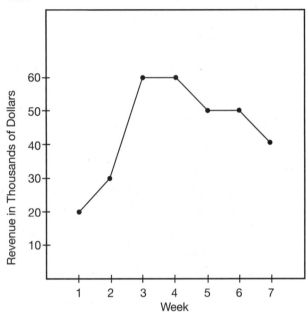

The graph shown here represents the total weekly revenue of a company over several weeks. For which of the following periods has the weekly revenue increased?

a. between weeks 2 and 3

b. between weeks 3 and 4

c. between weeks 4 and 5

d. between weeks 6 and 7

27. Circle the line in the coordinate plane below that represents the graph of the equation $3x - 2y = 1$.

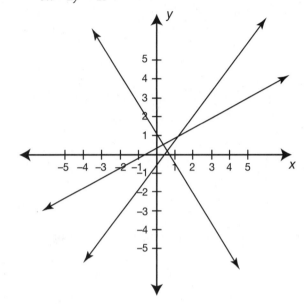

28. A line z is perpendicular to the line $y = -x + 5$. If z passes through the points $(0,-2)$ and $(x,5)$, what is the value of x?

a. 0

b. 3

c. 7

d. 10

29. Which of the following is equivalent to the numerical expression $\sqrt{2}(\sqrt{18} - \sqrt{6})$?

a. $4\sqrt{3}$

b. $5\sqrt{6}$

c. $6 - 2\sqrt{3}$

d. $6 - \sqrt{6}$

30. A beauty-product manufacturer has been researching the way that people use various beauty products. After several surveys, it has collected the data shown in the scatter plot below, which shows the time that participants spent on their beauty routines on a typical morning versus the amount of money the participants spent per month on beauty products.

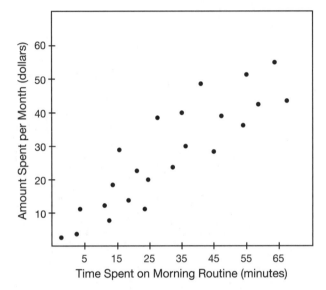

Given this plot, which of the following best describes the relationship between the amount of time spent and the amount of money spent?
a. In general, the longer people spent on their morning beauty routine, the more money they spent per month on beauty products.
b. In general, the longer people spent on their morning beauty routine, the less money they spent per month on beauty products.
c. In general, the amount of time people spent on their morning beauty routine was about the same as the amount of money they spent in dollars on beauty products.
d. In general, there is no clear relationship between the amount of time people spent on their beauty routine and the amount of money they spent per month on beauty products.

31. A walking trail is 11,088 feet long. If a mile is 5,280 feet, how many miles long is the walking trail?
a. 0.2
b. 0.5
c. 1.6
d. 2.1

32. The product of $x^2 - 6$ and x^4 is
a. $x^8 - 6$
b. $x^6 - 6$
c. $x^6 - 6x^4$
d. $x^8 - 6x^4$

33. The table below indicates the behavior of the price of one share of a given stock over several weeks.

END OF	CHANGE
Week 1	Increased by $5.00
Week 2	Decreased by 10%
Week 3	Decreased by $1.10
Week 4	Doubled in value

If the stock was worth $10.15 a share at the beginning of week 1, what was the value of one share of this stock at the end of week 4?

a. $25.07
b. $29.46
c. $32.20
d. $50.12

34. What is the mode of the data set 9, 4, −1, 12, 4, 8, 7?
a. −1
b. 4
c. 7
d. 13

35. There are 48 total applicants for a job. Of these applicants, 20 have a college degree, 15 have five years of work experience, and 8 have a college degree and five years of work experience. If an applicant is randomly selected, what is the probability, to the nearest tenth of a percent, that he or she has a college degree or has 5 years of work experience?

a. 41.7%

b. 56.3%

c. 72.9%

d. 89.6%

36. A customer uses two coupons to purchase a product at a grocery store, where the original price of the product was $8.30. If the final price paid by the customer was $7.00 and each coupon gave the same discount, what was the value of the discount provided by a single coupon?

a. $0.65

b. $0.90

c. $1.30

d. $2.60

37. Lee is planning to buy a new television and has been watching the price of a particular model for the past month. Last month, the price was $309.99, while this month, the price is $334.99. To the nearest tenth of a percent, by what percent has the price increased over the past month? Write your answer in the box below.

%

38. Which of the following are the two solutions to the equation $x^2 - 2x - 3 = 0$?

a. 3 and −1

b. −3 and 1

c. −3 and −2

d. 2 and 2

39. Which of the following represents the solution set of the inequality $x + 2 > 5$?

a. $\{x: x > 10\}$

b. $\{x: x > 7\}$

c. $\{x: x > 3\}$

d. $\{x: x > 2.5\}$

40. What is the value of $\frac{x-5}{x^2-1}$ when $x = \frac{1}{2}$?

a. −10

b. $\frac{3}{2}$

c. 6

d. 0

41.

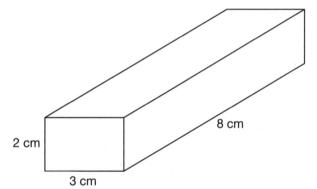

2 cm
3 cm
8 cm

What is the volume of the figure above?

a. 6

b. 24

c. 48

d. 108

42. The bar chart represents the total dollar value of sales for four product versions in July.

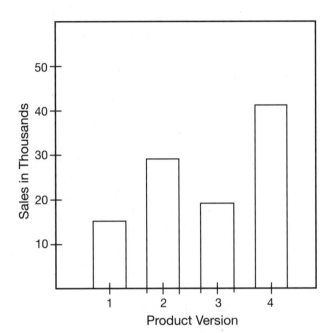

Which two products have combined sales of more than $50,000 in July?
a. Products 1 and 2
b. Products 2 and 3
c. Products 2 and 4
d. Products 1 and 3

43. The surface area of a sphere is 36π cubic meters. To the nearest meter, what is the diameter of this sphere?
a. 3
b. 6
c. 12
d. 24

44. What value of x satisfies the system of equations $x - 2y = 8$ and $x + 2y = 14$?
a. −6
b. 11
c. There are infinitely many values of x that satisfy this system.
d. There are no values of x that satisfy this system.

45. $(x^2 + 5) - (x^2 - x) =$
a. $5 + x$
b. $5 - x$
c. $2x^2 - 5x$
d. $2x^2 + x + 5$

Answers and Explanations

1. Choice b is correct. "10 fewer than" implies that 10 should be subtracted from the next stated term. That term is "2 times the number of video games that Joseph owns," or $2v$.

Choice **a** is incorrect. This expression represents 2 fewer than 10 times the number of video games Joseph owns.

Choice **c** is incorrect. This expression represents 2 times 10 fewer than the number of video games Joseph owns.

Choice **d** is incorrect. This expression represents 10 times 2 fewer than the number of video games Joseph owns.

2. Choice c is correct. The product in the numerator can be written as $\sqrt[3]{3 \times 3 \times 3 \times 6}$ $= 3\sqrt[3]{6}$. The 3 in the denominator cancels out the 3 in front of the root.

Choice **a** is incorrect. The numerator is made up of a product. The denominator can only cancel one factor of the numerator.

Choice **b** is incorrect. The denominator cannot cancel out a factor within a cube root.

Choice **d** is incorrect. The cube root of 9 is not 3.

3. Correct answer: $\sqrt{2}$

Two factors of 72 are 2 and 36. Further, $\frac{\sqrt{a}}{\sqrt{b}} = \sqrt{\frac{a}{b}}$ for positive numbers a and b. Using these properties, $\frac{\sqrt{72}}{\sqrt{36}} = \frac{\sqrt{2 \times 36}}{36} = \sqrt{2}$.

4.

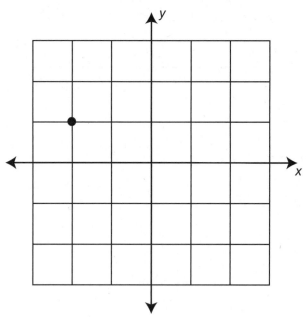

The first term of the ordered pair is the x-coordinate. Since this is negative, the point will be on the left-hand side of the y-axis. The second term is the y-coordinate. This indicates how many units above the x-axis the point is located.

5. Choice b is correct. To cube means to take the number to the third power. Adding 5 to this yields the expression $x^3 + 5$. Finally, multiplying this by 2 yields $2(x^3 + 5)$.

Choice **a** is incorrect. This represents multiplying the number by 3 as the first step. To cube means to take the number to the third power.

Choice **c** is incorrect. This represents multiplying by 2 before adding 5.

Choice **d** is incorrect. Two times x cubed is not equivalent to x to the 6th power.

6. Choice c is correct. The original statement can be written as $n + 4 < 5m$. Given the value of m, $5m = 5 \times 6 = 30$, therefore $n + 4 < 30$. This can be simplified further, to $n < 26$.

Choice **a** is incorrect. The original statement can be written as $n + 4 < 5m$. This statement can be used to show what n is less than, but it can't indicate what n is greater than.

Choice **b** is incorrect. The original statement can be written as $n + 4 < 5m$. Given the value of m, $5m = 5 \times 6 = 30$, therefore $n + 4 < 30$. While $n < 26$, it is not necessarily true that $n + 4 < 26$.

Choice **d** is incorrect. The original statement can be written as $n + 4 < 5m$. This statement can be used to show what n is less than, but it can't indicate what n is equal to.

7. Correct answer: $490.80. The employee is paid a 4% commission on his sales of $1,020. Therefore, he will be paid $0.04 \times \$1,020 = \$40.80$ for the sales. This is on top of his regular pay of $450. Therefore, his total paycheck will be $450 + $40.80 = $490.80.

8. Choice b is correct. The radius of the circle is 5, and the circumference is $2 \times \pi \times$ (radius), or 10π. This can also be found simply by multiplying the diameter and π.

Choice **a** is incorrect. The radius of the circle is 5 and must be doubled in order to find the circumference.

Choice **c** is incorrect. This is the area of the circle, which is found by squaring the radius and multiplying by π.

Choice **d** is incorrect. The diameter does not need to be squared in order to find the circumference.

9. Choice a is correct. Applying an exponent to a fraction is equivalent to applying that exponent to the numerator and denominator.

Choice **b** is incorrect. An exponent of 3 is not equivalent to multiplication by 3.

Choice **c** is incorrect. The exponent must be applied to both the numerator and the denominator.

Choice **d** is incorrect. An exponent of 3 is not equivalent to multiplication by 3 and would be applied to both the numerator and the denominator.

10. Correct answer: (0,–14)
Since n is parallel to the given line, it must have the same slope, 3. Given this and the point that n passes through, we can use the point-slope formula to determine the equation for n.

$$y - 1 = 3(x - 5)$$
$$y - 1 = 3x - 15$$
$$y = 3x - 14$$

Now that the equation is in the form $y = mx + b$, we can see that the y-intercept is -14. By definition, this means that the line passes over the y-axis at the point $(0,-14)$.

11. Choice a is correct. The answer choices are in the form $y = mx + b$. Using the given information, when $x = 4$, $y = 0$, and the slope is $m = -\frac{1}{2}$, this gives the equation $0 = -\frac{1}{2}(4) + b$, which has a solution of $b = 2$.

Choice **b** is incorrect. When solving for the y-intercept b, the -2 must be added to both sides of the equation.

Choice **c** is incorrect. The given point $(4,0)$ is not a y-intercept; it's an x-intercept. The equation $y = mx + b$ uses a y-intercept.

Choice **d** is incorrect. If the x-intercept is $(4,0)$ as given, the y-intercept will be -4 only if the slope is 1. Here the slope is $-\frac{1}{2}$.

12. Choice d is correct. Substituting −1 for the x, $f(−1) = 3(−1 − 1)^2 + 5 = 3(−2)^2 + 5 = 3(4) + 5 = 12 + 5 = 17$.

Choice **a** is incorrect. When substituting −1 for x, $x − 1$ represents $−1 − 1 = −2$, not multiplication.

Choice **b** is incorrect. It is not true that $(x − 1)^2 = x^2 + 1$.

Choice **c** is incorrect. By the order of operations, the subtraction within the parentheses as well as the squaring operation must be performed before the multiplication by 3.

13. Choice c is correct. Using the slope formula first, $m = \frac{5 − 1}{4 − (−2)} = \frac{4}{6} = \frac{2}{3}$. Now, applying the point-slope formula, we have:

$$y − 1 = \frac{2}{3}(x − (−2))$$
$$y − 1 = \frac{2}{3}(x + 2)$$
$$y − 1 = \frac{2}{3}x + \frac{4}{3}$$
$$y = \frac{2}{3}x + \frac{4}{3} + 1 = \frac{2}{3}x + \frac{7}{3}$$

Choice **a** is incorrect. In the point-slope formula, the x_1 and y_1 must come from the same point.

Choice **b** is incorrect. When the point $(−2,1)$ is used in the point-slope formula, the result is $y − 1 = m(x − (−2))$. On the right-hand side of this equation, the 2 ends up being positive.

Choice **d** is incorrect. The slope is found using the change in y on the numerator: $\frac{5 − 1}{4 − (−2)} = \frac{4}{6} = \frac{2}{3}$. In the point-slope formula, $\frac{4}{3} + 1 = \frac{7}{3}$.

14. Choice c is correct. Using the Pythagorean theorem, the hypotenuse of the right triangle formed by the ladder and the building is 9, while the length of one leg is 6. This yields the equation $6^2 + b^2 = 9^2$ or $b^2 = 81 − 36 = 45$. Therefore, $b = \sqrt{45} \approx 6.7$.

Choice **a** is incorrect. The terms in the Pythagorean theorem are squared.

Choice **b** is incorrect. Applying the Pythagorean theorem to this problem yields the equation $6^2 + b^2 = 9^2$. The exponent of 2 indicates to multiply the term by itself twice, not multiply by 2.

Choice **d** is incorrect. The length of the ladder represents the hypotenuse, or c, in the Pythagorean theorem.

15. Choice b is correct. The rate of cooling indicated in the graph is the slope of the line passing through the points $(0,200)$ and $(4,0)$. This slope is −50, which implies the material is losing 50 degrees every hour. The slope of the equation in this answer choice is −60, which implies the material is losing 60 degrees every hour, a faster rate of cooling.

Choice **a** is incorrect. This slope would imply that the material is losing 25 degrees every hour, which is a slower rate of cooling.

Choice **c** is incorrect. This slope would imply that the material is losing 10 degrees every hour, which is a slower rate of cooling.

Choice **d** is incorrect. This slope would indicate the material is losing 50 degrees every hour, which is the same rate of cooling that is given in the graph.

16.

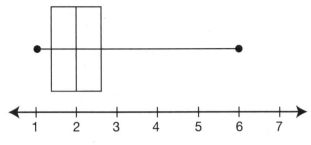

Hours per Day Spent on E-mail

The statement "50% spent more than 2 hours a day composing or reading emails" indicates that the median of this data set is 2. This is typically indicated on a box plot by a vertical line in the center of the box.

17. Choice a is correct. Using the two given points, whenever y increases by 2 units, x increases by 5 units. This means the slope must be $m = \frac{2}{5}$ (the change in y divided by the change in x). Further, the y-intercept is $b = -2$. Using the equation $y = mx + b$, we have $y = \frac{2}{5}x - 2$.

Choice **b** is incorrect. The line rises from left to right; therefore, the slope must be positive.

Choice **c** is incorrect. The x-intercept is not used when writing the equation as $y = mx + b$. In fact, b represents the y-intercept.

Choice **d** is incorrect. The line rises from left to right; therefore, the slope must be positive. Additionally, the y-intercept is -2 and not 5.

18. Choice b is correct. Rewriting the equation by subtracting 14 from both sides yields the quadratic equation $x^2 - 5x - 14 = 0$. The left-hand side of this equation can be factored into $(x - 7)(x + 2)$, indicating that the solutions are 7 and -2.

Choice **a** is incorrect. Once the quadratic equation is rewritten and factored, the zero product rule states that $x - 7 = 0$ or $x + 2 = 0$. Therefore one of the solutions is -2 instead of 2.

Choices **c** and **d** are incorrect. To factor the rewritten quadratic equation, find factors of 14 that sum to -5 instead of numbers that sum to -14.

19. Choice d is correct. To find the slope of the line with this equation, move the y-variable to one side on its own to put the equation in the form $y = mx + b$, where m is the slope. Adding y to both sides and subtracting 2 from both sides gives the equation $y = 10x - 2$, so the slope is 10.

Choice **a** is incorrect. The coefficient of x, not the coefficient of y, represents the slope when the equation is written in the form $y = mx + b$.

Choice **b** is incorrect. The slope cannot be read from the equation in the form it is currently written.

Choice **c** is incorrect. When solving for y to find the slope, 10 will be divided by 1 and not by 2.

20. Choice c is correct. When multiplying terms with the same base, the exponents are added. Therefore $5^{\frac{1}{2}} \times 5^2 = 5^{\frac{1}{2} + 2} = 5^{\frac{1}{2} + \frac{4}{2}} = 5^{\frac{5}{2}}$.

Choice **a** is incorrect. When multiplying terms with the same base, the exponents are added, not subtracted.

Choice **b** is incorrect. When multiplying terms with the same base, the exponents are added, not multiplied.

Choice **d** is incorrect. When multiplying terms with the same base, the exponents are added, not divided.

21. Choice c is correct. $1.2 \times 10^{-3} = 0.0012$ and $10 \times 0.0012 = 0.0120$.

Choice **a** is incorrect. It is not possible for the thickness of ten parts to be smaller than the thickness of one part.

Choice **b** is incorrect. This is the thickness of a single part.

Choice **d** is incorrect. This is the thickness of a stack of 100 such parts.

22. Choice d is correct. The slope will be the negative reciprocal of the given slope, and b in the equation $y = mx + b$ is -4.

Choice **a** is incorrect. The slope of a perpendicular line will be the negative reciprocal of the slope of the original line.

Choice **b** is incorrect. Parallel lines have the same slope, while perpendicular lines have negative reciprocal slopes.

Choice **c** is incorrect. The term added to the x-term will be the y-intercept, which is not -1.

23. Choice a is correct. The division is equivalent to $\frac{3}{x} \times \frac{2}{5x} = \frac{6}{5x^2}$.

Choice **b** is incorrect. The division of two fractions is equivalent to multiplying the first fraction by the reciprocal of the second fraction.

Choice **c** is incorrect. This is the result of multiplying and not dividing the fractions if the 5 canceled out. There are no terms that would cancel with the 5.

Choice **d** is incorrect. This is the result of multiplying the two fractions.

24. Correct answers: 910 and 1,115. The minimum number of items the factory could produce in this time frame is $16 \times 8 \times 7 = 896$ items, while the maximum is $20 \times 8 \times 7 = 1,120$. Any whole number value in between these numbers is a possible number of items the factory could produce over the given time frame.

25. Choice b is correct. The price per ounce is found by dividing 3.45 by 32.

Choice **a** is incorrect. Dividing the number of ounces by the cost will give the number of ounces per cent.

Choice **c** is incorrect. Subtracting terms will not give an interpretable value.

Choice **d** is incorrect. Adding these two terms will not give an interpretable value.

26. Choice a is correct. The revenue is increasing whenever the graph is rising from left to right. This occurs between weeks 2 and 3.

Choice **b** is incorrect. The revenue is increasing whenever the graph is rising from left to right. This does not occur between weeks 3 and 4.

Choice **c** is incorrect. The revenue is increasing whenever the graph is rising from left to right. This does not occur between weeks 4 and 5.

Choice **d** is incorrect. The revenue is increasing whenever the graph is rising from left to right. This does not occur between weeks 6 and 7.

27.

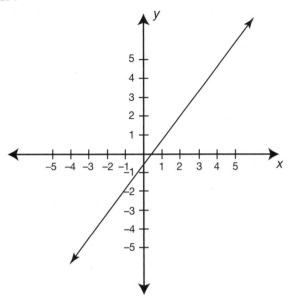

Each of the given lines has a different y-intercept. Solving for y in the given equation will put the equation in $y = mx + b$ form, where b is the y-intercept. In this case, that equation is $y = -\frac{1}{2} + \frac{3}{2}x$. The line given in the image above is the only line with a y-intercept of $-\frac{1}{2}$.

28. Choice c is correct. Since z is perpendicular to $y = -x + 5$, it must have a slope of 1. The given point $(0, -2)$ is a y-intercept since the x-value is 0, so the equation of z must be $y = x - 2$. Plugging in the given y-value of 5 in the point $(x, 5)$ yields the equation $5 = x - 2$, which has the solution $x = 7$.

Choice **a** is incorrect. The y-intercept of the line is –2 and not 5. A perpendicular line does not necessarily have the same y-intercept. Further, the 5 in the point $(x, 5)$ is a y-value and not an x-value.

Choice **b** is incorrect. The 5 in the point $(x, 5)$ is a y-value and not an x-value.

Choice **d** is incorrect. The y-intercept of the line is –2 and not 5. Two perpendicular lines do not necessarily have the same y-intercept.

29. Choice c is correct. Distributing the square root of 2 and simplifying:
$$\sqrt{2}(\sqrt{18} - \sqrt{6}) = \sqrt{36} - \sqrt{12} = 6 - \sqrt{4 \times 3}$$
$$= 6 - 2\sqrt{3}.$$
Choice **a** is incorrect. Radicals and whole numbers are not like terms and therefore cannot be combined.

Choice **b** is incorrect. The square root of 2 must be distributed to both terms. Additionally, the radical and the remaining whole number are not like terms.

Choice **d** is incorrect. The square root of 2 must be distributed to both terms in the parentheses.

30. Choice a is correct. The pattern in the scatter plot has a general upward trend from left to right. This indicates a positive relationship. As one variable increases, the other variable also increases.

Choice **b** is incorrect. A negative relationship would be indicated by a pattern that is generally falling from left to right.

Choice **c** is incorrect. This would be true if, for each point, the x- and y-coordinates were the same. But there are many points where this is not the case.

Choice **d** is incorrect. A general sloping pattern indicates a relationship between the two variables.

31. Choice d is correct. The conversion given can be written as a ratio, 1 mile : 5,280 feet. Using this to cancel out units: $11,088 \text{ ft} \times \frac{1}{5,280} = \frac{11,088}{5,280} = 2.1$.

Choice **a** is incorrect. There is no need to divide by 12 since the units are not in inches.

Choice **b** is incorrect. Dividing 5,280 by 11,088 leaves the units in terms of $\frac{1}{\text{miles}}$, which doesn't make sense.

Choice **c** is incorrect. Subtracting the two values will not give an interpretable value.

32. Choice c is correct. The two steps are to distribute and add exponents. $x^4(x^2 - 6) = x^{4+2} - 6x^4 = x^6 - 6x^4$.

Choice **a** is incorrect. When two terms with the same base are multiplied, their exponents are added. Further, the term x^4 must be distributed to every term in the given binomial $x^2 - 6$.

Choice **b** is incorrect. The term x^4 must be distributed to every term in the given binomial $x^2 - 6$.

Choice **d** is incorrect. When two terms with the same base are multiplied, their exponents are added.

33. Choice a is correct. After increasing by $5.00, the share was worth $15.15. It then decreased in value by 10%, or by $0.1 \times 15.15 = 1.515$. Therefore, at the end of week 2, it was worth $15.15 − $1.515 = $13.635 a share. At the end of week 3, it was worth $13.635 − $1.10 = $12.535. Finally, it doubled in value and was worth $2 \times$ $12.535 = $25.07 per share.

Choice **b** is incorrect. The stock decreased in value by $1.10 at the end of week 3. This represents subtraction in the problem.

Choice **c** is incorrect. A 10% decrease can be found by multiplying 0.9 and the current value. This answer comes from using 1% or 0.01 as the decrease.

Choice **d** is incorrect. To double means to multiply by 2 and not 4.

34. Choice b is correct. The mode is the most commonly observed value. In this case, 4 occurs the most number of times.

Choice **a** is incorrect. This is the minimum value of the data set.

Choice **c** is incorrect. This is the median of the data set.

Choice **d** is incorrect. This is the range of the data set.

35. Choice b is correct. Given the final question is about an "or" probability, the correct formula to use is $P(A \text{ or } B) = P(A) + P(B) − P(A \text{ and } B)$, where $P(A)$ stands for the probability of the event A occurring. Applying this here:

$P(\text{degree or five years}) = P(\text{degree}) + P(\text{five years}) − P(\text{degree and five years}) = \frac{20}{48} + \frac{15}{48} - \frac{8}{48} = \frac{27}{48} = 0.5625$

Finally, 0.5625 is equivalent to 56.3%.

Choice **a** is incorrect. Although this is an "or" probability, the numbers for college degree and five years of work experience must be included.

Choices **c** and **d** are incorrect. When finding "or" probabilities, the probability of the "and" event must be subtracted.

36. Choice a is correct. If x represents the discount provided by a single coupon, then $2x$ represents the combined discount provided by both. Given the prices before and after, the following equation can be written and solved:

$8.3 - 2x = 7$
$-2x = -1.3$
$x = 0.65$

Choice **b** is incorrect. If each coupon gave a 90-cent discount, the final price would have been $8.30 − $1.80 = $6.50.

Choice **c** is incorrect. This is the value of both coupons together.

Choice **d** is incorrect. The coupons provide a discount of $1.30 together, so it is not possible that one coupon by itself has a larger discount value.

37. The correct answer is 8.1%.

The percent increase can be found by finding the difference between the two prices and then dividing by the original price:

$\frac{334.99 - 309.99}{309.99} = 0.0806$.

Multiplying by 100 to convert this to a percentage yields 8.06%. Rounded, this is 8.1%.

38. Choice a is correct. The equation can be factored and rewritten as $(x - 3)(x + 1) = 0$.

Using the zero product rule, this results in the equations $x - 3 = 0$ and $x + 1 = 0$. The solutions to these equations are 3 and –1, respectively. Choice **b** is incorrect. After factoring, the zero product rule must be applied. This will result in the equations $x - 3 = 0$ and $x + 1 = 0$. Choices **c** and **d** are incorrect. The solutions can't be read off the coefficients. Instead, factoring, the quadratic formula, or completing the square should be used to solve a quadratic equation like this.

39. **Choice c is correct.** Subtracting 2 from both sides yields the solution $x > 3$.

Choice **a** is incorrect. In this inequality, the 2 is added to the variable. Therefore, when attempting to isolate the x, both sides should not be multiplied by 2. Instead, 2 should be subtracted from both sides.

Choice **b** is incorrect. In this inequality, the 2 is added to the variable. Therefore when attempting to isolate the x, 2 should be subtracted from both sides instead of being added.

Choice **d** is incorrect. In this inequality, the 2 is added to the variable. Therefore, when attempting to isolate the x, both sides should not be divided by 2. Instead, 2 should be subtracted from both sides.

40. **Choice c is correct.** After plugging in the given value of x, we must simplify the result using basic operations with fractions:
$$\frac{\frac{1}{2} - 5}{\frac{1}{4} - 1} = \frac{\frac{1}{2} - \frac{10}{2}}{\frac{1}{4} - \frac{4}{4}} = \frac{-\frac{9}{2}}{-\frac{3}{4}} = \frac{9}{2} \times \frac{4}{3} = \frac{36}{6} = 6$$

Choice **a** is incorrect. When plugging in the given value of x, the 5 is subtracted, not multiplied.

Choice **b** is incorrect. When simplifying a fraction over a fraction, the fraction in the numerator is multiplied by the reciprocal of the fraction in the denominator. Dividing the fractions piece by piece is not a valid method.

Choice **d** is incorrect. Taking a value to the power of two is not the same as multiplying it by two. Furthermore, a fraction with a denominator of zero is undefined, not equal to zero.

41. **Choice c is correct.** The area of the base is $2 \times 3 = 6$ square centimeters. Multiplying this by the height of 8 cm gives us the volume in cubic centimeters: $6 \times 8 = 48$.

Choice **a** is incorrect. This is the area of one of the smaller faces.

Choice **b** is incorrect. This is the area of one of the larger faces.

Choice **d** is incorrect. This is the surface area of the given shape.

42. **Choice c is correct.** Since product 2 had almost $30,000 in sales and product 4 had over $40,000 in sales, the total must be more than $50,000.

Choice **a** is incorrect. The total sales in July for these two products was about $45,000.

Choice **b** is incorrect. The total sales in July for these two products was slightly less than $50,000.

Choice **d** is incorrect. The total sales in July for these two products was about $35,000.

43. Choice b is correct. Using the surface area formula:

$$36\pi = 4\pi r^2$$
$$9 = r^2$$
$$r = 3$$

Since the radius is 3, the diameter is $3 \times 2 = 6$.
Choice **a** is incorrect. This is the radius of the sphere. The diameter is twice as large as the radius.
Choice **c** is incorrect. When solving the equation $36\pi = 4\pi r^2$, divide, do not multiply, both sides by 4. Additionally, the diameter will be two times as large as the radius.
Choice **d** is incorrect. When solving the equation $36\pi = 4\pi r^2$, divide, do not multiply, both sides by 4.

44. Choice b is correct. Using the addition method, adding the two equations yields the equation $2x = 22$, which has a solution of $x = 11$.
Choice **a** is incorrect. Subtracting the two equations will eliminate the x from both equations, making it where y must be found first.
Choice **c** is incorrect. If there were infinitely many solutions, the equations would be multiples of each other.
Choice **d** is incorrect. If there was no solution, the equation would yield an incorrect statement such as $0 = 1$ or $-5 = 3$.

45. Choice a is correct. Distributing the negative and combining like terms yields $(x^2 + 5) - (x^2 - x) = x^2 + 5 - x^2 - (-x) = 5 + x$.
Choice **b** is incorrect. The negative must be distributed to every term in the parentheses.
Choice **c** is incorrect. Since the second term is being subtracted, the x^2 terms will cancel out. Further, the 5 and the x are not being multiplied.
Choice **d** is incorrect. Since the second term is being subtracted, the x^2 terms will cancel out.

APPENDIX:
MATHEMATICAL REASONING
FORMULAS SHEET

The following are the formulas you will be supplied with on the GED® Mathematical Reasoning test.

Area

Parallelogram: $A = bh$

Trapezoid: $A = \frac{1}{2}h(b_1 + b_2)$

Surface Area and Volume

Rectangular/right prism:	$SA = ph + 2B$	$V = Bh$
Cylinder:	$SA = 2\pi rh + 2\pi r^2$	$V = \pi r^2 h$
Pyramid:	$SA = \frac{1}{2}ps + B$	$V = \frac{1}{3}Bh$
Cone:	$SA = \pi rs + \pi r^2$	$V = \frac{1}{3}\pi r^2 h$
Sphere:	$SA = 4\pi r^2$	$V = \frac{4}{3}\pi r^3$

(p = perimeter of base B; $\pi \approx 3.14$)

Algebra

Slope of a line: $m = \dfrac{y_2 - y_1}{x_2 - x_1}$

Slope-intercept form of the equation of a line: $y = mx + b$

Point-slope form of the equation of a line: $y - y_1 = m(x - x_1)$

Standard form of a quadratic equation: $y = ax^2 + bx + c$

Quadratic formula: $x = \dfrac{-b \pm \sqrt{b^2 - 4ac}}{2a}$

Pythagorean theorem: $a^2 + b^2 = c^2$

Simple interest: $I = prt$

(I = interest, p = principal, r = rate, t = time)

Using the code below, you'll be able to log in and access additional online practice materials!

Your free online practice access code is:
FVELYI7GXX6T72PNFR24

Follow these simple steps to redeem your code:

- Go to **www.learningexpresshub.com/affiliate** and have your access code handy.

If you're a new user:
- Click the **New user? Register here** button and complete the registration form to create your account and access your products.
- Be sure to enter your unique access code only once. If you have multiple access codes, you can enter them all—just use a comma to separate each code.
- The next time you visit, simply click the **Returning user? Sign in** button and enter your username and password.
- Do not re-enter previously redeemed access codes. Any products you previously accessed are saved in the **My Account** section on the site. Entering a previously redeemed access code will result in an error message.

If you're a returning user:
- Click the **Returning user? Sign in** button, enter your username and password, and click **Sign In**.
- You will automatically be brought to the **My Account** page to access your products.
- Do not re-enter previously redeemed access codes. Any products you previously accessed are saved in the **My Account** section on the site. Entering a previously redeemed access code will result in an error message.

If you're a returning user with new access codes:
- Click the **Returning user? Sign in** button, enter your username, password, and new access codes, and click **Sign In**.
- If you have multiple access codes, you can enter them all—just use a comma to separate each code.
- Do not re-enter previously redeemed access codes. Any products you previously accessed are saved in the **My Account** section on the site. Entering a previously redeemed access code will result in an error message.

If you have any questions, please contact Customer Support at Support@ebsco.com. All inquiries will be responded to within a 24-hour period during our normal business hours: 9:00 A.M.–5:00 P.M. Eastern Time. Thank you!